# THE LEGAL HISTORY OF
# DISASTERS

THOMAS J. SHAW

# THE LEGAL HISTORY OF
# DISASTERS

Cover images:

First column, first row: Versailles train.
First column, second row: RMS Titanic.
Second column, first row: The Hindenburg.
Second column, second row: Three Mile Island.

The materials contained herein represent the opinions of the author and should not be construed to be the views or opinions of the companies with whom the author is associated with or employed by.

Nothing contained in this book is to be considered as the rendering of legal advice for specific cases, and readers are responsible for obtaining such advice from their own legal counsel. This book is intended for educational and informational purposes only.

© 2024 Thomas J. Shaw. All rights reserved.

No part of this publication may be reproduced, stored in a retrieval system, or transmitted in any form or by any means, electronic, mechanical, photocopying, recording, or otherwise, without the prior written permission of the publisher or author.

Printed in the United States of America.

ISBN 979-8-34209-980-6

# Contents

| | |
|---|---|
| Dedication | vi |
| Foreword | vii |
| About the Author | xii |

*Chapter 1*
**BEFORE 1900** — **1**
1.1 Railroads — 3
1.2 Ships — 26

*Chapter 2*
**1900 – 1924** — **51**
2.1 Buildings and Mines — 53
2.2 Transportation and Disease — 79

*Chapter 3*
**1925 – 1949** — **117**
3.1 Buildings and Aircraft — 119
3.2 Industry and Engineering — 146

*Chapter 4*
**1950 – 1974** — **177**
4.1 Nature and Environment — 179
4.2 Airborne and Industry — 204

*Chapter 5*
**1975 – 1999** — **231**
5.1 Environment and Nature — 233
5.2 Structures and Flight — 261

Afterword — **299**

Index — 301

# *Dedication*

This book is dedicated to all the victims of disasters, in their untold numbers, some of whose stories are recounted here.

I would also like to thank my daughter for her help with the proofreading.

# *Foreword*

After I had launched my new "Legal History Of" series, I was considering the topic of my next book. I had gone through the list of future books I had jotted down over the years, but none seemed like the right time to tell those stories. Then, suddenly, a topic I had not listed came into my head. Perhaps it was from re-watching the movie *Titanic*. But that was not the image that came first to mind, which was of the *Hindenburg* (who could forget those newsreel images and that radio reporting). Then I had memories of the nuclear accident in Japan I personally lived through and other disasters I was proximate to. A rudimentary outline coalesced into a whole book. This then is the legal story of those and many other disasters.

This book is the sixth in a series of legal history books on the legal issues that arose around significant periods in American, and global, history. These all examine how the law responds when people are placed into dynamic, and typically unexpected circumstances. I began this series by looking at the legal issues of the Second World War. Next, I wrote about the legal issues around the First World War. The third book continued back further in time to the legalities of the American Revolutionary War. The fourth book presented the legal issues of pirates and privateers, from the 16th century England to 19th century America. The fifth book covered the legal issues that arose for the key protagonists on the American frontier, from 1775 to 1899. These books tell the legal side of the stories of varied adventurers, and of average citizens, from the 16th to the 21st century.

Like the five books that preceded it, what hopefully makes this new book unique is its legal focus on well-known, or forgotten, stories. It presents, in the 19th and 20th centuries, a legal perspective of both the growth of new technologies and the consistent forces of nature, and their occasional negative impacts. It brings together in a single volume the major legal issues surrounding varied types of disasters, of which I have tried to cover as many as possible. In doing so, I have often used the word "disaster" and "accident" interchangeably but to be clear, every disaster is an accident but not vice versa. A disaster had a significant impact on human life, health, property, or the environment. There were no pre-set limits though, as I was more interested in identifying legal issues arising from different types of disasters, not in limiting them. Disasters include the origins and consequences of both natural and human-assisted disasters, with the former focusing usually only on the impacts, as the cause is typically clear, while the latter focuses on both the causes and effects.

The book is organized by chapter using 25-year periods to group different types of disasters together and the legal issues they implicate. The first chapter covers all years before the 20$^{th}$ century, but in effect is the 50-year period from 1850 to 1899. The sections describe the general categories of disasters, and the sub-sections present the specific types of disasters. Within the chapters, the disasters are not necessarily in date order, but typically are. It was more important to have a sequence of the different types of disasters than to have the disasters in chronological order. Regardless, all the disasters occurred within the date period of the chapter. There is no significance attached to a certain disaster type not appearing in a period. Also, some disaster types may occur more than once, to tease out unique legal issues. I have tried to find as many unique types of disasters as possible in these time periods but not every type is in each period. If the legal issues of a disaster type are different in a later period, a certain disaster type may be presented more than once.

The presentation focuses on the common law countries of the United States and the United Kingdom, due to the higher frequency of litigation arising from disasters. I could have included disasters from other countries, as catastrophes historically have occurred across the globe. However, because the legal approaches and mechanisms would be different, I have decided to limit it to these two countries, to maintain a consistent narrative on the legal issues. Also, it is important to understand that this is not an encyclopedia of disaster law, tort law, accident law, or workplace law. It merely describes representative legal issues around disasters, choosing examples that may or may not be well-known, but that illustrate unique legal issues over the history of the last two centuries. No attempt is being made to consolidate this law. Also, to the extent possible, this focuses only on civilian, not military, disasters, due to the type of law being explored, and the lack of litigation arising from most military disasters.

Each of the disasters chosen could easily have been the subject of an entire book. Many have been. It is not possible in the five pages or so devoted to each disaster to address all the legalities in much depth. At best, the disaster can be introduced, with a portrait of the impact on victims provided, before out of necessity moving on to the relevant legal topics. The cases, investigations, inquests, and statutes are the focus of this book, so a fuller understanding of human, social, financial, and other impacts of each disaster presented are best found elsewhere. While I may present the recommendations for statutory change, following all the actual implementations into new or revised laws would again have encompassed a whole additional book. The same would be true to tracing all the subsequent events of each story. While as interested as anyone in the whole story, including what happened to the varied protagonists, this must be followed up on by the reader if interested. Often there were later legal proceedings that I have not included, if they were of lesser significance.

The results of some, if not many, of the disasters are not legally or morally satisfying. In earlier cases, the law of torts was not sufficiently developed to deal with plaintiffs seeking compensation. Statutes often did not specify with sufficient clarity the legal duties of owners and operators. This often led to the people who should have been held responsible avoiding liability completely, both penal and financial. High-powered lawyers found loopholes in poorly drafted state laws or municipal ordinances, defendants wore down grieving plaintiffs through delay and costs, and overly conservative judicial panels seemed intent on siding with monied interests. There are sufficient quotes and holdings from such courts, so the reader can decide for themselves whether justice was ever served. Commonly though, disasters did spur updated legislation and revised codes, to ensure the same type of disaster would not re-occur, at least in that jurisdiction. There are also some important disasters that were not included because there was not a sufficient legal dimension to discuss.

Also, a word about looking for legal conclusions to each disaster. Often, the legal aspects in a civil case will play out and then, based on which way things go, the defendant may decide to settle. This could be before any litigation begins or could be after a defeat on preliminary motions, such as the dismissal of a complaint, striking certain counts, or changing venue. That may be the end of what we publicly see in a case, as the settlement will occur confidentially and the terms of these will never be seen, so only obscure references to the conclusion will be publicly known. While frustrating to us all, this is how the legal process works and so what will be discussed are the publicly visible workings of the law, most typically in court cases. Also, death tolls are commonly approximated, because it is rarely certain how many people were killed in a disaster. I have also included a few cases sprinkled across the book not directly part of presented disaster but were relevant to the topic. These were included because they were entertaining, drawing on either unusual and unknown stories or well-known stories not told from a legal manner before.

I did consider changing the Afterword to a Chapter 6, 2000-2024, but did not, because I wanted to keep the book a certain size and deal as much as possible with settled litigation. I may do this in a future edition. Also, besides avoiding presenting disasters that are the result of armed conflict between adversarial nations, I have also intentionally avoided discussing acts of terrorism, although clearly disasters. Although many legal issues are involved with such events, but these are intentional criminal acts, a different area of the law. While criminal law is discussed, it is principally involuntary manslaughter that is invoked, as it was not the intention of the perpetrator to inflict the resulting harm. It is typically negligence that is the central legal issue of the disasters covered, not intentional harm to others.

I have often found that the joy of writing legal history comes from listening directly to those who lived long ago. I find that their voices are the truest, and sometimes no amount of explanation could substitute for their original words. It also is a chance to hear directly from superior writers, writing on matters occurring in their times. Therefore, I often use longer quotes from court cases when that is the best explanation for the relevant topic. Given the subject of this book, I also found it meaningful to give voice to the victims of disasters where it made sense to, often through newspaper articles reporting in situ during or just after the event, to be able to reflect accurately the human emotion. This does mean that there are often what we would modernly consider grammar and spelling errors included within the quoted verbiage, both from the court cases, and from the newspaper accounts. To provide the truest sense of what was being expressed then, I have left these completely untouched, if the meaning is clear to the reader, so to not interfere with those speaking in their time.

Have these stories been told before? Most definitely, especially for the more famous disasters. What makes this book different is bringing so many scores of different stories together into a single narrative, to find the statutes, regulations, inquiries, investigations, and trials that explain the legal response to disasters. There are more than 50 disasters presented, selected from hundreds or thousands of possibilities. Each demonstrates at least two legal issues, even though there may be more issues not noted expressly but will come out upon reading each of the sections. These are presented through different legal response mechanisms, most often legal cases for damages but sometimes coroner's inquests, government or regulatory investigations, revised legislation or codes, or criminal trials. I also tried to go into detail on the various aspects of the legal process in at least one disaster, such as legal complaints, settlement types, etc. Finally, records are not always extant or never were or are kept hidden away, so it only possible to work with the materials that can be reasonably accessed.

My intent with this book, as always, is to entertain, educate and inform readers, which I can only wish I have achieved in some measure. While my target audience with this type of book is those who enjoy legal history, hopefully the book's materials are at a level that can be read easily by those generally interested in this topic or these periods of history. My goal is to create a single source to reinterpret often-told, mis-told, or ill-remembered tales of disasters, looking at them through the lens of the law. I again hope that I have accomplished this in some small way.

*Thomas J. Shaw, Esq.*
October 2024

# About the Author

**Thomas J. Shaw, Esq., Author, Lawyer, CPA, DPO**

Thomas J. Shaw is an EU-based lawyer and the author of a dozen books on legal history and on technology and privacy law, including books describing the legalities involved with pirates and privateers, global wars and wartimes, disasters, and the adventurers, speculators, settlers, and natives who populated the American frontier.

He can be reached at thomas@tshawlaw.com.

## *Chapter 1*

# BEFORE 1900

It was the King's fête, a spring celebration for the ruler of France. May 8 would, a century later, become synonymous with victory in Europe. In 1842, monarch Louis Philippe I, dubbed *le Roi Citoyen* (the Citizen King), had come to the throne rather unusually, voted in by the Chambre des Députés. As part of the festivities, large crowds had come to Versailles, the former residence of the kings of France. As the fountain displays (*Grandes Eau*) finished, the large crowd moved on to take the trains back to nearby Paris. The crowd was so large that the train, traveling along the banks of the River Seine, required two engines to pull the 16 to 18 carriages of passengers, all locked into their carriages as was the norm at the time.

On the return trip to Paris, traveling at 25 miles per hour, the axel of the leading locomotive broke, the second engine crashed into the first, and the leading passenger carriages crashed successively into the engines and each other. A great fire broke out, with embers from the engine's fireboxes consuming the wooden, freshly painted carriages. More than 50 people are known to have died but the actual number was unascertainable, due to the significant fire and collision damage. Among the dead was Jules Dumont D'Urville, the explorer responsible for retrieving the Venus de Milo statue for the Louvre. As one passenger recounted his experience,

> We did go on quickly for in less than ten minutes we were half-way on the road. The train from Paris passed. I had but just turned round, when I felt a violent shock. Two others followed, then stopped. First there was a dead silence, then the most dreadful cries. Still I thought the danger passed, as nothing moved, but it was only after I had with much trouble succeeded in forcing my way out of the window that I

found the dreadful position we were in. The engines, the coal carriage, and the four or five first waggons were an immense heap of ruins, under which more than 100 passengers lay buried. Some succeeded in disengaging themselves from the ruins, and ran about in agony. But soon the spectacle became still more terrific; this heap became a furnace. The burning coal, excited by the violence of the wind, had spread itself to the mass of overturned carriages, in which the passengers were burning.[1]

This accident would help kickstart what would become the science of metal fatigue, identifying cracks in materials caused by cyclic loading (repeated use). The French *Académie des Sciences* began an investigation, whose report cited these main causes of the disaster: the use of 4-wheel instead of 6-wheel locomotives; using two locomotives instead of one; locking the passengers inside the carriages preventing their escape; and not isolating the carriages from the locomotives. The report then notes,

It is worthy of remark, that if all those causes had not existed together, and if only a single precaution had been taken, the accident would not have happened. If the first engine had been furnished with six wheels when its axle broke, it would not have lost its equilibrium. If a second locomotive had not been employed, the only consequences of the accident would have been a shock; and even admitting that the first two causes of accident existed, had the doors of the waggons not been locked, a number of the passengers might have escaped the flames. In fine, the interposition of the elastic system would have saved the train, even if no other precaution had been observed.[2]

From this early rail disaster, a new threat announced itself. That of large-scale death arising from the products of the emerging industrial revolution. As mechanization of transport and industry exposed humans to greater risks, institutions struggled to respond. Disasters brought about new legal issues. A nascent regulatory environment was defined by investigations, inquests, statutes, regulations, and court cases. The first section addresses legal issues arising from railroad disasters. The second section discusses legal issues connected with ship-related disasters.

---

[1] *Dreadful Railroad Accident Near Paris – Immense Loss of Life*, THE EXAMINER (May 14, 1842), p. 12.
[2] *Id.*

## 1.1 RAILROADS

### A. Early Cases

| LEGAL ISSUES |
|---|
| ❖ Strict liability or negligence for latent defects<br>❖ Liability standards for carriers of goods vs people |

The liability for the operators of railroads carrying passengers was first fully litigated in 1845, but for coach operators. In *Ingalls*,[3] the supreme judicial court in Massachusetts was reviewing an appeal where the plaintiff, Henry Ingalls, was a passenger on a coach traveling from Boston to Cambridge in September 1841. He was sitting on the top of the coach with other passengers when the rear axle broke, and one wheel came off. Fearing for his safety, he, along with others, jumped down onto the pavement for his safety, but injured his arm in doing so.

In the court of common pleas, the defendant showed that they were diligent in ensuring that the coach was made of high-quality materials and was in a safe and roadworthy condition. They had performed careful inspections and examinations externally. The evidence showed that the accident was caused by a small fracture in the iron in the internal part of the axel, likely created at the time it was forged. The defect was surrounded by good quality iron a quarter inch thick, so the flaw would not have been found by an external inspection or examination. Therefore, the defendant asked for a jury instruction that they would not be liable unless they were negligent in some manner. The judge did not agree, instead instructing the jury that there was an implied promise of roadworthiness.

The defendant also asserted that because Ingalls had jumped down unnecessarily (the coach had not overturned), they were not liable for his injuries. Instead, the judge instructed the jury that they were to evaluate the reasonableness of the plaintiff's act of preservation. If it was a reasonable act and the defendant had put him into this peril by their negligence, then they would be liable for his injury. This was true even though in retrospect it appeared that he could have kept his seat and not jumped. The jury's verdict was for the plaintiff and the defendant appealed.

---

[3] Ingalls v. Bills, 50 Mass. 1, 9 Met. 1 (1845).

The supreme judicial court contrasted the current state of the law, under which common carriers of goods were responsible for all harms except those originating from acts of God or enemies. That degree of responsibility had not been assigned to those who carried people, because passengers could be vigilant about their own rights, unlike goods' owners. It then discussed all the historic cases involving the carrying of passengers.

In the English case *White v. Boulton* in 1791, the negligence of the driver led to a broken arm for a passenger on a mail coach. The instant court viewed this as correct, as it involved negligence. In *Aston v. Heaven*, in 1797, the issue was again negligence of the driver leading to injury, with the English judge differentiating the carrying of goods and people, and negligence required for the latter. In 1803, in *Israel v. Clark,* an overturned coach led to injuries, with the court ruling that the coaches had to be of sufficient strength and "landworthy," an obvious reference to the seaworthiness requirement for ships. The instant court viewed this obligation as not reaching the level of warranty. In *Christie v. Griggs*, in 1809, the axel of the coach in England had, like the present case, broken without the negligence of the driver. The plaintiff had been thrown from the top of the coach. The court instructed the jury as follows,

> as the driver had been cleared of negligence, the question for the jury was as to the sufficiency of the coach. If the axletree was sound, as far as human eye could discover, the defendant was not liable. There was a difference between a contract to carry goods and a contract to carry passengers. For the goods, the carrier was answerable - at all events, but he did not warrant the safety of the passengers. His undertaking as to them went no further than this, that, as far as human care and foresight could go, he would provide for their safe conveyance. Therefore, if the breaking down of the coach was purely accidental, the plaintiff had no remedy for the misfortune he had encountered.[4]

In *Bremner v. Williams*, in 1824, the court said that the coach company "warrants to the public that his stage coach is equal to the journey it undertakes." In *Crofts v. Waterhouse*, in 1825, the same English court held that the coach company was required to use the utmost diligence and care in the carrying of passengers but at least one opinion said that negligence

---

[4] *Id.* at 9-10.

was the appropriate standard. This was described in a case that year to mean carrying the passengers safely. In 1833, in *Sharp v. Grey*, a similar situation occurred, a coach axle breaking whose defect was not obvious. The court issued varied opinions, including one justice who wrote,

> a coach proprietor is liable for all defects in his vehicle, which can be seen at the time of construction, as well as for such as may exist afterwards, and be discovered on investigation. The injury in the present case appears to have been occasioned by an original defect of construction; and if the defendant were not responsible, a coach proprietor might buy ill-constructed or unsafe vehicles, and his passengers be without remedy.[5]

The instant court rejected these analyses, saying,

> But we incline to believe the learned judges gave too much weight to the comparison... that a coach must be roadworthy on the same principle that a ship must be seaworthy. We think the comparison is not correct, and that the analogy applies only where goods are carried, and not where passengers are transported. And no case has been cited, where a passenger has sued a ship owner for an injury arising to him personally in not conducting him in a seaworthy ship. If more was intended by the learned court, than that a coach proprietor is bound to use the greatest care and diligence in providing suitable and sufficient coaches, and keeping them in a safe and suitable condition for use, we cannot agree with them in opinion.[6]

The instant court then turned to American caselaw, citing first *Camden & Amboy Rail Road Co. v. Burke*, in 1835. This case said that for passenger injuries, such companies were only liable if they did not use the appropriate care and diligence. In *Hollister v. Nowlen*, in 1838, that court ruled that,

> stage coach proprietors, and other carriers by land and water, incur a very different responsibility in relation to the *passenger* and his *baggage*. For an injury to the passenger, they are answerable only where there has been a want of proper care, diligence or skill; but in relation to baggage, they are regarded as insurers, and must answer

---
[5] *Id.* at 11.
[6] *Id.* at 12.

for any loss not occasioned by inevitable accident or the public enemies.[7]

The instant court then summarized these prior holdings,

> if such a warranty were imposed by force of law upon the proprietors of coaches and other vehicles for the conveyance of passengers, they would in fact become the warrantors of the work of others, over whom they have no actual control, and—from the number of artizans employed in the construction of the materials of a single coach — whom they could not follow. Unless, therefore, by the application of a similar rule, every workman shall be held as the warrantor, in all events, of the strength, sufficiency and adaptation of his own manufactures to the uses designed — which, in a community like ours, could not be practically enforced — the warranty would really rest on the persons purchasing the article for use, and not upon the makers.[8]

The remaining issue the instant court had to address was the requirement for seaworthiness of ships, and how that should be applied to the requirements for "landworthiness" of coaches,

> But as it respects the seaworthiness of a ship, the technical rules of law respecting it have been so repeatedly examined, and the facts upon which they rest so often investigated, that the questions which arise are those of fact and not of law, and in a vast proportion of instances depend upon the degree of diligence and care which are used in the preservation of vessels, and practically resolve themselves into questions of negligence; so that the evils are very few that arise from the maintenance of the doctrine that a ship must be seaworthy in order to be the subject of insurance.[9]

The instant court concluded negligence was the appropriate standard,

> On the other hand, where the accident arises from a hidden and internal defect, which a careful and thorough examination would not disclose, and which could not be guarded against by the exercise of a sound judgment and the most vigilant oversight, then the proprietor is not liable for the injury, but the misfortune must be borne by the

---

[7] *Id.* at 13.
[8] *Id.* at 14.
[9] *Id.*

sufferer, as one of that class of injuries for which the law can afford no redress in the form of a pecuniary recompense.[10]

There was one other important early case. In *Farwell*,[11] in 1842, the supreme judicial court of Massachusetts was reviewing the liability of a railroad operator for the negligence of its employee. But instead of a duty being owed to its passengers, this was for harm to another employee. The plaintiff was an engineer on a train which, due to another's negligence in operating the switches, ran off the tracks and caused the plaintiff's injury. The court ruled this was not a case of *respondeat superior*, a master liable for the acts of his servant to strangers. Instead, it was a matter of contract,

> The general rule, resulting from considerations as well of justice as of policy, is, that he who engages in the employment of another for the performance of specified duties and services, for compensation, takes upon himself the natural and ordinary risks and perils incident to the performance of such services... it is the ordinary case of one sustaining an injury in the course of his own employment, in which he must bear the loss himself, or seek his remedy, if he have any, against the actual wrongdoer.[12]

Decades later, in *Warner*,[13] in 1868, an appeals court looked at the liability of a railroad company for the death of an employee. In this case, a timber bridge collapsed as the train passed over it, while the decedent was acting as a baggage man on the train. The bridge collapse was the result of decay in the timbers supporting the bridge. The jury instruction was to consider whether the company was to be considered negligent for not ascertaining that there was a decay in the bridge's support structure. The trial court had found that there was no defect in the original composition of the bridge, the competence of the defendant's employees was not impeached, and that regular, sufficient tests of the various parts of the bridge had not found the decay. Believing that the trial court's instructions made the defendant a warrantor and finding no such negligence on the part of the company, the appeals court reversed, directing a new trial be held using this view of corporate liability for the employee's death.

---

[10] *Id.* at 15.
[11] Farwell v. Boston & Worcester Railroad Corporation, 4 Metcalf (Mass.) 49 (1842).
[12] *Id.* at 52.
[13] Warner v. The Erie Railway Co., 39 N.Y. 468. (N.Y. Sept. 1868).

## B. Coupling Loss

| LEGAL ISSUES |
|---|
| ❖ Recreating an accident to verify witness testimony<br>❖ Negligence in braking train leading to criminal liability |

Early train travel in the U.K. was full of hazards in the mid-19th century, operating over a small landmass but moving many passengers. A string of fatal accidents plagued U.K. railways. Near Brighton, on August 25, 1861, a collision of two trains inside a tunnel killed 23 people. On September 2, 1861, near London, an excursion train collided with a freight train, killing 16 people. In Abergele, Wales, on August 20, 1868, carriages of a goods train carrying paraffin came loose and collided with a passenger train causing a fire where 33 people perished. On September 10, 1874, mail and express trains collided on a single-track line in Norfolk, leading to the death of 25 people. In Oxfordshire, on December 24, 1874, a passenger train derailment killed 34 people.

On August 12, 1858, near the Round Oak train station, parts of two trains of the Oxford, Worcester and Wolverhampton Railway collided. Fourteen people were killed and at least 50 injured. This special day excursion was supposed to be only for children and their teachers from Worcester to Wolverhampton. In the event, due to the very low fares, 1,506 people were ticketed, as many adults as children. On the return from Wolverhampton, they were spread over two sets of railway carriages. The leading train, which had 28 carriages and two brake vans, arrived first at the Round Oak station, up an incline. The trailing train, with a single engine, 14 carriages, and two brake vans, was just arriving back at the Brettel Lane station, one and a quarter miles away, down the incline.

The trains operated on a time interval system. Being a little over 10 minutes behind, the second engine then began to make its way out of Brettel Lane station in the dark. As it was doing so, one of the couplings joining the cars together on the uphill train snapped while still at the Round Oak station. This sent 17 passenger carriages and the rear brake van hurtling down toward the oncoming trailing train. The effort of the clerk at Round Oak to telegraph this emergency to the Brettel Lane and other stations did not receive an answer. The uphill train, carrying about 450 passengers, smashed into the second train's engine, causing the three leading cars and the brake van to be destroyed. In addition to the deaths and injuries noted, 170 people applied for compensation for injuries to their clothes or themselves.

The inquiry, authorized by statute,[14] was led by Capt. Henry Whatley (later Sir) Tyler of what would be called the Railway Inspectorate. He noted that three times on the journey before the final plunge, couplings had broken. These had all occurred at the rear part of the train, which the inquiry noted was unusual. This would be expected to occur toward where the engine was, as it provided all the force to get the carriages moving. Couplings breaking near the rear indicated to the investigator that the manual hand brake in the rear brake van "had been employed in a most injudicious manner."[15] This led suspicion to fall on the guard responsible for the brake in the rear van, as described in the report,

> A good deal of suspicion, therefore, to say the least of it, must fall upon the hind guard, Frederick Cook, as to the mode in which the [brake] of the last van was employed on the journey towards Worcester; and this suspicion is by no means lessened by the circumstance that he permitted half-a-dozen passengers to ride with him in his van, and that he employed one of their number, according to his own admission, to take the [brake] off in two cases. There is evidence, also, of his having been smoking and drinking with the passengers in his van, which leads to the belief that his conduct must have been altogether highly irregular.[16]

Further complicating the situation were not only the inclines, broken couplings and snapped side chains, but also the many curves on the route, as well as smoke from factories diminishing visibility, and the dark night. The first train had arrived at 20:10 at Round Oak and the second train arrived at 20:11 at Brettel Lane and departed at 20:14 for Round Oak. The fireman in the second engine of the first train had noticed a sudden jerk, as if the rear brake had been taken off and the carriages then moved backward under their own weight. Cook claimed he had applied the brake

---

[14] An Act for regulating Railways, 3&4 Vict. c. 97; An Act for the better Regulation of Railways, and for the Conveyance of Troops, 5&6 Vict. c. 55.
[15] Capt. H.W. Tyler to the Railway Dept., Board of Trade (Oct. 16, 1858).
[16] *Id.*

when he realized the situation, but he had later jumped off just before the collision, after advising the nearest passengers to do likewise.

During the coroner's inquest, Cook had testified,

We left Brettel Lane at 8.03 and arrived at Round Oak at about 8.10. On going to Brettel Lane I found the train was coming back, and I put my brake on to stop it, but it was to no effect. I put my brake on before the train parted. It is a usual thing to put the brake on before we reach the station. I put my brake off when I thought the train had stopped, and then I discovered the train was coming back, and I again applied the brake. When I put on the brake after the train had parted, it seemed to draw them up a bit, but they got a head afterwards. The brake was a good one and acted very well, but the weight was too much for it. We generally start about ten minutes from each other. I called out to the passengers and told them to jump out, saying, "Please to jump for your lives". I jumped out about ten yards from the spot where the collision took place. I saw the other train coming up, and put out my hand lamp, which is a red light, and waved it above the van; I also sounded my whistle. When I jumped out I left the brake on.[17]

Capt. Tyler undertook a series of experiments and calculations to test Cook's testimony. He loaded weights representing the prior occupants into the same number of carriages and had these travel down the same stretch of rail to check the velocity reached and braking distance. These experiments showed that the speed of 10 mph, which is what Cook claimed the train was traveling at, was reached in 440 yards. Applying the brake allowed the train to stop in 883 yards, which was 111 yards short of the point of collision. When the brake was applied as Cook stated, just after the carriages started heading back down the incline, the stopping distances were much shorter. Through calculations, at 1,434 yards to the collision site, the maximum velocity of the train could have been 18 mph, reduced by any wind resistance.

From all this testing evidence, Capt. Tyler stated,

---

[17] *The Late Fatal Railway Catastrophe Near Dudley, The Adjourned Inquest*, Wolverhampton Chronicle (Sept. 8, 1858).

The conclusion, therefore, is hardly, as far as I can see, to be avoided, that Cook was not in his van at all while the carriages were running backward; and that, no [brake] having been applied to prevent it, the carriages, acquiring fresh velocity at every turn of their wheels as they descended towards Brettle Lane, came into collision with the train somewhat behind them at a speed somewhat under 18 miles an hour, more or less, according to the strength and direction of the wind.[18]

The position of the brake screw also clearly showed that the brake had been off at the time of the collision. Tyler concluded that Cook had left the brake van when it reached Round Oak station without setting the brake. This led to the carriages moving forward towards the engine, then rebounding backwards, causing the coupling to snap. Tyler believed that although the couplings gave way under the weight of the passengers and the steep incline, when handled by competent men, the couplings should not break under normal stress loads. He laid further blame on the company that employed Cook for not discerning his true character, and for not employing more brake guards.

Tyler then concluded on the cause of the accident,

A man was selected by the company for the important duty of head guard, to a heavy train who proved to be anything but trustworthy and careful, and who, in not performing that duty with the attention that it required, caused the fracture of a defective coupling, and permitted the greater part of his train to run backwards down a steep gradient, on which it came into violent collision with a following train.[19]

The coroner's jury believed that Cook should be indicted for manslaughter. However, he was not billed by a grand jury, which seemingly believed that he had been at his post at the brake, as he testified. As the judge had instructed the jury, that while his efforts may have proven insufficient, they were likely rooted in his fears, as another member of the brake van had testified to, rather than a level of negligence sufficient to comprise manslaughter. Tyler's experiments, while factual, were done without the stress of being in a real disaster, and so did not account for the human fear factor, as the testers knew they would not be dying.

---

[18] Capt. H.W. Tyler to the Railway Dept., Board of Trade (Oct. 16, 1858).
[19] *Id.*

## C. Train Collision

| LEGAL ISSUES |
|---|
| ❖ Duty to deploy improvements in safety technology<br>❖ Creating common operating rules and regulations |

Through the balance of the 19th century, as American railroads build up their capacity, and passenger traffic greatly increased, so did the number and size of railway accidents. Some of the most severe were those with the highest toll on human life. In Norwalk, Connecticut, on May 6, 1853, a train went through an open draw bridge and 46 people died. On July 17, 1856, in Camp Hill, Pennsylvania, a head-on collision killed 66 people. In Mishawaka, Indiana, on June 28, 1859, a bridge collapse led to the death of 41 people. On December 18, 1867, in Angola, New York, a derailment on a bridge led to 42 deaths. In Ashatabula, Ohio, on December 29, 1876, a bridge collapsed while a train was passing over it and 86 people died.

On August 26, 1871, in Revere, Massachusetts, an accommodation (local) train operated by the Eastern Railroad Company was rear-ended by an express train. This resulted in the death of 29 people, with 57 more injured. The report from the railroad commissioners' investigation stated, "The collision was the result of a combination of fortuitous circumstances deeply implicating the management of the road."[20] This was part of 280 total injuries on Massachusetts' railroads that year. Half were passengers, one-fifth employees, and the remainder wandered on to the tracks or were struck at crossings. Of the 157 who were killed in the state in 1871, about one-quarter were passengers, mostly from this one accident.

The report noted that the company relied on a fixed schedule for their trains, neglecting to use a telegraph system to communicate the actual departure times of the trains to stations up the track. This was despite the railroad having mostly single tracks along their road, shared by trains moving in both directions. Being the busy summer holiday season, the rolling stock of the railroad was already over-stretched with added passengers, and any delays made it worse. Most trains leaving the Boston station were late due to the congestion, but there was no communication of these late departures to the varied stations they would pass ahead.

---

[20] *The Collision at Revere*, THIRD ANNUAL REPORT, BOARD OF RAILROAD COMMISSIONERS, p. xcv (Jan. 1872).

The accommodation train was scheduled to leave Boston station at 19:15, and the express train, which had a separate destination, was scheduled to depart Boston at 20:00. Their actual departure times were 19:40 and 20:04, respectively. Complicating this were two other trains on the same northbound track, which were to depart the main line at the branch at Saugus. The branch line operated as a single track, under the company rule that no outbound train could go onto the branch track until all inbound trains on that branch track had passed. However, no siding was provided to allow an outbound train to wait on. The usual switchman had outbound trains wait on the branch track or the southbound track of the main line, under a flag, but he was ill on August 26. His replacement simply followed company policy, having trains wait on the main northbound track.

In all, three trains ended up waiting there on the main track for an inbound branch train. The express train eventually caught up to these others and was stopped by the flagman of the train ahead of him. However, that train was not the accommodation train, as per the schedule, but one of the branch trains that was behind schedule. The engineer of the accommodation train assumed the train behind him was the express train, which would then be aware of his delays. This was important, as they would be on the same track after the branch. But the express train did not know this, and no message was given to the station manager at the branch to pass on. The express was now only a few minutes behind the accommodation train, not the 45 minutes stated in the timetable.

When the accommodation train pulled into Revere station, the express train was less than a mile behind it. However, its engineer was likely unable to make out the dim taillights (ordinary red lanterns without reflective power) of the accommodation train at the station in the darkness and fog. He also had to check a light signal on a masthead that the track was clear ahead. When the express engineer again looked ahead, and saw the accommodation train's lights, he quickly reversed the engine, but it was too late to stop his train, then traveling at 20-25 mph. The whistle for brakes did not allow for sufficient setting of hand brakes in several cars, and regardless, the engineer had jumped off before setting the locomotive brake. The few brakes that were set slowed the oncoming train to only about 10 mph, as the tracks were slippery with the damp conditions.

The locomotive plowed into the back car of the accommodation train at 20:15, pushing itself two-thirds of the way into that unfortunate car. Then a fire broke out as the kerosene lanterns used for illumination fell and broke, fed by the coal in the engine. There were 65-70 people aboard the accommodation train's back car, where all the fatalities occurred. People died from crushing, by scalding from the engine's boiler steam, and fire. The accident's causes attributed to operator Eastern Railroad were:

- Laxity of discipline in train movement and operating the road
- A rolling stock deficiency for the increase in summer travel
- The lack of siding at the branch junction
- Non-use of the telegraph to eliminate waiting at the branch
- Providing extra services at the expense of regular services

The commission listed the following causes of a general nature common to all railroad companies that contributed to this crash:

1st. A deficiency in the system of signals by which an interval either of space or of time was insured between trains following each other;

2d. The want of a complete telegraph system which should keep the central office fully advised at all times of the exact position of each train on the road, and in communication with all of such trains at the several stations;

3d. An insufficiency of brake power;

4th. The use of taillights of insufficient penetrating power.[21]

The commissioners regarded as their mandate, after an accident was reported to them, and investigated, to recommend possible changes to the law to increase railroad safety. They listed 15 causes of accidents which could be laid to some defect, in the following two categories:

Derailment by:
1. breaking of axle or rail
2. expansion of rail
3. defective switch
4. reason of insufficient cattle-guards.

---

[21] *Id.*, p. cxxix-cxxx.

Collisions caused by:
5. carelessness of employees
6. imperfect regulations
7. defective signals
8. want of telegraphic communication
9. want of brake power
10. railroad grade-crossings
11. breaking through bridges owing to want of guards
12. falling of train through draw
13. concussion in starting or stopping train
14. falling between cars while passing through train in motion
15. explosion of locomotives.

In conjunction with the railroad companies, the commission's recommendations addressed causes 6, 7, 8, 9, 13, and 14. Causes 1, 2, 5, and 15 were deemed to be beyond the control of legislation. Causes 3, 4, and 12 were already addressed under statute. Causes 10 and 11 had previously been strongly recommended by the commission, without avail.

The final recommendations included: adoption of brakes that could be operated by the engineer; construction of passenger cars to prevent telescoping; standardized heating devices to prevent fires during accidents; use of candles or other devices with a high ignition temperature for illumination; specialized lanterns for taillights; the deployment of a signal brakeman on the last car of each train; and the use of the telegraph system. The commission also created a set of operating regulations to be used by all railroads in the state. There were recommendations that the railroad companies would not accept, such as more fully integrating the telegraph into railroad operations. The commission was emphatic on what was needed, looking to the blocking system in England, where a train could not enter a space of track until the prior train had telegraphed that it had cleared that space.

The commission had noted the number of statutes passed in the prior six years in the commonwealth of Massachusetts included 49 general laws and resolutions but 294 special laws. It viewed the latter disdainfully, and wished a single general law for railroads, stating "the mass of special railroad legislation tends steadily to increase, and it is a notorious fact that it is now almost impossible to say what the exact position or rights of any given railroad corporation are; in some cases these depend on the construction of a hundred special laws."[22]

The rules and regulations agreed between the commission and the railroads addressed several areas. The first was signaling, which included whistles for braking and when approaching crossings; colors and combinations of flags (in daylight) and lanterns (in darkness); and special signals at drawbridges, junctions, and crossings. The second was the telegraph, which must be used for all dispatch orders. The message must be confirmed and then a copy each given to the conductor and engineer. Any accident or detention of a train off its schedule must be quickly notified to the closest station, who must telegraph the central or terminal station, and to any location where the approaching trains may be signaled.

The third was train services, which had many facets. Passenger trains had precedence over freight trains, and passenger and freight trains were to have 10-minute intervals between them. Accommodation trains could run five minutes behind an express train but there had to be a 15-minute interval if running ahead of an express train. Express trains were not to pass a station it was not stopping at with a speed over 10 mph. Speeds were to be regulated, and drawbridges were to be approached carefully and at a moderate and uniform speed. Additional rules were provided for meeting and passing and for operating on a single track.

The fourth was a set of rules for each category of employees. This list included specific rules for: conductors (overall responsible for the entire train and its safety), engineers and firemen, brakemen, baggage masters, station agents, section masters, flagmen and gate tenders, and draw tenders. Generally, they were all told,

> The safety of the passengers is the first consideration; to this, together with the safety, regularity and punctuality of the trains, and the comfort and convenience of passengers, all operations of working or repairing the road must be completely and entirely subordinate. All employees are expected to exercise the greatest care and watchfulness to prevent injury to persons or property; and they must in all cases of doubt take the course which involves no danger.[23]

---

[22] *Id.*, p. x-xi.
[23] *Id.*, p. cclvi.

## D. Bridge Collapse

| LEGAL ISSUES |
|---|
| ❖ Bridge designer being culpable after collapse<br>❖ Use of statutory courts of inquiry |

On December 28, 1879, a train was crossing a railroad bridge in Scotland when it collapsed in a storm, killing around 75 people, everyone aboard. The total number included 67-68 people who purchased tickets for Dundee and other locations, two with season tickets, and five employees of the railway. The Northen British Railways service from Burntisland to Dundee was crossing the Tay Railway Bridge. This bridge had been designed by a well-known figure, Sir Thomas Bouch, who oversaw construction and then the maintenance up to the collapse. The bridge was built by the firm Hopkins, Gilkes & Co., not the originally selected contractor firm, which had withdrawn due to the illness of its principal partner.

A court of inquiry was called, as specified under statute, when a formal investigation was commenced.[24] This court was comprised of three persons: the wreck commissioner, Henry Cadogan Rothery, the railways chief inspector, William Yolland, and the head of the Institute of Civil Engineers (ICE), William Henry Barlow. In three different sets of meetings, spread over several months and locations, they interviewed witnesses to the events of the day and the construction and maintenance of the bridge. This included Bouch and the contractors. They also appointed Henry Law of the ICE to do detailed analyses and asked the railway company for specific information.

The report issued by the court of inquiry described the bridge. It was 3,465 yards long, supported across 85 piers, on which each had from three to six vertical columns. The horizontal girders were of wrought iron lattice work. The land on the south shore was much higher than the land on the north shore, as the bridge rose to its summit of 88 feet above the water between piers 30 and 36. Between piers 28 and 41, the road was raised to allow for the passage of ships. This area was 3,149 feet long, comprised of 13 sections, 11 of 245 feet and 2 of 227 feet. It was this area of the bridge that fell.

---

[24] An Act to amend the Law respecting the Inspection and Regulation of Railways, 34&35 Vict. c. 78.

As it was the girders of the highest sections that fell, the report looked at their supporting piers. These were first built on cast iron caissons 31 feet in diameter surrounded by brick that were floated out and dropped into place, and concrete was used to fill them. On top of those, hexagonal shaped piers, 27.5 feet long and half the diameter, 15.5 feet, were then set on top. To the six faces of the pier were placed six cast-iron columns. On top of the columns were cast iron girders, which was topped by a cast iron table, on which sat the main girders forming the sides of the bridge. The report noted there were imperfections in some of the workmanship and in the various fittings.

The bridge had been inspected by a railway inspector but on a day of lighter winds. Use of the bridge was then approved, with the stipulation that trains should not exceed 25 mph. On the dark and stormy night of the accident, the train, consisting of an engine, five passenger carriages and a guard's van, was observed by a railway employee from the south end. From some distance away, he saw sparks coming from its wheels. After three minutes, there was a bright flash of light then total darkness. The engine was found with its throttle fully open, and the brake was not deployed, indicating that the engineer had no warning.

The report then turned to the ability of the bridge to withstand the forces of the wind, the so-called "wind loading." On a different bridge design project in Scotland, the Forth Bridge, a series of leading engineers had taken part and even turned to the Astronomer Royal, Sir George Biddell Airy, for an opinion, extracted as follows.

> We know that upon very limited surfaces, and for very limited times, the pressure of the wind does amount sometimes to 40 lbs. per square foot, or, in Scotland, probably to more. So far as I am aware, our positive knowledge, as derived from instrumental record, goes no further; but in studying the registers it is impossible not to see that these high pressures are momentary, and it seems most probable that they arise from some irregular whirlings of the air which extend to no great distance, I should say certainly to no distance comparable to the dimensions of the proposed bridge; and I think that the fairest estimate of the pressure on the entire bridge would be formed by taking the mean of the recorded pressures at one point of space for a moderate extent of time as representing the mean pressures on a

moderate extent of space at one instant of time. Adopting this consideration, I think we may say that the greatest wind pressure to which a plain surface like that of the bridge will be subjected in its whole extent is 10 lbs. per square foot.[25]

Apparently, influenced by this report, Bouch made no special provision for the winds in designing the Tay Bridge. This was considered by the inquiry to be a misunderstanding by Bouch, as he did not account for the 40 pounds of pressure from gusts, nor the fact that while the gusts may be localized in the 1,600-foot spans of the Forth Bridge, they would be more significant in the 245-foot spans of the Tay Bridge. Cumulatively, the problems with the incorrectly made and installed ties of the columns, combined with the gusting wind, the weight of the train, the larger surface area the train provided for the wind gusts, and the vibrations caused by the train on the rails, most likely led to the collapse of the bridge.

The conclusions, in material part, were,

5th. That the iron piers used in place of the brick piers originally contemplated were strong enough for supporting the vertical weight, but were not of a sufficiently substantial character to sustain, at so great a height, girders of such magnitude as those which fell. That the cross bracing and its fastenings were too weak to resist the lateral action of heavy gales of wind.

6th. That the workmanship and fitting of the several parts comprising the piers were inferior in many respects.

7th. That although a large staff of assistants and inspectors was employed, we consider that a sufficiently strict supervision was not exercised during the construction of that part of the work made at the Wormit foundry. We think that the inequality of thickness in some of the columns, the conical holes cast in the lugs, and several imperfections in workmanship which have been ascertained by this inquiry, ought to have been prevented.

8th. That the arrangements for the supervision of the bridge after its completion were not satisfactory…

---

[25] Tay Bridge Disaster: Report Of The Court of Inquiry, and Report Of Mr. Rothery, Upon the Circumstances Attending the Fall of a Portion of the Tay Bridge on the 28th December 1879, p. 10.

12th. That the fall of the bridge was occasioned by the insufficiency of the cross-bracings and its fastenings to sustain the force of the gale on the night of December 28, 1879, and the bridge had been previously strained by other gales.[26]

The court's final report was signed only by Yolland and Barlow, as Rothery submitted his own. His report noted that the opinion of the Astronomer Royal that Bouch claimed to rely on was sent in April 1873, nearly two years after the contract with the original contractors was signed. This implied that the astronomer's report had no influence on his original bridge design. Further, in current testimony from the Astronomer Royal, he asserted that his opinion had to do only with the Forth Bridge, which was a suspension bridge which could flex with the wind. However, the Tay Bridge, built on piers and columns, would not be able to return to its original position after a strong wind (i.e., it did not flex with the wind).

Rothery believed the terms of reference for the court of inquiry allowed assigning culpability, which the other members did not, and so he proceeded to identify who that was,

> The conclusion then, to which me have come, is that this bridge was badly designed, badly constructed, and badly maintained, and that its downfall was due to inherent defects in the structure, which must sooner or later have brought it down. For these defects both in the design, the construction, and the maintenance, Sir Thomas Bouch is, in our opinion, mainly to blame.
>
> For the faults of design he is entirely responsible. For those of construction he is principally to blame in not having exercised that supervision over the work, which would have enabled him to detect and apply a remedy to them. And for the faults of maintenance he is also principally, if not entirely, to blame in having neglected to maintain such an inspection over the structure, as its character imperatively demanded.[27]

---

[26] *Id.* p. 15-16.
[27] *Id.* p. 15-16.

## E. Derailment

| LEGAL ISSUES |
|---|
| ❖ Common carriers' passenger liability<br>❖ Leaseholders of railroads having legal liability |

Like many nascent railroads during the growth of rail in the United States in the 19th century,[28] the Pickering Valley Railway Company started with a special act of the Pennsylvania state legislature.[29] This allowed the railroad to run from a point on the road of its de facto parent, the Philadelphia and Reading Railroad Company (PRR), for up to 20 miles, with branches that could extend up to 10 miles. It was subject to the 1849 state act regulating railroads and could sell its capital stock to any other railroad company. The PRR bought most of the capital stock, guaranteed the bonds to be used for construction, and took out a 29-year lease on the railroad. It opened for service in 1871, carrying passengers and agricultural and mining products.

On October 4, 1877, a passenger train on this line was involved in an accident that killed seven people and injured many more. The train derailed during a severe storm, which had washed out part of the embankment on which the track sat. The rain in the hour before the derailment was about 2 inches, and nearly 5 inches during the day. The coroner's inquiry noted that the amount of land draining into the gully under the railroad that night had increased by half due to a diversion caused by a wooden trough under the railroad, so a significantly higher amount of water moved in the direction of the eventual washout.

The verdict of the coroner's jury[30] also discussed the unusual formation of the cars in the train, with the tank (tender) running first, the engine running second in a reversed direction, then the gentlemen's car, the ladies' car, and the milk car. Company policy specified the engine should be first, followed by the tank, then the milk car, the ladies' car, and the gentlemen's car. This would have led to fewer casualties, as the milk car did not derail, and this should have been the gentlemen's car instead. Six men had died, including the engineer and brakeman but the conductor

---

[28] For a deeper discussion of American railroad industry expansion during the 19th century, *see* THOMAS J. SHAW, THE LEGAL HISTORY OF THE AMERICAN FRONTIER.

[29] Pub. L. 1869, 686, An Act to incorporate the Pickering Valley Railroad Company (Apr. 1869).

[30] *Pickering Valley*, RAILWAY WORLD (Oct. 27, 1877), p. 1028.

located in the milk car was uninjured. The verdict also decried the use of iron rods on the outside of windows, as the escape of passengers from the carriages after an accident would be hindered.

From this accident, a legal case was filed in the court of common pleas for a trespass on the case (modernly, a tort) for injuries suffered by Harman Anderson, based on the negligence of the PRR. The car he was riding in was thrown from the track and he pleaded counts: of negligence of the PRR and its employees in the management of the train; that there was a duty of care to maintain its tracks, align its cars properly, and have the engine's light casting forward to see the track and it was the failure of this duty that led to his injuries; and there was a duty of care to keep the track, embankment, culverts, and drains in good repair, with the latter two erected appropriately to pass water under the embankments, and it was the failure of this duty that led to his car being thrown from the track.

The PRR asserted this was caused by an act of God it could not be held responsible for. The verdict in the court of common pleas was for the plaintiff Anderson, in the sum of $3,500, which led the PRR to appeal. In *Anderson*,[31] the supreme court of Pennsylvania heard the appeal. The PRR, as appellants, asserted, on prior caselaw, that the railroad did not warrant its cars and road but only that it acted with due care. A passenger alleging damages for injuries must do more than just show he was a passenger. The defendant should not have to prove both a lack of negligence and an act of God. By providing drainage for the embankment as designed by a competent engineer, the defendant should be relieved of all liability.

The plaintiff, appellee here, contended that the contract between the carrier and the ticket purchaser required that there was no negligence in the construction or maintenance of the road or the rolling stock or the operation of the trains. Further, the position of the defendant as a lessee of the railroad had no implication on the defendant's liability. The supreme court first ruled on the primary errors raised by the appellant, paraphrasing what the trial court judge had said,

> that where for a consideration a railroad company undertakes to transport a passenger from one point of its line to another, there arises an implied contract, upon part of the company, that it has, for

---

[31] Philadelphia & Reading Railroad v. Anderson, 94 Pa. 351 (Pa. May 1880).

that purpose, provided a safe and sufficient road, and that its cars are sound and roadworthy; that where the passenger is injured by any accident arising from a collision or defect in machinery, he is required, in the first place, to prove no more than the fact of the accident and the extent of his injury; that a prima facie case is thus made out, and the onus is cast upon the carrier to disprove negligence; that, in the case trying, the legal presumption was that the injuries to the plaintiff were caused by the negligence of the defendant, and that this presumption continued until a countervailing presumption of fact was established. To this the learned judge added, that this prima facie presumption might be overthrown by proof, to the satisfaction of the jury, that the injury complained of resulted from inevitable accident, or from something against which no human prudence or foresight could provide.[32]

The court wholly concurred with the direction of the trial court, which had utilized many of its own prior rulings. It then quoted from its own cases regarding the liability of passenger carriers,

But though in legal contemplation they do not warrant the absolute safety of passengers, they are yet bound to the exercise of the utmost diligence and care. The slightest neglect against which human prudence and foresight may guard, and by which hurt or loss is occasioned, will render them liable to answer in damages. Nay, the mere happening of an injurious accident raises, prima facie, a presumption of neglect, and throws upon the carrier the onus of showing it did not exist. This punctilious attention to the safety of the passenger embraces the duty of providing strong and sufficient carriages, or other conveyances for the journey, in every respect, sea, road and river worthy; safe and steady horses, or other means of progression, and skilful drivers, conductors and other agents, whose duty it is to use every precaution against danger.[33]

The court then moved on to another exception raised, that if the road and drainage were designed by a competent engineer and implemented according to his design, and if a violent storm washed away the embankment, the defendant should not be liable for the error of the

---
[32] *Id.* at 357.
[33] *Id.* at 358.

engineer. Here, the court differentiated between an employee and a passenger when assessing liability for an accident,

> But this doctrine can have no application to the case in hand, and for the very good reason that a passenger is not an employee. The one by his contract is presumed to run the ordinary risks of the machinery and appliances he is engaged to supervise or use; he is also held to a knowledge of the character and obvious defects of such machinery and appliances, as well as the skill and habits of his co-servants. A passenger, on the other hand, neither can know, nor is presumed to know, anything about these things. He has paid for his passage, and he is wholly passive in the hands and at the mercy of the transportation company and its agents. The doctrine advocated by the defendant's counsel, by which the passenger would be put on a par with an employee, will not do; it accords neither with reason nor precedent.[34]

The appellants had argued the key point that this involved an act of God which they should not be liable for. The court disagreed, noting that the trial court had differentiated that from the negligence of how the drainage of the embankment was constructed. If the jury found the latter was true, then it being an act of God would not suffice as a defense to liability. The court than turned to other assignments of error regarding the order of the cars in the train,

> These points required the court to instruct the jury, that there was no evidence from which they could find the defendant liable to the plaintiff for alleged negligence in running the locomotive backwards, with the tender in front and milk-car in the rear. The answer was as follows: "We answer these points affirmatively. The matters contained in these points would not be sufficient without proof that they caused the accident, or contributed directly to it; but the jury will consider the evidence relating to the matters contained in these points with other evidence in the case, in deciding whether or not defendant has been guilty of negligence." This answer is somewhat ambiguous, but as it is more favorable to the defendant than it ought to have been, we cannot understand why it is complained of. Three locomotive engineers say that an engine running backwards cannot be so readily

---

[34] *Id.* at 359.

handled as when in its proper position, and that the light is unsteady and unreliable. Indeed, any one might know that running an engine hind end foremost, with the tender in front, especially at night and in a storm, when the utmost vigilance is required, was, in itself, a dangerous circumstance. Then, as to the position of the milk-car, it is sufficient to say that the defendant's own rules condemned that, and pronounced such an arrangement dangerous.[35]

The supreme court had previously ruled that the fact that the defendant only leased the road was not relevant as it was the contracted common carrier. The lower court's decision was affirmed, and a later motion for re-argument was refused.

---

[35] *Id.* at 361.

## 1.2 SHIPS

### A. Lake Collision

| LEGAL ISSUES |
|---|
| ❖ Rules for avoiding collisions between ships <br> ❖ Mutual liability for damages in collisions |

Maritime disaster has been present from the start of European settlement in the New World. In the 19th century, many ships in the United States were lost, for a variety of reasons. On September 27, 1854, the steamship *Arctic*, sailing to the United States from Liverpool, collided with a smaller fishing vessel, killing 350 people. Off the Carolinas, on September 9, 1857, the *Central America* sank during a hurricane, killing more than 400 people. On April 24, 1859, the immigrant ship *Pomona* coming to the United States sank off the west coast of Ireland, killing almost 400 people. On April 27, 1865, a boiler explosion on the Mississippi River killed more than 1,500 on board the *Sultana*. The steamship *Pacific* was hit by a ship of sail on November 4, 1875, off the U.S. Pacific coast, killing upwards of 300 people.

On August 20, 1852, the *Atlantic*, a paddle steamship, collided with a screw propellor steamship, the *Ogdensburg*, on Lake Erie near Canada. The *Atlantic* was traveling southwest, from Buffalo to Detroit, via Erie. More than 250 passengers were initially on board and a like number came on at Erie, significantly more than the ship's normal capacity. The *Ogdensburg* was traveling northeast, from Cleveland to Ogdensburg, New York. In the middle of the night, they collided, ripping a hole in the *Atlantic*. Both ships continued on until the *Ogdensburg* came back to the sinking *Atlantic*, saving passengers still on the ship or those in the water who had not drowned. The number who perished was upwards of 200 people.

In *Ward*,[36] the owners of the *Atlantic* libeled[37] the *Ogdensburg* for the $75,000 cost of their ship. The district court instead awarded the $3,000 sought by the respondents for damage to their vessel. The case was appealed to the circuit court, which analyzed in detail what had caused the collision. In the days transitioning from sailing ships to internally powered ships, identification of the type of the other ship was critical to avoid

---

[36] Ward v. Chamberlain, 29 F. Cas. 169 (Cir. Ct. S.D. Ohio May 1855).
[37] For a deeper discussion of the libel process involving ships, *see* THOMAS J. SHAW, THE LEGAL HISTORY OF PIRATES & PRIVATEERS.

collisions, given the differences in speed and power. The proper signal lights were essential at night. All ships had some form of white lights, but the newer steam-powered ships used colored lights, required by law.

An 1838 statute mandated those steamships running in the dark carry signal lights visible to other ships on the same waters.[38] In 1849, this was clarified to include ships traveling on lakes at night.[39] Ships on a starboard tack (her right side exposed to the wind) must show a red light while those on a port tack (left side exposed to the wind) must show a green light. A white light signaled traveling with the wind or being at anchor. Powered ships were to have a triangular light on the stern, a green light on the starboard side and a red light on the larboard (port) side. Lights had to be big enough to ensure a good and sufficient luminosity. The owners of non-compliant vessels were liable for all loss or damage caused to other ships.

The court summarized the *Atlantic*'s case as pursuing a southwest by west course, when the *Ogdensburg's* two lights were seen off the port bow. These lights were three-fourths of a point (a point on the compass rose is 11.25 degrees, 1/32 of the full 360 degrees) off their direction of travel. The initial order given was to port the wheel and then, when the lights appeared closer, to hard a-port the wheel (this would turn the ship to the right, avoiding the collision). Seeing it was too late, the second mate, in charge then, decided to let his ship proceed ahead. The *Ogdensburg* crashed into the port side of the *Atlantic*. The latter ship's bow sunk within a few minutes but the stern stayed above water until the next morning.

The respondent's case was they were traveling northeast by east, when they saw the lights of the *Atlantic* 2-2.5 points off the starboard bow. No course change was made, until the collision seemed inevitable, when a hard a-starboard command for the wheel was given (turn to the left). The engines were stopped and reversed. The *Atlantic* crew said they had their full running lights on, and the *Ogdensburg* crew claimed the same. The court reviewed the course that second mate McNatt and master Richardson claimed and said such a course would have seen them miss the collision by ten miles. Far from being on a parallel course, as claimed,

---

[38] An Act to provide for the better security of the lives of passengers on board of vessels propelled in whole or in part by steam, c. 25, s. 2. ch. 191, § 10.
[39] An Act making Appropriations for Lighthouses, Lightboats, Buoys, &c., and providing for the Erection and Establishment of the same, and for other Purposes, c. 30, s. 2. ch. 105, § 5.

McNatt could not have seen the red port lights of the other ship over his starboard bow unless he was coming at an angle from the south below that ship. He would have instead seen the green starboard lights.

The court concluded, on the evidence and McNatt's statements, that he intended to pass around the bow of the other ship but could not after the *Atlantic* ported the wheel. Several witnesses testified the lights of the *Ogdensburg* were so dim, they could not be seen from more than a ship's length away. The lights had not trimmed that night and only were when ordered by the captain after the collision. These were white lights, not the colored lights required for a powered ship. The court found fault with the *Ogdensburg* because it had not ported her wheel when it first saw the lights of the *Atlantic*, to pass by its stern. The court said there was no rule of navigation that supported McNatt in steering the course he did.

The court referred to a Supreme Court case describing how to avoid collisions. In *St. John*,[40] the collision was between a steam-powered ship and a wind-powered ship. Ships with the wind had to yield to ships against the wind. If both ships were in the same position versus the wind, the ship on the larboard tack had to give way. When a steam-powered ship encountered a sailing vessel, the latter could keep their course, the steamer had to avoid colliding. Two steamships must both perform a helm a-port. The Court referred to the masters of Trinity House, the British organization created under royal charter by Henry VIII. His daughter Elizabeth had them design signals ensuring ships reached their destinations safely.[41] Trinity House also licensed pilots on the Thames.

This led the instant court to quote from that case,

The Trinity masters say: "We beg to observe to this court, that the golden rule so long established, must be strictly adhered to; it is this, that the larboard tack is to give way, and the vessel on the starboard tack to hold on." This rule when applied to the open sea is pregnant with danger, as above observed. It is salutary, no doubt, when applied in a narrow river, where its shores show the position and course of each vessel. But the masters say: "And the new rule which has been lately made for steam vessels, namely, each to put the helm a-port

---

[40] St. John v. Paine, 51 U.S. 557 (1850).
[41] An Act concerning sea-marks and mariners, 8 Eliz. I ch. 13.

under all doubtful circumstances." This rule is founded on common sense and common prudence. It was disregarded by the propeller.[42]

The court felt *Ogdensburg* was also at fault with its signal lights. Being barely visible, the other ship believed it was a sailing ship. The court, though, believed that the entire fault did not lie with the *Ogdensburg*. The second mate oversaw the *Atlantic* during the collision. Although the court agreed he had acted correctly if ascertaining that the other ship was a ship of sail he could outrun, he did not know that for certain. The crew owed a significant responsibility to the 500 passengers aboard, believing that it was not sufficient just to be within the rules of navigation. They also had a responsibility to ascertain the type of vessel in front of them.

Quoting again from *St. John*, the court wrote,

> speaking of the Trinity rules, the court say: "These rules have their exceptions in extreme cases, depending upon the special circumstances of the case, and in respect to which no general rule can be laid down or applied. Either vessel may find herself in a position at the time when it would be impossible to conform to them without certain peril. These cannot be anticipated, and therefore cannot be provided for by any fixed regulation. They can only be examined, and the management of the vessel approved or condemned, as the case may arise."[43]

And then from another Supreme Court case,[44]

> the court say: "Neither can the order to stop the engine and back, instead of changing the course of the steamship, be regarded as a fault. It would evidently have been unwise to change her course until the course of the approaching vessel was ascertained. She might be approaching at an angle that would clear the steamship, and a change in the course of the latter might produce a collision, instead of preventing it."[45]

The court believed that the rule of porting the helm would suffice if ships were on parallel courses but when they approached at an angle, the

---

[42] Ward v. Chamberlain, 29 F. Cas. 169, at 173.
[43] *Id.* at 174.
[44] Peck v. Sanderson, 58 U.S. 178 (1854).
[45] Ward v. Chamberlain, 29 F. Cas. 169, at 174.

only safe course was to stop and reverse engines until the situation cleared itself, and the ship's master was called to take command. With the fault being mutual, the court ruled the damages were to be divided equally, and not apportioned according to culpability. The district court's decree was reversed accordingly. This meant the owners of the *Ogdensburg* owed the owners of the *Atlantic* $36,000.

Appealed to the Supreme Court,[46] the *Ogdensburg* was found at fault because of they did not have a competent office on the deck, because the signal lights were not displayed in accordance with the law, and because the mate had not taken the steps to avoid the other ship when he first saw their lights. The Court interpreted the 1849 statute to mean that,

> Failure to comply with the regulation in case a collision ensues is declared to be a fault, and the offending party is made responsible for all loss or damage resulting from the neglect; but it is not declared by that section or by any other rule of admiralty law in the jurisprudence of the United States that the neglect to show signal lights on the part of one vessel discharges the other, as they approach, from the obligation to adopt all reasonable and practicable precautions to prevent a collision. Absence of signal lights in cases falling within the act of Congress renders the vessel liable to the extent already mentioned, but it does not confer any right upon the other vessel to disregard or violate the rules of navigation or to neglect any reasonable and practicable precaution to avoid a collision which the circumstances afford the means and opportunity to adopt.[47]

The Court then found fault with the *Atlantic* because the officer in charge did not ascertain the type of ship approaching, he did not take sufficient steps to avoid the collision, and because there was not an assigned lookout, just the officer in charge. The led the Court to affirm the ruling of the circuit court, that the total damages and loss should be equally apportioned between the parties. This case was the appeal of the respondents. The libelants had also appealed to the Supreme Court,[48] stating the *Atlantic* was not at fault, but using the same reasoning, the Court rejected this claim.

---

[46] Chamberlain v. Ward, 62 U.S. 548 (1858).
[47] *Id.* at 567.
[48] Ward v. Chamberlain, 62 U.S. 572 (1858).

## B. Fog Collision

| LEGAL ISSUES |
|---|
| ❖ Rules for avoiding collision between ships in fog<br>❖ Differences between two nations' maritime judgments |

On June 15, 1869, in a heavy fog, the British sailing bark *Mary A. Troop*, destined for New York, was struck by the British propellor steamship *Pennsylvania*, 200 miles off Sandy Hook, New Jersey. Six of the bark's crew drowned, four others survived. Within a week, the owners of the bark had initiated a libel against the steamship in federal district court.[49] The facts presented were that the bark was essentially laying to, moving very slowly, ringing her bell. The owners of the bark asserted that the steamship was moving at too high a speed, did not have a proper lookout, and did not change her course in time to miss the bark. The owners of the steamship responded that they were running at a reduced speed, they had a lookout, the fog had reduced visibility to one ships-length, that upon hearing the bell they had hove to, and had stopped and backed their engine and ported the helm but were too near the bark to avoid it. Further, because the bark had lashed its helm, it was unable to also port, and traveling at five knots, came into the slowing steamship.

The district court first said that neither of the ships said the accident was unavoidable, so it must look to the faults of each. For the faults of the bark, it said that although the bark had its helm lashed, it was not at anchor and was moving through the water. The use of a bell was only for ships at anchor. Ships moving had to use a foghorn, according to international navigation rules, to warn other ships. However, the court ruled that the use of a bell, which indicated a ship unable to get out of the way, was essentially its condition with its helm lashed, so the steamship should not have been misled in hearing the bell. The crew of the bark had believed that the bell they used could be heard further away than the foghorn they had on board. The court said that a ship's crew in such a vulnerable position would hardly have chosen to use the lesser effective of two methods of warning others.

---

[49] The Pennsylvania, 19 F. Cas. 180, 4 Ben. 257 (E.D.N.Y. June 1870).

The court also did not believe the steamship's assertion that the bark had no lookout, as it took a person standing on the forecastle, where the bell was located, to ring the bell. The court therefore found no fault with the actions of the bark. Although the varied testimonies were not all aligned, the steamship, upon seeing the bark appears to have done a hard a-port, then a hard a-starboard, then a final port of the helm. The one witness aboard who would discuss the speed said the steamship was going seven knots, which is what was needed to keep the ship traveling straight. The court took this to be the steamship's actual speed but did not necessarily concur with the necessity of that speed to remain in control.

In finding for the libellant bark, and thereby condemning the steamship to be sold to compensate the bark's owners, the court concluded,

> it was the clear duty of this steamer, under the circumstances to reduce her speed to the lowest point, consistent with steerage way. There is, I am aware, a notion entertained by some commanders, that they are justified in running at full speed in fog at sea, upon the ground that the time of exposure to peril is thereby lessened, and, if a collision does occur, the chance of injury to the steamer is diminished. But such a practice, if safer for the steamers, is full of danger to all smaller vessels, and cannot be upheld. The maritime law imposes upon a steamer, running in a thick fog at sea, the duty of at least slackening her speed to the lowest possible point, consistent with steerage way.[50]

The case was then appealed to the circuit court.[51] That court found similar fault with the steamship, including for not responding appropriately when the bell was first heard, instead of later when the bark was first seen through the fog. However, the circuit court also found fault with the bark and the use of the bell instead of the foghorn,

> They regarded themselves as lying to; and, in this, they are supported by other witnesses, who are experienced mariners. They appeared to have regarded the term "under way," in the rule, as the opposite of "lying to." But, in this they were mistaken, if the term "lying to" was at

---

[50] *Id.* at 182.
[51] The Pennsylvania, 19 F. Cas. 184, 9 Blatchf. 451 (Cir. Ct. E.D.N.Y. Feb. 1872).

all apt to describe their condition. The rule is, that, in a fog, sailing ships under way shall use a fog-horn; when not under way, they shall use a bell. Here, the barque, although having some of her sails reefed, and her helm lashed, was on her starboard tack, and making not less than a mile an hour. True, she was not under full headway, but she was, nevertheless, under way, and should have used her fog-horn. Evidence was given, tending to show that the bell which she used could be heard at a greater distance than a fog-horn could be heard. But parties are not at liberty to disregard a distinct and explicit rule of navigation, upon their judgment that its disobedience will better subserve the purpose for which the rule is designed.[52]

The respondents had said that by not using a foghorn, it gave the steamship less time to respond and altered the type of response the steamship would have undertaken. The court, in the end, rejected this as assigning any fault to the bark, because the steamship had responded only from seeing the bark, and not from hearing its bell. No one on the steamship had responded when the sound of the bell was reported on board. The court also upheld the valuation of the bark as ordered by the lower court, as the valuation had been proved by varied witnesses at both the vessel's home port of St. Johns and at the destination port of New York, where it was libeled.

Not being satisfied with the circuit court's decision, the case was then appealed to the Supreme Court. However, in the meantime, this same case had been litigated back in the U.K. A libel had been initiated there in the high court of admiralty by the owners of the cargo, separate from the ownership of the ship. The U.K. court held that the steamship was at fault. This case was then appealed to the court of appeal or more formally, to the Lords of the Judicial Committee of the Privy Council.[53] This court evaluated the case on whether the collision was inevitable and then where did fault lie. The Privy Council court believed the fault lay with the steamship, for traveling at an excess speed for the conditions and that the foghorn would not have been heard at a sufficient distance to change the outcome.

---

[52] *Id.* at 185.
[53] National Steam Ship Company v Merry and another ("the Pennsylvania") (JCPC June 1870).

The court believed that it depended on the circumstances, so there was no hard and fast rule,

> But their Lordships are of the opinion that in a thick fog in the Atlantic Ocean, in the direct line to New York, about 200 miles to the east of Sandy Hook, where frequently there must be a great number of vessels congregated, seven knots an hour is too great a speed for a steamer to proceed at.[54]

The British court believed that contrary to the assertion that that speed was required for commerce across the Atlantic, steamships had to slow down or face the consequences of any collision. They concluded that the collision was not inevitable, but that the excess speed of the steamship was the principal cause. Crediting the nautical assessors who assisted the court in this case, the belief was that if the steamship had starboarded her helm when first seeing the bark, the collision could have been avoided. They also found it odd that, upon seeing a vessel on their starboard bow, a vessel would turn the helm to port (turn to the right), thereby heading directly into the other ship. Deferring to the high court of the admiralty, the Trinity masters, and their own nautical assessors, the appeals court affirmed the original judgement.

This British decision was made several years before the case reached the U.S. Supreme Court. In 1864, a U.S. federal statute had been passed that created a set of rules for avoiding maritime collisions.[55] One article dealt with signals in the fog (other sections dealt with rules for lights and for sailing and steering). This article, in full, stated,

> Whenever there is a fog, whether by day or night, the signals. fog-signals described below shall be carried and used, and shall be sounded at least every five minutes, viz: -
>
> (a) Steamships under way shall use a steam-whistle placed before the funnel, not less than eight feet from the deck.
>
> (b) Sailing-ships under way shall use a fog-horn.

---

[54] *Id.*
[55] An Act fixing certain Rules and Regulations for preventing Collisions on the Water, c. 38, s. 1, ch. 69.

(c) Steamships and sailing-ships when not under way shall use a bell.[56]

In the UK, essentially the same rule had previously been enacted under the Merchants Shipping Act, 1862,[57] which said,

> Whenever there is Fog, whether by Day or Night, the Fog Signals described below shall be carried and used, and shall be sounded at least every Five Minutes; viz.-
>
> (a.) Steam Ships under weigh shall use a Steam Whistle placed before the Funnel not less than Eight Feet from the Deck.
>
> (b.) Sailing Ships under weigh shall use a Fog Horn.
>
> (c.) Steam Ships and Sailing Ships when not under weigh shall use a Bell.[58]

So, when the case finally reached the U.S. Supreme Court,[59] the Court said speed should be reduced as the risk of encountering other vessels increase. It noted that the Privy Council had ruled in a prior case, that of *The Europa*,

> This may be safely laid down as a rule on all occasions, fog or clear, light or dark, that no steamer has a right to navigate at such a rate that it is impossible for her to prevent damage, taking all precaution at the moment she sees danger to be possible, and if she cannot do that without going less than five knots an hour, then she is bound to go at less than five knots an hour.[60]

Agreeing with testimony of the experienced seaman who was a passenger on the steamship, that there was no difficulty to use a lower speed, the Court ruled that the steamship was at fault for putting itself in the position of not being able to avoid the collision. Then looking to the fault of the bark, the Court said the use of a bell instead of a foghorn was a violation of the relevant statute, and further, the two different devices signaled a different status of the sending ship, one of being at rest and one

---

[56] *Id*. Article 10.
[57] An Act to amend "The Merchant Shipping Act, 1854," "The Merchant Shipping Act Amendment Act, 1855," and "The Customs Consolidation Act, 1853," 25&26 Vict. ch. 63.
[58] *Id*. Table C, Article 10.
[59] The Pennsylvania, 86 U.S. 125 (1873).
[60] *Id*. at 134.

of moving. Further, when in violation of a statute, the offender had to affirmatively prove that its violation could not have been a cause of the collision.

To show this, the Court again quoted from the Privy Council, in the case of *The Fenham*,

> It is of the greatest possible importance, having regard to the admiralty regulations and to the necessity of enforcing obedience to them, to lay down this rule: that if it is proved that any vessel has not shown lights, the burden lies on her to show that her noncompliance with the regulations was not the cause of the collision.[61]

Because the bark did not, and could not, prove the use of the bell did not contribute to the collision, the Court held that both vessels were at fault and the damages should be divided between the parties, according to admiralty rules. The decree of the circuit court was reversed, with directions to issue a decree in accord with this decision. The owners of the *Pennsylvania* then realized that they had to get their damages on the record, to be part of the apportionment. They were allowed to do so by the district court.[62]

As a closing remark, the Court noted the different decision they had reached on the same case, and facts, than had the court of the Privy Council,

> We have not overlooked the fact that in a libel by the owners of the cargo of the bark against the steamer for damages resulting from the same collision, it was held by the judicial committee of the Privy Council in England, that the disaster was chargeable to the steamer alone. But with great respect for the tribunal that thus decided, we do not feel at liberty to surrender our judgment, especially in view of the fact that the case is now more fully presented and the evidence is more complete than it was in the British court.[63]

---

[61] *Id.* at 136.
[62] The Pennsylvania, 19 F. Cas. 186, 12 Blatchf. 67 (E.D.N.Y. May 1874).
[63] The Pennsylvania, 86 U.S. 125, at 138.

## C. River Collision

| LEGAL ISSUES |
|---|
| ❖ Rights of way on rivers<br>❖ Final actions taken before collision defining legal liability |

In the United Kingdom, with its very long maritime history, shipwrecks were part and parcel for a seafaring nation with a global trade network. In the 19th century, there were many large losses of life at sea across the world, reflecting the vast extent of the British Empire. The *City of Glasgow* disappeared in January 1854, carrying nearly 500 people from Liverpool to Philadelphia. In February 1855, the *Guiding Star*, an immigrant ship on the way to Australia, was lost without explanation, with over 500 people dead. In October 1859, the *Royal Charter* broke up after hitting rocks off the coast of Wales, killing more than 450. The *Atlantic* hit rocks off Nova Scotia in April 1873 and sank, killing more than 500 people. In November 1874, rounding the Cape of Good Hope, the *Cospatrick* caught fire and more than 460 people died.

On September 3, 1878, the *Princess Alice*, a paddlewheel steamship which was returning from an excursion to Gravesend on the River Thames, was struck by a much larger propellor steamship, the collier *Bywell Castle*. Despite being on a river, this resulted in the deaths of more than 600 people from the *Princess Alice*, many whom were women and children. The ship broke up and quickly sank, leaving little time to lower the boats. Among the dead was the captain, William Grinstead. The location and timing of the accident, at around 19:45, coincided with the scheduled release of a large amount of sewage into the river near the Woolwich Arsenal. The *Bywell Castle* pulled survivors aboard, threw overboard ropes, chains, and anything that would float, put out its own boats, and blew its whistles for assistance from other nearby boats.

> "It's astonishing," said one of the boatmen, "how quick the poor creatures were gone. They cried out at first, but they were soon still. It was awful soon that we only heard our own voices. For you see, Sir, a great many of them were women and children, and the mothers would cling to the little 'uns, and so as a matter of fact they'd drown each other. One of the women as was saved said she had her child in her arms the minute before, and it was washed away. There's gents as

has lost their wives and children, and wives as has lost their husbands and little 'uns; there's families as have gone down together; there's some as is divided, half saved, half drowned. One man has lost all his family, and vice versa, so has one woman; it's most awful and peculiar how the misfortunes has worked; and I don't know who's most to be pitied, them as is gone, or them as is left behind. I never see so much crying and praying and misery, and never hope to again.[64]

The log of the *Bywell Castle* from the captain, Thomas Harrison, stated that it had ported its helm (turned to the right) on seeing the other ship, which had also ported its helm. Then, the *Princess Alice*, for unclear reasons, starboarded its helm (turned to the left), where its green running lights could be seen. This action led directly to the collision. The surviving officer from the *Princess Alice* gave a different account, saying that his ship had starboarded their helm because the other ship had done this first. Both ships claimed to have cut their engines before the collision. With the differing accounts, the legal battle would soon begin. In a strange irony, the ship's namesake, Princess Alice, the daughter of Queen Victoria, died, at the age of 35, just a few months after this disaster, while the legal process played out.

The coroner's jury listened to a vast amount of testimony, producing more than 5,000 pages of evidentiary record. After a long deliberation, the jury found that the ships should have both stopped and either reversed or gone astern, and that more stringent rules should be laid down for steam navigation on the Thames. They also added that the *Princess Alice* was seaworthy, but was not sufficiently manned, had more passengers than was prudent, and did not have sufficient safety capabilities.

A Board of Trade inquiry ruled that the *Princess Alice* had violated Rule 29, Section (d) of the Board of Trade Regulations and the current Regulations of the Thames Conservancy Board, which required each vessel coming in opposite directions to pass each other on its port side. Instead, the *Princess Alice* had gone helm a starboard, crossing in front of the bow of the *Bywell Castle* from right to left, and so was solely at fault for the collision. Instead of sharing the blame, as the coroner's jury had determined, the Board of Trade inquiry found fault solely with one ship.

---

[64] *Six Hundred Lives Lost*, N.Y. TIMES (Sept. 15, 1878).

The case was first tried before the new probate, admiralty, and divorce court, which had recently subsumed the long-standing role of the high court of admiralty.[65] The admiralty court was assisted by elders from Trinity House (see above). The court said the ships were initially red light to red light (each was on the left side of the other). Within a distance of 100 to 400 yards, the *Princess Alice* suddenly turned hard a-starboard (to the left), thereby leading to the accident. The court held that the *Princess Alice* was to blame for the collision, having not given due regard for the speed or in posting sufficient look-outs when travelling on the river. However, the court then looked at the actions of the *Bywell Castle* just prior to the collision. The court ruled that, after seeing the green light (starboard side) of the *Princess Alice*, the hard a-port command was the worst action to take. If it had not been done, many lives would have been saved. So, the court assigned blame to both vessels.

This decision was appealed and the three justices of the court of appeal each wrote separate opinions, assisted by two nautical assessors.[66] The opinion of the first justice, William James, agreed with the admiralty court as to the guilt of the *Princess Alice*, as the ship was being navigated in a careless and reckless manner. *Bywell Castle* was being navigated with due care and skill, up until the final moment, when it performed the hard-a-port. This court's naval assessor agreed with the admiralty court and its Trinity masters that this was the wrong thing to do. The assessors believed the *Bywell Castle* should be absolved of contributory negligence, as her final hard a-port maneuver would not have changed the outcome. The court adopted this opinion as its own but then went on to say,

> But I desire to add my opinion that a ship has no right, by its own misconduct, to put another ship into a situation of extreme peril, and then charge that other ship with misconduct. My opinion is that if, in that moment of extreme peril and difficulty, such other ship happens to do something wrong, so as to be a contributory to the mischief, that would not render her liable for the damage, inasmuch as perfect presence of mind, accurate judgment, and promptitude under all circumstances are not to be expected. You have no right to expect

---

[65] For a deeper discussion of the English admiralty courts, see THOMAS J. SHAW, THE LEGAL HISTORY OF PIRATES & PRIVATEERS and THOMAS J. SHAW, THE LEGAL HISTORY OF THE REVOLUTIONARY WAR.
[66] The Bywell Castle, LR 4 PD 219 (July 1879).

men to be something more than ordinary men. I am therefore of opinion that the finding of the Court below, that the *Bywell Castle* was, for the purposes of the suit, to be considered to blame, must be overruled, and that the *Princess Alice* was alone to blame.[67]

The opinion of the second justice, William Brett, found four findings of fact: that the ships were red light to red light, the *Bywell Castle* was traveling at half speed and the *Princess Alice* at full speed, the *Bywell Castle* was navigated with due care and skill up to just before the accident, and that the last-minute helm hard a-port was wrong. After reviewing what he believed the most likely courses of the vessels that night, he also found no fault with the *Bywell Castle*.

The third justice, Henry Cotton, concurred with his colleagues, saying,

For in my opinion the sound rule is, that a man in charge of a vessel is not to be held guilty of negligence, or as contributing to an accident, if in a sudden emergency caused by the default or negligence of another vessel, he does something which he might under the circumstances as known to him reasonably think proper; although those before whom the case comes for adjudication are, with a knowledge of all the facts, and with time to consider them, able to see that the course which he adopted was not in fact the best. In this case, though to put the helm of the *Bywell Castle* hard a-port was not in fact the best thing to be done, I cannot hold that to do so was under the circumstances an act of negligence on the part of those who had charge of that vessel.[68]

This ruling came into U.S. jurisprudence, when the Supreme Court noted approvingly a few years later that it was,

a well-considered judgment by Lords Justices James, Brett and Cotton, in the Court of Appeal, and the rule there formulated is, that "where one ship has, by wrong manœuvres, placed another ship in a position of extreme danger, that other ship will not be held to blame if she has done something wrong, and has not been manœuvred with perfect skill and presence of mind.[69]

---

[67] *Id.*
[68] *Id.*
[69] The Elizabeth Jones, 112 U.S. 514 (Dec. 1884).

## D. Running Aground

| LEGAL ISSUES |
|---|
| ❖ Protection from legal liability by statute<br>❖ Federal maritime and admiralty law overriding state law |

On January 18, 1884, the passenger steamship *City of Columbus* ran aground off the Massachusetts coast on a submerged reef named the Devil's Bridge, leading to the deaths of more than 100 people. This occurred at night, off the cliffs of Gay Head on the western end of the island of Martha's Vineyard. The ship was traveling from Boston to Savannah with more than 80 passengers and 45 crew members, in a storm. Less than half the crew and only about a dozen passengers eventually survived, drowned in the ship or swept off as a giant wave hit those who came topside. With the ship taking on water and only its masts out of the water, most of those who survived had climbed up onto the rigging. Some stayed there for up to 12 hours in the winter cold, later having to jump into the water and swim to a revenue cutter that had arrived on the scene.

When the grounding happened, the second mate, Edward Harding, was in charge, with the captain, Schuler E. Wright, down below. During the inquest before the local board of inspectors for steam vessels, the captain was unable to account for the accident. If his steering instructions had been followed, the ship would have cleared Gay Head by several miles. He had directed west-southwest but believed the ship must have gone south-west half west instead. He had ordered passengers to put on lifejackets and ordered the boats be launched but did not know what had happened after that, as he saw no boats there the next morning. He claimed that the very powerful light in the lighthouse at Gay Head did not help when too close to it. The next morning, another ship passed the 30-40 men struggling to hang onto the ship's rigging but did not stop to assist.

Libels were soon filed against the shipowner,

> a libel… against the Boston and Savannah Steamship Company to recover $50,000 damages for the loss of the life of Sampson Fawcett, of Lawrence, Mass., by the City of Columbus disaster. It is claimed by the parties who bring this suit that the act limiting liability has no application to the claims of passengers, and especially to those whose

lives were sacrificed. The vessel was substantially insured, and they contend that the law and justice of things do not allow a company to get full indemnity for its vessel and then invoke a statute to hide it from the consequences of its failure to protect its passengers. James Brown, one of the saved, has filed a similar libel for $25,000 for personal injuries alleged to have been received in the disaster.[70]

The statute referred to was enacted in 1851, which said in part,

That the liability of the owner or owners of any ship or vessel, for any embezzlement, loss, or destruction, by the master, officers, mariners, passengers, or any other person or persons, of any property, goods, or merchandize, shipped or put on board of such ship or vessel, or for any loss, damage, or injury by collision, or for any act, matter, or thing, loss, damage, or forfeiture, done, occasioned, or incurred, without the privity or knowledge of such owner or owners, shall in no case exceed the amount or value of the interest of such owner or owners respectively, in such ship or vessel, and her freight then pending.[71]

In *Butler*,[72] the Boston and Savannah Steamship Company's (BSSC) libel would reach the Supreme Court. BSSC had filed the libel seeking protection under this statute, asserting there was no fault of the owners or any of its officers or crew, and the losses claimed by the plaintiffs was much greater than the value of the owner's total interest in the ship. It asked that, if it was found to have any fault, that its liability be limited to its interest in the ship after the loss and the total value of the freight it was carrying at the time. An injunction against lawsuits had been granted.

Despite the injunction, in September, the administrators of the estate of Elizabeth R. Beach, one of the women lost on the ship, sued on behalf of her niece and aunt, who had relied upon Elizabeth for support. Among the allegations was the negligent operation of the ship, the lack of discipline of the crew, and that no efforts were made to save the passengers. Further, Harding was not a licensed pilot for these waters, there was no proper apparatus to launch the six boats, and there was no proper bulkhead. This in total constituted negligence or carelessness on the part of the owner.

---

[70] *The City of Columbus Sufferers*, N.Y. TIMES (Mar. 14, 1884).
[71] An Act to limit the Liability of Ship-Owners, and for other Purposes, c. 31, s. 2, ch. 43, § 3.
[72] Butler v. Boston & Savannah Steamship Co., 130 U.S. 527 (Apr. 1889).

Under Massachusetts statute,

> If the life of a passenger is lost by reason of the negligence or carelessness of the proprietor or proprietors of a steamboat, or stagecoach, or of common carriers of passengers, or by the unfitness or gross negligence or carelessness of their servants or agents, such proprietor or proprietors and common carriers shall be liable in damages not exceeding five thousand nor less than five hundred dollars, to be assessed with reference to the degree of culpability of the proprietor or proprietors or common carriers liable, or of their servants or agents, and recovered in an action of tort, commenced within one year from the injury causing the death, by the executor or administrator of the deceased person, for the use of the widow and children of the deceased, in equal moieties, or, if there are no children, to the use of the widow, or, if no widow, to the use of the next of kin.[73]

The plaintiffs, asserting that Elizabeth "suffered great mental and bodily pain upon the vessel, and was afterwards washed into the sea, and drowned,"[74] sought $5,000 under Massachusetts law and $50,000 under general admiralty jurisdiction of the United States, plus $150 for her clothing and baggage. They further asserted that an 1871 statute[75] regarding steamship safety required there be licensed pilots on steamships. Owners were fully liable to passengers for injuries suffered due to non-compliance with the statute. The plaintiffs also appeared on the BSSC's original libel, claiming that BSSC had been insured for the ship and its contents and so were indemnified against their losses suffered. The circuit court held for the BSSC, so both cases went to the Supreme Court.

The argument of the plaintiffs was that the limitation of liability applied only to property and did not extend to personal injuries. The Court held otherwise, saying that this was the general maritime law that the statute merely adopted.[76] It referenced the *Epsilon*,[77] where the court focused upon the statute's wording, believing it included personal injuries

---

[73] *Id.* at 533.
[74] *Id.*
[75] An Act to provide for the better Security of Life on board of Vessels propelled in Whole or in Part by Steam, and for other Purposes, c. 41, s. 3, ch. 100.
[76] For a better explanation, *see* Norwich Company v. Wright, 80 U.S. 104 (1871).
[77] The Epsilon, 8 F. Cas. 744 (E.D.N.Y. Feb. 1873).

"for any loss, damage, or injury by collision, or for any act, matter, or thing, loss, damage, or forfeiture, done, occasioned, or incurred."[78]

In general, that court had said,

> the ground for all the opposition which has been made to the rule of limited liability, and they have, in most countries, been overpowered by the strong public interest to encourage the investment of capital in ships. It is, of course, highly important to protect the persons of those who are carried in ships, but, in order that there may be any persons carried, there must be ships to carry them. The act of 1851 does not apply to river or inland navigation, but is confined to a commerce where the amount of property and number of persons transported on each voyage is upon the increase, while the hazard of the navigation does not diminish... the investment of capital in such a commerce might well be deterred by a refusal to give the benefit of the act of 1851 in respect to demands for injury to the person.. The necessary protection of life against neglect may perhaps be better secured by criminal punishments inflicted on those guilty of the neglect than by increasing the risks of capital invested in navigation.[79]

The Court ruled the 1871 statute did not provide restrictions limiting liability, but negligence by the owner could prohibit a decree of limited liability. It ruled the lack of the mate's license was the captain's fault, not the owners, as the captain was licensed. For the receipt of insurance proceeds by the owners, the Court referred to its *City of Norwich*[80] case, which held that insurance proceeds had no bearing on the liability of the ship owner. Regarding use of the state statute, the Court said the ship,

> was on the navigable waters of the United States, and no state legislation can prevent the full operation of the maritime law on those waters... We have no hesitation, therefore, in saying that the Limited Liability Act applies to the present case notwithstanding the disaster happened within the technical limits of a County of Massachusetts and notwithstanding the liability itself may have arisen from a state law.[81]

---

[78] *Id.* at 745.
[79] *Id.* at 746.
[80] The City of Norwich, 118 U.S. 468 (May 1886).
[81] Butler v. Boston & Savannah Steamship Co., at 558.

E.  **After Death**

| LEGAL ISSUES |
|---|
| ❖  Right to administer a victim's estate<br>❖  Proving survivorship of shipwreck victims |

On September 8, 1860, while traveling at night during a gale on Lake Michigan from Chicago to Milwaukee, the paddle steamship *Lady Elgin* collided with the schooner *Augusta*. Efforts to plug the hole in the ship were unsuccessful, resulting in the sinking of the *Lady Elgin*. Most passengers were able to find something to float on but eventually some 300 lives were lost, many finally drowned or dashed upon the rocks the next morning. The disaster saw many people struggle throughout the night for life in the water, as recounted by a Lt. Hartsuff of the U.S. Army in his own harrowing experience,

> From a quarter to half an hour after she was struck she broke up, the hurricane deck floating off and the hulk going to the bottom with a tremendous noise. As she broke I jumped with my life-preserve -- a board six or eight feet long, and about one wide -- into the water, which was at this time only a few feet below us, and pulled with all my might to escape from the mass of the wreck. After the confusion had somewhat subsided, I heard the voice of Capt. WILSON cheering and encouraging the people on the wreck, telling them that the shore was but a few miles off, and that, if they kept calm and obeyed his directions, they might all be saved. I heard him speaking in this manner for perhaps ten minutes, and then I had separated so far from the hurricane deck, on which the Captain and a large number were, that I heard no more. All around me were numbers of persons floating on pieces of the wreck, until it became daylight. When it became so light that I could see some distance, I discovered a large mass of the wreck a little distance to the windward of us, covered with people.
>
> I then got on quite a large piece of wreck which was floating near me, and which contained no other person, and no person got on it after I did. The large mass to the windward, of which I have just spoken, now began to separate. I then left the piece I was on, and got on a large piece of the hurricane deck, on which there were four other persons -- don't know who they were. On this fragment I remained until we

reached about a quarter of a mile of the shore, when our raft broke up, and two of the four on it with me were washed off and drowned. A moment after the remainder of our party were washed off by a heavy sea, and one more of our little party drowned. My remaining companion contrived to regain the raft, and I again took to a life-preserver which I found afloat, and on this I floated to the shore just below the bluffs. From the time I was swept from the raft, until I reached the shore. I was several times hurled deep under the waves. When close in to the shore I was thrown from my life-preserver and went to the bottom, and although the water was not more than three or four deep. I was so exhausted as to be unable to rise, and crawled for some distance under the water until I reached dry land.[82]

The owner of the *Lady Elgin* quickly filed a libel against the *Augusta*, which survived the accident, for $4,200. The coroner's jury attributed the primary fault to the lighting arrangements required of sailing vessels by law. Additional factors identified were the schooner's second mate not immediately informing his captain of seeing the steamship's lights. The owners of the steamship were censured for allowing too many passengers while the captain of the schooner was censured for not dropping anchor to discover the injuries to the steamship. Further, the jury believed all passenger ships should be built with watertight compartments, which would have prevented the great loss of life in this disaster.

In *Lumsden*,[83] the supreme court of Louisiana considered the succession of a passenger lost aboard the *Lady Elgin*. Francis A. Lumsden, a partner in a publishing firm, his wife, and their only child, Frank Spedden Lumsden had perished. Within a month, administration of the father's succession was filed in the district court of New Orleans by the surviving partner in his firm. The same day, administration of the son's succession had been filed. As the deaths were considered as simultaneous, the parents had legally died first, with the son their heir. His grandmother, and legal heir, opposed an administration for the father, but it was rejected by the court. On appeal, the supreme court affirmed. Under state law, a surviving partner was allowed to first administer an estate to pay business debts before the estate's residuary was made available to the legal heir.

---

[82] *Still Later Particulars*, N.Y. TIMES (Sept. 12, 1860).
[83] Succession of Lumsden, 17 La. Ann. 38 (La. May 1865).

On October 6, 1866, the steamship *Evening Star*, traveling from New York to New Orleans, sank in a hurricane, taking more than 280 people to their deaths. As few passengers and crew survived, after days at sea, picked up by various ships, some of which were also in disrepair. One passenger, merchant W. H. Harris, recounted his ordeal's first few hours.

> In an instant the sea swept me clear of the deck, and carried me down some twenty-five feet I thought. When I came to the surface I found myself fin the midst of the wreck of the vessel, surrounded by floating spars and drift wood. Men and women were floating all about, clinging to anything they could lay hold of. All shouts for aid were drowned by the fury of the hurricane. I secured a piece of the wreck with which to support myself, but I had to abandon this owing to the danger I was in of being struck by pieces of the flying wreck, which were being hurled about in all directions by the wind and the waves. I then got hold of a piece of the fragments of the saloon, upon which I pulled myself, but was thrown off again and again by the violence of the waves, in each new effort to regain my position, lacerating my hands and limbs on the nails and splinters in the pieces of the wreck. In this way I clung to life for two or three hours.[84]

The government investigation into the disaster by the Treasury Department produced a final report. Its key points were that while the ship had the required number of boats, this was not sufficient for everyone on board. It was estimated that half the people on board could have survived if the boats had been given the legally required attached apparatus, were properly launched and manned, and were supplied with food and spars. The principal cause was attributed to an error in judgement on the part of the captain, in not moving the ship to a better location when it became clear that a severe storm was coming. Further, the crew was undermanned, especially in not having a carpenter aboard, and in not having a sufficient supply of spars, lumber, and sail.

In *Robinson*,[85] the heirs of a husband and a wife who both died on the *Evening Star* litigated over their property. The heirs of the wife, Catharine R. Gallier, were suing the heirs of her husband James Gallier Sr. for valuable New Orleans real estate and $5,000 in coin provided for the wife

---

[84] *The Evening Star,* N.Y. TIMES (Oct. 15, 1866).
[85] Robinson v. Gallier, 20 F. Cas. 1006 (Cir. Ct. La. Nov. 1875).

in his final will. The plaintiffs admitted that under Louisiana law, that if both died simultaneously, or if the husband died second, they had no case. Their entire case depended on proving the wife died second. To assist this, they noted that the husband was 68 years old and in feeble health, while the wife was 44 years old and better health. The plaintiffs introduced testimony from some of the few survivors that Mr. Gallier was not seen on deck the day of the sinking and that Mrs. Gallier was seen in the water, then was helped into a boat which capsized five times. Each time she made it back into the boat, except for the final time when she drowned.

In opposition, the defendants introduced testimony of a few survivors. A crew member and a passenger testified that three women were in the boat where Mrs. Gallier purportedly was and there were only three women ever aboard. Two survived and the third, who expired after several capsizes, was described as about 23 years old and 130 pounds, while Mrs. Gallier was 44 years old and 212 pounds. They also argued the other witness produced by the plaintiff was a Black actor in a minstrel show. The plaintiff asserted that under Louisiana law, when two people perished in the same event, the significantly younger spouse should have been presumed to have survived, while the defendant argued that the plaintiff was required to provide actual evidence of such survivorship. The judge instructed the jury to focus solely on whether they believed Mrs. Gallier survived her husband or not. The jury did not, finding for the defendants.

On May 7, 1875, the *Schiller*, a German steamship traveling between New York, Plymouth, and Hamburg, was lost at night off the coast of England after striking rocks in a thick fog, and sinking, leaving more than 330 people dead. The Board of Trade inquiry identified the site as near the Bishop's Rock Lighthouse, off the Scilly Isles. The court of inquiry said that the last observation was made on May 4, due to thick weather. If their calculation on May 7, taken by dead reckoning, had been accurate, they would have been 152 miles west of the lighthouse. Instead, that night in the fog, the ship passed inside of the lighthouse, without seeing its light or hearing the fog-bell, which was going at that time.

Despite later slowing their speed, the court said if a cast of the lead had been down before their final course correction, they would have understood their situation. The ship had instructions for the English Channel on board, which directed avoiding a northerly setting around the

Scilly Isles and the careful use of a lead in thick weather. The company had also set out maneuvers appropriate when approaching land. The court ruled that it was the neglect of these precautions that was the sole cause for the disaster. The court also tried to dispel the rumor that the ship had used its distress signals, done by the firing of guns, to announce their arrival. This would explain the lack of a rapid response, but the court said this could not be imputed to either the captain or the owner of the ship.

In *re Ridgway*,[86] the surrogate court in New York was handling a matter relating to the sinking of the *Schiller*. Mary Ridgway was a passenger on the *Schiller* who did not survive. Her will had her two grandchildren, Joseph R. Walter and Mary R. Walter, as beneficiaries of a trust set up for them, with the residue of her estate. They would receive the corpus of the trust at a certain age, but if the grandchildren died without issue, contingent beneficiaries would receive the proceeds from the trust instead. The grandchildren, along with their father Charles W. Walter, were also passengers on the ship who did not survive. They were all on the ship's deck when a wave hit and the grandmother was swept away but because it was night, it was not clear whether she was washed out to sea or another part of the deck. The other three were seen on the pavilion on the deck 10-15 minutes later before they too were swept away.

The court discussed the related case on the will of the grandchildren's mother, Elizabeth M. Walter. Her will had similar provisions, where it was held that legal title vested in the trustees immediately upon the testatrix's death and remained with them until the grandchildren's deaths. Having died without issue, they had nothing to transmit, and the residual went to the contingent beneficiaries. The grandchildren were also to receive certain jewelry and paintings from their grandmother, if they survived her. Their heirs at law asserted that as they were the last seen alive, they would have survived their grandmother. The court felt otherwise, saying,

> When two persons are lost by the same calamity, at sea, it does not follow, in my opinion, that the one last seen alive is necessarily or probably the survivor; otherwise a person escaping from a sinking ship by a life-boat might be adjudged to have first perished, because, an instant after, his companion may have been seen on the ship, which

---

[86] In re Ridgway, 4 Redf. 226 (N.Y. Surr. Ct. Mar. 1880).

immediately thereupon went down with all on board. Indeed, I am of the opinion that it is the general experience of seamen in such a disaster that they are safer at the mercy of the waves, and have a better chance of rescue through the instrumentality of some floating object, than by remaining on the ship until its last plunge. The facts of this case seem to me to indicate the instant and inevitable doom of the children, with hope of rescue or at least some continuance of life on the part of the grandmother. At all events, I am of the opinion that the parties alleging survivorship have not satisfactorily proved the fact.[87]

The highest court in New York reviewed[88] the case of the mother's will, coming to the same conclusions, while laying out two other key points regarding the survivors of shipwreck victims,

> 1st. That the appellants who claim through a survivorship must prove the survivor-ship.
>
> 2d. That there is no presumption in law of survivor-ship in the case of persons who perish by a common disaster, as in this case, by shipwreck, without other evidence tending to prove the fact, and hence that the party upon whom the *onus* lies fails to establish it.[89]

---

[87] *Id.* at 231.
[88] Newell v. Nichols, 75 N.Y. 78 (Nov. 1878).
[89] *Id.* at 86.

## *Chapter 2*

## **1900 – 1924**

Disaster, the source of so much unintended death, can occasionally be connected to intentional death. And so it was with the homicide of William March Rice, occurring just after the first great disaster of the new century, the flood of Galveston, Texas in 1900. Rice, the founder of his eponymous university, was a wealthy merchant with interests in real estate, transportation, and lending. He married his second wife, Elizabeth Brown, in 1867 in Texas. However, the marriage frayed and near the end of her life, while on an 1896 trip to their second home in Texas, she created a new will that, under Texas' community property laws, allowed her to give away her half of the couple's assets acquired during the marriage.

Elizabeth passed away that same year, but Rice sued to prove that he was a resident of New York, not Texas. As part of the litigation, his lawyer hired a former Texas lawyer now in New York, Albert T. Patrick, to assist. Patrick would become attracted to Rice's wealth to such an extent that he contrived a plot to have Rice murdered. But only after Patrick had forged a new will naming himself the residual beneficiary. Patrick had been trying to get Rice's valet to slowly poison Rice, which made him ill but did not kill him. After the storm and flood in Galveston and a mill fire in Houston caused significant damage to Rice's Texas property holdings, he decided to transfer large sums from his bank to rebuild his properties. The imminent loss of these funds caused Patrick to accelerate his plan to murder Rice.

The varied litigations for Patrick's criminal murder trial, Rice's attempts to defeat his deceased wife's new will, Patrick's attempts to get the fraudulent will accepted, and the attempts by Elizabeth's New York beneficiaries to defeat the Texas administration of her will[1] all went on over the course of several years in the early 1900's. After her death, her Texas executor was granted administration and filed a lawsuit against Rice for Elizabeth's share of the community assets. Rice countersued, and these lawsuits were pending at Rice's death in September 1900. While the battle of the wills was being contested in New York, the Texas administrator of Rice's estate settled with the administrator of his deceased wife's estate for a specified sum and an agreement that the lawsuits would proceed to judgment specifying that Elizabeth's claims were invalid.

In the murder trial against Patrick, the valet accomplice admitted he had chloroformed Rice to his death, as part of a conspiracy hatched by Patrick to acquire Rice's wealth. The court of appeals affirmed the trial court's guilty verdict of first-degree murder, based upon the corpus delecti, the corroboration of the testimony of the accomplice, and the several forgeries. "The evidence, independently of the testimony of the accomplice, is fraught with a crushing implication of the defendant in the deliberate purpose to kill Rice, in order that he might possess his estate."[2]

The month after Rice's death, his valid 1896 will was introduced for probate but Patrick objected, pleading the forged 1900 will. The proceedings were delayed while Patrick was tried for murder. After a year, the surrogate court had waited long enough and ruled the 1896 will was the valid and admitted it to probate. The appeals division affirmed, saying

> The name of William M. Rice appears four times upon the alleged will of 1900, and upon a critical examination of these four signatures it will be found that they correspond almost exactly—a coincidence which could not possibly happen in the case of four genuine signatures of a person upwards of 80 years of age; and for this reason it does not need the testimony of experts to demonstrate that these signatures were not genuine, but tracings.[3]

This chapter presents both natural and manmade disasters. The first section covers building and mine disasters while the second addresses disasters involving transportation and disease.

---

[1] Baldwin v. Rice, 89 N.Y.S. 738, 44 Misc. Rep. 64 (June 1904).
[2] People v. Patrick, 19 N.Y. Crim. 136, 182 N.Y. 131 (N.Y. Ct. App. June 1905), at 176.
[3] In re Rice's Will, 81 N.Y.S. 68, 81 App. Div. 223 (N.Y. Sup. Ct. Mar. 1903).

## 2.1 BUILDINGS AND MINES

### A. Flood

| LEGAL ISSUES |
|---|
| ❖ Acts of God not always a defense<br>❖ No responsibility for unauthorized post-disaster acts |

As the water rose on September 8, 1900, ten Sisters of Charity nuns of the St. Mary's Orphans Asylum tied themselves to their children via clothesline rope. It was to no effect, as almost all would perish as their dormitory was swept away. The residents of Galveston, Texas, had long been assured that they did not need a seawall to protect them from potential hurricanes, as they had survived tropical cyclones before without serious damage. Lying on an island off the coast of Texas, south of Houston, this city was very hard hit when a hurricane made landfall that day, leading to the deaths of 6-8,000 people, possibly more. The storm surge, sea water that is pushed ashore by winds, was estimated to have reached modern category 4 levels. That surge plus rainfall from the storm itself caused wide-spread flooding across the low-lying island. Washed away were railroad tracks, bridges, telephone, telegraph, and electrical poles and wires, gas and water works, and most of the buildings, including homes, churches, and schools. As this was a natural disaster instead of a man-made one, it was unnecessary to probe further for the cause. However, the flooding was to have significant legal impacts in many ways, especially commercially.

In *Missouri, Kansas & Texas Railway*,[4] the plaintiff had shipped wheat using the defendant railroad to a flour milling company at its grain elevator in Galveston. Instead, the railroad delivered the grain to the elevator of a different wharf company, located a distance from the flour mill's elevator, held for the plaintiff's account. This was due to a mistake by the defendant's agent, who believed the flour mill's grain elevators were full. There were 300 rail cars sitting on its side tracks with unloaded customer wheat, which could not be stored in the mill's elevator. The plaintiff's cars of wheat at the wharf company were not unloaded before the arrival of the September 8 flood and were consequently destroyed. If the flour mill had been notified by the railroad, the wheat would not have been

---

[4] Missouri, Kansas & Texas Railway Co. v. Seley & Early, 31 Tex. Civ. App. 158 (Jan. 1903).

destroyed, as their railroad tracks were not washed away, nor was their grain elevator. The elevator space for the 300 cars of customer wheat waiting to be unloaded was full but only for customer wheat. The flour mill had a separate space in the elevator for its purchased wheat, where it would have unloaded the plaintiff's wheat if timely notified by the railroad.

In addition, the bill of lading declared that there was no liability for an act of God, which the defendant asserted. The court of appeals took a different view, that by not delivering the wheat to the intended flour mill, it had technically converted the wheat. This was despite the wheat being held by the wharf company on account of the shipper. The court ruled that because the wheat was already converted, it could not use the storm as a defense to liability. It had lost control of the wheat when it was delivered to the wharf company. The railroad could not force a business relationship on the shipper without their knowledge or consent. The court was also doubtful that the defendant would prevail even if the railroad had left the wheat with the wharf company on its own account but as that was not the case, it affirmed the judgment of the lower court.

In *Brown*,[5] plaintiff A. A. Brown sued the city for the $200 value of his horse which he claimed had been impressed by the chief of police to assist in removing the dead and taking care of the sick, and subsequently worked to death. Two horses were taken from the plaintiff and worked for six days unendingly. This had been done without the knowledge and consent of the plaintiff, and his demand for a return of the horses was refused by the patrol wagon driver. The court noted that a municipal corporation is liable for the tortious acts of its agents when these have been authorized and it is within the powers granted to it by the state. No authorization to impress personal property was found in the city's charter and the city council had not authorized any impressing. The seizures and continued possession were done by a policeman and patrol wagon driver, on the orders of the mayor and chief of police, who had no authorization. As such, the court held for the city.

In *Bartlett & Lucas*,[6] the defendant had applied to purchase a lot in the city and required a loan to be able to pay the plaintiff contractors to construct a house there. He had an oral agreement on the lot purchase and

---

[5] City of Galveston v. Brown, 28 Tex. Civ. App. 274 (Feb. 1902).
[6] Bartlett & Lucas v. Bisbey, 27 Tex. Civ. App. 405 (Dec. 1901).

loan from its owner and a written contract with the builders. Three progress payments were to be made. This was followed by a written contract for the purchase of the lot and a house constructed on it. After it was completed, the buyer would make a down payment and receive a loan, which would be extended for each phase. The work on the first phase was completed, approved, and paid for. The work on the second phase was completed and approved but not yet submitted for payment when the storm struck and swept away the unfinished house. The current owner and the buyer both refused to pay the contractor for the second phase of work. The court ruled that the contractor had committed to build a house and was liable to still do that, despite the flood. Further, he could not collect money due him for the second phase of work done, as he committed to deliver an entire house. It might be different if the contracted work was for repairs to a house that had washed away. Also, the contract stated that fire and acts of God would only delay the completion, not completely excuse it.

In *the Hyades*,[7] the district court was asked to determine liability for the loss of wheat sent from Galveston to New York and damaged by the storm. The main issue was whether the hatch coverings were properly sealed. The plaintiffs asserted they were not properly sealed while the defense maintained they were and this loss was merely a result of the perils of the sea, from the storm that hit Galveston. The bill of lading specified no liability for the carrier for causes beyond its control, for perils of the sea, or unseaworthiness of the vessel, provided all due diligence was exercised to make it seaworthy, and the vessel was in compliance with the Harter Act. This statute said in relevant part,

> That if the owner of any vessel transporting merchandise or property to or from any port in the United States of America shall exercise due diligence to make the said vessel in all respects seaworthy and properly manned, equipped, and supplied, neither the vessel, her owner or owners, agent, or charterers shall become or be held responsible for damage or loss resulting from faults or errors in navigation or in the management of said vessel nor shall the vessel, her owner or owners, charterers, agent, or master be held liable for losses arising from dangers of the sea or other navigable waters, acts of God, or public enemies, or the inherent defect, quality, or vice of

---

[7] The Hyades, 118 F. 85 (S.D.N.Y. Oct. 1902).

the thing carried, or from insufficiency of package, or seizure under legal process, or for loss resulting from any act or omission of the shipper or owner of the goods, his agent or representative, or from saving or attempting to save life or property at sea, or from any deviation in rendering such service.[8]

The district court believed the sealing of the hatches met the due diligence standard of the act. The ship had been forced to hove to for three days while fighting the storm and endured significant damage, despite being a new and strongly built ship. The crew made additional efforts to keep the hatches battened down but were only partially successful. The court also rejected evidence of another ship, which had left two days prior, which successfully delivered its wheat undamaged by using tarpaulins instead of hatch covers. The court discounted this comparison, saying that there is no proof that they were subjected to the same weather conditions and even if they were, the power of individual waves is such that it is not possible to compare the injury on one vessel to another. The court held this damage was due to the perils of the sea, not negligence and the court of appeals affirmed.[9]

In *Cameron Mill*,[10] the exporter plaintiff was asserting that the title to wheat that was shipped to Galveston had not yet passed when it was damaged sitting in the railway cars during the storm, and so the defendant was liable for the amounts already paid. The parties had entered an oral agreement, which was then followed up by respective letters. The plaintiffs asserted that the 10,000 bushels had to be inspected, graded, and weighed and delivered into the grain elevator in Galveston. The defendants countered that the contract was already made and paid for and that it was merely acting as a bailee of the grain during shipment and delivery. The trial court held for the exporter plaintiff against the defendant mill, that delivery to the elevator was required under their agreement. The letters seemed to merely fill in various details of the sale which occurred over the telephone. The court of appeals was not impressed by the vagueness in the letters,

---

[8] An Act relating to navigation of vessels, bills of lading, and to certain obligations, duties, and rights in connection with the carriage of property, c. 52, s. 2, ch. 105, § 3.
[9] The Hyades, 124 F. 58 (2nd Cir. July 1903).
[10] Cameron Mill & Elevator Co. v. Chas. F. Orthwein's Sons, 120 F. 463 (5th Cir. Feb. 1903).

Plaguing difficulties like those presented in these skeleton letters are often imposed on trial courts, when traders, trusting their ventures to the vagaries of such hastily formed commercial instruments, find it desirable, after the unforeseen happens, and losses to either side follow, to invoke the courts to determine for them, from enigmatical contracts, made up of such letters, where or in whom was the title and risk when the loss was incurred. We are not impressed by the vague language of these letters, nor by the want of words which seem necessary to clothe the skeleton, or fill the blanks with sentient thought, with the presumption of fact that their authors respectively intended, or were endeavoring to reduce, concretely, to writing, or even to state intelligibly, all the understandings which they had with each other in making the verbal contract of sale.[11]

The court of appeals, in analyzing the two letters, found that one stated the delivery was to the "elevator at Galveston" and the other merely stated "Galveston." The former gave the location of delivery, while the latter was apparently intended to set the pricing used for that location. The trial court had not allowed parol evidence to further clarify these conflicting documents but instead determined that delivery to the elevators was what was agreed. The court of appeals, given the ambiguity of the key terms in the confirmatory letters, reversed the lower court and ordered a new trial where parol evidence could clear up the meanings.

In *Hildenbrandt*,[12] the issue was survivorship. Frank Doll had taken out a $2,500 life insurance policy, payable to his wife Minnie if she succeeded him. Both perished in the storm, so the only legal question was whether there was sufficient evidence of the wife living longer. The evidence produced showed that Frank had departed a grocery store using the store's wagon and headed in the direction of his home at around 13:00 to get his wife. At 16:00, witness saw the horse, a block past the Doll's residence, in belly high water, moving as if it was being guided and driven, with the reins and harness going up and down as if driven. Due to the wagon cover, the witness could not see who in the wagon, if anyone, was driving the horse. The court ruled this evidence insufficient to challenge the survivorship, holding the wife's interest was contingent and had failed.

---

[11] *Id.* at 466.
[12] Hildenbrandt v. Ames, 27 Tex. Civ. App. 377 (Dec. 1901).

## B. Theater Fire

| LEGAL ISSUES |
|---|
| ❖ Duties owed to a theater audience<br>❖ Requirements to indict for manslaughter due to fire |

On December 30, 1903, a fire broke out in the Iroquois Theatre in Chicago, resulting in the deaths of more than 600 people. There were more than 2,000 people in the theater, including many mothers and children attending an afternoon performance, and several hundred without seats. There were also 300 performers and theater employees. The fire started from an arc light, which caught on to muslin used for stage decorations and from there to the rest of the sets. An asbestos laden curtain was to come down and separate the stage from the audience in case of fire, but it malfunctioned. The audience in the three seating levels of orchestra, first balcony, and second balcony had different experiences, with those on the highest levels being burnt as the flames rushed at them after external doors were opened. People died of flames, asphyxiation or being trampled, on stairways, on unfinished fire escapes, or in front of locked doors. Many early jumpers perished, while later jumpers used those bodies as cushions.

The blame came fast and furious. There were allegations of building code violations, as there were no automatic sprinklers; the fire alarm was not connected to the city fire alarm; there was no ventilating shaft at the rear of the stage to conduct fire away from the audience; all exits were not marked so as to be found in the dark; and there were seat rows that did not have aisles when the seats were occupied. A coroner's jury was quickly convened to investigate whether the steel doors on the first and second balconies were locked, to prevent patrons from descending to the higher priced seats; why the asbestos curtain had not lowered; the usage of arc lights; and why ushers closed the doors after the fire was declared. Fifteen people on stage then, including the stage manager, electrician, light operator, and carpenter, were arrested and charged with manslaughter, while fifteen singers on stage were arrested as witnesses without charge. All theaters without asbestos curtains were ordered closed. The chief usher was arrested and charged with manslaughter. Other men were arrested for destroying evidence regarding the sealing of the skylights.

The theater was owned by a syndicate of two New York groups (J. Fred Zimmerman, Sr. and Samuel F. Nixon, Marc Klaw and Abraham Erlanger) and one in Chicago (William J. Davis and Harry Powers). At the insistence of a man who lost his wife, and three children, Davis and Powers were arrested and charged with manslaughter, as was building commissioner George Williams. Davis and business manager Thomas J. Noonan admitted the employees were not trained for fires, there were not sufficient aids available to fight fires, many exits were locked, and no one had operated the stage ventilators. The coroner's jury found violations of building ordinances and fire regulations, leading to the arrests of several men.

Arrested were mayor Carter H. Harrison, fire chief W. H. Musham, Davis, Williams, building inspector Edward Laughlin, theater fireman William Sallers, stage manager/carpenter James E. Cummings, and light operator William Mullen. A special grand jury then indicted Davis, as the active manager, Cummings, and Noonan for manslaughter for not supplying the safety apparatus to extinguish the fire, and Williams and Laughlin for misfeasance in not complying with city inspection ordinances. Another grand jury indicted Davis for involuntary manslaughter and Willaims and Laughlin for neglect of duty but not Klaw, Erlanger, Powers, Cummings, Noonan, or Sallers.

The special grand jury had indicted Davis, Noonan, and Cummings in February 1904. In late September 1904, as they were about to go to trial on manslaughter charges, Noonan and Cummings asked for a change of venue, based on prejudice against the defendants in Cook County. They gave a long series of reasons, including: their long residence and work in Cook County; more than 100 witness who appeared before the grand Jury; the fire happening in Chicago and being charged with manslaughter for it; stories on this topic carried for several months in all the local newspapers with their large circulations; more than 200 witnesses subpoenaed by the coroner, whose inquest was open to the public in Cook County; much publicity about the theater's initial opening; public periods of mourning; the widely written about and discussed negligence of the defendants; the creation and publicity of the Iroquois Memorial Association; the shutting of local theatres; the widespread condemnation of the defendants; etc.[13]

---

[13] People v. Davis, 1 Ill. Cir. Ct. Rep. 191 (Ill. Cir. Ct. Oct. 1904).

The public fervor had significantly decreased after the indictments in February. However, just before the trial was to begin, the theater reopened after repairs, with a new name, but the public condemnations started all over again. The defendants introduced thousands of affidavits demonstrating the local prejudice against them. The prosecutor had originally opposed the motion but later withdrew his opposition on seeing the affidavits, except on the ground of additional costs. The court granted the change in venue, as increased trial costs were not a sufficient reason to deny the change in a criminal trial. The trial was moved to Peoria County, to be heard before a judge from that county and one from Cook County. Davis moved to quash the indictment before the Cook County judge.[14]

The indictment noted the ordinances that the defendants were accused of violating included having a metal flue pipe and dampers above the stage to channel smoke out of the building in case of fire, an automatic sprinkler system, and for stationary scenery, a portable fire extinguisher. Davis, responsible for the whole building and theater, Noonan, responsible for the business of the building and theater, and Cummings, in charge of the stage, did not supply these items required under the city ordinance. Because of the lack of those varied apparatus to put out the small stage fire before it grew, the flue to channel the smoke, and the fire sprinklers to put out the flames, the named victim, Viva R. Jackson, while witnessing the show, had been burned, and asphyxiated, leading to her death.

The court first looked at the difference between common law and statutory involuntary manslaughter. The state's case was that at common law, gross negligence was required but under statute, it was less, a lawful act without due caution and circumspection. The defense argued the opposite, that the statutory definition was narrower and required direct violation of a statute. The court found four different statutory definitions for manslaughter and excusable homicide, which it would try to harmonize while using a few rules of construction. These rules were that the common law would not be repealed by implication or any further than it was explicitly declared. And that statutes could not legalize acts which at common law were opposed to public policy. The court said the common law was still in force in its view for the manslaughter provisions, requiring an unlawful act or omission to be the proximate cause of death.

---

[14] People v. Davis, 1 Ill. Cir. Ct. Rep. 217 (Ill. Cir. Ct. Feb. 1905).

The court said that the city ordinances did not name who had the responsibility for the duties it set out, so it must be the owner or lessee of the building. As the three defendants were indicted as the general manager, business manager, and carpenter, they were not under that legal duty. The court said that in an indictment, the facts must stand or fall on the face of the indictment and courts in the state did not take judicial notice of municipal ordinances. Ruling that the defendants did not have these legal duties under the pled ordinances, and had not taken the duties on voluntarily, the court held the indictments were not sufficient to sustain a conviction for violating the city ordinances. Nor did the indictment sufficiently plead violation of a common law duty. The court deemed it better to quash an improperly drafted indictment before an expensive trial and have it re-drafted. The indictment of Davis was quashed by the Cook County judge and the other two's by the Peoria County judge.

A second indictment was then returned against Davis the following month. It contained six counts, the first four of which were for violation of the city ordinances and the final two for violation of a common law duty. The first count identified Davis as the president, director, and general manager of the Iroquois Theatre company and general manager of the building with full authority and control. The ordinance required buildings of this class to have a flue, a switch operating the dampers, automatic sprinklers, and fire extinguishers, hooks, and axes upon the stage, to employ an expert fireman, and a diagram of the building to be printed on the programs. Penalties were laid out for non-compliance, it was Davis' duty to comply, and he was negligent for not doing so, leading to the death of Viva R. Jackson. The second count was the same, except naming Davis as a manager and agent of the building and theatre. The third count named Davis owner and occupant of the theater. The fourth count named Davis as being in control of the building and theater on behalf of the owners. The fifth and sixth counts specified Davis' legal duty in his roles in which he was negligent, causing Jackson's death, without reference to the ordinances.

The court held that there was no common law duty to provide safety for fires and so quashed the fifth and sixth counts. The defense raised the same question, that the ordinance did not name who was responsible to supply the fire suppression devices. The court said that it was its duty to uphold statutes where possible, acknowledging the lesser legal skills of those drafting municipal ordinances. Further, knowing that the building had been constructed without these devices, the legal duty of the defendant was to not occupy a building that violated the ordinances. The defense also argued the fire, not lack of safety apparatus, was the direct and proximate cause of Jackson's death. The court said that the violation of municipal ordinances was prima facie evidence of negligence. The court overruled the motion to quash for the first four, leaving for a jury to determine if the defendant exercised due caution under these laws.

Davis then moved for a change of venue, submitting more than 12,000 affidavits in support. The court granted the motion.[15] The trial of Davis was held in Vermilion County,[16] finally facing a jury trial for the four counts of the indictment for manslaughter based on violating the ordinances. The defense moved to suppress the introduction of the municipal ordinances, as void. This was because the state only delegated to the city the power to set a geographic fire limit within which wooden buildings could not be erected. However, this did not apply to other delegated powers like the fire apparatus regulations. The state law gave city councils the powers,

> To prevent the dangerous construction and conditions of chimneys, fire places, hearths, stoves, stove pipes, ovens, boilers and apparatus used in and about any buildings and manufactories, and to cause the same to be removed or placed in a safe condition when considered dangerous; to regulate and prevent the carrying on of manufactories dangerous in causing and promoting fires; to prevent the deposit of ashes in unsafe places, and to cause all such buildings and enclosures as may be in a dangerous state to be put in safe condition.[17]

Because the Chicago ordinances applied only within the specified fire limits and did not apply equally to the whole city and all people within it, the defense asserted it was void. This court, in a weak legal argument heavily reliant on other judges' analyses and without its own in-depth synthesis of the relevant law, agreed with the defense. It also held that there was no explicit legal duty specified for Davis in the ordinance. Without the evidence of the ordinances, the court then directed the jury to return a not guilty verdict. The 600 victims of the fire had found no justice.

---

[15] People v. Davis, 1 Ill. Cir. Ct. Rep. 207 (Ill. Cir. Ct. June 1906).
[16] People v. Davis, 2 Ill. Cir. Ct. Rep. 395 (Ill. Cir. Ct. Mar. 1907).
[17] *Id.* at 422.

## C. Earthquake & Fire

| LEGAL ISSUES |
|---|
| ❖ Limitations on fire insurance liability for earthquakes<br>❖ Replacing legal records loss in a conflagration |

On the morning of April 18, 1906, an earthquake registering nearly 8.0 on the Richter scale occurred along the San Andreas fault in California. The epicenter may have been off San Francisco Bay, as the destruction in the city was significant. The earthquake though was just the beginning of the disaster, with worse to follow. The toppling of chimneys and the breaking of water mains and gas lines set the stage for the Great San Francisco[18] Fire that ensued. Deaths have been modernly estimated at around 3,000, due to a significant undercounting in the minority communities at the time. The destruction to buildings was immense, with so many homes lost that more than half the population was immediately made homeless.

More than 50 fires broke out across the city. Despite nearly 40 fire engines and 600 firefighters, the vast number of wooden structures, many shabbily constructed, provided the necessary kindling for the fire. Without water, firefighters and the military were forced to use dynamite on buildings, to create a sort of crude firewall. As reported by Jack London,

> The earthquake shook down in San Francisco hundreds of thousands of dollars worth of walls and chimneys. But the conflagration that followed burned up hundreds of millions of dollars' worth of property There is no estimating within hundreds of millions the actual damage wrought. Not in history has a modern imperial city been so completely destroyed. San Francisco is gone. Nothing remains of it but memories and a fringe of dwelling-houses on its outskirts. Its industrial section is wiped out. Its business section is wiped out. Its social and residential section is wiped out. The factories and warehouses, the great stores and newspaper buildings, the hotels and the palaces of the nabobs, are all gone. Remains only the fringe of dwelling houses on the outskirts of what was once San Francisco.[19]

---

[18] For a deeper understanding of San Francisco during its formative years, *see* THOMAS J. SHAW, THE LEGAL HISTORY OF THE AMERICAN FRONTIER.
[19] Jack London, *The Story of an Eyewitness,* COLLIER'S WEEKLY (May 5, 1906).

In the *Charles Nelson*,[20] a damages libel was filed by steerage class passengers on a ship out of San Francisco just after the fire. Passenger numbers were limited by the quantity specified on its inspection certificate. Not only were there more people than licensed, but there were shortages of food, water and coal onboard. These were exacerbated by bad weather which made the journey last longer than planned. The libel was rejected by the court, "It is the opinion of the court, however, that the extraordinary conditions existing at San Francisco when the voyage, was undertaken justify and require the exercise of judicial discretion and that according to principles of equity the libelants are not entitled to prevail."[21]

The court explained why more tickets had been sold than licensed,

a few days prior to the sailing of said vessel the city of San Francisco was practically destroyed by earthquake and fire; that the docks in said city were largely destroyed, and the place of business of the claimant was totally destroyed; that the usual ticket agencies in San Francisco where the claimant sold tickets for voyages to Puget Sound were destroyed by fire; that for the accommodation of parties desiring to leave San Francisco by steerage on the vessel *Charles Nelson*, and in the light of the great disaster in San Francisco, the claimant reduced the fare for steerage passengers on said trip, and to accommodate intending purchasers offered tickets for sale at Oakland, as well as at its office and at the dock in San Francisco; that the claimant, on account of the destruction of its place of business, was at that time unable to obtain offices in the city of San Francisco, and was maintaining an office in Oakland, Cal.; that up to a time subsequent to the time when said vessel sailed there was no telegraphic or telephonic communication between Oakland and San Francisco, and no means of communicating other than by special messengers, and on account of the confusion due to the fire and, earthquake it was exceedingly difficult to communicate with the claimant's several agencies by private messenger; that a few hours before said steamer sailed there had been sold at its Oakland office for said voyage 15 steerage tickets, and the claimant learned that 7 tickets had been sold at the Stewart Street Dock in San Francisco; that as soon thereafter as

---

[20] The Charles Nelson, 149 F. 846 (W.D. Wash. Dec. 1906).
[21] *Id*. at 847.

it was able to get into communication with its agencies in San Francisco the claimant withdrew all tickets from sale, and directed the agents to refund to holders of tickets above 16 the purchase money.[22]

The ship departed at night, when all gas and electric lights plants in San Francisco had been destroyed, so there was no light on the pier. The crew was instructed that steerage passengers above 16 were to be sent back to travel agencies for refunds. When tickets were taken the next morning, 27 passengers had steerage tickets, plus three stowaways. By then the ship was too far out at sea to return. The stowaways were put to work and housed with the crew. The steerage passengers were served meals in the crew mess, but apparently preferred to eat elsewhere. The ship could not obtain fresh water or coal in San Francisco. Only the condenser provided water but due to the extended nature of the voyage, condenser use had to be economized to save coal to reach the destination.

Dismissing a libel it was clearly indignant of, the court concluded,

The appalling disaster which suddenly rendered a great multitude of people in San Francisco homeless and destitute is a matter of common and general knowledge, and due credit should be given to the generous impulses of officers and managers of railroads and steamship lines which prompted them to make extraordinary exertions to facilitate the emigration of the many who hastened to leave the ruins and desolation which surrounded them in that city. It is plainly apparent that the desire of the libelants to get away from San Francisco was too strong to admit of any questioning of the sufficiency of the accommodations afforded by the *Charles Nelson* before going aboard of her, and their demands are as ungracious as would be the case if they had been castaways, and were suing a rescuing ship which had brought them away from a desolate shore. The evidence proves that the officers of the *Charles Nelson* did not intend to oppress the libelants, nor to violate the law by receiving on board an excessive number of passengers, and that the overcrowding of the ship was occasioned by the intrusion of those who came on board in the darkness.[23]

---

[22] *Id.*
[23] *Id.* at 848-49.

In *Baker & Hamilton*,[24] the court analyzed a fire insurance policy covering the loss of goods in the great fire. The policy read, in part,

> This company shall not be liable for loss caused directly or indirectly by... or for loss or damage occasioned by or through any volcano, earthquake, or hurricane, or other eruption, convulsion, or disturbance; or by theft; or by neglect of the insured to use all reasonable means to save and preserve the property at and after a fire or when the property is endangered by fire in neighboring premises; or (unless fire ensues, and, in that event, for the damage by fire only) by explosion of any kind.[25]

The company asserted it had no liability because the loss was caused by the earthquake. The court concluded that "occasioned by or through" was equivalent to "caused" and so if the fire was not directly caused by the earthquake, the defendant insurer was liable. Only an earthquake that was the direct, immediate, and proximate cause of a fire that led to the loss would the insured not be covered. The general rule was to construe insurance provisions in the light most favorable to the insured. In *Henry Hilp Tailoring*,[26] a different judge left it to the jury to interpret this phrase, saying it would suffice if a fire from another building started by the earthquake destroyed the plaintiff's premises. It was up to the defendant to prove that the loss was occasioned by or through the earthquake.

In *Richmond Coal*,[27] the latter case's judge explained, using examples,

> If you find and believe from the evidence... that the earthquake of April 18, 1906, caused directly or indirectly in the city and county of San Francisco a fire in the vicinity of Fourth and Natoma streets; or a fire in the vicinity of Third and Minna streets; or a fire in the vicinity of Third and Howard streets; or a fire in the vicinity of First and Mission streets; or a fire in the vicinity of Market and Fremont streets, in... Mack & Company's drugstore; or a fire on Fremont street, between Howard and Mission streets, in... the Martel Power Company's plant; or a fire at No. 117 Steuart street, in the place known as Alice's; or a

---

[24] Baker & Hamilton v. Williamsburgh City Fire Ins., 157 F. 280 (Cir. Ct. N.D. Cal. Aug. 1907).
[25] *Id.*
[26] Henry Hilp Tailoring Co. v. Williamsburgh City Fire Ins., 157 F. 285 (Cir. Ct. N.D. Cal. Aug. 1907).
[27] Richmond Coal Co. v. Commercial Union Assur. Co., 159 F. 985 (Cir. Ct. N.D. Cal. Jan. 1908).

fire at No. 48 Steuart street, between Market and Mission streets, in... Brown's store; and that those fires, or any one or more of them so-caused, spread by flame, spark, or heat, and burned uninterruptedly from building to building, or block to block, until they or any one or more of them reached and destroyed plaintiff's property located and situated on the northwest corner of Howard and Spear streets — then I charge you that it is your duty, and you must be governed by what the evidence shows, to return a verdict in favor of the defendant insurance company and against the plaintiff coal company.[28]

The federal court of appeals[29] then weighed in, saying that if a fire started in another building and spread to the insured's premise, the earthquake would not be direct cause. Citing *Baker & Hamilton* approvingly, the change of wording of the clause from "directly and indirectly" in the prior phrase had to imply some meaning. This meaning was that the earthquake had to be the direct cause of the fire. The court of appeals believed that if the insurance company intended something else, it could have easily used clearer wording in its policies to indicate this.

In *Levey*,[30] the plaintiff landlord sued its tenants for a subletting of the tenancy, asking for rent, eviction, and forfeiture of the lease. The eviction notice came within three months of the fire. When the trial court only awarded the rent, the plaintiff appealed. After the great fire, the two tenants in a building on Fillmore Street in San Francisco took on three subtenants, all on different terms, two of which had the tenants paying some form of rent. This was undoubtedly due to the complete lack of office space after the fire. The court of appeals reversed the lower court's judgment, holding that a forfeiture of the lease should be declared.

In *in re the Estate of Heywood*,[31] Agnes Heywood, the widow of Franklin Heywood, had petitioned the court for a probate homestead, an exempt personal property set off, and a family allowance. This was refused by the superior court in San Francisco in November 1905 and orders set out. A bill of exceptions was served in March 1906 and was not settled by the time of the great fire the next month, which destroyed all the official

---

[28] *Id.* at 988.
[29] Williamsburgh City Fire Ins. Co. of Brooklyn v. Willard, 164 F. 404 (9th Cir. Oct. 1908).
[30] Levey v. Hockwald, 6 Cal. App. 417 (D. Ct. of App. Sept. 1907).
[31] In re the Estate of Heywood, 154 Cal. 312 (Cal. Oct. 1908).

records. The appeal required the orders of November 1905 to be restored. Under a June 1906 act of the California legislature,[32] court records lost to conflagration not the fault of the applicant could be officially restored from a certified copy of the original. If none was available, and the applicant would be damaged without restoration, the court could make an order as to the substance and effect of the lost record. The supreme court dismissed this appeal, as it was the appellant's responsibility, not the court's, to apply for the lost court records, and it had been too long.

In *Napoli*,[33] the defendant was convicted of second-degree murder and his motion for a new trial was denied. Before his bill of exceptions could been allowed by the trial court for an appeal, all the records of the trial were destroyed in the great fire. The next year, the defendant motioned for a new trial under a new 1907 law. This statute[34] allowed a new trial in the case where a bill of exceptions or statement of the case was lost due to conflagration and could not be restored and a motion for a new trial was pending. The appeals court rejected his motion, saying that when the trial court originally rejected his motion for a new trial, it lost jurisdiction and a motion for a new trial was no longer pending.

In *Bodkin*,[35] the defendant Cordelia Bodkin was convicted of first-degree murder for sending poisoned candy through the mail to Mary Elizabeth Dunning of Dover, Delaware in 1898. The defendant asked for a reversal of judgment due to loss of certain evidence in the great fire. These were photographic copies of exhibits showing her handwriting used as evidence in the trial. The defendant asserted that because the full record was not available, the judgment should be reversed, and a new trial ordered. The court of appeals noted no authority for this assertion and held that this was not sufficient for a new trial. The original jury had heard from the witnesses who testified whether her handwriting matched the exemplars and had made their decisions accordingly. The loss of evidence on appeal did not mean she had not received a fair trial.

---

[32] An Act relating to the restoration of court records which have been lost, injured or destroyed by conflagration or other public calamity, ch. 55 (1906).
[33] People v. Napoli, 7 Cal. App. 79 (D. Ct. of App. Dec. 1907).
[34] An Act providing for the disposition of actions and proceedings in which bills of exceptions and statements on motion for a new trial have been lost or destroyed by conflagration or other public calamity, ch. 537 (1907).
[35] People v. Botkin, 9 Cal. App. 244 (D. Ct. of App. Oct. 1908).

## D. Mine Explosions

| LEGAL ISSUES |
|---|
| ❖ Explosions in mines generating legal liability<br>❖ Differing judicial interpretations of operator's liability |

The month of December 1907 was a particularly grim one for coal miners in the United States. On December 1, there was an explosion at the Naomi Mine in Pennsylvania operated by the Hillman Coal and Coke Company, resulting in the deaths of at least 35 miners. On December 6, there was an explosion at the Monongah Mine in West Virginia operated by the Fairmont Coal Company, with at least 362 miners, and likely more, killed. On December 16, an explosion at the Yolande Mine in Alabama operated by Yolande Coal and Coke Company saw at least 55 miners lose their lives. On December 19, an explosion at the Darr Mine in Pennsylvania operated by Pittsburgh Coal Company led to the deaths of 239 miners.

These, and the very long list of other mining accidents, would eventual lead to the creation of a federal Bureau of Mines in 1910, charged with making investigations "especially in relation to the safety of miners, and the appliances best adapted to prevent accidents, the possible improvement of conditions under which mining operations are carried on, the treatment of ores and other mineral substances, the use of explosives and electricity, the prevention of accidents and other inquiries and technologic investigations pertinent to said industries."[36] This did not give the bureau any right of inspection of mines within the states. So, miner safety rested upon state laws, and the judicial interpretations thereof.

In 1893, Pennsylvania passed a statute addressing the health and safety of coal miners.[37] Among the many provisions were: allowing a maximum of 20 workers at a time unless there were two openings to the surface, one an airway and the other for ingress and egress; miners were to be raised and lowered by machinery if the mine's vertical depth was more than 75 feet, which was to be inspected daily; the operator was to provide ample means of ventilation, with the fans to operate 24 hours a day; working areas were to be kept free of standing gas, any working area

---

[36] An Act to establish in the Department of the Interior a Bureau of Mines, c. 61, s. 2, ch. 240.
[37] An Act relating to bituminous coal mines, and providing for the lives, health, safety and welfare of persons employed therein, c. 48 (1893).

with firedamp (methane) was to be inspected before each shift, and areas with explosive gas required locked safety lamps; safety lamps were the property of the mine operator; a mine foreman required a certificate of competency and was responsible for ventilating apparatus and airways, timber to support the shaft, cut-throughs, rock overheads, weekly air measurements, and removing all dangers; superintendents (operator's agents) were responsible for keeping a full supply of safety materials on hand; and no powder or explosives were to be stored in a mine.

In *Saylor*,[38] a miner's widow asked the court for damages based on the operator's negligence leading to her husband's death in an explosion. The court explained that the bituminous coal mine in question had two shafts, one for the miners and one for air, connected by a cut-through. As the mine's face was moved forward, new cut-throughs were required but the old one must be bratticed (closed) to make the new one effective. The evidence of witnesses showed that the cut-throughs had not been bratticed, which was the responsibility of the mine foreman. However, the foreman had asked the operator's agent (superintendent) for the necessary materials three weeks prior and while promised, none had been received. This explained the unclosed cut-throughs and the lack of circulation for the explosion. The court of appeals upheld the jury's verdict that the mine operator was negligent, awarding the widow $1,000.

In *Sloss-Sheffield Steel*,[39] the plaintiff was injured by a fire resulting from an explosion in the Bessie Mine in Alabama in July 1907. The plaintiff had asserted he suffered injuries that made it difficult to resume work and that the defendant was at fault due to violation of a state statute. This law required mine operators to supply sufficient air to carry off all noxious gases in a mine. The claim by the plaintiff was for the fault on not brushing out noxious gases or other explosive substances, which led to the explosion and therefore his injuries. The supreme court of the state ruled that while the statute did specify a duty to remove noxious gases, it did not create a duty to do the same for explosive substances. That was beyond what the statute specified. Because both were included in the count of the complaint, the entire count must fail.

---

[38] Saylor v. Chartiers Coal & Coke Co., 31 Pa. Super. 447 (Super. Ct. Pa. Oct. 1906).
[39] Sloss-Sheffield Steel & Iron Co. v. Sharp, 156 Ala. 284, 47 So. 279 (Ala. July 1908).

In *Davis*,[40] plaintiff George Davis worked as a shot-firer in a coal mine, putting gunpowder into pre-drilled holes and lighting the fuses to bring down certain portions of a mine in a controlled manner. On January 25, 1906, he was engaged in this role when an explosion of coal dust severely burned him. Davis sued for damages under a state law that required operators to avoid coal dust explosions. The manager of the mine testified that the track over which mules pulled the coal cars was sprinkled once a week to keep the coal dust down. He, the company's mine examiner, and the state mine inspector analyzed the accident and concluded the problem was improper timing between the firing of the shots, causing a gas explosion. The state supreme court did not find material contributory negligence by the plaintiff. It was the operator's responsibility to keep the coal dust sprinkled and not having done so recently, led to the explosion and injuries. The lower courts' judgement for the plaintiff was affirmed.

In *Elvis*,[41] the plaintiff was injured by the explosion of an air compressor in a coal mine on February 22, 1907, when he, in his role as a mule driver, was seventy feet away from it. The explosion was caused by the pooling of unconsumed oil from the compressor cylinders, which was not drained for three days when it should have been drained each day. The other workers in the area were all covered by the oil after the explosion. The plaintiff asserted and the appeals court agreed that this was a case of *res ipsa loquitur* and prima facie case for negligence had been made out and it was up to the operator to disprove this. The operator said this rule did not apply to employer-employee relationships, but the court held that because a mule driver had no relation to the operation of an air compressor, that rule should apply just as it would to a rail passenger.

In *Bisko*,[42] the plaintiff was injured by an explosion on March 19, 1906, while working in a Pennsylvania coal mine. Gas in a pocket where he was working was ignited by the open lamp in his hand. The plaintiff sued, asserting that the mine operator was negligent in not providing adequate materials to ventilate the mine, providing a safe working place, or ventilating the mine. The state supreme court said that state law required mine owners to keep on hand a supply of materials for the health and

---

[40] Davis v. Illinois Collieries Co., 232 Ill. 284 (Ill. Feb. 1908).
[41] Elvis v. Lumaghi Coal Co., 140 Ill. App. 112 (Ill. App. Mar. 1908).
[42] Bisko v. Braznell Gas Coal Co., 223 Pa. 186 (Pa. Jan. 1909).

safety of workers as ordered by the mine foreman. Because the foreman had not ordered such materials based upon the requirements of the workers, the court ruled the mine operator was not negligent for that. In any event, the lack of material is not what caused the accident. As to the second assertion, the rest of the mine was considered safe and although the statute did not allow workers to be sent to unsafe places in a mine, it did allow it if the intent was to make the area safe. For the final assertion, there was not sufficient evidence that the mine was not ventilated properly. Even if there had not been proper ventilation, by raising his hand to where the gas pocket was, contrary to his foreman's instructions, the miner contributed to his own injury. The supreme court reversed and entered a judgment for the defendant operator.

In *Edwards' Administrator*,[43] the decedent James Boyd Edwards had been killed on November 21, 1907, in an explosion and fire in a mine in Kentucky. By state statute, mine operators were required to provide 100 cubic feet of air per minute per person working in a mine and to provide an abundant supply of air through artificial means. Contrary to the plaintiff argument that the air in the mine was not good on that day, the defendant operator claimed it was good, and that the explosion was caused by miners not leaving sufficient time between firing off the shots. The trial court held for the defendant, but the court of appeals reversed, holding the jury instructions were invalid, as not fully stating the law. The court also said the instructions were flawed in that they did not show the responsibility of the operator to properly space timings of firing the shots five minutes apart or in sequence starting from those closest to the mine entrance, so the fumes would flow out of the mine.

In *Cody*,[44] the plaintiff was required to buy his own tools and blasting materials as an employee of the defendant's coal company. He purchased 50 feet of fuse from the company's commissary store. Upon trying to light the fuse, it did not take after three attempts. On the fourth attempt, the blast immediately exploded, leaving the plaintiff with severe injuries. The defendant countered that the plaintiff was contributorily negligent in staying so close to a lit fuse and the injuries were not the natural result of a defective fuse. The court of appeals noted that the warranty on the fuse

---

[43] Edwards' Admr. v. Lam, 132 Ky. 32 (Ken. App. Feb. 1909).
[44] Cody v. Norton Coal Co., 110 Va. 363 (Va. Nov. 1909).

assumed a reasonable and proper usage and that damages needed to be reasonably anticipated. The court viewed the lack of smoke in the three earlier attempts as a misunderstanding by the plaintiff, as this likely indicated that the fuse was doing exactly as intended, consuming the fuse efficiently. The court held the contributory negligence of the plaintiff was the proximate cause,

> Nothing could have been more imprudent and reckless than the conduct of the plaintiff. To put flame or fire to a fuse connected with dynamite, the object of which was to explode the dynamite, and to remain by it until the explosion occurred, upon the unwarranted assumption that the fuse was defective, instead of seeking a place of safety and there awaiting the result, was to invite and court disaster.[45]

In *Dickinson*,[46] a father was suing over the death of his minor child in a coal mine in West Virginia. Dallas E. Love was 11 years old when he was killed in a mine explosion. One question the court had to consider was whether the employment of such a youth would be considered negligence, as it was in violation of state law. Unlike adults, who were assumed to take on the risk of injuries due to the negligence of their fellow workers, minors of this age could not. The court held that the father, as a party to the unlawful employment contract and recipient of any damages, would be held contributorily negligent sufficient to preclude recovery.

Regarding the explosion equating to negligence, the court said,

> The fact of the explosion is not, as plaintiff's counsel affirm, even *prima facie* evidence of negligence, calling for explanation. In other words the rule *res ipsa loquitur* does not apply. We take judicial notice that explosions occur in the best equipped, best regulated and perfectly ventilated mines. Moreover, the owner or operator is not liable when the explosion is the result of negligence of a fellow servant, and not of its neglect to furnish a reasonably safe place in the first instance, or to employ a competent mine boss or fire boss, or to perform some other statutory or common law duty imposed.[47]

---

[45] *Id.* at 368.
[46] Dickinson v. Stuart Colliery Co., 71 W. Va. 325 (W. Va. Nov. 1912).
[47] *Id.* at 327.

## E. Factory Fire

| LEGAL ISSUES |
|---|
| ❖ Owner's liability for locking in factory workers<br>❖ Proving guilt as a public nuisance |

On March 25, 1911, the Triangle Waist Company, on the top floors of the 10-story Asch Building in New York, caught fire and burned, resulting in the deaths of more than 140 people. Most of them were young women engaged in sewing and assembling shirtwaists (blouses) for other women. They had been locked into the factory by owners who would soon face criminal charges. There was only a single internal fire escape in this tall building and fire engine ladders could not reach the fire on the eighth, ninth, and tenth floors. Elevators took as many as possible while still operating but filled up each time upon reaching the eighth floor, never reaching the ninth. The owners escaped the fire, going from the tenth floor to the roof, on a route unknown to most of the young women workers.

> At 4:40 o'clock, nearly five hours after the employes in the rest of the building had gone home, the fire broke out. The one little fire escape in the interior was never resorted to by any of the doomed victims. Some of them escaped by running down the stairs, but in a moment or two this avenue was cut off by flame. The girls rushed to the windows and looked down at Greene Street, 100 feet below them. Then one poor little creature jumped. There was a plate glass protection over part of the sidewalk, but she crashed through it, wrecking it and breaking her body into a thousand pieces. Then they all began to drop. The crowd yelled "Don't jump!" but it was jump or be burned – the proof of which is found in the fact that fifty burned bodies were taken from the ninth floor alone. They jumped, they crashed through broken glass, they crushed themselves to death on the sidewalk… A thirteen-year-old girl hung for three minutes by her finger tips to the sill of the tenth-floor window. A tongue of flame licked at her fingers, and she dropped to death. A girl threw her pocketbook, then her hat, then her furs from a tenth-floor window. A moment later her body came whirling after them to death.[48]

---

[48] *141 Men and Girls Die in Waist Factory Fire*, N.Y. TIMES (Mar. 26, 1911).

Multiple investigations and inquests started, including those by the attorney general, the coroner, the fire department, the city bureau of buildings, and the state department of labor. The latter two engaged in a public dispute over who had the responsibility for the fire escapes. The labor department claimed it had this responsibility for factories everywhere in the state except New York City, due to a 1903 decision by the state courts. In *Sailors' Snug Harbor*,[49] the jurisdiction over factory fire escapes had been given by general statute to the labor department's factory inspectors but a special statute gave those powers in the city to the bureau. The bureau had the fire department perform onsite building inspections. The fire department had reported nearly 14,000 buildings needing additional means of egress to protect lives, but the Asch Building was not among them. The labor department was responsible for factory doors, which were to be outwardly opening, except when not practical.

Within a few weeks, after the district attorney's agent had found a fastened lock in the ruins, the owners of the company, Isaac Harris and Max Blanck, were indicted for first- and second-degree manslaughter by the grand jury. The coroner's jury found the death of one girl due to criminal negligence was the responsibility of the company's two owners in not following the legal requirement to keep the doors unlocked. There were two stairways, one leading to Greene Street and one to Washington Place. The former had quickly been engulfed in flames for the girls on the ninth floor, precluding its use. It was the Washington Place door, inwardly opening, that they tried to use but the surviving girls claimed it was locked. The locking of this door would become the key contention in the trial.

Preliminarily, the defendants moved to have demurrers issued against the charges.[50] Seven indictments were handed down by the grand jury, each with identical charges but a different deceased girl named on it. There were six counts, two sets of three, with the first set addressed to first-degree common law manslaughter and the second set to second-degree manslaughter. The first count was that the defendants did willfully suffocate the victims by fire and smoke, causing them to die. The

---

[49] City of New York v. Trustees of Sailors' Snug Harbor, 83 N.Y.S. 442, 85 App. Div. 355 (N.Y. App. Div. July 1903).
[50] People v. Harris, 26 N.Y. Crim. 472, 74 Misc. 353 (N.Y. Crim. Nov. 1911).

defendants asserted this must be proved the likely result, but the court rejected the demurrer, as not being the time to raise the need for proofs.

The second count alleged that defendants willfully killed the victims while in commission of a misdemeanor. The consolidated laws of the State of New York used (and uses) different chapters to group the law in an area, two of which were the Labor Law (modernly chapter 31) and the Penal Law (modernly chapter 40). The misdemeanor was the violation of the Labor Law, which did not allow the locking of factory doors during working hours, under article 6. The Penal Law specified that anyone violating article 6 of the Labor Law had committed a misdemeanor. The Penal Law also specified that causing the death of a person while committing a misdemeanor affecting that person was manslaughter in the first degree. Because of the locked door, the victim was unable to leave and burned to death. The defendants asserted this did not apply because they were tenants in the building, but the court rejected this, as the law applied to the owners of factories, whether building owners or tenants. The defendants also asserted the Labor Law section implied that only one door had to be unlocked to comply but again the court rejected this attempt at wordsmithing, saying that in a factory all doors had to remain unlocked.

The third count alleged manslaughter based on not keeping the factory safe for their employees and violating the legal duties of owners in the operation of factories. This equated to a public nuisance, which was a misdemeanor, manslaughter in the first degree, as in the second count. The failure of their duties included not keeping their workers safe from fire and the factory free from the unnecessary accumulation of combustible (flash point above 37.8 °C/100 °F) and flammable (flash point below 37.8 °C/100 °F) materials while workers were in the factory. This was primarily remnants and clippings of cloth used in making the shirtwaists, plus other rubbish, left to obstruct doorways, leading to the death of the victim. The defendants asserted there was nothing in the statute that specifically labels this violation of a duty a misdemeanor nor was it within the definition of a public nuisance.

The court responded that by failing to keep the door unlocked, this constituted a public nuisance. In explanation, the court noted that the concept of public nuisance, through the common law, could be an injury or annoyance that affected a considerable portion of the community.

Manufacturing establishments have been prolific of public nuisances, such as offensive odors, noxious gases, disturbing noises, smoke, cinders and fire which disturbed repose and comfort or menaced health or rendered life insecure to any considerable number of persons in the community. A careful examination of authorities fails to disclose a case in which the owner of such a place was held for maintaining a public nuisance because of the injury which it worked upon the laborers and employees at the source of the annoyance and within the confines of the factory. But the common law in its progress has been applied to new conditions as they presented themselves. It is not an inflexible instrument which will not bend to correct a wrong because precedent is lacking. In the manufacturing establishments of the present time there are frequently more human beings engaged than there are inhabitants in the entire population of villages where the common law theory of "public nuisances" applies. Whether or no[t] our penal statute which defines "public nuisances" is an extension of the common law doctrine of public nuisance it seems to be in accord with the reason of that doctrine. In my opinion it covers the allegation in this count that the defendants kept locked and bolted a door in their factory during the hours of labor.[51]

The Penal Law had defined a public nuisance as an act or omission that "Annoys, injures or endangers the comfort, repose, health or safety of any considerable number of persons; or... *In any way renders* a considerable number of persons insecure in life."[52] The court concluded that keeping the door locked during working hours made a considerable number of people insecure in life. Because this was the commission of a misdemeanor while causing the death of the victim, the court rejected the demurrer on the third count. The court allowed the demurrer to the fourth count, which it viewed as not having sufficient facts and evidence for manslaughter in the second degree. The court did not allow the demurrers to the fifth and sixth counts for second-degree manslaughter. It was based on the commission of unlawful acts, the omission to perform certain duties, the gross negligence that the victim could not safely leave when the fire broke out, and the negligence for the speed and violence with which the fire spread.

---

[51] *Id.* at 481.
[52] *Id.* at 481-82.

In the subsequent trial on one of the seven indictments, after much proof and many objections from the defense, the prosecutor was able to get the door frame and lock, which was still engaged, into evidence, based on the testimony ultimately of the men who had installed and sold the locks. Many surviving workers testified that the doors were locked. There was testimony that the sister of one of the owners had faced a locked door on the eighth floor and it was only by the intervention of a machinist with a key that the door was opened on that floor. The defense introduced witnesses who claimed the door was never locked, including Harris who said the doors were never locked but he did have workers' bags checked for possible theft. He also said there had been five other fires since 1902.

The jury acquitted the defendants, likely due to the stringent instructions from the judge on what constituted guilt for these charges,

> Because they are charged with a felony, I charge you that before you find these defendants guilty of manslaughter in the first degree, you must find that this door was locked. If it was locked and locked with the knowledge of the defendants, you must also find beyond a reasonable doubt that such locking caused the death of Margaret Schwartz. If these men were charged with a misdemeanor I might charge you that they need have no knowledge that the door was locked, but I think that in this case it is proper for me to charge that they must have had personal knowledge of the fact that it was locked.[53]

The prosecutor attempted to try the remaining indictments in 1912. The same judge ruled the 1911 jury's verdict had determined the door was not locked, so a new jury could not re-determine this issue, and the case must fail.[54] Three years after the fire, lawsuits against the building owner were settled for $75 per victim, paid by the accident insurance company. From June 1911, the repaired premises were offered to the company by the owner. However, the repairs for the legally mandated new stairs and outwardly opening doors took until September. The court held the owner could not collect rent for months when the building was untenantable.[55]

---

[53] *Triangle Owners Acquitted by Jury*, N.Y. TIMES (Dec. 28, 1911).
[54] People v. Grzesczak, 27 N.Y. Crim. 520, 77 Misc. 202 (N.Y. Cty. Ct. 1912), at 525.
[55] Gerson v. Blanck, 79 Misc. 24 (N.Y. Sup. Ct. Jan. 1913).

## 2.2 TRANSPORTATION AND DISEASE

### A. Iceberg

| LEGAL ISSUES |
|---|
| ❖ Limitation of liability for foreign ships striking an iceberg<br>❖ Passenger ticket provisions excluding negligence |

Late on April 14, 1912, on a voyage starting in the United Kingdom, with a destination in the United States, the *RMS Titanic* hit an iceberg and sank on April 15, taking the lives of more than 1,500 passengers and crew. Inquiries began both in the United States and the United Kingdom. Because the survivors were already in New York, the U.S. Senate started first, on April 19, lasting for more than a month. After interviewing more than 80 witnesses, the committee's final report found the ship did not slow after receiving ice reports, that no general alarm was issued, there was a lack of lifeboats and drills, and many boats went out unfilled. Recommendations included sufficient crewed lifeboats for all aboard, drilling for lowering and rowing lifeboats, 24-hour wireless communications, and direct communications with the bridge, electric searchlights, no firing of rockets except as distress calls, and sufficiently watertight ship skin and bulkheads.

The British inquiry ran for two months from the start of May, calling nearly 100 witnesses. Unfortunately, it was called by the Board of Trade (BoT), which had been responsible for approving the Titanic before it sailed. This was a conflict of interest from the start, as the BoT issued the 26 questions for the inquest to answer, many easy technical queries. The final report's answer to whether the ship met all safety regulations was, of course, answered affirmatively. It did regard the excessive speed as the primary factor in the collision, while saying that the captain had made a mistake but could not be blamed, as it was common shipping practice. Recommendations included watertight ship subdivisions, sufficient lifeboats, boats drills, continuous wireless operation, and moderating speed at night when ice was present. The report exonerated two male passengers, J. Bruce Ismay and Cosmo Duff-Gordon. The latter escaped in a mostly empty lifeboat with his wife, Lucy Duff-Gordon, who would become legally famous within a few years in her role as a rising fashion designer.[56]

---

[56] Wood v. Duff-Gordon, 222 N.Y. 88 (N.Y. App. Dec. 1917).

Significant U.S. litigation soon followed the 1912 disaster. The *Titanic* was owned by the Oceanic Steam Navigation Company Ltd. The latter went to court in New York to stem the tide of lawsuits, invoking the 1851 limitation of liability statute discussed in Chapter 1, which said, in part,

> That the liability of the owner or owners of any ship or vessel... or for any loss, damage, or injury by collision, or for any act, matter, or thing, loss, damage, or forfeiture, done, occasioned, or incurred, without the privity or knowledge of such owner or owners, shall in no case exceed the amount or value of the interest of such owner or owners respectively, in such ship or vessel, and her freight then pending.[57]

While it considered the limitation of liability, the district court, in October 1912, issued a monition (notice) to all claimants to bring their claims to this court and an injunction to stop litigation elsewhere. Elizabeth H. Natsch, executrix of Charles Natsch, who perished on the *Titanic*, sued in the state supreme court. Other claimants motioned for the injunction to be modified to allow them to also initiate common law actions within the permitted time to not lose their legal rights.[58] The district court would not allow other courts to claim jurisdiction over lawsuits regarding the *Titanic* sinking, saying all claims and limitations needed to be tried by the same district court that was charged with determining the limitation of liability.

A. Leonard Brougham was the lawyer who had initiated the lawsuit on behalf of Elizabeth H. Natsch. He was cited for contempt for disobeying the court's injunction against litigation, responding he did not read the order and monition before filing suit. The court said he could purge his contempt by withdrawing the suit. When he was later fined $200, he appealed the contempt order. The court of appeals[59] looked at whether the district court had the necessary jurisdiction. Finding that it clearly did, it said that obeying the injunction was not to be based on whether the limitation of liability would be subsequently granted. The court of appeals, ruling Brougham had sufficient knowledge, and its modification of the injunction (see below) did not act as a pardon, affirmed the contempt order.

---

[57] An Act to limit the Liability of Ship-Owners, and for other Purposes, c. 31, s. 2, ch. 43, § 3.
[58] The Titanic, 204 F. 295 (S.D.N.Y. Nov. 1912).
[59] Brougham v. Oceanic Steam Navigation Co., 205 F. 857 (2nd Cir. May 1913).

A claimant motioned[60] for the *Titanic's* tonnage to be entered on the record. This was due to the difference between the American and British laws limiting liability, as discussed in Chapter 1. The U.S. statute limited liability to the value of the ship and freight, while the U.K. statute[61] allowed for liability up to a rate per tonnage of the ship (£8 for goods or £15 for loss of life or injury, per ton). The claimant's theory was that the ship was British owned, British registered, and lost in collision with an iceberg, not the ship of another nation. As such, they should not enjoy the protections of U.S. law. The court rejected this, as when sued in the United States, the owners had the right to the full effect of U.S. law, including the limitation of liability based on the rem (what physically remained after the disaster).

An appeal was made by the Long Island Loan & Trust Company, as executor for the estate of Wyckoff Van Derhoef, who died on the *Titanic*. The appeal was for the rejection of a motion in the district court to modify the injunction to allow the bringing and prosecuting of suits. The court of appeals[62] was cognizant of the problem for claimants in losing legal rights if they did not sue within twelve months of the accident, by April 15, 1913. The court held, if the decision on whether Oceanic Steam would be granted a limitation of liability would not be finalized in time, then the district court had the power, without much adverse impact, to modify the injunction to allow such lawsuits to be filed by claimants to not lose all legal remedy. If the court found the petitioner was entitled to a limitation of liability, then the other suits would end. If it did not, the district court would deal with all damages directly and the other suits would also end. It was only if the district court rejected the limiting of liability but then could not proceed for whatever reason or did so in coordination with other courts that these legal issues would be important. A request for a writ of mandamus to the court of appeals on the same issue was later rejected.[63] This trust company had also sought to dispose witnesses in England.[64]

Two of the claimants, William J. Mellor, a British national, and Harry Anderson, an American, filed exceptions to Oceanic Steam's petition, asserting that the owner of a British registered ship lost in the mid-Atlantic

---

[60] The Titanic, 204 F. 298 (S.D.N.Y. Jan. 1913).
[61] An Act to consolidate Enactments related to Merchant Shipping, 57&58 Vict. c. 60.
[62] In re Oceanic Steam Navigation Co., 204 F. 260 (2nd Cir. Feb. 1913).
[63] The Titanic, 218 F. 990 (2nd Cir. Oct. 1914).
[64] The Titanic, 206 F. 500 (S.D.N.Y. July 1913).

could not take advantage of American limitations on liability, and that British law should apply.[65] The petitioners, Oceanic Steam, had,

> prayed that an appraisement be made of the value of the petitioner's interest in the Titanic, and of her pending freight; that an order be made authorizing the petitioner to file a stipulation for the payment into court of the amount of said value whenever the court should order; that the court issue a monition requiring claimants to appear before a commissioner and prove their claims; that an injunction issue restraining the prosecution of suits against the petitioner except in the present proceeding, and that the court adjudge that the petitioner's liability be limited to the value of the petitioner's interest in the steamship at the end of the voyage.[66]

The district court analyzed a long series of cases, including those of the Supreme Court,[67] to hold that a collision with an iceberg was analogous to colliding with a ship of one's own country, and in such a case, the case precedents seemed to indicate that the law of that ship's country should apply. As to the two claimants, their exceptions to the petition were sustained, and the court dismissed the petition of Oceanic Steam for limitation of liability for these two only. The court of appeals then certified several questions for the Supreme Court for these exceptions:

> A. Whether in the case of a disaster upon the high seas, where (1) only a single vessel of British nationality is concerned and there are claimants of many different nationalities; and where (2) there is nothing before the court to show what, if any, is the law of the foreign country to which the vessel belongs, touching the owner's liability for such disaster, such owner can maintain a proceeding under sections 4283, 4284 and 4285, U. S. Revised Statutes and the fifty-fourth and fifty-sixth Rules in Admiralty?

> B. Whether, if in such a case it appears that the law of the foreign country to which the vessel belongs makes provision for the limitation of the vessel owner's liability, upon terms and conditions different from those prescribed in the statutes of this country, the owner of

---

[65] The Titanic, 209 F. 501 (S.D.N.Y. Apr. 1913).
[66] *Id.* at 502.
[67] The Scotland, 105 U.S. 24 (1881).

such foreign vessel can maintain a proceeding in the courts of the United States, under said statutes and rules?

In the event of the answer to question B being in the affirmative:

C. Will the courts of the United States in such proceeding enforce the law of the United States or of the foreign country in respect to the amount of such owner's liability?[68]

The Supreme Court answered the three questions as Yes, Yes, and the law of the United States. The limitation of liability discussed in both *The Scotland* (see footnote above) and *La Bourgogne*[69] was based,

> Not on their being subject to the act of Congress or any law of the United States in their conduct, but if not on that ground, then it must have been because our statute permits a foreign vessel to limit its liability according to the act when sued in the United States.[70]

The defendant was now liable only for the appraised value of the remaining lifeboats, passage money, and pending freight, about $92,000. Prepaid passage money was the main component, even after deducting the passage money for the "transportation of passengers who were saved and carried to their destination."[71] This would grow to about $118,000 with interest. More than $16.6 million in claims had been filed with the commissioner by the one-year anniversary of the sinking. Additional time extensions through November 1913 brought 51 more claims for $321,000.

The trial began in June 1915, trying to litigate the facts and the unresolved legal issues. While this was going on, a committee of plaintiffs' counsel had been meeting with the defendant's representatives all the while, trying to increase the pressure to enlarge their proposed settlement amount. By December 1915, the committee believed they had reached the point where the settlement offer would not further increase and so recommended that all the claimants accept the offer, which would release Oceanic Steam from all liability anywhere. The amounts of the settlement, and allocations, were as follows:

---

[68] The Titanic, 209 F. 513 (2nd Cir. Nov. 1913), at 513-14.
[69] La Bourgogne, 210 U.S. 95 (May 1908).
[70] Oceanic Steam Navigation Co. v. Mellor, 233 U.S. 718 (May 1914), at 733.
[71] In the matter of Final Decree. The Petition of the Oceanic Steam Navigation Company, Ltd., for limitation of its liability as owner of the steamship Titanic (S.D.N.Y. July 1916).

the Steamship Company offered to pay $664,000 to settle the entire litigation arising from the sinking of the "TITANIC".

This sum was to be made up as follows:

About $119,525 was to take the place of the bond given in the limitation of liability proceedings as the value of what was saved from the "TITANIC" and freight and passage moneys; $50,000 or so much thereof as was needed was to be used for settlements of claims which had been filed in the limitation liability proceedings and upon which suits had been brought in England; counsel fees and expenses were to be paid out of the fund to proctors who had taken an active part in the case; the balance of the fund to be prorated among all the claimants who should come in and accept the settlement.

In order to have any settlement whatever the Steamship Company required that substantially all proctors who had filed answers in the case should agree to the settlement and should sign consents to the entry of a decree or decrees exonerating the Steamship Company from any liability.

If all the claimants join in this compromise, then the whole fund of $664,000, subject to the deduction for English claimants and allowances to counsel and their expenses, is to be divided immediately among all the claimants *pro rata*.[72]

The court's final decree in July 1916 fully released Oceanic Steam from all liability for the sinking, acknowledging they had no privity or knowledge. Perhaps sensing this outcome, several claimants had previously sought to withdraw their claims before the district court,

"It is asserted that the object of the claimant is to get permission to prosecute her suit in England. This may be true, but whether true or not is, in our view, immaterial. The motion is that the claimant have permission to withdraw her claim in the District Court. We do not see that she is called upon to state her reason for this motion, but it is easy to infer that her reason, as well as that of the other claimants, is

---

[72] Letter from George Betts et al of the Titanic Survivors committee to all claimants (Dec. 20, 1915).

that she is satisfied that she can get no adequate redress in the courts of the United States."[73]

In 1913, four lawsuits[74] of a similar nature were filed in the U.K., seeking damages for the lost lives of relatives under the Fatal Accidents Act of 1846.[75] This law allowed the executor or administrator of the deceased to act for the benefit of the parents, spouse, or children of the deceased to seek damages, in a case where the wrongful act or negligence of a defendant caused the death. The lead case was initiated by Tommy Ryan, for the death of his son Patrick Ryan. As the facts were essentially similar among the four cases, the parties had agreed that the jury findings on Ryan's case would apply to the others, except for how the tickets were presented to each, as Denis O'Brien had a ticket pre-paid in the United States, which would require a separate finding by the jury.

The plaintiffs argued that the company was negligent because the ship was traveling too fast for the conditions, which it had been warned of by telegrams from other ships, and that there were insufficient lookouts. The plaintiff noted that there were five ice warning telegrams, three that were received by ship officers, but the officers' receipt of the other two was disputed. The wireless operator who sent one of the disputed two to the *Titanic* said he received an acknowledgement of its receipt, and it would be normal to deliver it right away to the captain. The wind was in a dead calm, and there was haze, making it difficult to spot the icebergs, so maintaining 22 knots was negligent in those conditions. Further, an additional lookout was not posted in the stern, more level with the icebergs. Testimony was introduced from wireless operators and lookouts. The plaintiffs also argued that the decedents had no notice of the terms on the back of the tickets.

The defense asserted that it was not negligent, this speed was typical, as sailing practice was to get through ice fields as soon as possible, and that the ice warning telegrams from other ships had not reached the captain. If it was negligent, passengers were held to the limitation of liability printed on the back of the tickets. The defense said that the telegraph operators were employees of the Marconi Company and if there was negligence for messages not delivered to the captain, it was Marconi's

---

[73] The Titanic, 225 F. 747 (2nd Cir. June 1915).
[74] Ryan v. Oceanic Steam Navigation Company, Limited, [1913] ___ KB ___.
[75] An Act for compensating the Families of Persons killed by Accidents, 9&10 Vict. c. 93.

negligence. Testimony was heard from other wireless operators, lookouts, and the *Titanic's* second through fifth officers, and many experienced ship captains. Most said they would continue at speed if the weather was clear but slow in a haze. They also did not see the value in a lookout in the stern.

The jury decided the ship had been traveling too fast for the conditions and that the victims had not had adequate notice of the terms printed on the back of the tickets, except for O'Brien, as his terms were printed on the front of the ticket. However, the court ruled that the form with these conditions had not been approved by the Board of Trade, as required, and as such was invalid. Judgments were entered for each of the plaintiffs, with their families to be compensated £100 each. Oceanic Steam then appealed the verdict, asking for a new trial.

In *Ryan*,[76] the form of the contract ticket for steerage passengers, as required by the Board of Trade, was titled "Steerage Passenger's Contract Ticket", followed by seven directions and a notice in the left-hand margin that said, "These directions and the notice to steerage passengers below form part of, and must appear on, each contract ticket."[77] The first direction stated, "1. A contract ticket in this form must be given to every person engaging a passage as a steerage passenger in any ship proceeding from the British Islands to any port out of Europe, and not within the Mediterranean Sea, immediately on the payment."[78] The seventh condition stated, "7. A contract ticket shall not contain on the face thereof any condition, stipulation, or exception not contained in this form."[79] After the directions and before the notice to steerage passengers was wording that began "I engage that the person named in the margin shall be provided with a steerage passage to, and shall be landed at, the port of ____."[80] This section ended with the date and the issuer's signature.

On the Titanic steerage tickets, the "These directions" wording was omitted, with the words "See back" added instead, with a slip attached that read in part "Your attention is specially directed to the conditions of

---

[76] Ryan v. the Oceanic Steam Navigation Company Limited, Ryan v. Oceanic Steam Navigation Company, Limited, [EWCA 1914] 3 KB 731.
[77] *Id.* at 733.
[78] *Id.*
[79] *Id.* at 734.
[80] *Id.*

transportation in the annexed contract." The notice to passengers had ten conditions, of which the third one stated,

> Neither the shipowner, agent or passage broker shall be liable to any passenger carried under this contract, for loss, damage or delay to the passenger or his baggage, arising from the act of God, public enemies, arrests or restraints of princes, rulers or people, fire, collision, stranding, perils of the seas, rivers, or of navigation of any kind, accidents to or from machinery, boilers, steam, latent defects, even though existing at the beginning of the voyage, or from causes of any kind, beyond the carrier's control even though the loss, damage or delay may have been caused or contributed to by the neglect or default of the shipowner's servants or of other persons for whose acts he would otherwise be responsible, and whether occurring on board this or any other vessel on which the passenger may be forwarded under this contract. All questions arising under this paragraph of the contract shall be decided according to English law with reference to which it is made.[81]

The court of appeal affirmed the judgment of the trial court by 2-1, with each of the three judges issuing an opinion. Justice Roland Vaughan Williams' opinion initially said he did not believe it was necessary to determine if the plaintiffs had adequate notice. He noted the plaintiffs' assertions that words of the exemption clause were not actually part of the contract and that if they were, they were excluded by the section 320 of the Merchant Shipping Act 1894 (see above). He held that neither the directions nor the notice to steerage passengers were part of the contract, which started with the words "I engage" and finished with the signature of "Joseph Bruce Ismay for and on behalf of the Oceanic Steam Navigation Company Limited of Great Britain."[82] He said the notice was not the subject of contract but instead was in response to legislation.

He then turned to the second assertion, noting that section 320 read,

> The contract ticket shall be in a form approved by the Board of Trade and published in the London Gazette, and any directions contained in

---

[81] *Id.* at 735-36.
[82] *Id.* at 748.

that form of contract ticket not being inconsistent with this Act shall be obeyed as if set forth in this section.[83]

As there had been no express approval of the exclusion clause, it was invalid. He also found there was sufficient evidence of negligence for that to go to the jury. In total, he believed the appeal should be dismissed.

Justice William Kennedy said there was no ground to impeach the verdict of the jury as being against the weight of the evidence. For the jury finding there was sufficient evidence of a lack of notice to the three victims, he again said there was sufficient evidence, and in one of his citations, noted that "The ticket in question in this case was for a steerage passenger — a class of people of the humblest description, many of whom have little education, and some of them none."[84] He also agreed that the exclusion clause was not approved by the Board of Trade and therefore could not be used to defend against plaintiff O'Brien. He viewed the term "face" in the seventh direction of the Board of Trade standard form as meaning not "front" but anywhere in the document. If the Board of Trade had intended there to be additions to the standard form, they would have left space for such conditions and exceptions in the standard form. He also believed the appeal failed in all four actions and should be dismissed.

The *Titanic* has, then and since, played an outsized role in the imaginations of millions. It also played such a role in the mind of at least one newspaper. In *Murphy*,[85] plaintiff Margaret Murphy, aged 24 and a New York resident of several years, was a *Titanic* survivor on a brief visit to see her family. The New York Press used these headlines for her story,

> Gave his Life to Save that of his Sweetheart. Young Irishman Fought His Way to Titanic's Lifeboat. They Eloped from Ireland. Girl Tells of Heroism Displayed by the Man she had Selected for her Mate.[86]

The story described its fabricated version of her fateful experience,

> here was told by Margaret Murphy, nineteen years old, a bright and prepossessing girl, the story of love, courage, and self-sacrifice that ranks with the foremost deeds of heroism of the many recorded in the

---

[83] *Id.* at 749.
[84] *Id.* at 762.
[85] Murphy v. New York Press Co., 143 N.Y.S. 1051 (Sup. Ct. App. Div. Nov. 1913).
[86] *Id.* at 1052.

wreck. Deeply religious, and firm in her belief that her sorrow is a visitation earned because she ran away with her sweetheart from their home in Fostra, County Longford, the young woman grieves for the loss of one who gallantly died after fighting desperately to carry her to a boat through the struggling passengers in the steerage. After leading her safely to the boat deck, the young man, John Kiernan, unstrapped the life belt he wore and tied it on the girl. He reached the deck in time to catch a boat that just was being sent away. There was room for one more and into it he forced her despite her protests. There was little time in which to say good-by but in the fleeting moments the youth caught the girl in his arms, pressed his lips to hers, and half flung her into the boat as it swung outward from the davits.

The hum of nervous voices, the rumbling of the boat falls in the blocks as the boat was lowered away, drowned the parting message of the youth as he leaned over the rail, his form silhouetted in the starlight night, gazing at the upturned face of the girl he loved, as the distance between them gradually increased. In the confusion none but the girl in the boat heard the young man shout: "Don't worry, I'll be saved." But he died with those who unselfishly thought of the safety of others.

The boy and girl were playmates in childhood in their native town. The girl in her humble state was above the youth socially for he was employed in her father's grocery store. They loved each other and agreed to elope to America. They little dreamed of the tragic fate awaiting one of them. When the ship was stabbed fatally by the hidden spur of the iceberg they were with hundreds of others in the steerage on the fifth deck of the liner. Those who were able grabbed life belts. The young man got one, his sweetheart did not.

Lest they should be separated in the crowd, Kiernan held the girl and fought his way with her to the boat deck. "One of us must go," he told her quietly, "you haven't a life belt, I have." Quickly he took the life preserver from his body and wrapped it around his sweetheart. She resisted and hampered his work, clinging to him and saying she would not go without him. By force he put her in the boat.[87]

The court held the story to be libelous pe se and granted her motion.

---

[87] *Id.*

## B. Triple Collision

| LEGAL ISSUES |
|---|
| ❖ Neglect of train signaling rules causing legal liability<br>❖ Signalman criminal liability not extended to railway |

The *Titanic* tragedy was soon followed by an intractable war and disasters in prosecuting that war. Not directly combat related, but involving soldiers on their way to Gallipoli, was the collision of three trains in Quintinshill, Scotland, on May 22, 1915. The troop train first collided with a standing train, which was then hit by an oncoming train, resulting in the deaths of 226 people. This rail disaster was followed by investigations, coroners' inquiries, and trials. Amidst the tragedies of World War I[88] that had already occurred, and those to come, this disaster was the most easily prevented.

The investigation was started by the Railway Inspectorate of the Board of Trade. Their final report noted a special troop train with 21 carriages was traveling south from Larbert (northwest of Glasgow), when it collided with a stationary local train with four carriages at 06:50. This wreck was then hit by a two-engine express passenger train heading north from Carlisle with 13 carriages. There were violations of Rule 55, a requirement for trains waiting at a signal box, a small building just off the tracks where traffic was controlled by setting points and signals. A crew member from a waiting train was sent to the box to wait there until the train was given permission to depart. Or they had to ensure a collar was put on the lever controlling their section of track (a block), so it could not be pulled without the intent to let them depart. Signing the train register was also required.

The relevant parts of Rule 55, quoted in the report, were:

(b) When a train or vehicles have passed a Home Signal, and are waiting to be crossed to another Line, or to be let into a Siding, or have been shunted on to the opposite Running Line, or placed on either a Main or Branch Line at a Junction, or when a train or vehicles have been shunted from a Siding on to a Running Line and are waiting to be crossed to another Line, the Guard, Shunter, or Fireman must, when the train or vehicles come to a stand, proceed immediately to the

---

[88] For a deeper understanding of the legal issues of wartime involved with this conflict, *see* THOMAS J. SHAW, THE LEGAL HISTORY OF WORLD WAR 1.

Signal-box, and remind the Signalman of the position of the train or vehicles, and, except as provided for in clause (f), remain in the Box until the Signalman can give permission for them to proceed or to be shunted clear of the Running Lines...

(f) Where mechanical or other appliances are provided to serve as a reminder to the Signalman that certain Signals must not be lowered or turned off, he must make prompt use of such appliances; and the... Fireman who has gone to the Signal-box in accordance with clauses (a) and (b) must return to the train after receiving an assurance that the Signalman has protected it by such appliances.[89]

There were many players involved in this disaster, but the three principal ones were signalmen James Tinsley and George Meakin and fireman George Hutchinson. Meakin was to work the night shift at the Quintinshill signal box until 06:00, with Tinsley to start work from 06:00. However, Tinsley came late, as usual, arriving at 06:32 to start his shift, coming on the same local train from Gretna Junction. Because this train was dispatched before faster express trains coming behind, it was typically shunted to the side (or loop) tracks for northbound trains. However, there was already a goods train standing in that space since 06:14, so Meakin had the local train back across the connection between the northbound and southbound tracks, stopping it in front of the signal box at 06:32, facing north on the southbound tracks. Meakin had the empty coal train moved to the loop tracks on the southbound side at 06:33.

The status of these three trains had the northbound loop track occupied by the goods train, the southbound loop track occupied by the coal train, and the southbound main track occupied by the local train, pointing north. All might have been well if the correct signals had been set and maintained. Meakin handed the responsibility over to Tinsley by 06:35 or 06:36, but the turnover was not crisp. In their private system of Tinsley starting work late, contrary to company rules, Meakin recorded the movements of the three trains between 06:00 and 06:30 on a separate piece of paper. Tinsley then would enter these into the register, so it would show as being done in his handwriting, to demonstrate he had been working since 06:00. This is what he was focused on at the start of his shift.

---

[89] CALEDONIAN RAILWAY ACCIDENT REPORT, LT. COL. EDWARD DRUITT, RAILWAY INSPECTORATE TO BOARD OF TRADE (June 17, 1915).

In 1889, after the Armagh accident killed 80 people, a revised railways regulation law was enacted,[90] allowing the Board of Trade to require the block system, interlocking points and signals, and use of continuous brakes. The block system required acceptance by signalmen to enter their block. At 06:38, the local train's fireman, George Hutchinson, entered the signal box and signed his name but not the time. As his last act on duty, Meakin accepted an express train from Carlisle to enter his block. That train passed his signal box, as the northbound track was clear. Tinsley, at 06:42, accepted the troop train from Kirkpatrick heading southbound, forgetting about the local train standing on the southbound tracks, thereby initiating the inevitable collision. He also accepted a second northbound express.

After the first collision, several men on the two trains on the loop tracks ran down the tracks to try to warn the second northbound express train but there was insufficient time to stop, and it ran into the wreck of the two trains that had collided less than a minute before. The signalmen had not reacted quickly enough to close the signals to this express train to avoid the second collision. Most of those killed were on the troop train, dying either from the initial collision, from the second collision inside the remnants of the trains or when walking away on the tracks, or by the subsequent fire, trapped inside the wrecked train. Neither of the two trains had been able to slow sufficiently to less than 40 mph. Nine passengers on the local and second express trains were killed, and three railway workers.

The report held both Meakin and Tinsley separately responsible. Meakin had not protected the local train. In the short handover period, one of them (neither admitted it) sent an "out of section" message to Kirkpatrick for the coal train on the loop track at 06:34. So that it was clear that southbound track was not clear, a "blocking back" signal had to follow this up. It was not sent. Meakin explained he had not sent it, because at the time the empty coal train was still on the southbound main track. After he moved it to the southbound loop track, he expected Tinsley, in the takeover, to send "out of section" message for the coal train, followed by the "blocking back" message for the local train. If a lock had been maintained on a blocking back signal for the local train, it would have been impossible for Tinsley to accept the troop train.

---

[90] An Act to amend the Regulation of Railways Acts; and for other purposes, 52&53 Vict. ch. 57.

The relevant regulation was:

> Blocking Back.-(a) When it is necessary, after the passing of one train, and before permission is given for another to leave the Signal-box in the rear, to obstruct the Line inside the Home Signal by allowing vehicles or a train to be crossed from one Line to another, or to leave a Loop Line or Siding for the Main Line for shunting purposes, or before the Line Clear Signal is received from the Signal-box in advance, the Blocking Back Signal (2-4) must, unless instructions are issued to the contrary, be given to the Signal-box or boxes in the rear... and the same must be acknowledged.[91]

Tinsley was held responsible not only for spending time forging entries in the register, but also for focusing on accepting the northbound express train from Gretna and the southbound troop train from Kirkpatrick, without noticing the local train sitting 60 yards or so directly in front of the signal box where he was. Hutchinson was held responsible for not obeying Rule 55 by not ensuring there was a collar on his train's lever in the signal box, to prevent the signal from being changed until the train departed. The relevant regulation for a train shunted to the opposite track was:

> For each of the operations mentioned above, or in any other case of the Line being blocked, the Signalman must place the Lever Collar over the handle of the Lever working the Signal which protects the Line upon which the obstruction exists, and so prevent the Signal from being lowered until the Collar is removed. When a " Lever Collar " has been used for the protection of a Train in accordance with the foregoing, the Signalman must not remove it from the handle of the Lever until he is personally aware that the Train has been shunted clear of the Line on which it had been standing, or he has been informed by the Shunter or Guard that this has been done. When the Guard, Shunter, or Fireman has satisfied himself, in accordance with the provisions of Rule 55, that his Train has been protected by the use of a Lever Collar... he may return to his Train.[92]

Other brakemen and Meakin were cited for lingering too long in the signal box, reading newspapers and chatting about war news, when they

---

[91] CALEDONIAN RAILWAY ACCIDENT REPORT.
[92] *Id.*

were required to depart after completing their shifts or Rule 55 duties. The report noted that this situation of having to put a local train on the northbound tracks due to the loop track being occupied had happened four times in the prior six months and in each case, the blocking back signal had been sent to the Kirkpatrick signal box, stopping southbound trains.

The 213-yard running length of the engine and fifteen carriages of the troop train involved (six had detached) after the collision only stretched to 67 yards, with the use of weak wooden carriages implicated. The ensuing fire from the engines and the tenders of the three trains became too great to fight, with the limited fire extinguishers available. The use of gas for lighting fed the fire, as did the flammable wood. The recommendations from the report included making carriages only out of steel and that all wood should be non-flammable; doors should not jam during accidents and windows should be openable; gas lighting should be abolished in favor of electric lighting; and the appropriate tools and appliances for extinguishing fires should be present in all the cars in a train.

Subsequent coroner's inquests were held in Scotland and England, as some victims had been taken across the nearby border to hospitals in Carlisle before expiring. These inquests found that Meakin and Tinsley should be tried for culpable homicide (Scotland) or manslaughter (England). They were eventually criminally tried in Scotland, along with Hutchison. Tinsley and Meakin were found guilty and sentenced to three years and eighteen months imprisonment, respectively, while Hutchinson was found to have no case to answer and was adjudged not guilty.

The inquests, trial, and a later inquiry into the crew deaths on the troop train all adopted the same view as the Railway Inspectorate had, that the actions of Meakin and Tinsley were to blame. Significantly, no blame was assigned to the railway for its crowded scheduling and train priorities during wartime, the design and usage of its tracks, its lax employee oversight, the outdated carriage technologies employed, or its non-use of modern electric circuit signaling technology. Nor was any fault assigned to the government, which in 1914, at the start of the war, had taken over the railways under an 1871 statute.[93]

---

[93] An Act for the better Regulation of the Regular and Auxiliary Land Forces of the Crown; and for other purposes relating thereto, 34&35 Vict. ch. 86, § 16.

## C. Torpedo

| LEGAL ISSUES |
|---|
| ❖ Putting a monetary value on lives lost at sea<br>❖ Sailing a ship into a warzone generating legal liability |

In the same month as the triple collision, the United Kingdom was to experience disaster again, when the RMS Lusitania was sunk by a German submarine torpedo. Owned by Cunard Steamship, the ship went down on May 7, 1915, off the coast of Ireland while traveling from New York to Liverpool, England, killing nearly 1,200 people. This caused an instant uproar and while the United Kingdom was already at war with Germany, this would be one of many acts that would eventually lead to American involvement in the First World War.[94] Legally, the response involved varied investigations, including inquests by the U.K. Board of Trade, court trials in the United States, and international committees formed to arbitrate unresolved claims from the war, occurring both during and after the hostilities had concluded.

The Board of Trade inquiry was once again led by the wreck commissioner, John Charles Bigham, Lord Mersey, who had led the *Titanic* inquiry just a few years before. It was similarly handled, with a series of question posed by the Board of Trade for the inquiry to answer. The most important of those answers listed in the final report[95] stated: there were no troops aboard and the ship was not armed; the ship was not flying the flag of any nation; that there was no warning given or a chance to heave to; no opportunity was provided for the passengers to disembark the ship; that there were no actions taken by the passenger ship to evade capture, escape, or resist the submarine; and that the sinking was caused entirely by the torpedo and there was nothing else that caused the explosions and damage leading to the loss, i.e., there were no secret munitions on board that acted as a contributing factor.

---

[94] To understand how the Lusitania impacted American involvement in the war, *see* THOMAS J. SHAW, THE LEGAL HISTORY OF WORLD WAR 1.

[95] LOSS OF THE STEAMSHIP *LUSITANIA*, REPORT OF A FORMAL INVESTIGATION INTO THE CIRCUMSTANCES ATTENDING THE FOUNDERING ON 7TH MAY, 1915, OF THE BRITISH STEAMSHIP *LUSITANIA*, OF LIVERPOOL, AFTER BEING TORPEDOED OFF THE OLD HEAD OF KINSALE, IRELAND, WRECK COMMISSIONER'S COURT OF INQUIRY (July 17, 1915).

With the damages' litigation started, Cunard did what the owners of the *Titanic* did, they initiated a legal action for a limitation of liability under the 1851 U.S. statute discussed above. This was brought in the same district court, and before the same judge, as the *Titanic's* petition to limit liability,[96] although the issues litigated had a somewhat different emphasis. The claimants in this case tried to focus on the negligence of the captain in several aspects to have the petition rejected. To analyze the issues, the district court used the testimony before the Board of Trade inquiry, in addition to its own examination of witnesses. The ship was evaluated seaworthy, unarmed, without explosives, and the military munitions it carried could not be exploded by impact or fire. The ship and equipment had been checked out before sailing, its officers were experienced and crew, given wartime needs, was as good as could be expected. It ran at a lower speed than it was capable of, to save cost and war materials.

In response to a similar British proclamation, in February 1915, the German government had declared the seas around the British Isle a war zone, where British merchant ships would be sunk without warning. About 20 such merchant and passenger ships were sunk in the next few months within 100 miles of the *Lusitania's* usual course. As a precaution, the ship would sail further off Ireland's coast, and when in the danger zone, swing out its boats, maintain radio silence, and go straight to its berth in Liverpool. The British government advised making landfall at night and arriving to their ports at dawn, to avoid prominent landfalls, and to engage in zigzagging. By newspaper advertisement, travelers were warned by the German government of the risk of going to Great Britain on this vessel.

As the ship approached Ireland on this fateful trip, the British government warned it of submarines, to avoid headlands, to pass harbors at full speed, and to steer a mid-channel course. More submarine warnings in that area were given the morning of May 7. On a bright day when it obvious which ship it was, one or two torpedoes hit the starboard side. Unable to heave to and listing badly to starboard, the boats were difficult to launch, as port side boats swung inboard, and starboard side swung out. Collapsible boats were freed. Despite sufficient boat spaces, the court rejected crew negligence or lack of drilling to explain why so many died.

---

[96] The Lusitania, 251 F. 715 (S.D.N.Y. Aug. 1918).

The one question of fact the court then focused on was the potential negligence of Capt. William Turner in not following the directions of the Admiralty. The court listed those key instructions: avoid headland, mid-channel course, maintain speed, zigzag, make ports at dawn, and get to the berth in Liverpool without waiting for a pilot to come aboard. The court felt what was most important was the captain's judgment as an experienced seaman, within the advice given. While he had turned inland before being torpedoed, this was reasonable given the warning about submarines mid-channel ahead. The court deferred to the Board of Trade inquiry regarding the captain's competence, saying he,

> "was fully advised as to the means which, in the view of the Admiralty, were best calculated to avert the perils he was likely to encounter… It is certain that in some respects Capt. Turner did not follow the advice given to him. It may be (though I seriously doubt it) that, had he done so, his ship would have reached Liverpool in safety. But the question remains: Was his conduct the conduct of a negligent or of an incompetent man?... I have sought the guidance of my assessors, who have rendered me invaluable assistance, and the conclusion at which I have arrived is that blame might not… be imputed to the captain. The advice given to him, although meant for his most serious and careful consideration, was not intended to deprive him of the right to exercise his skilled judgment in the difficult questions that might arise from time to time in the navigation of his ship. His omission to follow the advice in all respects cannot fairly be attributed either to negligence or incompetence. He exercised his judgment for the best. It was the judgment of a skilled and experienced man, and although others might have acted differently, and perhaps more successfully, he ought not, in my opinion… be blamed."[97]

The court believed zigzagging would not have made a difference, as there were multiple submarines which could torpedo the ship. The court held the captain, and the petitioner, were not negligent. Further, torpedoing a passenger ship without warning was against international law, so an illegal act. Legally, when a third-party committing an illegal act intervenes, a first party cannot be guilty of negligence, no longer being the proximate cause. Cunard's petition for limitation of liability was granted.

---

[97] *Id.* at 730-31.

Before the United States entered the war, diplomats on both sides had tried to address the American lives lost on the *Lusitania*. In one communique, the German ambassador to the United States wrote a note to the U.S. secretary of state, saying,

> The Imperial German Government having subsequent to the event issued to its naval officers the new instructions which are now prevailing, expresses profound regret that citizens of the United States suffered by the sinking of the Lusitania, and assuming liability therefor, offers to make reparation for the life of the citizens of the United States who were lost by the payment of a suitable indemnity.[98]

This was later disavowed[99] and claims regarding the *Lusitania* were to be made to the Mixed Claims Commission,[100] created by agreement between the United States and Germany after the war. Americans were able to make wartime claims, which were settled by a court comprised of an American commissioner, a German commissioner, and an umpire to settle disagreements between the commissioners. Death benefits were based on the present value of what the decedent would have contributed to the claimant in money, care, education, and supervision, plus the mental suffering of the claimant. The factors they had to consider were:

> *(a)* The age, sex, health, condition and station in life, occupation, habits of industry and sobriety, mental and physical capacity, frugality, earning capacity and customary earnings of the deceased and the uses made of such earnings by him;
>
> *(b)* The probable duration of the life of deceased but for the fatal injury, in arriving at which standard life-expectancy tables and all other pertinent evidence offered will be considered;
>
> *(c)* The reasonable probability that the earning capacity of deceased, had he lived, would either have increased or decreased;
>
> *(d)* The age, sex, health, condition and station in life, and probable life expectancy of each of the claimants;

---

[98] Count Johann von Bernstorff to Robert Lansing (Feb. 4, 1916).
[99] United States *ex rel.* Maid [sic] Thompson de Gennes v. Germany (Mar. 11, 1925).
[100] To further understand the workings of the Mixed Claims Commission, *see* THOMAS J. SHAW, THE LEGAL HISTORY OF WORLD WAR 1.

(e) The extent to which the deceased, had he lived, would have applied his income from his earnings or otherwise to his personal expenditures from which claimants would have derived no benefits;

(f) In reducing to their present cash value contributions which would probably have been made from time to time to claimants by deceased, a 5% interest rate and standard present-value tables will be used;

(g) Neither the physical pain nor the mental anguish which the *deceased* may have suffered will be considered as elements of damage;

(h) The amount of insurance on the life of the deceased collected by his estate or by the claimants will not be taken into account in computing the damages which claimants may be entitled to recover;

(i) No exemplary, punitive, or vindictive damages can be assessed.[101]

Examples of some of claims submitted by the survivors of those lost include the following. First-class passenger Charles Klien, 48 years old, was a successful British playwright who left behind a wife, who subsequently remarried, and two children, ages 26 and 6. The wife was British, but the children were U.S. citizens. The wife did not claim, only the American children. The older child was employed by his father and claimed a potential, but uncontracted, role to exploit his father's copyrights, but this was not binding and considered too remote. The younger child was awarded $30,000 and the older child $20,000.[102] Second-class passenger Annie MacHardy was 31 years old, married and worked as a waitress and was a mother to a child who lived in Scotland. Her husband received $4,000 but the estate received nothing, as their daughter was British.[103] Third-class passenger Mary Ferguson was a 23-year-old mother to her 15-month-old son. The husband received $10,000.[104] Third-class passenger Florence Lockwood and her two children perished, and her brother put in a claim, because her husband was not American. This claim was rejected.[105]

---

[101] Mixed Claims Commission (United States and Germany), Opinion in the *Lusitania* Cases. (Nov. 1, 1923).
[102] United States *ex rel.* Philip Klein and John Victor Klein, a minor, by his Guardian v. Germany (Feb. 25, 1925).
[103] United States *ex rel.* Peter Kenneth MacHardy, individually and as Administrator of the Estate of Annie R. MacHardy, Deceased v. Germany (Feb. 21, 1924).
[104] United States *ex rel.* Samuel James Ferguson v. Germany (Feb. 14, 1924).
[105] United States *ex rel.* George Robshaw v. Germany (Jan. 7, 1925).

Charlotte Luck was a 34-year-old homemaker, and her sons were 12 and 8 years old. Her husband/their father received $20,000 and her mother/their grandmother received $5,000.[106] Albert Lloyd Hopkins was 44 years old and a company president earning $25,000 a year. He left behind a wife, who later remarried, and a seven-year-old daughter. His wife was awarded $50,000 and his daughter $80,000.[107] Arthur Foley was a 51-year-old traveling salesman earning $3,000. He left behind a wife, two adult children and a 15-year-old daughter. His wife was awarded $25,000 and his minor child $5,000.[108] Third-class passenger Catherine Henry was pregnant and returning to Ireland to visit her mother. She survived the sinking after five hours in the water, claiming she had lost her life savings and property of $4,700. She also claimed $10,000 for injuries and her husband John claimed $5,000 for loss of her services. Saying there was insufficient evidence of any permanent injuries (she had three children in the interim) or the loss of money or property, they were jointly awarded $7,500.[109]

One of the claimants above, Thirza Ann Foley, had previously filed a lawsuit against her husband's company, claiming he died in the line of his work and so was due workmen's compensation. She asserted that the company was negligent for letting him travel on a British flagged ship, a country at war while there was an American flagged ship making the same journey at that time that he could have taken instead. The state supreme court reviewed the decision of the lower court that had dismissed the suit, holding that this was not a case of negligence of the employer. The supreme court viewed this differently, as merely a question of whether it was an accident arising out of employment, regardless of negligence. The supreme court reversed, holding that this was an accident arising out of his employment, as the risk of loss to for a ship traveling into a warzone was foreseeable by the employer.[110] This decision was later affirmed by the state's highest court.[111]

---

[106] United States *ex rel.* Arthur Courtlandt Luck and Frances Lapham Field v. Germany (Feb. 21, 1924).
[107] United States *ex rel.* May Davies Hopkins Gilmer, Administratrix of the Estate of Albert Lloyd Hopkins, Deceased, and May Davies Hopkins v. Germany (Feb. 21, 1924).
[108] United States *ex rel.* Thirza Ann Foley, individually and as Executrix of the Estate of Arthur R. Foley, Deceased v. Germany (Feb. 21, 1924).
[109] United States *ex rel.* Catherine Henry and John Henry v. Germany (Feb. 14, 1924).
[110] Foley v. Home Rubber Co., 89 N.J.L. 474 (N.J. Sup. Ct. Jan. 1917).
[111] Foley v. Home Rubber Co., 91 N.J.L. 323 (N.J. Oct. 1917).

Another of the claimants above, May Davies Hopkins, had sued her husband's life insurance company in 1916.[112] Before traveling aboard the *Lusitania*, he had obtained an accident insurance policy that paid his wife $40,000 in case of his death by accident. He also signed a rider that disallowed such a payment if it was directly or indirectly related to an act of war by the nations then at war. His wife asserted that, inter alia, because the rider was not filed with the superintendent of insurance, it should fail. These claims were rejected by the court. The appellate division reversed.[113] Then the court of appeals reversed that decision, reinstating the trial court's judgment, as the only penalty for not filing was a fine, looking instead for any provision that conflicted, which the rider did not.[114]

The will of *Lusitania* victim Charles F. Fowles, an art dealer, was revised in view of this upcoming voyage, had an unusual provision,

> In the event that my said wife and myself should die simultaneously or under such circumstances as to render it impossible or difficult to determine who predeceased the other, I hereby declare it to be my will that it shall be deemed that I shall have predeceased my said wife, and that this my will and any and all its provisions shall be construed on the assumption and basis that I shall have predeceased my said wife.[115]

The court ruled the provision against public policy. Trying to make it legal, the court interpreted its meaning to be that in the incapacity of his wife, this gift would go to whoever she designated in her will. Both died without proof of who predeceased. The court decreed for her executors. The appellate division reversed, saying such construction was not possible.[116] The court of appeals again reversed, holding this a gift to his wife and affirmed the surrogate court's decree.[117] His American daughter later claimed and received $10,000 from the Mixed Claims Commission.[118]

---

[112] Hopkins v. Connecticut General Life Ins., 158 N.Y.S. 79 (N.Y. Sup. Ct. Mar. 1916).
[113] Hopkins v. Connecticut General Life Insurance, 174 A.D. 23 (N.Y. App. Div. July 1916).
[114] Hopkins v. Connecticut General Life Insurance, 225 N.Y. 76 (N.Y. Ct. App. Dec. 1918).
[115] In re Construe the Last Will & Testament of Fowles, 16 Mills Surr. 425 (N.Y. Sur. Ct. Apr. 1916), at 427.
[116] In re to Construe the Last Will & Testament of Fowles, 176 A.D. 637 (N.Y. App. Div. Mar. 1917).
[117] In re the Will of Fowles, 222 N.Y. 222 (N.Y. App. Jan. 1918).
[118] United States *ex rel.* Gladys Mary Baylies v. Germany (Feb. 11, 1925).

## D. Rapid Transit

| LEGAL ISSUES |
|---|
| ❖ Impact of venue change on jury verdicts<br>❖ Use of uncertified drivers creating operator criminal liability |

On November 1, 1918, an evening subway train in Brooklyn, New York derailed, resulting in the deaths of nearly 100 people. Only a few months after reporting dozens were injured in separate derailments,[119] local newspapers had to tell of a far worse disaster,

> Packed together as in a box without structural strength to give them any protection, the passengers in the first car were crushed and cut to pieces. No one is believed to have escaped. After breaking through the first car the rest of the train dashed it against the partition wall and strewed wreckage and passengers along the tracks ahead, where the wheels of the cars following passed over them. Only splintered fragments of wood and broken and twisted bits of iron and steel remained of the first car.
>
> The second and third cars, leaving the rails after their impact with the first, ran sidewise into a series of iron pillars supporting the roof of the tunnel at intervals beside the partition. The pillars cut great gashes in the sides of the cars, which were still traveling at high speed, and mowed down the passengers who were standing, striking the heads of some from their bodies. The left sides of the second and third cars were stripped away. Scores of men, women and children were flung by the impact out of these cars against pillars and the concrete wall, where they were killed instantly or ground under the wheels after falling back upon the tracks. Some who were not flung from the car were killed inside, when they fell upon the broken iron of seats, splintered timbers and iron beams which projected through the shattered bottoms of the car. Passengers on the platforms were nearly all killed instantly. One dead man was found impaled on a broken bar of iron, which had run underneath the car, but which broke and shot up into the air like a javelin in the crash.[120]

---

[119] *30 Hurt in Derailments*, N.Y. TIMES (July 23, 1918).
[120] *Scores Killed or Maimed in Brighton Tunnel Wreck*, N.Y. TIMES (Nov. 2, 1918).

There had been a strike of company motormen that had led to a dispatcher driving this train. The train crew and company executives of the Brooklyn Rapid Transit Company (BRT) were quickly arrested. The driver was a young dispatcher named Antonio Edward Luciano, who also would go by the name Anthony Lewis. Having just gotten off a dispatching shift, he admitted he had been traveling 30 mph on a curve rated at no more than 6 mph. He had never driven this train before and had only just taken a few hours of instruction. Passengers claimed he missed a switch, going down the wrong track before backing up his train to the proper track. After this, the train began to travel at high speeds, perhaps to make up time lost.

The mayor held a John Doe hearing to determine whether a crime had been committed, concurrent with the investigation by the county district attorney. The result of the mayor's hearing was,

> After presiding at this examination and listening to the evidence and proof adduced at the hearing under examination by District Attorney Lewis, and having given it careful consideration, I have come to the conclusion that the crime of manslaughter has been committed and there is reasonable ground to believe that Timothy S. Williams. John H. Hallock, William S. Menden, John J. Dempsey, Thomas F. Blewett and Edward Luciano, alias Anthony Lewis, committed it, and for that reason I will direct and sign the issuance of warrants for the arrest of Williams, Hallock, Menden, Dempsey and Blewett, and that the defendant Luciano, alias Lewis, be held for the action of the grand jury.[121]

Six men were soon indicted by the grand jury in Kings County: motorman Luciano/Lewis; Blewitt, Brighton Line superintendent; Dempsey, BRT superintendent of transportation; Williams, BRT president; Hallock, president of subsidiary New York Consolidated Railroad, responsible for elevated railways; and Menden, Williams' assistant and chief engineer of subsidiary New York Municipal Railways. The indictment listed two counts, first of which was for manslaughter in the first degree, as the defendants had wrongfully committed acts, or omitted to perform certain duties, endangering the health and safety of the passengers, leading to the deaths of all the victims. The second count charged that,

---

[121] *Hylan Orders Arrest of Five B. R. T. Heads for Brighton Crash,* N.Y. TRIBUNE (Dec. 12, 1918).

through the neglect of said defendants to discharge their duty in promulgating and enforcing reasonable rules for the employment of trainmen and motormen and for the safe operation of the lines upon said railroad, and in employing an inexperienced, unfit, untrained and incompetent motorman who operated the train in a culpably negligent manner and at a high, excessive and dangerous rate of speed, at or near Malbone street in Kings county, the train was wrecked and the persons named in said indictments who were passengers upon said train were killed.[122]

The precipitating event for the use of unqualified motormen was the motorman strike started that same day. The reason for their strike involved attempts to unionize railway workers and the First World War. Among the many organizations the government used during the war was the National War Labor Board, created by public proclamation in April 1918.[123] Its mandate included pursuing labor peace to keep the war effort humming, by avoiding strikes and allowing workers the right to organize. Co-chaired by former U.S. president William Howard Taft, it technically did not have enforcement powers but the power of persuasion and cooperation during wartime was usually sufficient.

The case brought to the board by the BRT workers was that 29 of their fellow workers had been terminated for joining the Brotherhood of Locomotive Engineers. The board seemed to agree with their arguments, as it ruled that not only were the 29 employees to be reinstated but the company could not interfere with the rights workers had to organize and collectively bargain, which had come down from President Woodrow Wilson. The company had asserted that all but four of the 29 had signed a statement saying there was no dispute, so the board did not have jurisdiction. The board dismissed this assertion, as it saw these men as victims of coercion by the company. After all, this was a company that admitted employing a secret service which it claimed only existed to protect its physical locations, not to interfere with workers' rights, despite evidence to the contrary. This decision was made just one week before the workers' November 1 strike, and just ten days before the war's armistice.

---

[122] People v. Williams, 106 Misc. 65 (N.Y. Sup. Ct. Jan. 1919), at 67.
[123] To further understand the origins of the National War Labor Board, *see* THOMAS J. SHAW, THE LEGAL HISTORY OF WORLD WAR 1.

After their criminal indictment, the six defendants moved for a change of venue. They cited press stories with accusatory headlines and vivid photographs of the crash and the bodies of victims, and the varied organizations arrayed against them, making it impossible to get a trial in the county where the accident occurred. Examples of the latter included actions attributed to the Brighton Elevated Wreck Victims and Passengers' Protective Association, such as having widows dressed in black appear at the mayor's hearings. Other denunciations of the defendants included accusations made against them in churches, the mayor's hearings, and union resolutions. Dueling affidavits citing local prejudice or non-prejudice were filed by both the prosecutor and defendants' counsel. The prosecutor also noted that when the company was a defendant in lawsuits in this county, it had demanded a jury trial 80% of the time.

The prosecutor had polled those who were to sit on criminal juries during the current term, who mostly said that they could fairly and impartially sit as jurors to render a just verdict. The court said it must guard against unconscious prejudice and bias, which would not necessarily come out in questionnaires. The court also said this was not a matter of judicial discretion, such that if there was prejudice and bias, the move to a new venue was required. The talesman for the potential juries could not be selected on whether they had no prejudice or bias in this case, as the selection process was prescribed by statute. Further, the ability to eliminate a juror was also dictated by law, using peremptory challenges but these were limited in number, so bias could not be avoided in the county.

The court concluded that a change is venue was appropriate, because,

It is difficult for me to understand how a campaign for the conviction of the defendants could have been carried on with more effectiveness than that which has been conducted in this county since the happening of the unfortunate accident. It rivals the efforts of a well organized corps of propagandists. Prejudice, insidious in its nature, was so gradually and firmly implanted into the minds of the people of the community, that it is difficult to remove it. The public press has lost no opportunity in proclaiming these defendants guilty. It has been openly and publicly charged that their guilt was based upon their failure to obey the order of the war board, upon their failure to provide cars of steel construction and upon their failure to use proper means to determine whether or not the motorman was competent to operate a train.[124]

The separate trials of Blewitt (March 1919), Luciano (April 1919), Dempsey (December 1919), and Menden (January 1920), were held in Nassau Country. None were successful, returning a not guilty verdict or a hung jury. The trials of Williams and Hallock never went forward. Despite Luciano having only a few hours of training and no motorman certificate, the difficulty that prosecutors faced was shown by the jury instructions in the Blewitt trial. Blewitt had been responsible for selecting the motormen,

> If the defendant knew Lewis was not competent, I charge you that it was unlawful to appoint him. If he did not know or omitted to exercise the highest degree of care and failed to learn of his competency, the charge has been borne out. If Lewis was competent and knew how to operate the train, it matters not why or how he was selected If he was competent, but his careless actions caused the wreck, the charge cannot be borne out.[125]

In his trial, Luciano testified he was trying to use the brake, but the power had been shut off. He could not recall several key points like the speed. Other defense witnesses claimed the issue was the design of the track, defective brakes, sunken rails, obstructions on the tracks such as children throwing sicks on them, improper makeup of the train by not having the two non-powered trailer cars in between the three powered cars, the motor of the crashed train had been set in reverse, and the train was running at a normal speed, according to its conductor. The prosecutor believed the venue change was wrong and the jury verdicts were against the evidence. By early 1921, he gave up, and had the remaining indictments dismissed, claiming the witnesses, connected to the railroads, were withholding information or interpreting it in ways favoring the railroads. While the criminal trials were unsuccessful, the civil damage lawsuits were more successful, bringing significant awards to the families of those who died or those injured. These claims were settled before the trials concluded, with the railroad admitting liability, which, added to other larger debts, led to BRT's receivership and then being taken over. The new entity, with Menden as president, finally paid out over $1.5 million in 1923.

---

[124] People v. Williams, 106 Misc. 65 (N.Y. Sup. Ct. Jan. 1919), at 76.
[125] *Blewitt Freed in B.R.T. Case*, THE SUN (Mar. 19, 1919).

## E. Pandemic

| LEGAL ISSUES |
|---|
| ❖ Challenging the public health officers' authority<br>❖ Impact of pandemics on contractual obligations |

Not every disaster was caused by nature or man. Throughout human history, viral and bacterial infections have brought about illness and death on a much larger scale than all other disasters. The 6th century CE Plague of Justinian caused at least 10 million deaths. The 14th century CE Black Death killed at least 25 million people. The 2nd century CE Antonine Plague caused at least 5 million deaths. Other plagues and epidemics have killed upwards of 1 million people. The most lethal was likely the "Spanish" flu pandemic at the end of the First World War, with at least 50 million deaths globally.

While the pandemic may have originated near U.S. army camps, the ravages of the war had a dramatic impact on its weakened victims. The widespread movement of soldiers arriving in Europe, and then returning home, while living in close quarters, plus refugees and other displaced and malnourished civilians across Europe, made transmission of the virus that much easier. In the United States, transmission started in military camps, then spread to East Coast embarkation points for Europe, and later made its way westward to the Pacific. All segments of the population were soon affected. As described by one army doctor, where the virus first took hold,

> These men start with what appears to be an ordinary attack of... Influenza, and... they very rapidly develop the most vicious type of Pneumonia that has ever been seen... and a few hours later you can begin to see the [change of body tissue color] extending from their ears and spreading all over the face... It is only a matter of a few hours then until death comes... It is horrible. One can stand it to see one, two or twenty men die, but to see these poor devils dropping like flies.... We have been averaging about 100 deaths per day... We have lost an outrageous number of Nurses and Drs. It takes special trains to carry away the dead. For several days there were no coffins and the bodies piled up something fierce.... It beats any sight they ever had in France after a battle.[126]

---

[126] John M. Barry, *1918 Revisited: Lessons and Suggestions for Further Inquiry* (2005).

There were many legal implications across a wide variety of areas. One of the first were the methods used to try and control transmission. Municipal authorities, having to address the public health aspects of hundreds of thousands or even millions of residents within their geographies, enacted a series of ordinances to keep people safe. These focused on erecting barriers between people to reduce transmission. Rules were promulgated closing businesses, schools, theaters, churches, and any other places of large gatherings. Parades were canceled, ill people were isolated in their homes, and incoming travelers were quarantined. Compliance or non-compliance varied widely and so did efficacy. Essentially, starting early to implement protective measures, ensuring as much compliance as possible, and sticking with it as long as tolerable were the keys to success. However, no large city was successful the entire time.

In a well-publicized comparison, Philadelphia waited to implement measures, allowing a parade of several hundred thousand people to take place, despite a significant outbreak in the local military installations. The result was a significant spike in cases and deaths. St. Louis, on the other hand, closed schools and public gatherings almost immediately. In this second wave of the pandemic, Philadelphia had twice the excess death rate as St. Louis. In Minneapolis and St. Paul, the health commissioners had different approaches, proactive (closing public spaces) vs. reactive (isolating cases). Eventually, each came closer to the other's viewpoint, with St. Paul finally closing schools, theaters, and churches after a spike in cases. Public transport windows had to be open, and passengers limited, while store and business hours were reduced, and public elevators closed.

New York, as a port city, had a long tradition of watching for disease on arriving ships. When sailors on different ships in August and September 1918 presented with influenza, they were sent to isolate in city hospitals by the Board of Health. This would remain city policy, to isolate the ill, along with some staggering of business hours to reduce crowding on public transportation, and closing theaters without proper ventilation. Schools remained open, as these were healthier environments than the tenements most children lived in. In San Francisco, the Board of Health first issued a series of recommendations to residents but when the situation became worse, ordered a closure of dance halls, theaters, and schools. Those in contact with the public were advised to wear facemasks. This soon became a general recommendation for anyone in public. After it was not fully followed, mask wearing became a requirement under city ordinance:

> Section 1. During the period of the epidemic of the so-called "Spanish influenza" which is now prevalent in the City and County of San Francisco, which for the purpose of this ordinance shall be deemed to exist until proclamation, provided for in Section 2 of this ordinance shall have been issued, every person appearing on the public streets, in any public place, or in any assemblage of persons or in any place where two or more persons are congregated, except in homes where only two members of the family are present, and every person engaged in the sale, handling or distribution of foodstuffs or wearing apparel shall wear a mask or covering except when partaking of meals, over the nose and mouth, consisting of four-ply material known as butter cloth or of fine mesh gauze, at the four corners of which are attached tape or other fastening so that the mask or covering can be made to firmly cover the nose and mouth, said mask to be not less than five inches in width and seven in length.
>
> Section 2. When the Board of Health shall determine that the said epidemic of Spanish influenza has ceased to exist in the City and County of San Francisco, said Board shall communicate its determination to the Mayor of the City and County of San Francisco, who thereupon shall issue a proclamation to the people of the City and County of San Francisco, proclaiming the fact that the Board of Health has determined that said epidemic has ceased to exist.
>
> Section 3. Every person who shall violate any of the provisions of Section 1 of this ordinance shall be deemed guilty of a misdemeanor and shall be punished by a fine of not less than five ($5) dollars nor more than one hundred ($100) dollars or by imprisonment in the county jail for a period of not exceeding ten days or by both such fine and imprisonment.[127]

---

[127] Providing for the wearing of masks or covering over the nose and mouth by certain persons during the prevalence of the epidemic of the so-called 'Spanish influenza' and prescribing the penalty for violation thereof, Journal of Proceedings, Board of Supervisors, City and County of San Francisco (Oct. 21, 1918).

Legal challenges brought related to the pandemic included challenging or responding to various restrictions by health officials, the impacts to contracts from the inability to complete work due to closures ordered by boards of health, the impact on contracts for failure to timely delivery due to a lack of able workers, life insurance companies being reluctant to pay benefits for soldiers' influenza deaths, and varied other causes of action.

In *Benson*,[128] a traveling amusement show was banned from putting on a show in North Carolina by the board of health due to the pandemic. Circuses and carnivals, as transmitters and spreaders of influenza, had been banned for a period of months. An injunction against the board of health had been vacated and the plaintiff appealed against that ruling, saying such an action was arbitrary and capricious. The court of appeals, believing the board of health had acted out of proper motive and was intent on trying to protect the public health, and finding no evidence that they acted in an arbitrary and capricious manner, affirmed the lower court.

In *Clayton*,[129] the defendant saloon keeper was convicted of inviting and having people congregate in his saloon, in violation of city ordinance. The supreme court of New Jersey disagreed that there was anything in the following provision that such behavior could violate, as there was no description of the number of people, facility size or ventilation, and affirmed the court of common pleas in setting the conviction aside:

> That whatever is dangerous to human life or health, whatever building, erection, or part or cellar thereof is not provided with adequate means of ingress and egress or is not sufficiently supported, ventilated, sewered, drained, cleaned or lighted; and whatever renders the air, food or water unwholesome, are declared to be nuisances and are prohibited. Any person violating any of the provisions of this section shall be liable to a penalty of not less than five dollars.[130]

In *Globe School District*,[131] the city school district was trying to prevent the city board of health from closing the school during the pandemic. The board of health had declared all public gathering places, including schools,

---

[128] Benson v. Walker, 274 F. 622 (4th Cir. May 1921).
[129] Board of Health v. Clayton, 93 N.J.L. 64 (N.J. June 1919).
[130] *Id.* at 64-65.
[131] Globe School District No. 1 v. Board of Health, 20 Ariz. 208, 179 Pac. 55 (Ariz. Mar. 1919).

constituted a nuisance. The defendant school district asserted the board of health did not have such a power and if it did, the regulation was void for uncertainty, as there was no stated duration. The supreme court of Arizona ruled the board did not have the power to declare a public nuisance. However, it did have the power related to the reporting of infectious or contagious diseases and children exposed to such diseases and importantly, it had the same powers as state health boards.

State health boards had the power "to make and enforce all needful rules and regulations for the prevention and cure, and to prevent the spread of any contagious, infectious or malarial diseases among persons."[132] The court also ruled that during an exigency, the health board's powers were superior to those of the school board. Given its statutory powers and the exigency, the court held that the city health board had this capability while the exigency lasted. In *Alden*,[133] the operator of a movie theater in the same city was appealing a misdemeanor conviction for violating a theater closure order. The closures were to be in effect during the pandemic. The supreme court of Arizona upheld the conviction, based on its reasoning in the school district case above.

In *Citrus Soap*,[134] on November 7, 1918, the plaintiff agreed to deliver to the defendant 12 drums of soap lye crude glycerin prior to December 31. The nine drums delivered from December 31 to January 7 were refused. During December, due to the public health situation in San Diego where the plaintiff was located, workplaces were required to shut for four days. Five additional days were then lost after that due to the pandemic. The defendant argued that those nine days were insufficient to account for non-delivery, when the total contract period was nearly two months and they had started making the glycerin early in that period. The contract stated if there was any interference in production, deliveries would be made after the interference was removed. The trial court held there was a breach of contract by the defendant, and the court of appeals affirmed.

In *Hetrick Manufacturing*,[135] the plaintiff cotton mill had an order for 400,000 yards of cloth, which it agreed to delivery regardless of any delays

---

[132] *Id.* at 216.
[133] Alden v. State, 20 Ariz. 235, 179 Pac. 646 (Ariz. Mar. 1919).
[134] Citrus Soap Co. v. Peet Bros. Mfg. Co., 50 Cal. App. 246 (Cal. App. Dec. 1920).
[135] Hettrick Mfg. Co. v. Waxahachie Cotton Mills, 3 Ohio Law Abs. 577 (6th Cir. Oct. 1924).

in shipment. When the pandemic hit its workforce and production decreased, it had to delay shipments to the manufacturer. Upon not receiving a reply to its telegram, the manufacturer canceled the contract and returned the invoices. The cotton mill sued for the difference between the adjusted contract price and what it eventually sold the cloth for, asserting that delays in shipment were already provided for in the agreement. The defendant said there was no consideration for this term and the contract required the shipment of the entire 400,000 yards, not just portions thereof. As delays were addressed in the contract, the trial court sided with the plaintiff, and the court of appeals affirmed.

In *Phelps*,[136] a schoolteacher sought her wages during the period when the school was closed by the pandemic. Gladys Phelps was employed at a salary of $50 per month, and her school was closed for two months, so she was seeking $100. The school was closed by the Illinois Board of Health. She said she was ready, willing, and able to teach during that time. The court noted that a contract performance only became impossible due to an act of God or a public enemy. In that case, the school district would not be liable to pay. However, when the school was closed due to an epidemic or fire, it was liable, with the court citing cases from other jurisdictions. It did not matter whether it was the school district or the health officials who closed the school. Without a stipulation that covered that situation, it was an unconditional contract for $50 a month that must be paid.

In *Crane*,[137] the plaintiff sought payment on a contract to transport children to school. Due to the pandemic, the defendant school district closed the schools from the middle of October 1918 to middle of February 1919. The plaintiff wanted to be paid for those four months, being ready to perform the contracted work. The defendant said that performance was impossible, due to the closure. The supreme court of Oregon ruled that the department of health had no power to close schools, only to quarantine for public health reasons. That power rested with the school boards. As such the school was not legally closed. Therefore, the defendant's contract could not be suspended. As the contract was unconditional, impossibility was not a defense. The court affirmed, holding for the plaintiff.

---

[136] Phelps v. School District No. 109, 302 Ill. 193 (Ill. Feb. 1922).
[137] Crane v. School District No. 14, 95 Or. 644, 188 Pac. 712 (Ore. Mar. 1920).

In *Montgomery*,[138] a driver in Ohio had contracted to take children to school, without any conditions. When the board of health closed his school, the school board did not pay him. During this time, he kept himself and a team of horses ready, which meant he could not undertake other employment. He won in the trial court but was reversed in the court of appeals, who said the performance was impossible. The state supreme court reversed again, saying that the condition was one that could have been put into the contract but was not. Citing cases in other states, the court said that the payment of teachers when a school was closed for contagious diseases was a well-established legal principle.

In *Frush*,[139] the widow of a solider who had died of the Spanish flu was trying to collect on his life insurance policy. The insurance company refused, as he had died while engaging in military service, which the policy did not cover. Walter Guy Frush was drafted into the military in July 1918 and was located at a base in his home state of Ohio, when he contracted influenza and died. His wife claimed that he was not engaged in military service and did not die of military service. The court found such a clause, if interpreted to reduce voluntary enlistments, as against public policy. Further, the insurance company could protect itself against a death in combat. However, it the death was one he could just as easily experience in the non-military world, such as dying from influenza, then the company would be liable. The court ordered the insurance company to pay her the full amount of the policy.

In *Starr*,[140] a solider insured his life in May 1918 before dying of influenza in a military hospital in October. When his administratrix tried to collect, the insurance company responded that its liability was limited to the legal reserve on the policy of $15. The policy only allowed coverage for military service in a time of war by receiving the company's permission and paying an extra premium. If this was not done, all that was owed was the legal reserve. The trial court did not agree, awarding the full $2,000, as his death was not from a risk peculiar to military service, but from an illness prevalent in both civilian and military populations at the time. The

---

[138] Montgomery v. Board of Education, 102 Ohio St. 189 (Ohio Mar. 1921).
[139] Frush v. Ohio State Life Insurance, 22 Ohio Nisi Prius (n.s.) 428 (Licking Cty. C.P. Jan. 1920).
[140] Starr v. Great American Life Insurance, 114 Kan. 315 (Kan. Oct. 1923).

supreme court of Kansas affirmed, saying that any ambiguity should be resolved against the insurer.

In *Gorder*,[141] the facts were similar, and the insurance company tried to show that those in military service was more conducive to getting the disease and dying of it. The supreme court of North Dakota rejected this, saying,

> He testified that the ships were crowded; that the men were obliged to sleep in quarters with little or no ventilation; that conditions were such as to increase the risks of transmission of communicable diseases to the highest point. In stating his opinion as to the cause of the spread of the epidemic of influenza-pneumonia among the troops, he ascribed it to close contact, constant movement of the troops, age of the individual, rapid movement of the troops, climatic conditions, and the short period of organization after reaching debarkation camps. In addition to this testimony the appellant relies upon statistics showing a much higher mortality rate for influenza-pneumonia in the army than is shown by statistics covering those in civil life. Some statistics offered would seem to show that there were about six deaths in the army from this cause to one in civil life among a similar number of people, and that the disease was much more prevalent in the army than in civil life. These statistics are admitted to be very unreliable; for, as is remarked in the report of the state board of health for the biennial period ending June 30, 1920, "Case reports were most inaccurate and thousands never saw a physician," whereas, in the army every man was under constant observation for pathological symptoms, and no case of disease would be likely to be overlooked. Furthermore, the age of susceptibility to the particular disease in question is greatest and the mortality highest among those of military age, and of these it has been observed that it bore heaviest upon the most vigorous... The outstanding fact in this case is that the hazard to the lives of both the military and civil population was increased several fold by the prevalence of the pandemic of influenza-pneumonia.[142]

---

[141] Gorder v. Lincoln National Life Insurance, 46 N.D. 192, 180 N.W. 514 (N.D. Dec. 1920).
[142] *Id.* at 198-99.

In *Dunwoody*,[143] a physician had taken out a rider on an accident policy regarding accidental septic poisoning from an external source. When examining a patient in October 1918, the patient coughed on the doctor, leading to him contracting influenza then pneumonia and dying in less than two weeks. The insurance company refused to pay the widow's claim and she sued. The patient who coughed on the doctor testified as to his symptoms at that time. Other doctors testified to the dying physician's illness. The jury agreed with the plaintiff that the patient's coughing was the cause of the decedent acquiring the disease, and that influenza constituted septic poisoning. The supreme court of Michigan, citing a long list of precedents, affirmed that the company was liable under the rider.

In *Davis*,[144] plaintiff Bessie Allen sued and was awarded $700, for a serious cold she had received from open windows on a train and in the train station during the pandemic. The open windows were a measure to increase circulation and decrease the likelihood of catching the flu. The plaintiff, her husband and two small children were taking a train for which they arrived 20 minutes in advance on the last day of November 1918. The train was 20 minutes late. During their time in the waiting room, the windows were open for ventilation and there was no fire in the cold waiting room, despite the cold wind. There was a warm store across a narrow bridge up to 400 feet away, but she declined to travel that far on account of the children. When the train arrived, they sat in the ladies' coach, but the windows were open and a request to start a fire was refused. After arriving shaking and shivering from the one-hour journey, she was soon confined to bed helpless for six weeks. The defendants asserted that that it was merely carrying out procedures intended to lessen the impact of the pandemic, and that the plaintiff was contributorily negligent. The court of appeals affirmed, finding no contributory negligence, saying it was still the railroad operator's duty to provide warmth for its passengers.

---

[143] Dunwoody v. Royal Indemnity Co., 218 Mich. 358 (Mich. June 1922).
[144] Davis v. Allen, 199 Ky. 442 (Ky. May 1923).

## *Chapter 3*

# 1925 – 1949

It was the Jazz Age, the era of Prohibition, and the craze of the Charleston. The Pickwick Club of Boston was one of three members' clubs in town, along with the Phalanx Club and the Lamb's Club, known to host late night dance contests. They operated under a different licensing scheme than cabarets and other places of amusement, with charters issued by the secretary of state. On July 4, 1925, in a dance hall full of people purportedly dancing up a Charleston storm at the Pickwick Club, the roof and the three unoccupied stories above collapsed. The building had recently experienced a fire in those upper floors. The dancers were stuck below on the second floor, which also then collapsed, leading to the deaths of 44 people. As the rescue and recovery efforts were described,

> As the flood of electric lights once more illuminated the scene new groups of victims were found among the tangled mass of timbers, iron beams, bricks and plaster. Every moment brought forth evidence of other victims still more deeply imbedded in the wreckage… which sent scores to their deaths… when it collapsed… The flood lights created a picture resembling the stage of a theatre without curtains. The scene was one of cross-sections, showing portions of rooms still hanging from the back walls of the wrecked building, with some furniture still in place and pictures hanging on the wall, while beneath the workers continued the task of recovering bodies. The balconies filled with spectators were real balconies, the fire escapes of the surrounding buildings, and one side, overlooking the whole area, was the Olympic Theatre with its signs completing the stage picture.[1]

---

[1] *Remove 41 Bodies from Boston Ruins,* N.Y. TIMES (July 6, 1925).

The other two jazz clubs, the Phalanx Club and the Lamb's Club, were closed, and the secretary of state was insistent that this should not land in his lap for his licensing scheme. A grand jury quickly indicted a dozen men. There were manslaughter charges, drawn under both statute and common law, but it was the latter that would be used. Indicted were Timothy and Daniel Barry, the club officers; Hyman Bloomberg, a sub-lessee; George Funk, architect of the repairs; Henry Haven, architect of a new garage in the adjoining lot; Nathan Fritz, a contractor who had repaired the fire damage; John Pultz, a general contractor who was constructing the garage in the adjoining site; John Tobin, Pultz's superintendent; Lawrence Perkins, Pultz's foreman; James Hendricks, a city building inspector who had just rated the building as safe; and Edward Roemer, superintendent of construction in the city's building department. The building, previously the Hotel Dreyfus, was owned by the estate of Albert Rosenthal. Bloomberg, the Barry brothers, and Nathan Ginsburg, the estate administrator, were charged with maintaining a common nuisance.

The trial began within two weeks. There was conflicting testimony from building experts on the principal cause of the collapse, whether lateral support was an issue or not, but it was agreed that a support pier had given way. There was testimony of widening cracks in the building that were seen before the collapse. The fire three months prior on the upper floors had weakened the support structure. The destroyed roof was replaced by a temporary one made of thin boards that allowed rain in, so the club far below had to close when it rained. Additionally, the building next door had been recently razed for the new garage being built, further weakening support for the Dreyfus building. With insufficient proof the defendants' conduct was wantonly or recklessly negligent, manslaughter charges could not be supported, and the judge ordered directed verdicts. Perkins and Hendricks were found not guilty by the jury.

Although others were later indicted for the construction of the defective pier, again no one was found at fault for a disaster in a big city building, despite the many fatalities and clearly deficient construction practices. This pattern would only change as the years passed with the Depression and a new global conflict in the Second World War. The first section of this chapter discusses disasters in buildings and during air travel and the second section presents industrial and engineering disasters.

## 3.1 BUILDINGS AND AIRCRAFT

### A. Airship Explosion

| LEGAL ISSUES |
|---|
| ❖ Airship explosion investigations not determining causation<br>❖ Consequences of violating airship conditions of passage |

On May 6, 1937, the 811-foot-long airship *Hindenburg*, traveling from Frankfurt, exploded and crashed in New Jersey while attempting to dock, killing 36 people. As described by Herbert Morrison's famed reporting,

> We've been told that the airship is going to make an attempted landing in the rain... Well, here it comes, ladies and gentlemen... And what a great sight it is, a thrilling one, just a marvelous sight... The ship is riding majestically toward us like some great feather... proud of the place it's playing in the world's aviation... It's practically standing still now; they've dropped ropes out of the nose of the ship, and it's been taken a hold of down on the field by a number of men. It's starting to rain again... The back motors of the ship are just holding it, just enough to keep it from -- It burst into flames! Get out of the way! Get out of the way!... It's burning and it's crashing! It's crashing terrible! Oh my, get out of the way please. It's burning, bursting into flames and it's -- and it's falling on the mooring mast... this is terrible. This is one of the worst catastrophes in the world.
>
> And oh, it's... burning, oh, four or five hundred feet into the sky. It's a terrific crash, ladies and gentlemen. The smoke and the flames now and the frame is crashing to the ground... Oh, the humanity and all the passengers screaming around here. I told you. It's -- I can't even talk to people whose friends were on there. It -- It's... I -- I can't talk ladies and gentlemen. Honest, it's completely a mass of smoking wreckage. And everybody can't hardly breathe. It's hard, it's crazy. Lady, I -- I -- I'm sorry. Honestly, I -- I can hardly breathe. I -- I'm gonna step inside where I cannot see it. Charley, that's terrible. I – I can't... Listen folks, I -- I'm gonna have to stop for a minute because I've lost my voice. This is the worst thing I've ever witnessed.[2]

---

[2] Herbert Morrison, Recording made on May 6 for broadcast on station WLS on May 7, 1937.

The crash became a source of intensive investigation, overlayed by the airship serving as a propaganda tool for the Nazi regime in Germany. Named after the late German president who facilitated Hitler's final rise to power, the airship flew the Nazi swastika on its tail. This was the first of many transatlantic trips planned for 1937, after the U.S. Navy granted a revocable permit to American Zeppelin Transport Inc. to use its Lakehurst Naval Station as a terminal for the trips. American Airlines had also contracted to take airship passengers from Lakehurst to Newark to connect to other airplane flights, creating a global air travel network. The *Hindenburg* had left Frankfurt on May 3, in its first U.S. flight that year, commanded by the experienced Capt. Max Pruss, under the even more experienced Capt. Ernst Lehmann. Americans had booked the return flight, to arrive in Europe in time for the coronation of the new British monarchs.

Theories were soon proposed for the explosion. Designer Dr. Hugo Eckener first believed in three possibilities: gas let off to lower the altitude of the airship had done so with such force it had ignited; gas had ignited during refueling; or escaping gas was ignited by lightning. Others believed it was related to the venting of flammable hydrogen gas during an electrical storm, with the airship's static electricity, the wet landing ropes, and ground crew contact creating a spark. A spark from engine exhaust was another early possibility. Sabotage was considered as well.

The *Hindenburg's* use of volatile hydrogen, primarily due to the United States' effective monopoly[3] on the safer helium, seemed to be at the center of all theories. A law was soon passed to loosen that monopoly for non-military purposes, subject to strict oversight by the National Munitions Control Board and the president, allowing helium sales only,

> for medical, scientific, and commercial use, except that helium may be sold for the inflation of only such airships as operate in or between the United States and its Territories and possessions, or between the United States or its territories and possessions and foreign countries: Provided, That no helium shall be sold for the inflation of any airship

---

[3] An Act Authorizing the conservation, production, and exploitation of helium gas, a mineral resource pertaining to the national defense, and to the development of commercial aeronautics, and for other purposes, c. 68, s. 2, ch. 426, § 4; An Act To amend the Act entitled "An Act authorizing the conservation, production, and exploitation of helium gas, a mineral resource pertaining to the national defense, and to the development of commercial aeronautics, and for other purposes," c. 69, s. 2, ch. 355, § 4.

operating between two foreign countries notwithstanding such airship may also touch at some point in the United States.[4]

Investigations were soon started by the U.S. Navy, the Commerce Department, and the Nazi government, with Commerce going first. Commander Charles Rosenthal, in charge of the naval ground crew, could not account for the fire, believing everything was handled appropriately by trained personnel. Dr. Ludwig Duerr, with the Zeppelin program since 1899, could not account for the explosion. Meteorologists testified there was no lightning near the station at the time. Dr. Eckener suspected a sharp turn caused a shear wire to rip a hole in a gas bag and the leak was ignited by ball lighting or another electrical source. Other experts pointed to St. Elmo's fire or continual seepage of hydrogen hiding under the internal walkways. Sabotage was raised as a possibility by Rosenthal.

The final report listed all the evidence and then considered alternative theories. No evidence was found for sabotage. The mixing of hydrogen and air and its subsequent ignition were considered separately. It was not believed the mixing occurred due to diffusion or osmosis from the gas cells. There was no evidence of a gas valve malfunction. Decreased scavenging of gas was not believed to be a cause. Other possible sources for a gas cell rupture included a piece of the propellor, the facture of a tension wire, or structural failure. For the ignition source, spontaneous combustion was considered unlikely. Engine exhaust sparks and heat from exhaust gases were considered improbable. Overheating of electrical wiring, electrical meters, radio waves, or cell fabrics were dismissed. The conclusion was,

> The cause of the accident was the ignition of a mixture of free hydrogen and air. Based upon the evidence, a leak at or in the vicinity of cell 4 and 5 caused a combustible mixture of hydrogen and air to form in the upper stern part of the ship in considerable quantity; the first appearance of an open flame was on the top of the ship and a relatively short distance forward of the upper vertical fin. The theory that a brush discharge ignited such mixture appears most probable.[5]

---

[4] An Act Authorizing the conservation, production, exploitation, and sale of helium gas, a mineral resource pertaining to the national defense and to the development of commercial aeronautics, authorizing the acquisition by purchase or otherwise, by the United States of properties for the production of helium gas, and for other purposes, c. 75, s. 1, ch. 895, § 3(b).
[5] DEPT. OF COMMERCE, REPORT OF AIRSHIP "HINDENBURG" ACCIDENT INVESTIGATION (Aug. 15, 1937).

The naval inquiry was brief, focusing on injuries to naval properties and personnel. The German inquest, which included lab testing, listed the likely causes as: sparks from the motors; breakdown of the propellors; atmospheric electric discharges through the landing mast; electric sparks within the airship; faulty balloon covering materials, faulty electrical wiring; wireless issues; globular lighting; or violating safety rules. Ruled out were sabotage or large gas leakages. Essentially, it concurred with the Commerce report that a leak was ignited by a brush charge or other spark. Different theories have been proposed, but none yet definitively proven.

Surprisingly, there is no record of U.S. litigation against the Zeppelin legal entities. These were: Deutsche Zeppelin Reederei, GmbH of Germany (DZR), the airship operator; American Zeppelin Transport, Inc. of New York, the holder of the permit to land at Lakehurst as DZR's agent; Luftschiffbau Zeppelin GmbH of Germany, the builder of the airship; and Hamburg American - North German Lloyd lines, the passenger and express agency. There also is no record of litigation filed by the 36 passengers, 19 were either German or other Europeans and a German Mexican family of five. The remaining twelve were American citizens, seven of whom survived. They do not appear as plaintiffs, despite being fashion designers, sons of diplomats, and businessmen. There is no litigation record of executors or administrators, excluding the decedent who was the passenger traffic manager for Hamburg American – North German Lloyd lines, and his wife.

It was likely due to settlements paid by DZR's insurance policies, RM6 million (£500,000) with Lloyd's of London, and with Allianz in Germany. An unwillingness to litigate against foreign corporations under a Nazi government, and World War II[6] may have contributed. However, the most likely cause is the contracts between the passengers and DZR, represented by the ticket they were issued. Printed in multiple languages it stated it was a Zeppelin ticket. Then below that it stated DZR was taking charge of the listed person's air transport, from Frankfurt to Lakehurst, on the *Hindenburg* from May 3, 1937, for a specified fee, which was subject to DZR's conditions of carriage. It was signed and dated by DZR. This created the contract between DZR and the passenger. The conditions of carriage would have specified this flight was subject to the Warsaw Convention.

---

[6] To understand suing enemy corporations during wartime, *see* THOMAS J. SHAW, THE LEGAL HISTORY OF WORLD WAR 2.

The Warsaw Convention of 1929[7] was an international air travel convention which entered into force in Germany in 1933 and in the United States in 1934. As discussed in section E below, it would have a significant impact on airplane travel. The convention stated, "This Convention applies to all international carriage of persons, luggage or goods performed by aircraft for reward."[8] The key word is "aircraft." Although commonly used in airplane travel, aircraft was inclusive of other forms of travel through the air, including lighter than air travel on airships and balloons, as well as heavier than air travel on powered airplanes and gliders. If there was international travel between two member states, that travel was subject to the limitations of the convention. One limitation fixed the carrier's liability, "In the carriage of passengers the liability of the carrier for each passenger is limited to the sum of 125,000 francs."[9] In 1937, about 22 French francs equaled one U.S. dollar, so equated to about $6,000. This was the only damages payment available to the American citizens on the *Hindenburg*, whether they initiated litigation or not against DZR or the other entities.

In *Reiner*,[10] the plaintiff had entered a contract with a newspaper to send and receive messages from friends by radio while flying on the *Graf Zeppelin* airship between Friedrichshafen, Germany and New York in October 1928, during a then record setting flight. The defendant asserted that the plaintiff knew the exclusive news rights of the flight had been acquired by a third party and as condition of his passage, he could not send reports of the passage en route or for eight days after. He did so, under the guise of communicating with friends. The defendant refused to pay, asserting he had committed fraud. The court said the plaintiff was liable to the exclusive rights holder for diminishing those rights, and the court would not enforce a contract bargained for to commit a tort. A concurring opinion added, "The contract in suit may have been made before the contract of passage on the *Graf Zeppelin*, yet performance of the contract in suit could be made only through fraudulent concealment of the fact that the plaintiff would repudiate the stipulations of the contract of passage."[11]

---

[7] Convention for the Unification of Certain Rules Relating to International Transportation by Air (Oct. 12, 1929).
[8] *Id*. art. 1.1.
[9] *Id*. art. 22.1.
[10] Reiner v. North American Newspaper Alliance, 259 N.Y. 250 (N.Y. June 1932).
[11] *Id*. at 266.

## B. Nightclub Fire

| LEGAL ISSUES |
|---|
| ❖ Disregard of patron's safety giving rise to criminal liability<br>❖ Altering approved construction plans causing criminal liability |

In Boston, 17 years after the Pickwick Club building collapse, a fire occurred in a city nightclub, the Cocoanut Grove, on November 28, 1942, which killed 492 people. Once again there were many safety violations, either de facto or de jure. There was only a single revolving door entrance/exit, while other exits had been walled over, draped off, locked, or were inwardly opened instead of outwardly opened. The exits were not easily found in the darkness that soon pervaded. Many of the decorations that would conduct the flames did not have current fire-retardant coatings. The stairwell up from the lower level where the fire started, to the street level ballroom where most of the patrons were, was not wide enough at only 4 feet across. But it was wide enough to carry the flames up to the ground floor, running up the false ceiling. People died of the flames, asphyxiation from the smoke, inhaling poisonous fumes from some of the combustible materials, and being crushed to death at the revolving door.

The entertainment licenses of restaurants, taverns and hotels were immediately suspended until they could undergo fire safety inspections. All city night clubs had their licenses suspended as well, closing them down. The Cocoanut Grove was involved with organized crime and its first owner had been gunned down. Its current owner was Barney Welansky, the former owner's lawyer. The club had passed building and fire inspections. When the investigations started, the building inspector claimed that there was no regulation prohibiting flammable decorations nor one requiring fire extinguishers or the marking of exits. The technical secretary of the National Fire Protection Association said this disaster was,

> clearly due to gross violation of several of the fundamental principles of fire safety which have been demonstrated by years of experience in other fires and which should be known to everybody... It is too soon to determine the responsibility, to evaluate the part that may have been played by the chaotic condition of Boston's building laws, incompetent enforcement, political influence and careless management, but the main lessons of the fire are clear... as a result of the Iroquois Theatre

fire which killed 602 in Chicago in 1903, theatres all over the United States were carefully regulated to protect the safety of their patrons, but that no such standards had ever been applied to night clubs, which by their nature... were far more dangerous places than theatres... Night clubs are commonly located in old buildings made over for the purpose and practically every known rule of fire safety is violated.[12]

The official report of the fire department noted the establishment was licensed for about 500, when there were about twice that many patrons and staff on the night of the fire. Most of the eleven fire extinguishers were found unused afterwards. One finding was that carbon monoxide in the space between the false and actual ceilings was the source of the fire moving so quickly from downstairs to upstairs. The narrow stairway acted like a chimney moving the gas upwards, as did a fan upstairs, with further fuel provided by artificial leather wall coverings. Many deaths were attributed to a lock on the fire escape door at the top of the stairs, while others were caused by the inability to find exits. The report concluded,

> I find, therefore, that the principal cause of the large loss of life was the extremely rapid spread of the fire throughout the premises, and the partial pouring of the fire through most of the available exits, including all exits normally open to the public. Such rapid spread and pouring of fire was attributable to the peculiar gaseous nature of the fire, and the high temperature and the pressure of the gaseous material. Persons unable to escape through the exit doors were thus exposed to the effects of the carbon monoxide gas, the superheated air, or the flames themselves, in various parts of the building.[13]

Ten indictments were soon handed down by the county grand jury. Charged with manslaughter were Barnett Welansky and his brother James and wine steward Jacob Goldfine. The Welansky brothers were charged with conspiracy to violate the city building laws. The city building commissioner James Mooney was indicted for neglect of duty in enforcing building laws and police captain Joseph Buccigross for neglect of duty of a public officer and corruptly failing to enforce fire laws. Fire department lieutenant Frank Linney was charged with willful neglect of duty and

---

[12] *Fire Deaths at 487; Grand Jury to Act*, N.Y. TIMES (Dec. 1, 1942).
[13] REPORT CONCERNING THE COCOANUT GROVE FIRE, NOVEMBER 28, 1942, WILLIAM ARTHUR REILLY, FIRE COMMISSIONER BOSTON (Nov. 19, 1943), p. 47-48.

accessory after the fact to manslaughter, for his inspection about a week prior to the fire. Building inspector Theodore Eldracher was charged with neglect of duty for failing to report building law violations. Contractor Samuel Rudick, contractor's helper David Gilbert, and decorator/designer Reuben Bodenhorn were all charged with conspiracy to violate the building laws.

The jury also made a presentment of the following to the court,

We have found among members of various departments charged with the protection of public safety, laxity, incompetence, failure to fulfill prescribed duties effectively, and also lack of complete knowledge of duties. We have found shifting of responsibility and a tendency by various officials in different important departments to rely too much on their subordinates without exercising sufficient and proper check on such subordinates. Officials in each department seemed to attempt to shift responsibility to some other department and vice versa. We have found no completed coordination between Building Department, Fire Department, Police Department and Licensing Board with respect to various types of inspection intended to be made to insure public safety in addition to protecting the public health, morals, etc.[14]

In the superior court trials, Barnett Welansky was found guilty of involuntary manslaughter, while his brother James and the wine steward Goldfine were acquitted, not having managerial responsibility for operations of the club. Welansky was sentenced to 12-15 years at hard labor. Motions for a new trial, continuance, and arrest of judgment were denied. Rudnick was also convicted and sentenced to two years for violating building laws, while Eldracher, Gilbert, and Bodenhorn were all acquitted, as was James Welansky on this charge as well. Linney and Mooney were acquitted and the charges against Buccigross dropped. Barnett Welansky appealed his manslaughter conviction.

In *Welansky*,[15] the defendant raised more than one hundred assignments of error. The court noted that Welansky dominated the corporation running the nightclub, effectively owning all the stock, owning or leasing the land, and taking all the profits. There was no proof that the

---

[14] *Ten Are Indicted in Nightclub Fire*, N.Y. TIMES (Jan. 1, 1943).
[15] Commonwealth v. Welansky, 316 Mass. 383 (Mass. June 1944).

responsibility for the number or condition of the safety exits had been delegated to anyone else. He had suddenly taken to the hospital twelve days before the fire and was not present then, having his brother and Goldfine take on some of his duties. The court held he could not use his non-presence and the fact that others temporarily took some of his duties as a defense, as nothing had really changed from the usual operations that he had set in place. This included the lack of fire safety doors.

The indictment had charged Welansky with manslaughter in that he wantonly and recklessly failed in his duty to use reasonable care to keep the night club premises he had invited the public to safe for use, which resulted in the deaths of the named victims. The court spent significant time describing the difference between the wanton and reckless aspects of involuntary manslaughter and negligence and gross negligence. In the court's view, the latter were not criminal, so to be criminal, wanton and reckless conduct was required. This conduct would be intentionally failing to provide such reasonable care to the public he invited to the premises or disregarding the likely harmful consequences of failing to do so.

The charge to the jury was deemed proper,

> To constitute wanton or reckless conduct, as distinguished from mere negligence, grave danger to others must have been apparent, and the defendant must have chosen to run the risk rather than alter his conduct so as to avoid the act or omission which caused the harm. If the grave danger was in fact realized by the defendant, his subsequent voluntary act or omission which caused the harm amounts to wanton or reckless conduct, no matter whether the ordinary man would have realized the gravity of the danger or not. But even if a particular defendant is so stupid [or] so heedless... that in fact he did not realize the grave danger, he cannot escape the imputation of wanton or reckless conduct in his dangerous act or omission, if an ordinary normal man under the same circumstances would have realized the gravity of the danger. A man may be reckless within the meaning of the law although he himself thought he was careful.[16]

The court described at great length the number of fire exits and how the following conditions made it extremely difficult and unlikely that a

---

[16] *Id.* at 398-99.

group of one thousand people without familiarity with the layout could safely get out of the premises in the event of a fire in the dark. These reasons included exit doors being locked, obstacles being placed in front of the doors, exits being unmarked or at the end of narrow corridors, exit doors opening inwardly, exits being known only to employees, or the small size of the exits. The indictment had charged the absence of the fire doors and properly maintained means of proper egress, along with faulty wiring, the installation of flammable decorations, and overcrowding of the premises. By wantonly and recklessly disregarding the safety of his patrons in a fire, despite not committing a wanton and reckless act that directly caused the fire, Welansky could be found guilty of manslaughter.

In *in re Welansky*,[17] he was appealing his disbarment. Welansky asserted that he was not guilty of any malpractice or other misconduct as an attorney that should lead to disbarment. The court had taken judicial notice of his being convicted of 19 counts of manslaughter. The issue was whether conviction following a not guilty plea was sufficient evidence of guilt in a disbarment hearing. The court said that the issue was public confidence, so it was not appropriate to have a convicted criminal on the bar rolls. Although other states allowed a criminal conviction to either be conclusive or prima facie evidence in a disbarment hearing, a felony conviction in the commonwealth of Massachusetts was held to not require a retrial to determine guilt or innocence. Even though not directly related to acts of a member of the bar, it did bring discredit to the profession and demonstrated unfitness to remain a member.

In *Rudnick*,[18] the contractor also appealed his conviction for conspiracy, in doing work without a permit, making alternations not in accordance with an approved building plan, and making openings for doors in party walls without installing fire doors. The installed variations from the approved plans included blocking passages to the street with toilets. The applications for the changes were signed by Welansky, who was his untried co-conspirator, and Rudnick. Sufficient other evidence was produced showing Welansky's involvement in the alternations. There was also sufficient evidence introduced that Rudnick was involved in the alternations, which both men knew was not legal. The court did not accept

---

[17] In re Welansky, 319 Mass. 205 (Mass. Feb. 1946).
[18] Commonwealth v. Rudnick, 318 Mass. 45 (Mass. Mar. 1945).

the contention that it was common practice in Boston to wait until work was complete before getting approval for an alternation. The court held the acquittal of co-conspirators on the same evidence did not impact Rudnick's conviction, because the jury found that he had criminal intent while they did not.

In *Ober*,[19] the question was whether the Cocoanut Grove would qualify for an accident insurance policy. The policy on the decedent Douglas Ober's life called for payment if the death resulted from "the burning of any church, theatre, library, school or municipal administration building in which the insured shall be at the beginning of such fire, and is burned by such fire or suffocated by the smoke therefrom."[20] To support this, the plaintiff referred to the entertainment license of the club, the use of an orchestra, band leaders, singers, actors and actresses, the dancing area, and advertisements promoting its varied entertainment attractions. The trial court judge directed a verdict without letting the meaning of theater be given to the jury. The supreme judicial court agreed, saying a night club was one where the admission was free, and the entertainment was incidental to the selling of food and drinks while a theater was not either.

Quoting from other cases and law dictionaries, the court described a theater as "a building especially adapted to dramatic, operatic or spectacular representations, a play house... room, hall, or other place... so arranged that a body of spectators can have an unobstructed view of the platform.... an edifice used for dramatic, operatic or other performances for admission to which entrance money is received... a restaurant which induced patronage of its main business of serving food by furnishing entertainment was not a theatre"[21] Because there was no special meaning attached to the meaning of theater, there was no need to give that question to the jury to decide. The court concluded the entertainment provided was merely incidental to its principal business of selling food and refreshments, so it was a restaurant or night club, not a theater. The refusal to pay the claim on the accident insurance policy was held proper.

---

[19] Ober v. National Casualty Co., 318 Mass. 27 (Mass. Mar. 1945).
[20] *Id.* at 28-29.
[21] *Id.* at 30.

## C. Circus Fire

| LEGAL ISSUES |
|---|
| ❖ Arbitration agreement to handle tort claims<br>❖ Paying off damage awards in installments |

On July 6, 1944, a fire broke out at a Ringling Bros. and Barnum & Bailey circus performance in Hartford. This resulted in the deaths of at least 167 people, most of whom were children, and serious injuries to countless more. There were nearly seven thousand paid admissions at this afternoon performance, about to watch the Flying Wallendas, when the fire broke out. It ran up from the ground, perhaps from an errant cigarette, up a side wall to the big top, variously measured at up to 600 feet by 200 feet, the largest in the world. It fell back flaming onto the audience below. They in turn tried to escape the burning canvas on top of them but ran into metal chutes left over after the circus animals had just performed. Smoke inhalation and the flames killed many while others died in the crush to rush towards the exits or when jumping down. It had taken only minutes.

People in the grandstand seats saw they had to get off the grandstand quickly. Not being able to descend its stairs where the flames were, many jumped, with adults tossing children before them. The Flying Wallendas, Karl, his wife Helen, his brother Herman, Helen's sister Henrietta Grotefent, and Joseph Geiger, slid down and successfully made it outside. As Karl himself described, "when the flames hit the roof we saw we had to get down fast... We slid down the ropes and headed for the performers' exit but people were so crowded there that we saw that we didn't have a chance. So we climbed over the cage that lines the exit. That was easy for us – we're performers. But the public couldn't get out that way."[22]

Warrants were soon issued for Ringling Bros. and Barnum & Bailey employees. These were vice-president James A. Haley, who was married into the Ringling family; general manager George Smith; head of canvas Leonard Aylesworth; head of wagons and trucks David Blanchfield; and chief electrician Edward Versteeg. The city building inspector had visited to check there were sufficient marked and unobstructed exits, but the city fire inspector had not visited nor were any fire vehicles stationed nearby.

---

[22] *Children Caught in Frenzied Mass*, N.Y. TIMES (July 7, 1944).

Lawsuits were filed seeking damages and liens. One asked for the maximum for accidental death, for the loss of the mother of eight children, alleging that the defendants "neglected to supply sufficient exists; that the exits were barred and obstructed; that adequate precautions were not taken against fire; that there was failure to have sufficient personnel on duty for the protection of the public; and that the defendants used dangerous and combustible materials and equipment."[23] Other lawsuits alleged the use of paraffin mixed with gasoline on the tents was negligent.

The difficulty for the claimants was that their claims, over $1 million, were against a defendant which was unable to generate any income while it just sat there idle. A decision was reached for a temporary receivership and to allow it to return to its home base in Florida. The liens on its physical assets were released so the nearly 100 train cars of the entourage could return home to start generating revenue again. It would only perform in large auditoriums in the future, without its big top. What would be left behind were certain pieces of evidence for the criminal proceedings and funds to address civil damage claims. The funds were comprised of a $380,000 check, an assigned $500,000 Lloyds of London liability policy, and an assigned $125,000 fire insurance policy. The sum of $5,000 was set aside for expenses of the court appointed receiver.

The circus then agreed to the local bar association's creative proposal for a three-member arbitration panel, with one circus representative. It would determine the liability for each claimant, and the claim would then be entered as a judgment of the court. It would admit to no liability for those who did not enter their claims in this process. Beyond what had already been pledged, the circus would contribute future net income and tax refunds and ensure there were no increases in salary allowed during this period, no extraordinary expenses, and no dividends paid. Even with this plan, the circus was only able to pay the claims received of nearly $4 million by installments, with interest. In 1950, it proposed a plan to pay off the final part of the accumulated claims and exit receivership, if accepted by all claimants. The circus would pay off the remaining balances owed, about 1/6 of the total claims, without accrued interest, to the claimants, representing the estates of the deceased or those injured.

---

[23] *Hartford Circus Fire Dead Reach 157; Churches Hold Services Amid Funerals*, N.Y. TIMES (July 10, 1944).

The investigation by local officials did not assign a particular source for the blaze or blame any local government department but determined that there was a lack of coordination and gaps in regulations controlling such events. Recommendations included adopting a standardized health and safety code, with temporary improvements suggested for the building, fire, police, and health departments. In the manslaughter trial, the men charged pleaded no contest and were sentenced to varied terms. General manager Smith and the head of tents Aylesford were sentenced to up to seven years in prison and vice-president Haley to was sentenced to up to five years in prison, with the others sentenced to up to a year. The Florida attorney general then asked for the pardons of the three serving longer sentences but was turned down by Connecticut. Eventually all three were paroled after serving the minimum terms of their sentences. Haley later served in the U.S. Congress for 24 years.

In *North*,[24] the executors of the estate of John Ringling were complaining about the impacts of this situation. The Ringling family seemed to be regularly in some kind of dispute with each other. At the time of the fire, all the Ringling brothers were dead. The circus was owned by the widows of two of the brothers, Edith and Aubrey, with the other significant share owned by the state of Florida via the Ringling estate. The executor was John North, the son of the only Ringling sister Ida. Edith wanted her son Robert Ringling to be involved, and Aubrey wanted her husband James Haley involved. Robert was the president when the fire occurred but escaped prosecution, while Haley served time in prison for it. North wished to be in control and so this litigation was in pursuit of that aim, by using his effective control of John Ringling's estate.

North brought a derivative suit using the 37% of the Ringling Bros. corporation belonging to John's estate. The motion to dismiss the suit by the corporation here was unsuccessful. On one of the causes of action, North complained about corporation money used to defend James Haley as a waste of corporate resources and demanded an accounting. On the second cause of action, asking for indemnity, North alleged negligence,

> the assemblage of many thousands of persons during performances creates serious hazards to life and property in the event of fire and

---

[24] North v. Ringling, 187 Misc. 621 (N.Y. Sup. Ct. June 1946).

other contingencies, which hazards require observance of precautions and safeguards... It is then alleged that defendants knew that failure to exercise such precautions would, in the event of an emergency, result in serious damage to the corporation... defendants' failure to observe the necessary precautions and to exercise due care and prudence, such as engaging insufficient personnel, overloading employees, not providing adequate fire prevention and fire extinguishing materials and facilities, employing an incompetent general manager, etc.... [it] alleges full knowledge of defendants as to the conditions therein described... [and] continues with allegations of the occurrence of the much publicized fire in Hartford, Connecticut, on July 6, 1944... that defendants permitted the conditions to exist which prevailed at the time of the fire... then sets forth the consequences flowing from the fire, such as the criminal proceedings against employees and executives of the corporation, the pleas of *nolo contendere,* the imposition of a fine, liability for deaths and injuries occurring in the fire, the arbitration agreement as to such claims, and the liability of the corporation for costs, expenses and fees in connection with the various proceedings resulting from the fire. These matters are pleaded as direct and proximate consequences of defendants' failure to exercise due care and prudence.[25]

In *Jacobs*,[26] one of the claimants was used by the company to complain about the fee for the receiver. Edward S. Rogin had been the receiver appointed during the entire six plus years of receivership for the Ringling Bros., until the claims were paid off. He claimed that he had put in about 5,000 hours and had neglected his own legal practice, so asked for a fee of $175,000. The circus strongly resisted the amount, feeling it grossly excessive. The court said he was a receiver in a limited capacity, as he did not have to liquidate assets or operate the business, just carry out the arbitration agreement. The court noted that it took skills to deal with the claims while not seeking too much money from the corporation, to keep it from the liquidation or bankruptcy it had committed to avoid. However, he still had to obtain sufficient funds to pay claims while ensuring that the in-fighting among the company's owners did not derail profitable operations.

---

[25] *Id.* at 623.
[26] Jacobs v. Ringling Bros.-Barnum & Bailey Combined Shows, Inc., 18 Conn. Supp. 134 (Conn. C.P. Aug. 1952).

The court also noted that his practice income during the receivership did not diminish but significantly increased over this period, while his time on the receivership decreased after the first few very active years. The court felt that he had understandably magnified the worth of his work. The court held, based on evidence, that it took 2,000 hours to do this work and $60,000 would be adequate compensation. The court closed its opinion by congratulating the lawyers involved in the arbitration, and the circus itself,

> of the co-operative spirit and effort of circus management through long and trying years. Quick to recognize their deep moral obligation to those who were sacrificed in death or injury, the officers of the circus corporation met their duty foursquare, and, insofar as money has been able to assuage grief and discomfort and misery, they have made complete reparation in honorable and forthright fashion.[27]

Both Rogin and Ringling Bros. appealed,[28] for the award either being too low or too high. The supreme court noted Rogin had gotten the company to make up the difference when the fire insurance only paid out $65,000 instead of $125,000. The court said the 2,000 hours were based on his written record but that he claimed 3,000 hours that were not documented. The court agreed with the lower court that Rogin was not merely a stakeholder who received and disbursed funds. However, it also agreed with the lower court that Rogin was a receiver for limited purposes. As it could not say whether the award was more or less than reasonable compensation, the $60,000 was affirmed and both appeals dismissed.

> A new national fire safety standard for circuses was soon promulgated,

> The result of a committee project inaugurated shortly after the circus fire in Hartford, Conn., on July 6, 1944, in which 168 lives were lost. This disaster showed that tents and other places of outdoor assembly have not in general been subjected to the same sort of regulation in the interest of public safety that has been applied to theatres, halls and other places of indoor assembly which are covered by building codes and other municipal and state regulations.[29]

---

[27] *Id.* at 140.
[28] Jacobs v. Ringling Bros.-Barnum & Bailey Combined Shows, Inc., 141 Conn. 86 (Conn. Mar. 1954).
[29] Standards for grandstands, tents and other places of outdoor assembly: [ASA Z-20], 1946.

D.  **Hotel Fire**

| LEGAL ISSUES |
|---|
| ❖ Equal protection violations arising from hotel fire<br>❖ Enforcing current fire codes on older buildings |

On December 7, 1946, a fire in the early morning hours at the Winecoff Hotel on Peachtree Street in Atlanta killed 119 people. The building was engulfed in flames on all the floors of the hotel, which ran from the 3rd to the 15th floor. The stories of those who survived and those who did not varied widely. Some left their rooms encompassed in flame to crawl on the window ledge to another room. Some who stayed in their rooms were able to keep the flames at bay using mattresses and water, before being rescued by firemen on ladders. Others forced out onto the ledges by the fire were fortunate enough to jump and land in a fireman's net. A few even survived jumps of up to ten stories or, shockingly, after hitting the pavement. But the jumps of many were not so fortunate, due to,

> flames shooting from the fourth, fifth and sixth floors. Dozens of guests, mostly women, lined the ledges above the flames. Improvised ropes of sheets and bedclothes dangles from many windows. Body after body hurtled down through the chill pre-dawn darkness. Some landed in outstretched lifenets, some struck the pavement. One woman's body struck a wire... just above the marquee, spun and then fell the remaining few feet. From as high up as the eleventh floor, some of the 285 ill-fated guests plummeted to their death in crazed fear. Another woman on the seventh floor clasped her hands as if in prayer, bowed her head for a moment and then fixed a stare skyward. A young girl at the next window wriggled feet-first over the ledge and started down a sheet-rope. Catlike, braced against the building, she began descending to an aerial ladder two floors below. She lost her footing and dangled, flames lapping at her feet. Then she hurtled down to the marquee awning. Another woman landed on a fireman descending a ladder with a woman. All three fell the several floors.... From the seventh floor, a woman threw two children, a boy of about 7 and a girl of 4 or 5, and then plunged after them to the sidewalk.[30]

---

[30] *Women Plunge Out of Inferno*, N.Y. TIMES (Dec. 8, 1946).

The investigations revealed that the hotel had no fire escapes and only a single internal stairway and no fire doors but had recently passed a fire safety inspection. Doors to guests' rooms were not built of fire-resistant material. The ladders used by the firemen were antiquated. The building's original owner, Willliam F. Winecoff, still resided there, dying in the blaze. He had sold the hotel in 1944 to W. H. Irwin, who had leased it to Arthur Geele, Sr. and Robert O'Connell. Within days of the fire, the building was sold to the new Arlington Corporation. Indictments were brought against the lessees, Arthur Geele, Sr., Arthur Geele, Jr. and Robert O'Connell, lessees since 1934. The counts charged included involuntary manslaughter in the deaths of a victim falling to their death, and for willfully and wantonly operating a hotel without external fire escapes. Also charged were failures to provide fire hoses, fireproof doors, a sprinkler system, fire escapes, a fire alarm system, and waiting to notify the fire department.

In *Geele*,[31] the supreme court of Georgia reviewed demurrers to the indictments, which were based on a 1910 state law requiring hotels with at least three stories and charging guests at least $2 per night to have fire escapes. J. R. Moody had fallen to his death trying to escape the fire due to a lack of fire escapes. His death was a result of the defendants' unlawful act, which they had willfully and wantonly engaged in, disregarding the probable consequences of not having such fire escapes to protect the lives of guests from fire. The demurrer asserted the 1910 law differentiated between hotels charging $2 a night and those charging less. Because the former required fire escapes, the law was arbitrary and bore no relation to the purpose of protecting guests, violating the U.S. and state constitutions. The relevant George code sections were: 52-201 (hotels charging $2 or more a night), 52-205 (hotels at least three stories required external fire escapes providing reasonable means of escape), and 52-9902 (a proprietor of such hotel who violates 52-205 is guilty of a misdemeanor).[32]

The supreme court started by noting that any basis for classification must relate to the purpose or object of the law. It quoted from both state and Supreme Court cases, "Such statutes and ordinances must make no discrimination which is not based upon some reason connected with or growing out of that paramount cause in which they find justification for

---

[31] Geele v. State, 202 Ga. 381 (Ga. June 1947).
[32] State of Georgia 1933 Code, Title 52.

their enactment... While reasonable classification is permitted, without doing violence to the equal protection of the laws, such classification must be based upon some real and substantial distinction, bearing a reasonable and just relation to the things in respect to which such classification is imposed."[33] Otherwise, it would violate the due process and equal protection clauses in the U.S. Constitution and Georgia's impartial protection provision.

The court said the classification for structures three stories in height and higher was related to the purpose of the law, as the lives of those below the third story were not in as much such danger. However, the amount a guest was charged did not relate to the danger of fire he might be exposed to. The prosecution asserted that to require fire escapes on hotels charging less than $2 day would require raising their rates above $2 a day, impinging the purpose of lower rates. This argument was rejected by the court, which held the law was arbitrary and therefore unconstitutional.

The state indicted the three men again for involuntary manslaughter while in commission of a lawful act without due caution or circumspection. They were criminally negligent due to: failing to provide serviceable fire hoses, fire-resistant doors on stairwells and guest rooms, or a fire alarm system; providing an open stairwell constituting a chimney that spread the fire, vertical pipe vents covered only by flammable wooden doors, and combustible wainscoting for the walls, corridors, stairways, and rooms; failing to maintain a fire watch, provide a sprinkler system, treat carpets to make them fire-resistant, or provide external fire escapes to all guest rooms and an internal fire escape of fire-resistant material; not discovering the fire and warning those who were killed; placing combustible mattresses in the hallways and corridors; operating a hotel, in light of these points showing a want of due caution and circumspection and creating a fire trap endangering the lives of the guests; and for not contacting the fire department immediately.

The case again came to the state supreme court.[34] That court said it was difficult to separate an unlawful act from a lawful act done in an unlawful manner but defined criminal negligence as being indifference to the results of the negligent acts. Indifference required a defendant knew,

---

[33] Geele v. State, 202 Ga. 381, at 385.
[34] Geele v. State, 203 Ga. 369 (Ga. Mar. 1948).

or should have known, his acts would probably endanger others. The instrumentality thereof must be dangerous in the manner it was handled, but these instruments listed were not dangerous. The court then said none of the charged acts of negligence were against a current state law. Further, the indictment did not allege knowledge of the defendants of these negligent acts. As such, the indictment did not allege facts showing criminal negligence and the lower court judgment was reversed. The court also rejected the state's assertion of the *Welansky* case, as too different on the facts. No criminal liability would be found in this case but this disaster would at least have an impact on revised national fire codes.[35]

In *Willis*,[36] to attach garnishments while they pursued their damages lawsuits, parents of the victims sued: the hotel owner (Annie Irwin); the Winecoff Hotel Company (a partnership of Geele, Geele, and O'Connell), as the hotel operators and lessee; and their insurance companies. There was a mortgage on the building, but it was believed the value of the property, and the fire insurance payouts would be sufficient to pay off the mortgage and to provide funds for the payouts from the damages' lawsuits. The plaintiffs further alleged the lessees had made no demand on the owner to repair the building, damaging their leasehold interests, that Annie Irwin had transferred the ownership of the building four days after the fire to the Arlington Corporation in a fraudulent transfer to strip her of assets to then declare her insolvent, so she did not have to pay damage awards, and that letting the property deteriorate would diminish the amounts plaintiffs could recover.

They asked that a receiver be put in charge of the property and to collect all the insurance proceeds and, inter alia, the fraudulent property transfer by Annie Irwin be canceled. When a receiver was appointed by the trial court, the defendants appealed. Pointing to the claim of the mortgagor on the building, that the garnishments the plaintiffs had obtained were not judgments, and the statements in court from the defendants that they would not act without court approval and would post necessary bonds, the supreme court of Georgia overruled the trial court on the need to appoint a receiver over all the defendants.

---

[35] NFPA, Building Exits Code, Ninth Edition: [ASA A9.1], 1948.
[36] Irwin v. Willis, 202 Ga. 463 (Ga. June 1947); Geele v. Torbert, 202 Ga. 482 (Ga. June 1947); Irwin v. Torbert, 202 Ga. 482 (Ga. June 1947).

In *Willis*,[37] the case was back before the state supreme court seven months later. The court now said that the facts it had previously seen only alleged the lessees had not had the building repaired. The following additional facts were now before it, which included the sale of equipment and liquor using lessees' wives to hide assets and the disposal of linens, furniture, and supplies. The fire insurance policies had been assigned to their lawyers, done after they were legally enjoined from making transfers under the prior receivership. They also transferred all the furniture and equipment in another hotel they owned to secure a loan and owned a third hotel in the names of their wives and girlfriends. Based on this evidence, the lower court had established a receivership over Geele, Geele, and O'Connell (but not Irwin). The supreme court affirmed.

In *Torbert*,[38] the supreme court ruled further on this case. First, because certain older building codes only applied to new buildings, the plaintiff could not assert negligence per se using them. Second, it rejected challenges to state and city laws as ultra vires, unconstitutional, an unlawful delegation of powers, or too vague or indefinite. Third, certain sections of the building code needed to be included in the petition. Fourth, the court reversed demurrers against common law negligence, saying all the parties (owners and lessees) could be tried on allegations of deficiencies and defects in the structure of the building, while the lessees could be tried on allegations of negligence in the operation of the hotel. Acts of commission and omission were unlawful if lacking in ordinary care.

In *Bates*,[39] the court of appeals, referring to the supreme court decisions, tried to bring some clarity to these many holdings, saying,

> From what we have said, the allegations of negligence per se for violations of the ordinances of the City of Atlanta referred to in the petition... constituted valid and germane allegations of negligence per se except as to those [on the unconstitutional fire escape statute] and which we have held are not valid allegations of negligence per se. And also the allegations of common-law negligence as alleged in the petition are good and valid allegations of common law negligence.[40]

---

[37] Irwin v. Willis, 202 Ga. 267 (Ga. Jan. 1948); Geele v. Torbert, 202 Ga. 267 (Ga. Jan. 1948).
[38] Torbert v. Irwin, 204 Ga. 111 (Ga. June 1948).
[39] Geele v. Bates, 77 Ga. App. 396 (Ga. App. July 1948).
[40] *Id.* at 400.

## E. Airplane Crashes

| LEGAL ISSUES |
|---|
| ❖ Proving airline negligence in plane crashes<br>❖ Applying the Warsaw Convention for international travel |

Commercial airplane travel first started in the 1930s but really began to accelerate after the Second World War ended. Air travel in its early days had a higher element of risk for passengers, in much the same manner as railroads did during their 19<sup>th</sup> century beginnings. So it was that airplane crashes were relatively common during this period, with large numbers of deaths. In the 1930s, there were several crashes of up to a dozen fatalities. During the war, there were several crashes of up to two dozen fatalities. However, after the war, these numbers increased significantly. For example, in 1947, 43 perished on UAL 521, 64 died on EAL 605, 50 were killed on PCA 410, and 52 died onboard UAL 608. In 1948, 30 perished on NWA 4422, 43 died onboard UAL 624, and 37 were killed on NWA 421. In 1949, 55 died on EAL 537, 35 perished on SAL 897R and 28 were killed onboard AAL 157. With the increasing numbers of fatalities came litigation. These cases present some of the legal issues in early commercial aviation, not necessarily in date order.

In *Wyman*,[41] the executor for the estate of Edward E. Wyman was suing about a flight from San Francisco to Hong Kong, the Hawaii Clipper service, which was lost without a trace over the Pacific Ocean in July 1938, with 15 people dead. The court first noted that the Warsaw Agreement of 1929[42], which had become U.S. law in 1934 by presidential proclamation, was applicable to international air travel. There was a presumption of liability by the airline, which paid out a fixed amount for injury or death. This was unless there was willful misconduct. However, there was no proof of such misconduct, or even negligence here. The plaintiff was seeking to set aside the award of $8,300, asserting that the plane was lost on the leg between the U.S. territories of Guam and the Philippines. The court held that the Warsaw Convention applied because the destination was Hong Kong, making it an international flight from the United States.

---
[41] Wyman v. Pan American Airways, Inc., 181 Misc. 963 (N.Y. Sup. Ct. June 1943).
[42] Convention for the Unification of Certain Rules Relating to International Transportation by Air (Oct. 12, 1929).

In *Faron*,⁴³ the plaintiff asked for damages of $300,000 in contract or negligence, for the death of her husband Scott on a 1946 flight from New York to Boston that crashed in Connecticut, killing 17 people. She also asked for $20,000 under Connecticut's wrongful death statute. The airline asserted she was only allowed the $20,000, as the crash happened in Connecticut. The court quoted from *Wyman*, "The right to bring a death action is purely statutory. It did not exist at common law... and depends upon the existence of a statute creating a right of action at the place where the force impinged causing injuries and death." Because of this, the negligence actions could not survive and as the contract action depended upon negligence, it could not survive either. As the recovery must be based on some statute, and New York's law only applied to deaths occurring within the state, the only law available to the plaintiff was Connecticut's.

In *Garcia*,⁴⁴ the executors of Manuel Diaz were seeking to have his flight from New York to Portugal be declared outside the Warsaw Convention. A flight was under the convention if it was between two member states, even if there were intermediate stops in non-member states. The United States was a member and Portugal was not. The flight was to travel from New York to Bermuda, the Azores, then Portugal, where it crashed in February 1943, with 24 fatalities. The plaintiff asserted it should be adjudicated under Portuguese law. The issue was whether the air travel contract was for travel originating in New York and terminating in Portugal or originating and terminating in New York. The flight cost equaled two one-way tickets, but the ticket's origin and termination listed New York, routed via Lisbon, and stated that it was under the convention. The court held the trip was under the convention.

In *Conklin*,⁴⁵ passenger Arthur V. Conklin was flying from Albany to Newark in April 1930 when his plane hit power lines in thick fog, causing his death, and three others. The airline was only willing to pay $5,000. On the ticket, it had stated that class A passengers were limited to this amount, with classes B and C limited to $10,000 and $15,000, respectively. Conklin was not given a choice of purchasing the other ticket classes, nor of being able to waive a limit altogether. Because he had no choice, and

---

⁴³ Faron v. Eastern Airlines, Inc., 193 Misc. 395 (N.Y. Sup. Ct. Nov. 1948).
⁴⁴ Garcia v. Pan American Airways, Inc., 269 A.D. 287 (N.Y. Sup. Ct. A.D. May 1945).
⁴⁵ Conklin v. Canadian-Colonial Airways, Inc., 266 N.Y. 244 (N.Y. Feb. 1935).

because the general trend in courts was not to allow common carriers to escape liability for their negligence, the court held that this restriction was against public policy and void. Further, because the contract was made in New York, the court ruled New York's law applied instead of where the accident occurred in New Jersey.

In *Goodheart*,[46] the plaintiff did not rely on res ipsa loquitur but instead introduced evidence that there was negligence. The flight from Newark to Buffalo in June 1934, crashed in the Catskill Mountains, killing seven people. The evidence was that the pilot deviated from the known course and flew over a dangerous mountain area with which he was not familiar, at an unsafe altitude. Several other flights had taken the same known route during that time without incident and the weather had not materially changed. The plane had all the essential equipment for flying in difficult conditions and had been inspected just before the flight. The defendant believed it had done everything it was required to do. The trial court submitted it as res ipsa loquitur, but the court of appeals believed this was error, as the evidence of negligence introduced should have been considered and ordered a new trial.

In *Caswell*,[47] Audrey M. Caswell was a passenger on UAL 521 that failed to get airborne at LaGuardia Airport on May 29, 1947, crashing and killing 43 people. The report[48] of the Civil Aeronautics Board (CAB) listed the only one to survive, with slight injuries, was the pilot. He had hit the brakes after the plane did not lift off. It noted there were two possible factors leading to the crash, both pilot error. One was in aborting after choosing a shorter runway for which the plane was overloaded. The other was that the gust lock (to keep control surfaces locked) had not been released by the pilot, Benton Baldwin, an experienced commercial and military pilot. The executor asked to interview the pilot, the airline president, the mechanic, the dispatcher, and anyone else with knowledge of the fact. The airline said they no longer employed the pilot, who was in Germany working for the federal government, and objected to the other requests, as inappropriate before a negligence trial. The court disagreed,

---

[46] Goodheart v. American Airlines, Inc., 252 A.D. 660 (N.Y. App. Div. Dec. 1937).
[47] Caswell v. United Air Lines, 191 Misc. 941 (N.Y. Sup. Ct. Apr. 1948).
[48] CAB SAFETY BUREAU, ACCIDENT INVESTIGATION REPORT, UNITED AIRLINES, INC., LAGUARDIA FIELD, NEW YORK, MAY 29, 1947.

It must be recognized that there is a vast difference between a situation where an airplane crashes with fatal results to most, if not all, of the passengers and the ordinary negligence action involving collisions between vehicles or pedestrians... Ordinarily, it is not necessary to examine the defendant to establish his negligence. The same can not be said to be true where a claim is asserted against a commercial airline. In the case of a commercial airline, even if there are survivors as a result of a crash, such survivors are laymen with no technical knowledge of the condition of the plane or its management and operation. Such knowledge is usually exclusively within the possession of the defendant and not in the possession of a survivor and certainly not in the possession of the representative of one who was killed in an airplane crash. If negligence there was, and proof thereof can be obtained by an examination of the defendant, neither a survivor nor the representative of a deceased person should be precluded from a right to recover by reason of restrictions upon an examination before trial of a defendant that are sometimes applied to the ordinary negligence case. The matter of the inspection of the plane before taking off on its flight, the condition of the plane and its parts, the weather reports received by the operator of the plane, whether or not there should have been a take-off at the particular time and place or on a particular runway, and other matters almost solely within the knowledge of the defendant and in the nature of things almost wholly impossible for the injured person or the representative of the deceased person to know, should be permitted to be established through the medium of an examination before trial.[49]

In *Johnson*,[50] 22 people on EAL 42 died when it crashed in South Carolina, en route from Miami to New York, on September 7, 1945. The executor sued for the wrongful death of his son. The defendant proved the plane had been inspected, certified as airworthy, and the pilot was experienced and competent. According to the court, the reason the pilot turned back before crashing was still unknown. The CAB, however, had found that there was a fire aboard and that all the people on the plane had crowded into the front part of the plane, likely to avoid the fire. Several fire

---

[49] Caswell v. United Air Lines, 191 Misc. 941, at 943-44.
[50] Johnson v. Eastern Air Lines, Inc., 177 F.2d 713 (2nd Cir. Oct. 1949).

extinguishers on board had been used.[51] The jury found for the defendant. The plaintiff had asked for a directed verdict, as the defendant did not show the pilot was not negligent. This was based on South Carolina law that presumed negligence on the part of a common carrier in accident. The court said while true, this was only to let it go to a jury to decide on this rebuttable presumption, not to get a directed verdict. To do so would make the airline essentially an insurer. The court of appeals affirmed.

In *McCusker*,[52] an early case set out the liability standard for common carriers in aviation. On May 22, 1930, Louise McCusker received a message her mother had been fatally injured in an accident, and requested that she travel from Illinois to Georgia. She arranged to fly that same night. She fell asleep and awoke in a hospital. The pilot, landing at an emergency airport for unknown reasons, clipped a tree which the defendant claimed was unmarked around a heavily lit airport. The pilot was killed, and the plaintiff seriously injured. The evidence showed the tree was outside the normal approach path to the airport. The defendant asserted it was a private, not a common, carrier, and was only held to the exercise of ordinary care, not the highest standard of care. Reviewing its many advertisements, it was clear the defendant was trying to entice paying customers to its services. The court described the history of common carriers,

> The term 'common carrier' is not of statutory origin. Its meaning is to be found in the history of the law of the early days when means of travel and communication were slow and uncertain and innkeepers and carriers were restrained from the robbery and ofttimes murder of those to whom they offered their hospitality or service, only by the imposition of heavy penalties and responsibility for the safekeeping of their patrons' goods and persons... With the development in traveling facilities from the post horse to the chaise, the stage coach and to the modern railroad train or steamboat, the term 'common carrier' has been applied to each new development catering to the public generally, and the strict rules of the old law have been relaxed but

---

[51] CAB, Accident Investigation Report, Eastern Air Lines, Inc., Florence, South Carolina, September 7, 1945 (July 16, 1946).
[52] McCusker v. Curtiss Wright Flying Service, Inc., 269 Ill. App. 502 (Ill. App. Feb. 1933).

little, for with the development came new dangers of a mechanical sort inherent to swiftly-moving machines.[53]

The court found that airplanes were now to be included as a common carrier, when they, for hire, transported people, and goods, from place to place. The pilot had not exercised proper care, the highest degree of care, on a lighted airport, with lights on his plane and green lights signaling where to line up to land. The court of appeals affirmed the trial court's award of $10,000. To the defendant's contention that passenger must bear the risks of such travel in this new mode of transportation, the court said,

> Aviation is no longer an experiment. Great airplane lines are engaged in the transportation of passengers, mail and express. Their service covers the entire country, and it is a matter of common knowledge that such lines are held out to the public to be a safe means of transportation. In the instant case defendant informed the traveling public that it would get its passengers to their destinations "speedily, *safely* and in comfort," and that it was willing to carry all who sought its service, and it comes with poor grace from defendant to argue that the general rules relating to the care that must be exercised by common carriers should not apply to it.[54]

In *Smith*,[55] the decedents were passengers on PCA 410 when it crashed in West Virginia on June 13, 1947, killing 50 people. The main issue was the use of res ipsa loquitur, which the court held was applicable to airlines as common carriers. The court also addressed use of CAB reports,

> It is further argued that since the Civil Aeronautics Board conducts an inquiry into every aircraft disaster and embodies its findings in a public report, the plaintiff and the defendant are on a parity in respect to access to information as to the causes of such catastrophe. If this line of argument were determinative of the question at issue, it would apply equally to railroad wrecks, since they are investigated by the [ICC]. This circumstance, however, has never been deemed a ground for denying the application of res ipsa loquitur to railroads.[56]

---

[53] *Id.* at 518-19.
[54] *Id.* at 527.
[55] Smith v. Pennsylvania Central Airlines Corp., 76 F. Supp. 940 (D.D.C. Apr. 1948).
[56] *Id.* at 944-45.

## 3.2 INDUSTRY AND ENGINEERING

### A. Mass Poisoning

| LEGAL ISSUES |
|---|
| ❖ Mass corporate poisoning bringing about criminal liability<br>❖ Impact on consumer protection statutes for drugs |

In September 1937, Tennessee pharmaceutical manufacturer S.E. Massengill Company (after founder Samuel Evans Massengill) manufactured and distributed its Elixir Sulfanilamide, leading to the deaths of more than 100 people. As its solute, this product used sulfanilamide, a known treatment for streptococcal infections. It would become a popular anti-infection drug treating wounded soldiers in the Second World War. It was made in either powder or tablet form, but there were requests to provide it in a liquid form, to address its bitter taste for children. The company chemist, Harold Cole Watkins, decided to employ, as a solvent, DEG or diethylene glycol, poisonous to humans, as was described in contemporary scientific journals. The solvent was 3/4 DEG and 1/4 colored and raspberry flavored water. This solution was not tested for toxicity before being shipped, checked only for flavor, fragrance, and appearance.

The Food and Drug Administration (FDA) soon identified this drug as the common factor in the deaths of 13 people in Tulsa and East St. Louis. So began a frantic effort to chase down every bottle that had been shipped out by the company to various parts of the country. Six more people were then reported dead within a few days, patients of one physician in Mississippi, which raised the death toll to 21. Within a few days, the toll had increased to 36 deaths, with field agents from the FDA hurriedly trying to track it down, by telephone and telegram, pushing the company to assist. More than 600 bottles that had been shipped to 15 states, so shipping records were checked, and salesmen and pharmacists interviewed. Because it was not always sold by prescription, there were not always records. Not all doctors, fearing liability, were forthcoming on their patients or prescriptions. The number soon reached 60, then by early November the death toll was at 67, partly due to reclassifying certain deaths previously assigned to other causes. By late November, 93 deaths were attributed to the prescriptions of Elixir Sulfanilamide. The final number of deaths was determined as 107, a third of which were children.

More than 234 of 240 gallons shipped out were recovered. Under the Pure Food and Drug Act of 1906,[57] DFA agents used allegations of misbranding to affect the seizures. This act did not allow the manufacture of adulterated drugs. Adulterated meant that it differed from the definition and strength, quality, and purity shown in the United States Pharmacopeia (USP).[58] It also prohibited the manufacture of misbranded drugs, which were false or misleading statements on the package or label. For drugs, this was "If it be an imitation of or offered for sale under the name of another article."[59] Any drug that was adulterated or misbranded was liable to be seized for confiscation. USP's definition of elixir was something that contained 25% alcohol. Because Elixir Sulfanilamide contained no alcohol, therefore it was misbranded and subject to being seized for confiscation.

The history of major U.S. drug legislation shows that Congress has only acted after a crisis. The 1906 act was passed after Upton Sinclair's exposé on the meatpacking trade (with Theodore Roosevelt's follow-up). In 1962, after the thalidomide disaster primarily hit Europe (FDA chemists had held up its U.S. approval), a new law required that safety and efficacy of drugs be proven in advance by those creating them. In 1938, this disaster spurred Congress into passing the Federal Food, Drug, and Cosmetic Act.[60] This law required an effective application before introducing a new drug, with:

> (1) full reports of investigations which have been made to show whether or not such drug is safe for use; (2) a full list of the articles used as components of such drug; (3) a full statement of the composition of such drug; (4) a full description of the methods used in, and the facilities and controls used for, the manufacture, processing, and packing of such drug; (5) such samples of such drug and of the articles used as components thereof as the Secretary may require; and (6) specimens of the labeling proposed to be used for such drug.[61]

---

[57] An Act for preventing the manufacture, sale, or transportation of adulterated or misbranded or poisonous or deleterious foods, drugs, medicines, and liquors, and for regulating traffic therein, and for other purposes., c. 59, s. 1, ch. 3915.

[58] An Act to prevent the Importation of adulterated and spurious Drugs and Medicines, c. 30, s. 1, ch. 70.

[59] *Id.* § 8.

[60] An Act To prohibit the movement in interstate commerce of adulterated and misbranded food, drugs, devices, and cosmetics, and for other purposes, c. 75, s. 3, ch. 675.

[61] *Id.* § 505.

In *Harper*,[62] the first prosecution under the Safe Food and Drug Act was against Robert Harper, for the manufacture and sale of a misbranded drug. On the carton and label, he called his drug "Harper's Cuforhedake Branefude" (assume hyphens after the second, fifth, and eighth letters of the second word and after the fifth letter of the third word). He also sometime switched "branefude" with "brain food." The court instructed the jury to view these words in their ordinary meaning to determine if they were indeed a cure for a headache, and if it was a food, and a food for the brain and not the whole body. If not, they were misleading. Also, the jury had to decide whether the claims on the box, label, and circulars, that the drug contained no poisonous ingredients, was a harmless relief, and contained 30% alcohol, were false and misleading. Harper was found guilty and fined $700, the maximum, despite evidence of deaths caused by his ingredient of acetanilide (along with lots of caffeine and alcohol).

In *Johnson*,[63] a few years later, the Supreme Court got involved with "Dr. Johnson's Mild Combination Treatment for Cancer." The district court had quashed the indictment, saying,

> "Having regard to the intendment of the whole act, which is to protect the public health against adulterated, poisonous, and deleterious food, drugs, etc., the labeling or branding of the bottle or container, as to the quantity or composition of 'the ingredients or substances contained therein, which shall be false or misleading,' by no possible construction can be extended to an inquiry as to whether or not the prescription be efficacious or worthless to effect the remedy claimed for it."[64]

The government appealed, asserting it was misbranding to claim his product cured cancer while knowing that such representations were false. The Court, in parsing the wording of the statute, held that misbranding applied only to its identity and perhaps to its strength, quality, and purity. Nothing beyond that, such as a claim to cure cancer, was within the statute's restrictions for drugs. Three justices dissented to this interpretation of the wording, noting that defendants in 30 prior cases had accepted misbranding to mean just what the prosecution alleged.

---

[62] United States v. Harper (Pol. Ct. D.C. Mar. 1908).
[63] United States v. Johnson, 221 U.S. 488 (May 1911).
[64] *Id.* at 500.

The criminal case against Massengill, trading as the S.E. Massengill Co., was under the Pure Food and Drug Act for misbranding and adulteration.[65] Brought by federal district attorneys, they were directed by the FDA under the Department of Agriculture. There were two prosecutions, one in Tennessee and one in Missouri,[66] as the Kansas City plant had also shipped out some of the elixir. The Tennessee prosecution was for shipments to 14 states, and the Missouri prosecution to 5 states. The first article charged that the Elixir Sulfanilamide was adulterated because its purity fell below the quality under which it was sold. This was because the representations made were that sulfanilamide was in a non-poisonous solvent, when in fact sulfanilamide was in a poisonous solvent of diethylene glycol and water.

The second article charged the statement "Elixir Sulfanilamide" on the bottle label was false and misleading, in that it was sulfanilamide in a nonpoisonous solvent when it was actually sulfanilamide in a poisonous solvent of diethylene glycol and water. Further, the statement "Quality Pharmaceuticals" on the sticker was false and misleading as a representation of superior grade, meaning a mixture of substances to cure, mitigate or prevent disease and suitable for such purposes, when it was not of a superior grade and did not consist of a mixture of substances suitable to cure, mitigate, or prevent disease, in that it was a poisonous mixture. The defendant demurred to all counts and the court sustained the demurrer for counts related to the statement "Quality Pharmaceuticals," but it overruled the demurrers for the other counts. This left 112 counts in the information in Tennessee and 62 counts in the information in Missouri. In its decision, the district court referred to the Supreme Court's *Johnson* decision (above) in outlining its reasoning for overruling the demurrers,

> The information charges that the word 'elixir' denotes a nonpoisonous vehicle or solvent. The defendant contends that the information makes no such charge, and that the word has no such meaning actually, and that is has acquired no such secondary meaning, and that so such secondary meaning is alleged or charged. I have reached the conclusion that a fair construction of the language of the information is that the word 'elixir' used in connection with the word 'sulfanilamide' constitutes a representation that the contents of the

---

[65] U. S. v. Samuel Evans Massengill (The S. E. Massengill Co.), No. 29751 (E.D. Tenn. Oct. 1938).
[66] U. S. v. Samuel Evans Massengill (The S. E. Massengill Co.), No. 29752 (W.D. Mo. Oct. 1938).

package or bottle contained no ingredient which used as elixirs as used by the profession, and as directed by the manufacturer, would either counteract the effect of the active drug sulfanilamide, or kill or seriously injure the patient. If this construction [is] correct, the charge clearly presents an issue of fact to be determined, and if determined in favor of the Government's contention, an offense against the act exists. I have very carefully considered the defendant's contention that such charged representation relates not to the character of the ingredient, but to the physiological effect of the ingredient; in other words, that it does not deal with the question of strength or purity, but rather comes with the class of cases of which the cancer case is typical, and is not, therefore, violative of the statute, which relates to drugs as distinguished from foods. I think the language employed... [in *Johnson*]... is authority for the conclusion I have reached.[67]

Under the act, the penalty was a maximum of $500 and up to 1 year imprisonment for each violation, at the discretion of the court, or up to $1,000 for subsequent violations. The district court settled on $150 per count, without imprisonment. After Massengill pled guilty to the counts of adulteration and misbranding "Elixir Sulfanilamide," his entire penalty totaled $26,100; $16,800 in the Tennessee prosecution and $9,300 in the Missouri prosecution. Civil litigation resulted in settlements, with varied estimates of the totals.[68] The chemist, Watkins, killed himself according to a coroner's jury. A few cases came to court, related to late filings. In *Cauley*,[69] the victim had died in Florida. The issue was whether Tennessee's 1-year statute of limitations for filing wrongful death suits applied or Florida's 2-year rule. The Tennessee court held *lex loci* did not apply, therefore the lawsuit was dismissed. In *Wilson*,[70] the victim had died in South Carolina, where the limit to file was 6 years but the district court dismissed. The court of appeals disagreed, reversed and remanded, holding the Tennessee law merely preserved a cause of action while South Carolina's created a new one for wrongful death, and *lex loci* did not bar it.

---

[67] U. S. v. Samuel Evans Massengill (The S. E. Massengill Co.), No. 29751.
[68] $500,000 per UNITED PRESS, reported in STOCKTON EVENING AND SUNDAY RECORD (Jan. 18, 1939); $150,000 per TIME (Oct. 17, 1938).
[69] Cauley v. SE Massengill Co., 35 F. Supp. 371 (D. Tenn. Mar. 1940).
[70] Wilson v. Massengill, 124 F.2d 666 (6th Cir. Jan. 1942).

Two cases were to arise under the new act for the sulfa drugs. In early 1941, several children who had received the drug sulfathiazole died and dozens more would follow. Winthrop Chemical Company had come to prominence acquiring the U.S. assets of the Bayer companies seized by the U.S. government during the First World War.[71] The company had discovered the problem, that sulfathiazole had been contaminated with phenobarbital, in late 1940. Unfortunately, the company did not notify the FDA or initiate a comprehensive recall, with more deaths after its first recall began than before. The FDA finally was notified and required the company to do an appropriate recall three months after discovery. The legal impact was two-fold. It was the first company to have a new drug application suspended under the new act. In pleading guilty, the company was fined $15,800 under the new act for adulteration and misbranding.[72]

In *Sullivan*, the case involved the illicit sales of sulfathiazole without prescription, by placing them in a small box outside the usual packaging. These pills were often sold to soldiers suffering from gonorrhea. The owner of this pharmacy was charged with misbranding for removing the labeling and for the use of the term "Sulfathiazal" on the box. The district court convicted the defendant for violations of the statute.[73] The court of appeals reversed,[74] holding the key issue was whether this occurred in interstate commerce, which the act controlled, or merely intrastate commerce. The Supreme Court reversed again,[75] saying that the intent of the act was avoiding misbranding from when the drugs were introduced into interstate commerce until they finally reached the end consumer. Being misbranded would include not bearing adequate use instructions nor warnings about dangers and unsafe dosages necessary to protect users of the drug. Regarding the unusual nature of these new powers given the FDA, the Court said, "When it is reasonably plain that Congress meant its Act to prohibit certain conduct, [nothing] justifies a distortion of the congressional purpose, not even... marked deviations from custom."[76]

---

[71] To read about American seizures of German intellectual properties, *see* THOMAS J. SHAW, THE LEGAL HISTORY OF WORLD WAR 1.
[72] U. S. v. Winthrop Chemical Co., Inc., No. 656 (S.D.N.Y. Jan. 1942).
[73] United States v. Sullivan, 67 F. Supp. 192 (M.D. Ga. June 1946).
[74] Sullivan v. United States, 161 F.2d 629 (5th Cir. May 1947).
[75] United States v. Sullivan, 332 U.S. 689 (Jan. 1948).
[76] *Id.* at 693.

## B. Silicosis

| LEGAL ISSUES |
|---|
| ❖ Diseases arising from tunnelling work resulting in legal lability<br>❖ Use of workmen's compensation laws to avoid liability |

In the early 1930s, the building of a tunnel at Hawk's Nest Ridge in West Virginia led to the workers developing silicosis from drilling through the silicon laced mountainside, leading to the deaths of over 400 and perhaps many more. To hold an inquiry into this matter, Congress passed a joint resolution that stated,

> * Whereas four hundred and seventy-six tunnel workers employed by the Rinehart and Dennis Company, contractors for the New Kanawha Power Company, subsidiary of the Union Carbide and Carbon Company, have from time to time died from silicosis contracted while employed in digging out a tunnel at Gauley Bridge, West Virginia; and
>
> * Whereas one thousand five hundred workers are now suffering from silicosis contracted while employed in the construction of said tunnel at Gauley Bridge, West Virginia; and
>
> * Whereas one hundred and sixty-nine of said workers were buried in a field at Summerville, West Virginia, with cornstalks as their only gravestones and with no other means of identification; and
>
> * Whereas silicosis is a lung disease caused by breathing silicate dust, this dust causing the growth of fibrous tissues in the lung gradually choking the air cells in the lung and bringing about certain death; and
>
> * Whereas this condition has existed for years and all efforts to expose it have been thwarted; and
>
> * Whereas there are other similar conditions existing in the United States in said industry.[77]

---

[77] Investigation Relating to Health Conditions of Workers Employed in the Construction and Maintenance of Public Utilities, Hearings Before a Subcommittee of the Committee on Labor, House of Representatives, Seventy-Fourth Congress Second Session on H. J. Res. 449 (Jan. - Feb. 1936), p. 1.

Congressional testimony from social worker Philippa Allen said,

> According to the estimates of contractors, 2,000 men were employed there over a period of about 2 years in drilling 3.75 miles of tunnel to divert water from New River to a hydroelectric plant at Gauley Junction. The rock through which the workmen were boring was of a high silica content. In tunnel no. 1 it ran from 97 to 99 percent pure silica, and the contractors neglected to provide the workmen with any sort of safety device. None of the workmen, who have lived around Gauley Bridge all of their lives, were aware of the risk they were running, despite the fact that sandstone outcroppings can be seen all over the roads.
>
> These were robust, hard-muscled workmen, and yet many of them began dying almost as soon as the work on the tunnel started. With every breath they were breathing a massive dose of silica dust. That was the true explanation of it. It usually takes from 10 to 20 years to develop fully in a man's lungs this condition, but the medical men said that these men were working under extremely dusty conditions and the doses they received were massive indeed. Silica dust is deadly in large doses. Every worker examined by a physician after working in the tunnel any length of time has been found to have this dreadful disease. It is a lung disease that cannot be arrested, once it is started. Ultimately, the victim strangles to death...
>
> Why did the Rinehart & Dennis Co., contractors, dare to treat the colored "worsen if they was mules"? Simply because these poor, ignorant men had no standing in the community and there was no friendly organization to which they could protest. Most of them were far from home... a steady stream of cheap labor kept pouring in, enabling the company to reduce the hourly wage until it reached a low of 25 cents. Unorganized workers everywhere are an easy prey for the large companies who rob working men. This greedy company of contractors, Rinehart & Dennis not only robbed its workers by a ridiculously low wage scale, but purposely doomed them to die when they neglected to furnish men respirators (masks) which would have kept them from inhaling the deadly silica dust in the tunnel headings[78]

---

[78] *Id.* p. 3, 9.

In *Jones*,[79] the plaintiff, Nora Jones, had lost her husband to this disease. She was alleging negligence in the failure to provide a safe workplace, experienced foremen, proper rules, warning and instructing on the dangers, proper tools and equipment, and proper air circulation. This was negligence in causing the air in the tunnel to be saturated with silica, leading to the decedent contracting silicosis and dying. The silica dust arose from drilling holes for dynamite, and water drilling or other methods were not used to protect the workers from the airborne silica. The defendants Rinehart & Dennis Co. demurred because there was no allegation that the defendant was not a member of the workmen's compensation program. The plaintiff responded this case was not controlled by the workmen's compensation program, as: at common law, an employee had a right of action for damages against a negligent employer; a wrongful death action can be brought by his administratrix; diseases due to the job but not to employer negligence or non-job diseases were not compensable under West Viriginia's compensation law; and the law only shields employers from common law liability if compensable.

The workmen's compensation statute, in relevant part, stated, "Any employer subject to this chapter who shall elect to pay into the workmen's compensation fund the premiums provided by this chapter shall not be liable to respond in damages at common law or by statute for the injury or death of any employee however occurring."[80] In a later provision, the same law stated, "The commissioner shall disburse the workmen's compensation fund to the employees of such employers as are not delinquent in the payment of premiums… and which employees shall have received personal injuries in this State in the course of and resulting from their employment, or to the dependents, if any, of such employees in case death has ensued."[81] The defendant's position was that the case was about the former provision, not the latter, in that it was not liable at common law or by statute for damages.

Agreeing with the first two assertions of the plaintiff, the state supreme court then framed the query before it: "Is disease which is contracted by an employee through an indefinite period of employment

---

[79] Jones v. Rinehart & Dennis Co., 113 W. Va. 414 (W. Va. Feb. 1933).
[80] *Id.* at 418.
[81] *Id.*

compensable under the workmen's compensation statute?"[82] It answered "No" to this query, that the statute dealt with injury but not with disease. The court noted that 41 of the 44 states that had enacted workmen's compensation laws addressed occupational disease, and the two others had the matter decided by the courts. Only in West Virginia was it not mentioned in the statute or decided by the courts. In addition, almost all states did not shield the employer from liability if the disease was not compensable under the workmen's compensation law. The court ruled that a common law remedy could not be taken away from workers without clear statutory language. The court interpreted the statute to mean that employers were not liable at common law or by statute only for compensable injuries but were liable for non-compensable disease or death caused by the employers' negligence. Rejecting the defendant's interpretation of the statutory language, the supreme court affirmed the lower court's overruling of the defendant's demurrer.

In *Shay*,[83] 60 of the personal injury lawsuits against the same defendants, for contracting silicosis from the defendants' negligence, were transferred from Fayette County, where the events took place, to Kanawha County for trial. The reason for the change in venue request by the plaintiffs was the cases were taking too long to try, given the vast number of cases the local courts had to deal with, as 200 cases remained in Fayette County even after these 60 were moved. The second reason was based on jury verdicts in two cases that had already been tried there. The appellate court held that such an order for change of venue was not reviewable, as it was not a final judgment. The court said this was for a good reason, as defendants would use them as a delaying tactic. The defendants' writ of error was dismissed.

In *Scott*,[84] the plaintiff worked on the tunnel from April 1930 to September 1931 but did not realize he had contracted silicosis until three months before he sued in October 1933. The defendants' asserted the statute of limitations as a defense, where actions had to be brought within one year of the cause accruing. The state supreme court described what accruing meant,

---

[82] *Id.* at 421.
[83] Shay v. Rinehart & Dennis Co., 116 W. Va. 24 (W. Va. Jan. 1935).
[84] Scott v. Rinehart & Dennis Co., 116 W. Va. 319 (W. Va. May 1935).

West Virginia courts of last resort have consistently held that the right of action accrues when the wrong is committed, and in the absence of some act of concealment by the wrongdoer, the mere ignorance of the injured party of the actionable wrong will not suspend the statute.[85]

The supreme court, noted that essentially the statute had not changed since 1819, the state legislature had a very long time to change it to deal with disease that arises later but had not, and this was the observed rule in other states.[86] Not being able to change the law, which was the legislative function, the court was forced to agree that the statute of limitations was a complete defense to silicosis arising after the statutory period had expired, despite the plea from the plaintiff,

> Counsel for plaintiff recognizes this tremendous weight of authority but demands a change in construction under "the rule of reason, the dictates of humanity, the principles of common justice and the development and progress of the law in step with changing conditions."[87]

In *West Virgina,*[88] the United States was suing the state because of its approval of this dam project at Hawk's Nest Ridge. The federal government had originally sought an injunction against the state, Union Carbide and Carbon Corp., its subsidiary Electro Metallurgical Company, and another subsidiary, the New-Kanawha Power Company. It was the latter which had contracted with Rinehart & Dennis Co. to build the tunnel, so that water could be diverted from the New River to a hydroelectric plant. The power from the plant was to be sold to the power company. The federal government was contending that the approval of the project by the state was an interference on a navigable river in interstate commerce. Further, it would impact with improvements to navigation and flood control on the New and Kanawha Rivers that the federal government had built or was in the process of building and must be federally licensed. The defendants denied that the New River was navigable and that states had a sovereign right over their rivers. As the acts were by corporations, and the state only issued the permit, the Court dismissed this action as not justiciable.

---

[85] *Id.* at 320.
[86] Wiersycki v. Pratt & Letchworth Co., 151 Misc. 207 (N.Y. Sup. Ct. Apr. 1934).
[87] *Id.* at 321.
[88] United States v. West Virginia, 295 U.S. 463 (May 1935).

## C. LNG Explosion

| LEGAL ISSUES |
|---|
| ❖ Construction of a faulty LNG tank giving rise to legal liability<br>❖ Use of new technology not part of custom leading to liability |

On October 20, 1944, there was an explosion at a liquified natural gas (LNG) plant in Cleveland, Ohio, killing 130 people, injuring hundreds more, and making many homeless. The plant, owned by the East Ohio Gas Company (EOG), was to liquify natural gas, store it, and then re-gasify the LNG during periods of peak usage back into the normal natural gas distribution system. The plant used several spherical tanks, operating at very cold temperature and low pressures, that each stored 50 million feet of natural gas (83,300 cubic feet of LNG), and a single cylindrical tank that stored 90 million cubic feet of natural gas (150,000 cubic feet of LNG). It was this latter tank that developed the leak leading to the initial explosion. One of the spherical tanks exploded 20 minutes later from an ensuant fire.

Because of the Second World War, sabotage was a leading theory. However, a detailed investigation by the Department of the Interior's Bureau of Mines came to a different conclusion. The report explained that this was the first large-scale industrial plant for LNG. Instead of deploying a high-pressure line, the decision was made to build a large-scale LNG plant, due to its lower cost. The spherical storage units were built first and later the cylindrical unit was added, increasing capacity for war-related industries. The process used refrigerated ethylene to liquify natural gas. Liquid ammonia cooled the ethylene, which in turn was produced by cooling ammonia gas with water. The four tanks were designed, fabricated, and erected by Pittsburgh-Des Moines Steel Co. (PDM Steel) and affiliates.

The new tank was cylindric because PDM Steel determined that it was easier to perform a stress analysis with greater certainty than on the spherical tanks, which had certain issues as they got larger. A repair had been made for damage in the cylindrical tank. At the time of the fire, the plant was shutting down, as the tanks had all been filled. After the cylindrical tank failed and the LNG escaped, it evaporated and the natural gas was ignited, from any of many possible sources, including open laboratory flames and electrical wiring, switches, and lights. It also combined with sewer gas and caused further explosions underground.

The report discussed the possible causes for the failure of the cylindrical tank, focusing on both external and internal causes. An explosion near or underneath any of the other tanks was considered unlikely. An abnormal shock to the cylindrical tank from an operational failure in the liquification equipment or a sudden release of pressure were likewise considered unlikely. Seismic shocks such as the passing of nearby trains or the dropping of a hammer were not dismissed, as this tank did not have the same cushioning cork foundation as the spherical tanks. A crack in the tank was discounted after investigation. No definite conclusion was reached, but operating or personnel failure, earlier explosion of a gas-air mixture, or sabotage were ruled out. That left the improper design of the cylindrical tank, using steel in constructing the tank, or some flaw in the tank or its welding. Recommendations included keeping such plants at least a half mile from inhabited areas, using dikes to contain LNG spills around tanks, further study of the metals used, preventing LNG from entering storm sewers, removing sources of electrical ignition, and providing a procedure for rapid egress of personnel in an emergency.

EOG paid death benefits to those were killed, employees and otherwise, except for those who could not be identified, as it was presumed some transients were among those who died. Litigation was initiated against the designer of the tanks, PDM Steel. In *Roberts*,[89] PDM Steel was being sued by many victims. As it turned out, EOG had contracted with the Gas Machinery Company to erect the four tanks for LNG. Gas Machinery had in turn contracted with PDM Steel to construct the tanks. The fabrication was done by Pittsburgh-Des Moines Company (PDM) in Pennsylvania and it was PDM Steel that erected the tanks. EOG was involved in the preparation of specifications and design of the tanks and approved them. The foundations for the tanks, certain tank parts, and the plant and equipment were all constructed by other companies. Gas Machinery observed, inspected, and accepted the construction of the tanks. The spherical tanks had been in place for several years and the cylindrical tank for more than a year before the explosion occurred. Therefore, it was EOG that had had possession and control of the tanks for a long period before the explosion occurred.

---

[89] Roberts v. Pittsburgh-Des Moines, Co., and 37 other cases; Victory v. Pittsburgh-Des Moines, Co., and 24 other cases, 6 F.R.D. 25 (W.D. Pa. Sept. 1946).

The long form of the complaint, used by 38 of the plaintiffs, alleged recklessness and negligence by the defendants,

(a) In designing and constructing said tanks, and particularly the cylindrical tank without adequate outside dykes to retain said liquid gas in the event of a rupture of the walls of the tank.

(b) In using steel of such defective composition and improper treatment that it was of insufficient strength and toughness to resist the strains created in said tank, and was likely to be brittle and to shatter upon slight impact or strain.

(c) In designing and building said tanks at a place where there was almost continuous vibration and ground tremors, such that the rock wool used as insulation for the cylindrical tank was likely to disintegrate and collapse and to lose a substantial part of its insulating effect; and so that the steel of the tank was likely to become fatigued and be rendered increasingly brittle and subject to fracture.

(d) In failing to reduce the strains and stresses which had been created in said cylindrical tank in the process of erecting it and welding its constituent parts by an appropriate heat treatment, passing or otherwise.

(e) In so designing and constructing said tanks that any spillage or drainage therefrom would be drained into a covered pit or sump, and in failing to provide an anti-flash-back guard for the said pit.

(f) In designing the said tank so defectively and improperly that great internal strains were set up by the presence of liquid gas therein, which strains were due to the differences in contraction of the component parts of said tank.

(g) In designing the connecting pipes and valves which connected the various tanks with the general liquefying system of said plant in such a manner that there was inadequate protection against sudden surges of pressure in said tank.

(h) In designing said tank in such a manner that no device was provided for agitating the liquid contents thereof or otherwise protecting against the hazards of vapor pressure within said liquids, and so as to avoid the hazards of surge or "bumping" arising therefrom.

(i) In failing to design or provide an effective cushioning device to protect the said tank and its constituent members, and particularly the inner shell thereof, from the dangers of continued vibration and the fatigue resulting therefrom.

(j) In designing said tank in the form of a cylinder instead of a sphere when said cylindrical form was likely to rupture when put to the use for which it was designed; and in further constructing said cylindrical tank without adequate engineering data warranting its substitution for the spherical form which had been formerly used.

(k) In failing to provide adequate supports or materials of *sufficient* strength to support the weight of said cylinder and its liquid contents, and in failing further to make adequate laboratory tests to determine the effect of extremely low temperatures upon the materials thus used in the presence of the strains incidental to the weight and support of such a structure and the' vibrations encountered at the site of said tanks.

(l) In using for insulation a substance untested for such purpose, and which the defendants knew or ought to have known was likely to disintegrate and lose much of its insulating value, and in failing to provide adequate insulation between the inner and outer walls of said tank.

(m) In so designing and erecting said tank as to make it difficult, if not impossible, to keep the insulation in proper position or to replace defective insulation or to repair adequately leaks in the structure of said tank when such leaks should appear.

(n) In failing to make adequate tests of the effects of liquid gas upon the materials and alloys used in said structure before attempting to erect said tank.

(o) In designing, planning and erecting said tank at a place and in such close proximity to other, gas tanks that any leakage from one or the other of said tanks was likely to cause conflagrations and explosions in the other tanks.

(p) In so designing said tank and other spherical tanks in the immediate vicinity without any adequate safety devices or safeguards around each of said tanks so as to permit said gas, in the event, of leakage, to be protected against fires and explosions; and particularly in failing to equip said tanks with outside sprinkler systems or with Fossite or carbon dioxide safety provisions.

(q) In so designing said tank that there was no adequate provisions to give warning by automatic machinery or otherwise of the fact that leakage was taking place from said tank, or that a. rupture or fracture of the inner shell of said tank had taken place.

(r) In giving instructions to the employees of The East Ohio Gas Company after leakage had begun, to cause the frost spots resulting from said leakage to be removed by the process of applying steam blowers, when said process was hazardous and dangerous and was likely to cause ruptures to be enlarged and made more dangerous; and when further, said employees of The East Ohio Gas Company ought to have been instructed immediately to withdraw said liquid gas from said tank.

(s) In designing said system of tanks in such a manner as to fail to provide a spare or storage tank available for the storage of liquid gas in the event that one of said tanks developed ruptures or leakage, such as to require an immediate and early emptying thereof.[90]

The response by the defendants was that they owed no legal duty to the plaintiffs, as the complaint did not specify what caused the tanks to break. The district court ruled against this objection, In that, parts or all of subsections (b-d) and (f-n) explained in sufficient detail the acts of negligent commission or omission by which the tank was caused to rupture. The defendants next objected to whether the public nuisance was the tank as delivered or the operations of the entire plant. The court said that subsections (a-q) and (s) concerned the construction and subsection (r) the defendant giving instructions to EOG personnel after the construction and delivery of the tank. It ruled these were respectively negligence in construction and negligence in instructions given. The next objection raised by the defendants concerned the legal relationship of the

---

[90] *Id.* at 27-28.

plaintiffs' decedents to the tank owner. The court ruled this was necessary to include, as liability might be different depending on that relationship.

The defendant then asserted there were no facts about any changes made to the tank after its delivery and installation, but the court ruled this was the plaintiff's discretion. This was also true for the lack of allegations against others who might have been involved in alleged negligence. The court noted that the construction was based in part on patents held by the defendants. The final objection was the lack of a legal duty to design and construct safety devices for operation of the plant, but the court rejected this, as the focus was on safety devices for the tanks. There was a short version of the complaint filed by the 25 plaintiffs in the related *Victory* lawsuit. The court responded similarly to the objections, noting the under the Federal Rules of Civil Procedure, the purpose of the complaint was to give a short and plain statement of the claim and that the pleader was entitled to relief. Technicalities were no longer of importance.

In *Moran*,[91] another lawsuit asserted the use of improper steel in the tank and deposed James O. Jackson, PDM Steel's chief engineer. Counsel objected to him answering these questions, being their technical expert:

1. Was there in your opinion as a designing engineer any particular grain size requisite for safe use of steel in that No. 4 tank?

2. As a designing engineer was it your opinion that the grain size was of relevance or importance in choosing or selecting steel to be used in the No. 4 tank?

3. Did you as a designing engineer have any opinion on whether or not it was important in designing this No. 4 tank and building it to have the steel normalized or not?[92]

The court rejected the defendants' motion, as he was not an outside expert hired to give advice for the litigation, which would be privileged, but a regular employee of the company. The court did, however, suggest a slight rephrasing of the questions, removing the references to him being the designing engineer and referring to any request for his opinion.

---

[91] Moran v. Pittsburgh-Des Moines Steel Co., 6 F.R.D. 594 (W.D. Pa. Mar. 1947).
[92] *Id.* at 595.

In *Foley*,[93] the executrix widow sued for wrongful death of Michael J. Foley against PDM, a corporation, which had designed and fabricated the tank and against PDM Steel, a partnership, which supervised the fabrication and erected it. The court of common pleas awarded her a verdict for $50,000 but then the en banc court granted the defendants' motion for a judgment notwithstanding the verdict (*non obstante veredicto*). The appeal came to the state supreme court, which laid out the following seven queries it had to answer to determine liability,

> (1) By the law of what State is defendants' liability to be determined? (2) Was the evidence sufficient to establish negligence on the part of defendants? (3) Was the evidence sufficient to warrant a conclusion that such negligence was the cause of the accident? (4) Was defendants' negligence superseded by any independent, intervening cause? (5) If the accident was the result of defendants' negligence, are they legally responsible therefor to this plaintiff? (6) Does liability extend to *all of* the defendants in this action? (7) Is plaintiff's right of recovery barred by the Statute of Limitations?[94]

To the first question, the unequivocal answer was *lex loci*, where the accident took place and the defendants' standard of care was prescribed. *Lex fori*, law of the forum, would apply to govern the rules of evidence, burden of proof, and statute of limitations. On the second question, the court noted the plaintiff was asserting negligence in the design, construction, selection of materials, and testing and the high degree of danger meant that there had to be a high level of care. She asserted that the design was unproven and only selected due to lower cost. The court said the allegations and the responses from the defendants on the design and construction were for the jury to determine. For materials selection, the issue was the use of rock wool instead of cork for insulation of the cylindrical tanks and the type of steel used for the inner tank. The steel was 3.5% nickel steel. Ordinary steel became brittle at the extremely cold temperatures required for LNG. The materials had to not fall below 10 foot pounds in a specialized test to be sufficient to hold LNG. The steel in the spherical tanks had only been rated at 2–4 foot pounds but the same steel was used in the cylindrical tank, as the other tanks had not had problems.

---

[93] Foley v. Pittsburgh-Des Moines Co., 363 Pa. 1 (Pa. Sept. 1949).
[94] *Id.* at 9.

This also was a matter for the jury to determine if failure to use a suitable steel was negligent. It was the same for the sufficiency of testing. On the third question, the court said expert opinion on the cause of an accident was always admissible when dependent on circumstantial instead of direct evidence. The plaintiff's expert testified to the danger caused by the angles at which the sides and bottom of the cylindrical tank were connected; that spherical tanks were preferred to avoid concentration of stresses at any one point. The stresses at the bottom of the tank led, through a series of steps, to the expulsion of the LNG and then ignition. The defendants blamed EOG, asserting an explosion instead of leaking from the tank, and proposed many theories. The court said that,

> It is true that where, of several theories advanced for the cause of an accident, one is as plausible as the other *and equally consistent with the factual* testimony,' so that the verdict would necessarily be a mere guess as to the real cause, no recovery can be allowed... the burden is on the plaintiff to individuate that one as the proximate cause of his injury and to exclude other causes *fairly suggested by the evidence* to which it would be *equally reasonable* to attribute the injury... But on the other hand, where the evidence points to a certain cause which would make the defendant liable the plaintiff will not be denied redress merely because there may be some other *possible* cause for the accident; in such a case the question is for the jury... the law does not require the elimination of every *possible* cause of the accident other than that on which the plaintiff relies, but only such other causes, if any, *as fairly arise from the evidence*... All that a plaintiff is required to do is to prove, to the satisfaction of the court and jury, that the act or neglect of the defendant was the proximate cause of the injury; if he does this he can recover, even though the evidence to sustain his burden of proof does not absolutely exclude every possibility other than the one sought to be established.[95]

For the fourth query, the defendants had asserted that EOG's lack of inspection was an intervening act of negligence that superseded their own. The court rejected this, as a manufacturer could not be relieved of liability through the failure of an intermediate vendee to inspect. For the fifth query, the court acknowledged that historically the duty was owed to EOG,

---

[95] *Id.* at 24-25.

not the plaintiff but that had changed with *MacPherson v. Buick Motor*,[96] and was no longer the law. Further, the passage of time did not break the chain of causation. For the sixth question, the court ruled the partnership and corporation were essentially the same, as the partnership existed to avoid having to register as a foreign corporation in each state. On the seventh question, the court rejected the defendants' assertion that the statute of limitations ran from when the tank was turned over to EOG, not the date of the accident, saying a cause of action cannot accrue until an injury occurs. The judgment notwithstanding the verdict was reversed and remanded for consideration of the defendant's request for a new trial.

In *Moran*,[97] the case of the administratrix widow suing for the wrongful death of her husband Patrick J. Moran next came before the federal court of appeals. The district court had granted an involuntary nonsuit and dismissed. The court of appeals noted the two different theories argued, that of creation of public nuisance, which the court held could not be pursued, and negligence, which it held could be pursued and the non-suiting was incorrect, so reversed and remanded. The Supreme Court then denied a writ of certiorari.[98] In a retrial, the jury found the defendants not guilty. The plaintiff motioned for a new trial,[99] asserting the court's refusal to submit the issue of negligence in designing and building the tank and excluding the Bureau of Mines report. The court ruled "Unless there is a safer method available or it has been established in the custom or trade that the safety factor would be promoted by the use of a sphere rather than the cylinder, or that the hazard was increased by the use of the cylinder rather than the sphere, negligence cannot be inferred from the failure to do an act in some other way not shown to be safer... Where prudent, careful and cautious men, equally competent to judge of a difficult and doubtful situation, hold diametrically opposite views as to which of the two courses is safer, the adoption of either course cannot be negligence. In such cases there is no normal from which to depart."[100] The court of appeals[101] ruled both rulings were error and reversed.

---

[96] MacPherson v. Buick Motor Co., 217 N.Y. 382 (N.Y. App. Mar. 1916).
[97] Moran v. Pittsburgh-Des Moines Steel Co., 166 F.2d 908 (3rd Cir. Feb. 1948).
[98] Pittsburgh-Des Moines Steel Co. v. Moran, 334 U.S. 846 (June 1948).
[99] Moran v. Pittsburgh-Des Moines Steel Co., 86 F. Supp. 255 (W.D. Pa. July 1949).
[100] *Id.* at 266.
[101] Moran v. Pittsburgh-Des Moines Steel Co., 183 F.2d 467 (3rd Cir. July 1950).

## D. Fertilizer Explosion

| LEGAL ISSUES |
|---|
| ❖ Negligence in government program resulting in legal liability<br>❖ Tort Claims Act limited by acts of discretion |

On April 16, 1947, several explosions on ships carrying ammonium nitrate, among other cargo, killed more than 500 people in Texas City, Texas. Ammonium nitrate could be used either as fertilizer or in explosives. A fire started aboard the French-registered ship *Grandcamp* which had more than 2,000 tons of Fertilizer Grade Ammonium Nitrate (FGAN). This was intended for Europe in the early days of aid for occupied territories. The ship had formerly belonged to the U.S. government as part of the Liberty cargo ship program to supply the Allies in Europe during World War 2. It was assigned to the French government in late 1946 and operated by the French Line (*Compagnie Generale Transatlantique*), principally owned by the French government. Another nearby ship, *High Flyer*, had nearly 1,000 tons of FGAN plus a larger amount of sulfur. The *Grandcamp* exploded after 09:00 in the morning, destroying vast numbers of buildings in the port and leading to fires that caused additional damage. The *High Flyer* exploded past midnight.

In *Texas City Litigation*,[102] nearly 300 lawsuits were filed under a recently enacted federal law. The Federal Tort Claims Act was passed in 1946,[103] giving plaintiffs the ability to sue in the district court of the claimant or where the incident took place. The defendant would be the United States federal government, for any loss to property, bodily injury, or death, due to the negligent act of omission of a federal government employee acting within the scope of his employment. There were about 8,500 claims: 1,500 for deaths, 1,000 for personal injuries, and 6,000 for property damage. The allegations were that FGAN was a known dangerous explosive and was negligently manufactured, transported, and loaded onto ships by the federal government or its agents or employees without sufficient warning to the public. A single test case was put forward to trial, with the result then applying to all the other now consolidated cases.

---

[102] In Re Texas City Disaster Litigation, 197 F.2d 771 (5th Cir. June 1952).
[103] An Act to provide for increased efficiency in the legislative branch of the Government, c. 79, s.2, ch. 753, Title IV.

The district court ruled for the plaintiff and the government appealed. Among the errors assigned were that the Tort Claims Act had exceptions when the federal government employee was acting with due care to carry out a statutory function or when carrying out a discretionary function. The court of appeals found that nothing in the act specified liability for the government acting as a manufacturer or shipper. It looked at the three categories of federal employees or agents the plaintiffs identified and ruled that they were engaged in discretionary functions, making policy decisions for the government. Courts should not review decisions of other branches, like using old munitions plants to manufacture FGAN to aid the populations of war-torn Europe in growing their own food. The discretion was seen in the different judgments made by varied leaders regarding the manufacture and transport of FGAN and due care was exercised by those beneath them.

In *Dalehite*,[104] the case then came before the Supreme Court. The background of these shipments of FGAN was further explained to be usually manufactured at reactivated ordnance plants operated by private firms like DuPont. When those plants could not initially produce enough, private producers were called on to provide FGAN. In return, the government was to allocate future quantities it made back to the private firms. The FGAN on this shipment was allocated to the Lion Oil Co., which in turn sold it to the French Supply Council of the French government, whom the FGAN was consigned to for export. It was later loaded on to the *Grandcamp* and the *High Flyer* by independent stevedores hired by the French government. The Court held that the district court did not have jurisdiction, as a matter of law, given these facts.

Looking to the legislative history, the Court quoted a key intention as,

a highly important exception, intended to preclude any possibility that the bill might be construed to authorize suit for damages against the Government growing out of authorized activity, such as a flood control or irrigation project, where no negligence on the part of any government agent is shown and the only ground for the suit is the contention that the same conduct by a private individual would be tortious... The bill is not intended to authorize a suit for damages to test the validity of or provide a remedy on account of such

---

[104] Dalehite v. United States, 346 U.S. 15 (June 1953).

discretionary acts, even though negligently performed and involving an abuse of discretion.[105]

The Court interpreted the exception of discretionary acts to include whether they were performed negligently or wrongfully by federal agencies of employees in the exercise of discretion. This widened the exception beyond the Cabinet level discretion to initiate the program,

> the "discretionary function or duty" that cannot form a basis for suit under the Tort Claims Act includes more than the initiation of programs and activities. It also includes determinations made by executives or administrators in establishing plans, specifications, or schedules of operations. Where there is room for policy judgment and decision, there is discretion. It necessarily follows that acts of subordinates in carrying out the operations of government in accordance with official directions cannot be actionable. If it were not so, the protection of § 2680(a) would fail at the time it would be needed -- that is, when a subordinate performs or fails to perform a causal step, each action or nonaction being directed by the superior, exercising, perhaps abusing, discretion.[106]

All the asserted acts of negligence were done according to specifications drafted by the field director. Further, the negligence asserted in fighting the fires could not be sustained under the act, because there was no such liability for a publicly employed fireman in failing to contain a fire. Two justices did not take part in the decision and three justices dissented, meaning only four out of the nine justices constituted the majority in this decision. The dissenters focused on the fact that the FGAN was manufactured at government-owned plants to government specifications and shipped in support of a government program, saying "one of the unanticipated consequences of the Tort Claims Act has been to throw the weight of government influence on the side of lax standards of care in the negligence cases which it defends."[107]

Decrying the majority's opinion that moved contrary to the judicial trend in holding large producers to higher standards of care,

---

[105] *Id.* at 30.
[106] *Id.* at 35-36.
[107] *Id.* at 50.

This is a day of synthetic living, when, to an ever-increasing extent, our population is dependent upon mass producers for its food and drink, its cures and complexions, its apparel and gadgets. These no longer are natural or simple products, but complex ones whose composition and qualities are often secret. Such a dependent society must exact greater care than in more simple days, and must require from manufacturers or producers increased integrity and caution as the only protection of its safety and wellbeing. Purchasers cannot try out drugs to determine whether they kill or cure. Consumers cannot test the youngster's cowboy suit or the wife's sweater to see if they are apt to burst into fatal flames. Carriers, by land or by sea, cannot experiment with the combustibility of goods in transit.[108]

We believe it is the better view that whoever puts into circulation in commerce a product that is known or even suspected of being potentially inflammable or explosive is under an obligation to know his own product and to ascertain what forces he is turning loose. If, as often will be the case, a dangerous product is also a useful one, he is under a strict duty to follow each step of its distribution with warning of its dangers and with information and directions to keep those dangers at a minimum... we find that those [findings] as to the duty of further inquiry and negligence in shipment and failure to warn are sufficient to support the judgment.[109]

Subsequently, Congress passed a new law to help the victims,[110] whereby Congress accepted responsibility for losses due to the explosions and fires at Texas City. Claims could be submitted to the secretary of the Army, but it had to have been part of the civil lawsuit already filed. No claim could exceed $25,000. These payments were to be reduced by any amounts received in settlements except for life insurance proceeds. Attorney fees of up to 10% of the amounts paid were allowed.

---

[108] *Id.* at 51-52.
[109] *Id.* at 53, 56.
[110] An Act to provide for settlement of claims resulting from the disaster which occurred at Texas City, Texas, on April 16 and 17, 1947, c. 84, s. 1, ch. 864.

In *France*,[111] the country of France and the French Line sought to limit their liability under statute (see Chapter 2), for the fire and explosion aboard the *Grandcamp*. The United States was interpleaded, seeking to recover from France its costs of $16 million under the Texas City Relief Act. It became the assignee for the claims of $70 million, the total damages claimed by assignors. The district court listed the varied roles involved, such as freight and shipping agents, government maritime and food departments, stevedores, and the ship's captain, and their connections to the French government. This implied they should have been fully aware of the dangers of the FGAN and acted accordingly. Because the captain had not precluded smoking on the ship, which the court found had started the fire, not spontaneous combustion, he was negligent. He should have foreseen the danger of fire and the possibility of explosion. He did not use accepted methods to put out the fire, ruled the proximate cause, so the petition to limit liability was denied.

The court of appeals[112] had to decide if this was clearly erroneous, as the claimants had all died from the explosion, not from the fire. The district court found foreseeability, but the appellants disagreed, as no one, experts included, believed FGAN could cause such an explosion. This court ruled there was no foreseeability, reversed, and held there would be no liability,

> "It would be ironic indeed if the United States were permitted to impose liability for these claims on the Republic of France and the French Line in this litigation by claiming now that, unlike the officials and employees of the United States, the officials and employees of the French Government and the master of the *Grandcamp* should have known that FGAN was a dangerous explosive and that an explosion from fire should reasonably have been anticipated."[113]

Certiorari was then denied by the Supreme Court.[114] The railway that was destroyed in the explosion, the last non-assignor in the above matter,[115] had previously reached a legal settlement with its insurers.[116]

---

[111] In re Republic of France, 171 F. Supp. 497 (S.D. Tex. Mar. 1959).
[112] Republic of France & Compagnie Generale Transatlantique v. United States of America, 290 F.2d 395 (5th Cir. July 1961).
[113] *Id.*
[114] United States v. Republic of France, 369 U.S. 804 (Feb. 1962).

## E. Dam Failure

| LEGAL ISSUES |
|---|
| ❖ Private claims process used to quickly provide relief<br>❖ Issuing bonds to fund the cost of claims |

On March 12, 1928, around midnight, the St. Francis Dam serving Los Angeles failed, sending a wall of water, billions of gallons in volume, cascading down the San Francisquito Canyon. It traveled all the way to the Pacific Ocean, sweeping homes off their foundations and killing more than 400 people in its race to the sea. Conceived by William Mulholland, who had given Los Angeles its aqueduct, the dam had only begun operating less than a year before. The dam was a solid gravity type, designed and built by the city, and was 205 feet high at its tallest and 175 feet thick at the base. Conclusions by the quickly assembled governor's commission, in their final report, noted that no witness to the collapse had survived to describe it. In doing its best to reconstruct what happened in the dark that night,

> The magnitude and violence of the wave released on the failure of this dam are hard to visualize even by engineers familiar with floods and flood conditions. The rush of water attained a maximum depth of about 125 feet in the deepest of four sections measured by the commission within three-fourths of a mile below the dam. In the vicinity of San Francisquito Power House No. 2, approximately 1.5 miles along the channel downstream from the dam, an even greater depth was reported. The flood wave completely carried away the heavy concrete power house down to the generator floor, together with the less substantial buildings occupied by the operators and their families. The flood followed down San Francisquito Creek 9 miles from the dam and then down the Santa Clara River 43.5 miles to the ocean.

> It seems probable that the flood peak immediately below the dam exceeded half a million second-feet and this, together with its occurrence in the darkness, and the suddenness and violence of the wave, was such that very few of the persons in the constricted valley

---

[115] Republic of France and Compagnie Generale Transatlantique v. United States of America, 307 F.2d 493 (5th Cir. Aug. 1962).
[116] Texas City Terminal Railway Co. v. American Equitable Assurance Co., 130 F. Supp. 843 (S.D. Tex. Apr. 1955).

below the dam escaped with their lives... Even at a construction camp of the Southern California Edison Company, 16.5 miles below the dam, more than 80 out of about 140 perished. The damage caused in the path of the waters 52 miles to the sea was very great. The record of known dead at this time is 236 and 200 are still missing... The total property loss of farms, orchards, small towns and public utilities will certainly be many millions of dollars.[117]

This build of this dam was considered conservative, so with good foundations it should not have collapsed. The final report found that the material on the west side of the dam was a reddish conglomerate that lost its rocklike characteristics when wet, so collapse was inevitable. Failure likely occurred on the west side, given how far downstream those concrete blocks had been moved. The east side blocks merely toppled over, and the central blocks stayed upright. Attributing the failure to the foundations, it absolved the dam design as a contributing factor. It did recommend state supervision and control over the building and maintenance of dams.

The coroner's jury concluded that "construction and operation of a great dam should never be left to the sole judgment of one man, no matter how imminent, without check by independent expert authority."[118] They also found no criminal liability, as the district attorney's advice was,

> If, in the selection of this dam site... Mr. Mulholland, who has frankly stated that he was responsible for the matter, made an error of judgment, an honest mistake, and a catastrophe resulted, of course there could be no criminal responsibility attached to it... they left it to the individual judgment of one man and he undoubtedly exercised an honest opinion... If a man went up there and knowing that put up a dam on that treacherous foundation and said, I don't know anything about it, I will put it there anyway, he would be guilty of manslaughter, but if he used all the care and prudence that he was capable of using and found afterwards that he had made a mistake, there could be no criminal negligence.[119]

---

[117] REPORT OF THE COMMISSION APPOINTED BY GOVERNOR C. C. YOUNG TO INVESTIGATE THE CAUSES LEADING TO THE FAILURE OF THE ST. FRANCIS DAM NEAR SAUGUS, CALIFORNIA (Mar. 24, 1928).
[118] St. Francis Dam Inquisition, In the matter of the Inquisition upon the Body of Julia Rising, Verdict of Coroner's Jury (Apr. 12, 1928).
[119] *Id.*, Transcript, Vol 2, p. 818-19 (Apr. 10, 1928).

Unlike many disasters, the city's claims process was non-adversarial but without admitting liability. The city set up claims processing locations, with the first claims investigated, settled, and paid within four months. The claims for those who were employed, such as employees of the Bureau of Water and Power and the employees of Southern California Edison, filed their claims through the Industrial Accident Commission. All other claims were made to the Sub-Committee on Death and Disability Claims, which was part of the Citizens Restoration Committee. On July 15, 1928, the sub-committee reported the following statistics on claims:

Settled death claims: 293 for a total of $884,000.

Damages requested in these 293 claims: $3,587,000.

Unsettled death claims: 34 for a total of $1,200,000.

Settled injury claims: 38 for $32,000.

Damages requested in these 38 claims: $87,000.

Unsettled injury claims: 4 for a total of $176,000.[120]

There were sometimes significant differences between the claimed and settled amounts. Crisostoma Alvarado claimed $75,000 for the death of one adult and four children and his injuries but was awarded $20,000. S.M. Anderson claimed $22,000 for the loss of two adults but was awarded $2,000. Mae and Stephen Averill claimed $21,000 for the loss of one child but were awarded $4,000. Leora Basolo claimed and was awarded $12,000. George P. Boardman claimed and was awarded $23,000. Juan and Marguerite Carrillo claimed $325,000 for the loss of one adult and seven children and their injuries but were awarded $20,000. Pedro Cerna claimed $50,000 for the loss of one adult but was awarded $500. Aaron Coffer claimed $102,000 for the loss of one adult and his injuries but was awarded $9,000. Emily and Jack Crumley claimed $50,000 for the loss of one adult but were awarded $13,000.[121]

In settling these claims, the sub-committee had to go to great lengths to ensure the identity of the claimant, the identities and relationships for the decedents they were claiming upon, proof of their deaths or injuries,

---

[120] All claims per Sub-Committee on Death and Disability Claims report to Citizens Restoration Committee (July 15, 1928); all dollar amounts rounded to thousands.
[121] *Id.*

dependencies upon decedents, decedent's earning capacity, and guardianships of children who lost parents. They also had to deal with extravagant claims and improper claims. One settled death claimant asked for $200,000 for the loss of two adults. An unsettled death claim asked for $253,000 for losing one adult and two children, while another asked for $366,000 for losing two adults and three children, and a third asked for $309,000 for the loss of one adult and four children. Such large claims were not awarded, as the largest death award was $25,000, for the loss of six family members. There were also some claims refused, such as claiming for grandchildren, siblings, or the requests from the Mexican Consulate.

With the cost of cleanup, repairs, restoration of water services, and other liabilities related to the dam failure, the city, needing new funds to pay for all this, issued $250,000 in municipal bonds. In *Shelton*,[122] a taxpayer in the city decided to oppose the issuance, seeking an injunction. The request for an injunction was dismissed in the lower court and came to the state supreme court on appeal. The water and power board had the power under the city charter to determine an emergency existed such that it could borrow money to repair works for supplying the city with power or water. The city council passed an emergency ordinance authorizing the issuance of such bonds, paid for out of the water revenues of the board.

> Whereas, the destruction of the St. Francis dam has caused a serious emergency by reason of the fact that it has decreased the water storage capacity and the water supply of the City of Los Angeles 38,000 acre-feet; that a portion of the Los Angeles Aqueduct and Power House No. 2 were destroyed; that the same or other works were and now are necessary to the proper and adequate service of the City of Los Angeles with water and electric energy; that unless immediately restored, the reserve supply of water and electric energy and the peace, health and safety of the inhabitants of the City of Los Angeles, will be jeopardized. That no funds are immediately available for the construction and acquisition of the necessary works to insure an adequate supply of water and electric energy.[123]

The plaintiff's assertion was that the amount of bonds being issued was more than the annual income produced by the city and board and so

---
[122] Shelton v. City of Los Angeles, 206 Cal. 544 (Cal. Feb. 1929).
[123] *Id.* 340-47.

contrary to the statutory authorization of the board and the state constitution, which did not let a city indebt itself to an amount greater than one year's revenue without a special election voting on a tax increase. The board responded that the bonds would be paid out of a special fund and were not obligations of the city. The supreme court agreed that the obligations of the board were not obligations of the city. It noted that a special fund, not commingled with others of the city, was set up where the income of the water and power board is received, to be used for necessary operating expenses and the payment of principal and interest on indebtedness the board had issued. The supreme court rejected the plaintiff's argument and affirmed the decision to not grant an injunction.

In June 1929, the state legislature approved a new law[124] regarding the supervision of dams. Among other powers, it allowed for state inspectors to examine dams that were previously completed and to require repairs if necessary, or their alteration or removal; the approval of plans and specifications of new dams and oversight of their construction; and oversight of the maintenance and operation of all relevant dams. In *Bent Bros.*,[125] after a state inspection under the new law, work done on a flood control dam for the city of Stockton required alterations, such as moving the center arch upstream, and the left abatement downstream. When the plaintiff did the work that included those revisions and presented its invoice, payment was refused. The reason stated was that the old contract was voided by the state inspector's revisions. The court of appeals said,

> It is the settled law of this court that the interdiction of statutes impairing the obligation of contracts does not prevent the state from exercising its police powers for the general good of the public through contracts previously entered into between individuals may thereby be affected.[126]

The court said the state engineer, through injunctions and suits, could prevent contracts from being performed that created a danger to life and property. However, the court ruled where unforeseen circumstances arise, further publicizing and bidding on contracts was not required. The court held this petition should be granted and ordered the payment to be made.

---

[124] Cal. Stats. 1929, p. 1505.
[125] Bent Bros. v. Campbell, 101 Cal. App. 456 (Cal. App. Oct. 1929).
[126] *Id.* at 463.

## *Chapter 4*

# 1950 – 1974

Sometimes disaster occurs when the deaths of a few in turn impacts millions. After the end of World War 2, with the new decade of the 1950s, came the emerging waves of the baby boom generation. Giving a rhythm to this large cohort of young people no longer under the oppression of war or depression was the new sound of rock-n-roll. One of its leading lights was a young Texan named Charles Hardin Holley, better known as "Buddy Holly." With already half a dozen songs high in the music charts, Holly was riding high professionally and personally, as he had recently married. To avoid the problems with a cold bus while touring in Iowa, he decided to travel instead on a small airplane. On February 3, 1959, a date that would become forever known as "the day the music died," Holly and fellow musicians J.P. Richardson aka the "Big Bopper" and Ritchie Valens, along with their pilot, were killed when the plane crashed in a snowstorm.

The Civil Aeronautics Board undertook an investigation into the causes of this disaster. It believed the crash of the Beech Bonanza aircraft was to be attributed to the decision making of the 21-year-old pilot flying at night in wintery conditions,

> This accident, like so many before it, was caused by the pilot's decision to undertake a flight in which the likelihood of encountering instrument conditions existed, in the mistaken belief that he could cope with en route instrument weather conditions, without having the necessary familiarization with the instruments in the aircraft and without being properly certified to fly solely by instruments.[1]

---

[1] CIVIL AERONAUTICS BOARD, ACCIDENT INVESTIGATION REPORT, BEECH BONANZA N 3974N, MASON CITY, IOWA, FEBRUARY 3, 1959, FILE NO. 2-0001 (Sept. 15, 1959).

The report noted two important weather advisories, the first which advised of snow and lower visibility conditions and the second which indicated low ceilings and visibilities, and freezing drizzle, snow, and fog. Neither of these seemed to have been communicated to the pilot or the owner of the plane. The report stated that the pilot likely entered an area of complete darkness with no definite horizon and no ground lights. This would have required the pilot to depend solely on the plane's instruments, for which he was not trained or certified. The gusty winds would also have made understanding the controls difficult for such an inexperienced pilot. Lack of familiarity with certain instruments like the plane's attitude gyro would have led to confusion in an already highly disorienting situation.

The estates and families of the musicians would later become involved in various types of litigation. In *Holley*,[2] the parents of Buddy Holly sought to receive workmen's compensation for him, as he was killed while being transported from one work location to another. They asserted dependency upon him and won an award before the compensation board, despite his wife also receiving an award. The appeals court investigated the alleged dependency and noted evidence that Holly had paid 85% of his parents' household expenses, bought them a car, and paid for his mother's hospitalizations. The appellant General Artists suggested that perhaps these amounts were remuneration for services rendered but this was rejected by the court. In affirming the award, the court also ruled the award did not have to start after the parents' share of the estate was gone. Future legal actions by their estates involved royalties[3] and trademarks.[4]

Death would soon come to another young rock-n-roll star on tour. On April 17, 1960, Eddie Cochran was killed near Chippenham, England, when the taxi he was riding in spun and crashed. It was determined that the 20-year-old driver had engaged in dangerous driving. He was found guilty, given a deferred sentence, a fine, and loss of driving privileges for 15 years. The youthful innocence this era began with was to know many such tragedies. The first section of this chapter presents disasters from nature and those affecting the environment, and the second section discusses disasters arising from industrial activity and when humans take to the air.

---

[2] Claim of Holley v. GAC Super Productions, Inc., 23 A.D.2d 928 (N.Y. App. Div. May 1965).
[3] MCA Records, Inc. v. Allison, No. B199801 (Cal. App. June 2009).
[4] Wells' Dairy, Inc., v. The Estate of J.P. Richardson, Jr., a/k/a Richardson Family Trust, p/k/a "The Big Bopper," 89 F. Supp. 2d 1042 (N.D. Iowa Mar. 2000).

## 4.1 NATURE AND ENVIRONMENT

### A. Hurricane

| Legal Issues |
|---|
| ❖ Weather forecasts and warnings giving rise to legal liability<br>❖ Misrepresentation exception to federal tort claims |

In late June 1957, a tropical depression in the Gulf of Mexico quickly developed into a tropical storm then into a hurricane. It would be named Audrey, and hit the U.S. coast in Louisiana and Texas, taking the lives of more than 400 people. The deaths, injuries, and property damage would arise mainly from the storm surge that pushed up to 20 miles inland. The U.S. Weather Bureau, in issuing its new long-range forecasting report the week prior, had said there would be a storm or two to hit the Gulf Coast. About two days before the storm hit the shore, a hurricane watch was issued by the bureau. Advisories reported the storm's advance. The day before, a hurricane warning was sent to all relevant media, advising people to move now to higher ground. Not everyone moved quickly enough or received the news timely, especially those in low areas along the coast.

The recriminations would soon begin,

The United States Weather Bureau said today that Hurricane Audrey had been "one of the best forecast, best tracked and most forewarned of hurricanes in in history." Its statement by implication strongly denied complaints by some survivors in the Louisiana costal area that there had not been adequate advance warnings. "From press reports, an estimated 75,000 people in the threatened areas evacuated to higher ground and escaped possible death or injury because they heeded weather bureau warnings and advisories," the bureau said. Residents of low-exposed areas were advised early Wednesday—June 26—twenty-two hours before the storm's center hit the coast—to move to higher ground to escape the forecast rising tides."... The specific complaint heard most often from survivors was that they had been told... the hurricane would not hit the coast until Thursday night... Others complained they had no warning of the "tidal wave."[5]

---

[5] *Storm Warnings Held Among the Best,* N.Y. TIMES (June 30, 1957).

In *Bartie*,[6] a father sued the weather bureau for wrongful death. Plaintiff Whitney Bartie, no longer able to escape the flood on the Thursday morning, went to the roof with his wife and five children as the flood waters from the storm surge rose and winds raged. Despite joining hands, they were one by one swept away. He survived when the house disintegrated by grabbing onto and floating on a freezer until he was able to climb onto a tree limb. He remained there for many hours until rescued. He sued under the Federal Tort Claims Act discussed in Chapter 3. He was alleging that federal employees in the bureau were negligent in providing the proper advisories and warnings about the tidal wave of the hurricane, such as its path, intensity, speed, and its very existence. He had relied on their guidance in deciding how to act. He also alleged that he did not feel he had to leave, because he did not reside on lower-lying ground.

The government responded that it was not negligent, and that Bartie was contributorily negligent for not leaving his home sooner. It also said that the statutory duty of the bureau to forecast the weather did not create a relationship between the bureau and those using its forecasts to make it liable in tort for a faulty forecast. It further responded that all the bureau's activities fell under the discretionary function exception and the misrepresentation exception. The latter was one of the listed exceptions under the statute, which did not allow claims that arose out of misrepresentation. The court started its analysis by reviewing the storm and the bureau's response. On June 24, the bureau found the storm due south of Cameron, Louisiana, issuing a bulletin saying it was likely heading northwards. The next bulletin, on June 25, said it was headed northward, beginning to intensify. By 16:00, the bureau had issued an advisory this was now a hurricane, with winds up to 100 mph. The message also said that tides would rise on the coast on that day and the next. At 18:00, a special bulletin warned of rising tides and that those in low and exposed places should act now to not get stranded. An advisory at 22:00 repeated the northward direction and the rising tides. An advisory the morning of the 26th warned of the storm increasing in size, the wind velocity, and the rising tides, which would be 2-3 feet above normal. By 10:00, the tides were expected to be 5-8 feet above normal, and warnings were again to go to higher ground. Gales would hit the coast that night.

---

[6] Bartie v. United States, 216 F. Supp. 10 (W.D. La. Mar. 1963).

The consistent refrain in the messages was that the storm was intensifying, heading northward, the tides were rising far above normal, the wind was increasing, and those living on the coast in exposed or low-lying areas should head inland as soon as possible. Local broadcasts on radio and television tried to downplay the urgency, but these were not controlled by the bureau. It was from these broadcasts late at night on the 26th that the plaintiff apparently made up his mind to wait it out. Just after midnight, another special bulletin said that the storm would hit his area before noon on the 27th. The court ruled that the bureau's reporting on the inception, location, and direction of the storm was prompt and accurate.

The court then discussed the bureau's reporting of the speed of the hurricane, and therefore when it hit land, was not entirely prompt or accurate. This was due to the fact of hurricane forecasting being based on complex models requiring many evaluations using judgment and discretion, and the difficulty of getting planes on hazardous routes into the hurricane. The ability to predict the course of hurricanes did not have a high accuracy rate at this time. Quoting from expert scientific testimony,

> "Meteorological prediction is in general less accurate than prediction in any of the physical sciences. This is due to two reasons primarily. One, we have an incomplete knowledge and understanding of the physical laws which govern the atmosphere at present; and secondly, we suffer from lack of data and information on which to make predictions based on these physical principles. This is particularly true over most of the tropical oceans and continental regions because of the scarcity of weather information that is typically available from these areas… It would be my opinion that the Weather Bureau forecasters in the New Orleans hurricane forecast office made forecasts of the future positions and other characteristics of Hurricane Audrey which were commensurate with the state of hurricane forecasting at that time which were well within the probable errors of such forecasts at that time, or for that matter, at the present time. In spite of certain conflicting information, they were able to exercise good judgment and make forecasts which were as accurate as could be expected at that time."[7]

---

[7] *Id.* at 15.

The court held the bureau had no duty to warn the plaintiff and the plaintiff had failed to establish the bureau's negligence. Regarding the affirmative defenses, the court found that the activities of the bureau consisted of setting policy, making judgments, and exercising discretion, so fell within this exception, as outlined in the *Dalehite* case (see Chapter 3). The court also held that the claim was based on misrepresentations made by the bureau and such claims were not actionable under the tort claims act. This was unsuccessfully appealed to the circuit court, which affirmed, saying the findings were fully justified by the evidence,[8] and the Supreme Court then denied certiorari.[9]

In *Boudoin*,[10] the plaintiff owned a wharf struck during the hurricane by a barge carrying an oil rig and owned by the defendant. When the hurricane warnings were sent out, the tug pulling the large barge was directed to Cameron, Louisiana, to the defendant's dock, located a mile inland from the gulf and a mile southeast of the plaintiff's wharf. When the storm hit, the tug did all it could to stabilize the barge with tow lines, to take the pressure off lines connecting the barge to the defendant's dock. Being dragged to land by the barge, which had broken its moorings, the tug finally gave up, saving the men on the tug. After the tow lines were cut, the barge, lifted by the tide and winds, was pushed a mile across the flat terrain all the way to the plaintiff's wharf. There the barge crashed into it, witnessed by a man clinging desperately to the top of a telephone pole.

The plaintiff contended that the barge should not have been moored at Cameron; that the standard of conduct of the master and owner required mooring the barge further inland to protect it. The defendant's response was that this was an act of God for which it could not be held liable. The court did not believe the master should be held responsible for determining where the storm would strike and further, that his judgment was reasonable in remaining at Cameron, as others did, instead of heading up the channel to Lake Charles. The court held that this event was ultimately an act of God, and the master could not be held liable for his act of discretion during the hurricane.

---

[8] Bartie v. United States, 326 F.2d 754 (5th Cir. Jan. 1964).
[9] Bartie v. United States, 379 U.S. 852 (Oct. 1964).
[10] Boudoin v. J. Ray McDermott & Co., 176 F. Supp. 900 (W.D. La. Sept. 1959).

The court of appeals reversed, disagreeing with the district court's inferences.[11] This court focused on the days preceding the hurricane coming onshore and whether the barge should have been where it was, noting the tug had settled into Cameron at 18:00 on June 25. The court reviewed the bureau warnings, concluding the master had sufficient time the day prior to heed these warnings. Further, the district court should not have evaluated the master's decisions against those of the civilians who decided not to depart Cameron timely, as he had a different duty of care. Because the upper part of the dock was 3 feet above the water and the draft of the barge was 3 feet, any tide over 6 feet would push the barge over the dock. The warnings were for more than 6 feet above normal. As testified by experienced masters, the prudent thing to do was to take the barge the 50 miles north to Lake Charles, as most large ships did on the 26th. It ruled the master had not done a critical evaluation of the weather data, and without that, a defense using act of God could not be successful.

In *Reed*,[12] parents sued a funeral home for the loss of the body of their daughter. The plaintiff claimed to have identified his daughter's body at a second funeral home. Their insurance policy dictated burial using the first funeral home, to which he requested retrieval of her body. The court held for the defendant, as it was likely the father had never identified the body,

> Mr. Reed was disturbed because the body of his daughter could not be found and that he attempted to find the little girl's body... but could not find or identify the body... there were many bodies located both [funeral homes]; that these bodies were brought in approximately two days after Hurricane Audrey and were in a decomposed state... it was very difficult to identify most of the bodies and... they had mass burials... [he] had hundreds of bodies brought to his funeral home... these bodies were placed in sheds and were staked out for identification and treatment for preserving them... it was some days later before the bodies were brought in... most of the bodies had changed color, probably due to the salt water and the sun, and it was very difficult to identify the bodies unless there was specific identification, such as rings, etc.[13]

---

[11] Boudoin v. J. Ray McDermott & Co., 281 F.2d 81 (5th Cir. July 1960).
[12] Reed v. Sacred Hope Service Insurance, 125 So. 2d 238 (La. App. Dec. 1960).
[13] *Id.* at 240.

## B. Air Pollution

| LEGAL ISSUES |
| --- |
| ❖ National, state and local laws to prevent air pollution<br>❖ Requiring implementation of pollution control devices |

Around Halloween 1948, a smog rolled into the small city of Donora, Pennsylvania and before it lifted, 20 people had died. In early December 1952, a smog took hold of London, with an estimated 4,000 victims. Around Thanksgiving of 1966 in New York, a smog settled over the city, leading to the deaths of more than 160 people. By the mid-20$^{th}$ century, air pollution had become a serious health hazard, although it did not always coalesce at one time as it did in these incidents. The causes could differ by locality, with weather interacting with local airborne pollutants. On top of existing pollution from industry and other burnings in cities, the widespread popularity of the automobile added another factor to air pollution, as seen in the car-saturated cities of California by the 1960s.

For the Donora incident, in a smaller city of 14,000, the cause could more easily be placed upon the local zinc works. Lawsuits were filed against United States Steel and its subsidiary American Steel and Wire, but both were settled for a fraction of the claimed damages. However, some years before this incident, American Steel had not settled a lawsuit based on its production. In *Procz*,[14] the plaintiff had sued for damage to his farm from smoke and fumes emitted from American Wire and Steel's zinc works. The plaintiff asserted that the emitted zinc oxide and sulfur dioxide compounds attacked his crops and settled in the soil, making vegetation stop growing. This led to erosion and the loss of the top soil, making it unfit for cultivation, despite being over a mile away from the works. This was testified to by experts, but the trial court would not allow their testimony of these compounds' effect on the soil, due to their missing qualifications.

The defendant asserted this meant they could not show the zinc works were the cause of the farm's damage. The state supreme court did not agree, as there was testimony from other farmers how the winds flowed from the mill, the effect it had, the plaintiff's farming abilities, and the exclusion of other potential causes. The judgement for the plaintiff was

---

[14] Procz v. American Steel & Wire Co., 318 Pa. 395 (Pa. Apr. 1935).

affirmed. Fifteen years prior, another plaintiff[15] had successfully sued the same mill for the same reason. The plaintiff's wife had been taken seriously ill after the startup of this zinc mill and the court held that there was sufficient evidence of the health impacts from the mill's emissions.

In New York,

> A blanket of warm air covered the city yesterday, trapping pollutants and sending the air-pollution index close to the danger mark. Officials warned persons with heart, lung or respiratory ailments to stay indoors. From 6 A.M. to 10 A.M., the amount of sulphur dioxide, carbon monoxide and dust-carrying haze was so high that... the Commissioner of Air Pollution Control, was on the verge of calling the first-alert stage of the city's air pollution warning system. The air became clearer in the late morning and early afternoon, but the pollution shot up again in the evening... between 8 and 9 P.M... the pollution count was possibly the highest in the city's history.[16]

A study that year had demonstrated,

> Examination of total deaths in New York City by day of occurrence shows periodic peaks in mortality which are associated with periods of high air pollution. These peaks are usually associated with periods of low wind speed and temperature inversion conditions which permit air pollution to build up to high levels. Unlike the experience of London, fog is not a necessary part of this picture, and therefore the presence of these episodes is often not apparent at the time to most inhabitants. A characteristic feature of these episodes is the immediate rise in mortality occurring on the same day as the peaks of pollution. A second characteristic is their frequent influence on death rates in the 45- to 64-year age group as well as in those over 65. These characteristics suggest that if these excess deaths are related to air pollution (as we believe to be highly likely)... affecting the course of a variety of different diseases.[17]

---

[15] Burkhardt v. American Steel & Wire Co., 74 Pa. Super. 437 (Pa. Super. Ct. July 1920).
[16] *Smog Here Nears the Danger Point; Patients Warned,* N.Y. TIMES (Nov. 25, 1966).
[17] James McCarroll and William Bradley, *Excess Mortality as an Indicator of Health Effects of Air Pollution,* AM. J. PUBLIC HEALTH, Vol. 56. No. 11 (Nov. 1966).

Based on the levels of pollution, the city could implement restrictions ranging from voluntary fuel and driving reductions in stage 1, banning the use of fuel oil and limiting industry and non-essential driving in stage 2, or stringently reducing car traffic, industrial activity, and public transportation in stage 3, along with initiating curfews on lighting and heating. The city implemented varied revisions to its municipal code, but it was at the state level where action was needed. The state, along with its nearby states of New Jersey and Connecticut, acknowledging that pollution knew no state boundaries, agreed to a compact to investigate the causes of air pollution, establish standards, and administer programs to achieve those standards,

> WHEREAS, the signatory parties recognize that they have certain serious problems in common with respect to pollution of the atmosphere by man-made contaminants; and WHEREAS, the nature and sources of air pollution are such that the states' efforts can be effectively supplemented by control measures applicable to regional airsheds which cut across state boundaries; and WHEREAS, the signatory parties recognize that the protection and improvement of the quality of their common atmosphere is vested with local, state and national interests, for which they have a joint responsibility; and WHEREAS, the signatory parties have determined to establish a federal-interstate agency, with jurisdiction and powers adequate to cope with interstate air pollution problems.[18]

In *Oriental Boulevard*,[19] the plaintiff apartment owner was challenging a city ordinance that required upgrading apartment incinerators to decrease the emission of particulates into the air. The city commissioner for air pollution control could seal incinerators not complying with the law within a certain timeframe. The plaintiffs challenged the fact of apartment incinerators contributing to air pollution. The court rejected this as within the police powers delegated to the city. The court also rejected assertions of discrimination for different deadlines based on each apartment complex's number of dwellings. Other challenges based on the cost to comply, and unlawful searches to identify and seize the incinerators were also rejected. The court did find two triable issues, regarding the time to comply and the sizes of penalties. It soon went to the state's highest court.

---

[18] Mid-Atlantic States Air Pollution Control Compact, N.Y. Env. Conserv. L. § 21-1501.
[19] Oriental Boulevard Co. v. Heller, 58 Misc. 2d 920 (N.Y. Sup. Ct. Jan. 1969).

The court of appeals[20] rejected the need for a trial, and the idea that apartment incinerators were a small part of the city's pollution, saying government was entitled to deal with large problems piecemeal. The court said the legislative function must be able to choose among reasonable alternatives. As the plaintiff had made no attempt to comply in several years, their time argument was not persuasive. The court also ruled the cost was not shown to be disproportionate to the benefits, "considering the serious health hazard represented by aerial pollution... it is hardly permissible to allow aerial pollution to continue untrammeled because the necessary outlays to avoid the condition would cut into profit margins."[21]

The 1952 incident in London, led to the Clean Air Act in 1956.[22] It prohibited emitting dark smoke from chimneys, which were to minimize grit and dust. Furnaces were not to emit smoke, and smoke was not to be emitted by chimneys in smoke control areas. Other smoke sources could be deemed a statutory nuisance. These prohibitions and restrictions also applied to railways and ships, and local councils could insist on higher chimneys. A clean air council would advise the government. In the United States, progressively stronger federal clean air laws were enacted in 1955,[23] 1963,[24] 1967,[25] and 1970,[26] and the Environmental Protection Agency (EPA) was tasked with enforcing them.[27] The 1970 act required states to formulate plans for ambient air quality supporting public health and welfare. Based on certain established criteria, the EPA administrator would approve them. Increasingly, the federal government would become involved in air pollution standards and enforcement.

---

[20] Oriental Boulevard Co v Heller, 27 N.Y.2d 212 (N.Y. Nov. 1970).
[21] *Id.* at 221.
[22] An Act to make provision for abating the pollution of the air, 4&5 Eliz. 2. c. 52.
[23] Pub. L. 84-159, An Act to provide research and technical assistance relating to air pollution control.
[24] Pub. L. 88-206, An Act to improve, strengthen, and accelerate programs for the prevention and abatement of air pollution.
[25] Pub. L. 90-148, An Act to amend the Clean Air Act to authorize planning grants to air pollution control agencies; expand research provisions relating to fuels and vehicles; provide for interstate air pollution control agencies or commissions; authorize the establishment of air quality standards, and for other purposes.
[26] Pub. L. 91-604, An Act to amend the Clean Air Act to provide for a more effective program to improve the quality of the Nation's air.
[27] Special Message from the President to the Congress About Reorganization Plans to Establish the Environmental Protection Agency and the National Oceanic and Atmospheric Administration (July 9, 1970).

In 1965, the federal government passed a revision to the Clean Air Act for automobile emissions.[28] Finding the big four American automobile manufacturers had conspired to avoid developing antipollution technology, the federal government took them to court. In a consent decree, they agreed to no longer do so.[29] The court did not allow in many potential intervenors, including states and New York City, believing their intent was to block the settlement to force a trial to get a guilty verdict, so they could then assert treble damages against the defendant under the Clayton Act. As the consent decree achieved the complaint's purposes, was a certain result, and much faster, the court held it was in the public interest and approved the decree. However, the grand jury records were not sealed.

With access to grand jury records, the intervenors, comprising states, counties, cities, and individuals representing farmers, sued[30] the automakers. Asserting automobile exhaust accounted for most air pollution, the court allowed them to sue for damages in class actions, on behalf of their constituents. The court of appeals[31] focused on the need to assert an injury to business or property and the injury arose by reason of an antitrust violation. Because the governmental entities did not allege injury to their or their constituents' business or property, they could not sue individually or as class representatives for damages. Farmers also could not, as their commercial activities were not in the target area of the carmakers' anticompetitive behavior. The court however did let the plaintiffs seek injunctive relief. The case returned to the district court[32] for injunctive relief requiring the automakers to retrofit pollution control devices on their brand of vehicles. The court held it only had the power to issue injunctions that cured anticompetitive behavior, not to require installation of pollution control devices, dismissing all the lawsuits asking for injunctive relief. With 22 states joining in, the court of appeals affirmed, that it could not require goals unrelated to the purposes of antitrust law.[33]

---

[28] Pub. L. 89-272, An Act to amend the Clean Air Act to require standards for controlling the emission of pollutants from gasoline powered or diesel powered vehicles, to establish a Federal Air Pollution Control Laboratory, and for other purposes.
[29] United States v. Automobile Manufacturers Ass'n, 307 F. Supp. 617 (C.D. Cal. Apr. 1969).
[30] In re Motor Vehicle Air Pollution Control Equipment, 52 F.R.D. 398 (C.D. Cal. Sept. 1970).
[31] California v. Automobile Manufacturers Ass'n, 481 F.2d 122 (9th Cir. June 1973).
[32] In re Multidistrict Vehicle Air Pollution, 367 F. Supp. 1298 (C.D. Cal. Nov. 1973).
[33] In re Multidistrict Vehicle Air Pollution. State of Washington v. Automobile Manufacturers Association, 538 F.2d 231 (9th Cir. June 1976).

## C. Landslide

| LEGAL ISSUES |
|---|
| ❖ Siting and managing coal tips defining operator legal liability<br>❖ Proof of negligence not required for damages |

On October 21, 1966, a landslide originating from a collapsed coal mine slag heap (spoil tip) at Aberfan, near Merthyr Tydfil, Wales, buried a school and homes below it, resulting in the deaths of 116 children and 28 adults.

> It was 9.15 and the school had just finished morning prayers when the million tons of coal waste, rocks, and water crumpled 800 feet down the Aberfan mountain. The children were due to start their week's half-term holiday at noon. But many children never reached school at all. Fog delayed a busload of 50 seniors and juniors from the village of Mount Pleasant near by. Some decided to walk - and arrived late enough to miss the landfall... A row of six cottages between the schools was buried, however, and a farmhouse farther up in the mountain swept away. Minutes before, the woman who lived there had taken her five children into Mountain Ash on a shopping trip. But possibly 15 adults died in the row of cottages and in another terrace of seven houses, a post office, and sweet shop in Moy Road just across the street...
>
> By dusk, more than 2,000 people were at work among the rubble. Miners abandoned shifts to come to the scene; factories closed to enable men to join the rescue work... Mothers and grandmothers scrambled at the rubble with their bare hands to find children lost somewhere in the waste of destruction... One of the bodies recovered was that of the deputy head teacher, Mr D. Beynon. A rescuer said: "He was clutching five little children in his arms as if he had been protecting them." Last night the parents of every schoolchild in Aberfan, Merthyr Vale, and Mount Pleasant met at Merthyr Vale school to hold a grim and final rollcall for all the children still "unaccounted for." Before the meeting Mr Griffiths appealed to outsiders to keep away from the meeting. "It will be a dreadful and emotional scene. But we have to find out."[34]

---

[34] *150 feared lost in Welsh landslip,* THE GUARDIAN (Oct. 22, 1966).

An inquest was called for by Parliament, under the Tribunals of Inquiry (Evidence) Act of 1921,[35] and the Welsh secretary appointed a three-member panel within days of the disaster. The tribunal sat for nearly three months taking evidence and visited both the site and the seven coal tips surrounding it. The tribunal would issue a report that went into great detail on all that happened that day and the years leading up to it.[36] The tribunal intended to answer four questions: 1. What exactly happened? 2. Why did it happen? 3. Need it have happened? (was it reasonably foreseeable) 4. What lessons can be learned? The report noted that there were no regulations regarding the safety of spoil tips and the issue was regularly ignored by those in the mining profession. The tribunal would conclude there was ignorance shown by those charged with the daily management of the tips; ineptitude shown by those supervising them; and a consistent failure to communicate shown by those with knowledge of tip safety.

The area had seven tips, the tallest of which was 171 feet and contained 706,000 cubic yards of material. Tip 7, the one that slipped, was the newest at about eight years old. It had grown to 111 feet tall, with about 297,000 cubic yards of material, with 30,000 cubic yards of that being comprised of tailings. The other tips did not contain tailings, the remnants of the mined minerals after the coal was extracted. The leftovers from the mining were taken by rail up to a crane on the side of the mountain, which would dump the contents onto the tip, growing it in size. The report noted that the key issue was water, and placing tips over places where water flowed, without adequate drainage. Prior tip slips at this site had occurred due to the placement of tips without considering water flows. Additional evidence showed that there were consistent sources of water below the tip. Locals regularly complained of flooding to the borough council, who passed this on the National Coal Board (NCB), as water would regularly saturate local homes. An understanding was never reached, and a permanent solution to the consistent water problems never implemented. NCB's not addressing the varied water issues at Aberfan was described by the tribunal as a "scandalous state of affairs."[37]

---

[35] An Act to make provision with respect to the taking of evidence before and the procedure and powers of certain Tribunals of Inquiry, 11&12 Geo. 5. c. 7.

[36] INQUIRY INTO THE ABERFAN DISASTER, REPORT OF THE TRIBUNAL APPOINTED UNDER THE TRIBUNALS OF INQUIRY (EVIDENCE) ACT, 1921.

[37] *Id.* p. 23.

Regarding the duty owed to those who populated the area around and below the tip,

> It has been asserted by many witnesses that no one could foresee that if there was a slide of No. 7 tip the village would be involved. Such an assertion can absolve no one from criticism for a failure to care for the stability of tips... Only a short way below the tip stood the old farmhouse of Hafod-Tanglwys-Uchaf which, as we know, was inhabited at the time of the disaster. Men and women, we have been told, took their leisure upon the mountain below the tip; children played and had lessons in nature study there. All these people were owed the duty of being kept free from harm from the tips. So that the debate upon whether anyone ever thought the material would slide as far as the village is unnecessary and largely irrelevant to determine what should have been foreseen in order to bring into being proper safety precautions. My lord, the place for colliery waste was upon the tip; the duty of the owners of it, the National Coal Board, was to keep it there. The moment this situation changed by a fall of the tip on the mountain land below, of no matter what dimensions, the danger of a breach of that duty arose, as did a situation which called for a careful and conscientious investigation.[38]

While generally the 500 or so tips in Wales had caused few problems, the fact that this area had had several slips in recent years should have called for a concerted response by those responsible. The tribunal rejected an assertion of villainy, instead saying this was a case of ineptitude, poor supervision, and the lack of heeding clear warnings. The report described how, after part of the tip liquified, thousands of tons of colliery rubbish slid down the mountain, taking out the mountain cottages, crossed an unused canal, surmounted a railway embankment, and buried a school and 18 houses. Just prior to the disaster, the men working on the tip first noticed a 10-foot depression in the tip and the rails used to hold the crane had fallen into this depression. By the time it was reported by workers, and they returned to the tip, it had increased to a 20-foot depression. The crane driver, who had been told to move the crane as far as possible from this hole, testified that,

---

[38] *Id.* p. 24-25.

> I was standing on the edge of the depression. I was looking down into it, and what I saw I couldn't believe my eyes. It was starting to come back up. It started to rise slowly at first. I still did not believe it, I thought I was seeing things. Then it rose up after pretty fast, at a tremendous speed. Then it sort of came up out of the depression and turned itself into a wave—that is the only way I can describe it—down the mountain... towards Aberfan village... into the midst.[39]

The feeling expressed by miners in the area was that although they knew there was a danger of the tip sliding, their insisting on fixing it might bring about the closure of the colliery. The local MP, S.O. Davies, expressing the fears of the miners, was asked, and answered,

> Then are we to understand that you went through the tortuous, and no doubt tortured, process of thought of weighing one against the other, the risk to life on the one hand and the risk of colliery closure on the other, and came down in favour of taking no action which might risk colliery closure? Mr Davies, think about the question. You understand it is a question of considerable gravity. [Davies] Yes, I have thought, if I may say so. But I had to consider the general feelings and the desires of the mass of people in that ward; and if I had had an official approach made to me about that tip, I should not like to tell the Inquiry that we could have stopped it, quite frankly. But if I had been *asked* to do so I would have done it.[40]

The tribunal found there were no statutory provisions for tip safety and so they were not part of regular mine inspections. The tribunal noted that the legal liability of the NCB for death, non-fatal injury, and property damage was clear. This was based upon the general principle established in the prior century, which stated "If a person brings, or accumulates, on his land anything which, if it should escape, may cause damage to his neighbour, he does so at his peril. If it does escape, and cause damage, he is responsible, however careful he may have been, and whatever precautions he may have taken to prevent the damage."[41] A 1921 decision reiterated this applied to tip owners, and negligence need not be proven.[42]

---

[39] *Id.* p. 30.
[40] *Id.* p. 33.
[41] Rylands v. Fletcher, L.R. 3 H.L. 330 (July 1868).
[42] Attorney-General v. Cory Brothers and Co., Ltd. 1921 1 A.C. 521.

The tribunal next turned to who was blameworthy, in a moral sense, not in legal liability. It started with the NCB, owners since nationalization in 1947. In 1944, tip no. 4 had seriously slipped but there seem to be no memory of it. Tip no. 5 started having the problem and despite assurances, was not regularly inspected and continued to be used. No precautions were taken against slippage and the same continued with the subsequent introductions of tips no. 6 and no. 7. There also was no civil engineering evaluation of the site of tip no. 7, which soon ran over an existing stream. It was based on a plan "he would have realized was utter nonsense had he cast even a superficial glance up at the mountain from his colliery office."[43]

The tribunal said that those who inspected the site,

"were jointly and severally quite unsuited by training to come to an unaided decision as to the suitability of the proposed site. To recapitulate: they had no Ordnance Survey map, and they took no plan with them, because none existed; they made no boreholes; they came to no conclusion regarding the limits of the tipping area; and they consulted no one else... They arranged for no drainage, for they considered none necessary. It was a case of the blind leading the blind... In our judgment, such inspection as... made was worthless."[44]

The tribunal focused next on the 1963 slip of tip no. 7 and the properties of tailings to increase the potential for slips. Experts testified that any experienced engineer would have immediately ordered a cessation to tipping on no. 7 but tipping continued, and there was no inspection by qualified engineers. Further incidents at tip no. 7 in the months and years before it slid and in nearby tips were sufficient to put the NCB on notice to a coming issue and the need to act. Its conclusions as to liability focused on the NCB, which had started the inquiry by blaming collective geological factors before finally accepting its fault at the end. Finding this disaster to be completely foreseeable, the tribunal assigned the blame to various NCB officials, and castigated its leader, Lord Roben. A new mining statute was soon enacted that addressed the safety of tips.[45]

---

[43] *Id.* p. 50.
[44] *Id.*
[45] An Act to make further provision in relation to tips associated with mines and quarries; to prevent disused tips constituting a danger to members of the public; and for purposes connected with those matters, 1969 c. 10.

## D. Well Blowout

| LEGAL ISSUES |
|---|
| ❖ Damage from oil well blowouts resulting in legal liability<br>❖ Requirement for public hearings before oil lease approval |

On January 28, 1969, a blowout occurred on an off-shore drilling platform near Santa Barbara, California, leading to an oil spill continuing into the next month. While no human deaths were recorded, it did lead to the deaths of thousands of local birds and other fauna and despoiled the beaches of local islands. The ability to drill for oil offshore in this area had a long legal history. In 1953, the federal government passed the Submerged Lands Act,[46] which gave the right and title to land lying under navigable water within a state's boundaries to each state. This included any natural resources located there, and the right to administer and lease such land and natural resources. The seaward boundary of a coastal state was three geographic miles off its coastline. The federal government retained the rights to natural resources outside this boundary on the Continental Shelf.

A second act, the Outer Continental Shelf Lands Act,[47] had the United States extend federal jurisdiction to all subsoil and seabed of the continental shelf seaward of those lands it had just granted to the states. Jurisdiction was also extended to artificial islands or fixed structures in this area. The secretary of the interior was given the power to grant mineral leases to these lands, and to promulgate rules regarding prevention of waste and conservation of natural resources. Adjacent state law was to become the United States law within these areas. There were other provisions regarding the bidding, leasing, and operations of mineral leases and the ability of the federal government to penalize violations or cancel such leases. Leases were to be let only at the current market value. The government retained the rights to certain minerals and gases, such as uranium and helium, and could require that lessees post surety bonds.

---

[46] Pub. L. 83-31, An Act to confirm and establish the titles of the States to lands beneath navigable waters within State boundaries and to the natural resources within such lands and waters, to provide for the use and control of said lands and resources, and to confirm the jurisdiction and control of the United States over the natural resources of the seabed of the Continental Shelf seaward of State boundaries.

[47] Pub. L. 83-213, An Act to provide for the jurisdiction of the United States over the submerged lands of the outer Continental Shelf, and to authorize the Secretary of the Interior to lease such lands for certain purposes.

In *California*,[48] the predecessor of these acts was a Supreme Court decision on who, the state of California or the United States, owned the land between the low-water mark and three miles off it. This suit concerned the oil and gas rights that lay beneath those waters. The federal government had filed suit because it claimed those lands out to three nautical miles, but California had been leasing these areas for oil and gas drilling and so was trespassing. The state's response was that an area to three English miles was granted to the original thirteen colonies and California had been admitted to the Union on an equal basis with those states. The Court rejected this, saying "And as peace and world commerce are the paramount responsibilities of the nation, rather than an individual state, so, if wars come, they must be fought by the nation… The state is not equipped in our constitutional system with the powers or the facilities for exercising the responsibilities which would be concomitant with the dominion which it seeks."[49] It held the United States owned these areas.

Improved technologies created the ability to drill for oil further offshore, which led to a new case that more clearly defined how the definitions of the state's coastlines were impacted by inland waters.[50] Federal leases were soon let in the areas owned by the United States, including one leased to partnership that included Union Oil. This company was drilling a new well called A-21 and had progressed down more than 3,000 feet, when, after removing the drill bit, a column of oil and natural gas exploded back up to the oil platform. When the workers were finally able to cap the wellhead, the real problem started. According to regulations, there was supposed to be 300 feet of conductor casing inserted into the borehole that was being drilled, to prevent the oil and gas from leaking into the bedrock outside the hole. There was supposed to be nearly three times that length of surface casing inside the conductor casing. Because of a waiver from the regulator, there was an insufficient amount of the conducting casing, and no surface casing. So, when the oil and gas, pushed upwards under intense pressure, found a capped wellhead, the pressure pushed the oil and gas out into the surrounding sandstone, as the borehole was not protected by sufficient casing. From this, the oil spill then grew.

---

[48] United States v. California, 332 U.S. 19 (June 1947).
[49] *Id.* at 35-36.
[50] United States v. California, 381 U.S. 139 (May 1965).

In *Santa Barbara*,[51] the court of appeals addressed requests for an injunction by the county and city of Santa Barbara and a former state senator against the secretary of the interior, other officials, and the oil companies. The court noted the secretary had entered leases with the oil companies pursuant to the Outer Continental Shelf Lands Act. After the blowout, the secretary ordered a halt to drilling and production in the Santa Barbara Channel, and called for recommendations to stop the current seepage and avoid future incidents. The district court, reviewing the applicable regulations, denied the injunction, finding no right to hearings before more drilling could occur, and that there would be no irreparable injury if such hearings did not take place. The court of appeals, limited in its review, found the district court had not abused its discretion.

In *Malley*,[52] the county sought to prohibit the Army Corps of Engineers from granting applications without a public hearing, based on regulations addressing national security and navigation. After certiorari was denied by the Supreme Court,[53] but before the court of appeals ruled, the regulations were revised to specifically exclude the hearings plaintiffs sought,

> 3) Since the Corps of Engineers considers only the effect on navigation and national security, public hearings will not normally be held in connection with applications for permits for artificial islands or fixed structures on Outer Continental Shelf lands under mineral lease from the Department of the Interior which has responsibility for other aspects of the public interest. Public hearings will be held by the Corps of Engineers only when in the District Engineer's judgment opponents have a reasonable complaint based on interference with navigation or on adverse effects on national security.[54]

---

[51] County of Santa Barbara, a Political Subdivision of the State of California, and the City of Santa Barbara, a Municipal Corporation of the State of California v. Walter J. Hickel, Secretary of the Interior, United States of America, Alvin Weingand v. Walter J. Hickel, Secretary of the Interior, William T. Pecora, Director, United States Geological Survey, D. W. Solanas, Regional Supervisor, Oil and Gas Division, United States Geological Survey, Lee A. Dubridge, Science Advisor to the President of the United States, John S. Steinhart, Office of Science and Technology and Executive Secretary to the Special Panel on the Future of the Union Oil Lease, Gulf Oil Company, Mobil Oil Corporation, Texaco, Inc., Union Oil Co., 426 F.2d 164 (9th Cir. Apr. 1970).

[52] County of Santa Barbara, a Political Subdivision of the State of California v. Robert J. Malley, Los Angeles District Engineer, Corps of Engineers, 426 F.2d 171 (9th Cir. Apr. 1970).

[53] County of Santa Barbara v. Malley, 396 U.S. 950 (Nov. 1969).

[54] *Id.* at 174.

In *Minier*,[55] the district attorney of Santa Barbara County had attempted to stop the drilling and production of oil in the channel using threatened legal action. He had been enjoined by the district court from doing so. The court of appeals noted this action concerned the leases to the partnership of Union Oil, Texaco, Humble Oil, and Phillips Petroleum, which had been involved in the blowout. The district attorney had served a notice on the oil companies and their executives to abate a nuisance. The nuisance was either the flow of oil and gas or the drilling for oil or gas. Similar nuisance notices were served on the businesses supplying the oil companies with products and services. These notices were based upon a provision in the California penal code,

> Every person who maintains, permits or allows a public nuisance to exist upon his or her property or premises, and every person occupying or leasing the property or premises of another who maintains, permits or allows a public nuisance to exist thereon, after reasonable notice in writing from a health officer or district attorney or city attorney or prosecuting attorney to remove, discontinue or abate the same has been served upon such person, is guilty of a misdemeanor, and shall be punished accordingly; and the existence of such nuisance for each and every day after service of such notice shall be deemed a separate and distinct offense.[56]

The district court held that the district attorney intended to bring as many prosecutions as possible to effectively shut down the operations in the channel. The district attorney asserted there were remedies available under state law to those notified. The court of appeals said that some small businesses might rather stop doing business with the oil companies instead of seeking that legal remedy, so the district court's ruling of irreparable injury was not clearly erroneous. The court of appeals said that the district attorney's actions were intended to frustrate a federal power. In affirming the district court, the court held that while a federal court could not issue an injunction to stay proceedings in a state court, these notices were not "in a state court" until a crime had been committed.

---

[55] Union Oil Company of California, a Corporation, and Fred L. Hartley v. David D. Minier, Phillips Petroleum Company, a Corporation, and Frank Davis v. David D. Minier, Texaco, Inc., a Corporation, and Wallace A. Avery v. David D. Minier, Crandall D. Jones and Humble Oil Refining Company, a Corporation v. David D. Minier, 437 F.2d 408 (9th Cir. Dec. 1970).
[56] *Id.* at 410.

In *Oppen*,[57] fishermen financially injured by the oil spill sued Union Oil for damages. Upon settling, the defendant objected to the district court agreeing that the oil spill leading to the reduction in aquatic life was a legally compensable harm. The court of appeals noted that negligence did not usually allow for pure economic losses but there were cases where it was allowed, such as in maritime cases and in California law, even when there was no privity, or when special relationships existed. The court framed the question as whether the oil companies owed a duty to the fishermen to refrain from negligent conduct in drilling operations which could foreseeably diminish the fish in the channel and so injure fishermen's livelihood. To this the court answered yes, as this was easily understood by the average schoolchild, thereby affirming the district court's decision.

In *Gulf Oil*,[58] the oil company tried to overturn the secretary of the interior's suspension of all oil drilling in the channel. The secretary cited an obligation to all natural resources on the continental shelf, not just the oil and gas resources. The National Environmental Policy Act of 1969[59] made environmental protection mandatory for all federal government organizations. He needed time to convince Congress to permanently cancel these leases. The court of appeals, noting risks if the leases were canceled and bore holes were not properly capped before abandonment, affirmed the suspension order, but said it had a limited life, as only Congress could permanently cancel leases. In *Union Oil*,[60] the four oil companies in the Santa Barbara partnership complained about the suspension order concerning platform C, which had not gone online before the blowout. The secretary determined it would not be consistent with protection of the environment. The court of appeals held that for the suspension to not be a permanent taking, the secretary's reasons had to not be arbitrary and capricious and be conditioned on the occurrence of future events. The oil companies finally agreed to pay damages to the county, city, and state.[61]

---

[57] Union Oil Company v. James J. Oppen and John J. Masterson, 501 F.2d 558 (9th Cir. June 1974).

[58] Gulf Oil Corporation v. The Honorable Rogers C. B. Morton, Secretary of the Interior of the United States of America, 493 F.2d 141 (9th Cir. Mar. 1974).

[59] Pub. L. 91-190, An Act to establish a national policy for the environment, to provide for the establishment of a Council on Environmental Quality, and for other purposes.

[60] Union Oil Company of California v. The Honorable Rogers C. B. Morton, Secretary of the Interior of the United States of America, 512 F.2d 743 (9th Cir. Apr. 1975).

[61] *$9-Million Ends Suit on Oil Spill*, N.Y. TIMES (July 24, 1974).

## E. Chemical Dumping

| LEGAL ISSUES |
|---|
| ❖ Limiting liability for chemical waste transferred<br>❖ Use of Superfund law to remediate and recover funds |

In April 1953, the Love Canal site (named after its founder) in the city of Niagara Falls, New York, was sold by the Hooker Chemical Company to the city for $1. This site was an abandoned canal that had been only partially dug out and subsequently was used as a landfill. The city had condemned other properties in the immediate area, intending to build a school for its growing population. A clause was added to the sale agreement absolving the company from liability. The reason was that the company had, over the prior years, been using the landfill site as a dumping ground for chemical waste products from its manufacturing processes, including some known carcinogens. Despite lining the landfill with clay, subsequent construction activity punctured the protective barrier. After a period of heavy rains, odd vapors appeared in the basements of homes adjacent to the landfill. Upon investigation, homes closest to the landfill had the most noxious vapors. Then, a series of birth defects and other health issues emerged over time among area residents. The state and federal governments became involved in both the cleanup and seeking remediation damages, and victims sued.

In *Hooker Chemicals*,[62] the federal government in 1979 and later the state of New York filed suit against Hooker and the city for costs and damages and an injunction for remedial actions. The city cross-claimed against Hooker. It was alleged the leakage from the plant entered the Niagara River and could enter the water supply and so violated the Safe Drinking Water Act, the Resource Conversation and Recovery Act, the Clean Water Act, and the Rivers and Harbors Act, plus various state statutes, and was a public nuisance. After years of varied litigation actions, a settlement discussion was initiated. At that time, four citizen groups sought permission to intervene, as did the Ontario government.

---

[62] United States of America, the State of New York v. Hooker Chemicals & Plastics Corp., Hooker Chemical Corp., Occidental Petroleum Investment Co., Occidental Petroleum Corp. & City of Niagara Falls, N.Y. ("S"-Area Landfill), Hooker Chemicals & Plastics Corp., City of Niagara Falls, New York, Niagara Environmental Action, Ecumenical Task Force of the Niagara Frontier, Inc., Pollution Probe Foundation, and Operation Clean Niagara, by Its President, Margherita Howe, 749 F.2d 968 (2nd Cir. Nov. 1984).

The permission for the Canadian province was granted, to represent the legitimate interests of that government and its citizens, but permission for the four citizen groups (two American, two Canadian) was denied. The district court believed their interests could be represented by their respective governments, but they could still serve as amicus, calling and cross-examining witnesses. The groups then appealed, asserting a right to intervene under the mentioned acts, but the court of appeals disagreed that a citizen could intervene in suits the government initiated under the emergency powers of those acts. They also asserted the right to intervene under the FRCP if their interests were not adequately represented by the parties. The court of appeals rejected this, not finding any abuse of discretion by the district court, quoting from a Supreme Court decision,

> Under the parens patriae concept, however, a state that is a party to a suit involving a matter of sovereign interest is presumed to represent the interests of all its citizens. Thus, to intervene in a suit in district court in which a state is already a party, a citizen or subdivision of that state must overcome this presumption of adequate representation. A minimal showing that the representation may be inadequate is not sufficient. The applicant for intervention must demonstrate that its interest is in fact different from that of the state and that that interest will not be represented by the state.[63]

The settlement was presented to the court for approval.[64] The court noted the defendant only agreed after Comprehensive Environmental Response, Compensation, and Liability Act (CERCLA) claims were added. The court listed the following in approving the settlement. There was concern over non-aqueous phase liquids (NAPL), comprising 15 compounds with a total weight of 25,000 tons. On top of the bedrock in the landfill were three areas, the top one of mostly man-made materials like wood and gravel, then a 16-foot layer of sand and silt, then a third layer of clay over varying thickness and with varied cracks and holes. The direction of the water was toward the river. The bedrock comprised dolomite of 125 feet and shale of 60 feet with top layers more permeable than the bottom ones. The water flow was away from the river, despite a slope towards it. The water treatment plant's intake pipes passed through the landfill.

---

[63] *Id.* 984-85.
[64] United States v. Hooker Chemical & Plastics Corp., 607 F. Supp. 1052 (W.D.N.Y. Apr. 1985).

The court determined that the settlement agreement addressed the current and future issues in both the landfill and the water treatment plant and approved it, despite Ontario having concerns that the NAPL could migrate under the river over to its side. The agreement focused on the remedial programs of containment, monitoring, maintenance, and environmental health and safety. Before initiating any remedial activity, Hooker had to submit detailed plans to the EPA and the state. If they rejected the plan, any party could petition the court to determine whether the remedial program was consistent with the agreement. The program was to continue for 35 years, and Hooker had to put up a $20 million surety to insure against its non-performance for financial reasons.

CERCLA was passed in 1980, giving authority to the president to take action,

> Whenever (A) any hazardous substance is released or there is a substantial threat of such a release into the environment, or (B) there is a release or substantial threat of release into the environment of any pollutant or contaminant which may present an imminent and substantial danger to the public health or welfare, the President is authorized to act, consistent with the national contingency plan, to remove or arrange for the removal of, and provide for remedial action relating to such hazardous substance, pollutant, or contaminant at any time (including its removal from any contaminated natural resource), or take any other response measure consistent with the national contingency plan which the President deems necessary to protect the public health or welfare or the environment.[65]

The state health department surveyed area residents in 1978 to determine the source of their health problems. Hooker then attempted to gain access to this medical information.[66] They based the request on its relevancy to the litigation, that it was not protected by state law, and privacy interests would be protected by a proposed protection order. Specifically, it needed the health data to adequately prepare a defense, but the state argued this data would not be used in its litigation. The court

---

[65] Pub. L. 96-510, An Act to provide for liability, compensation, cleanup, and emergency response for hazardous substances released into the environment and the cleanup of inactive hazardous waste disposal sites, § 104.
[66] United States v. Hooker Chemicals & Plastics Corp., 112 F.R.D. 325 (W.D.N.Y. Sept. 1986).

ruled the health data was relevant, as the state was trying to claw back monies spent on remediation and relocations based on health issues. Further, there was no other source from which Hooker could gain this data. Because of pending motions for summary judgment (below), the court decided not to issue an order pending the outcome of those rulings.

After years of legal wrangling over discovery and deposition issues, the government motioned for a partial summary judgment under CERCLA. This statute not only allowed the EPA to respond to hazardous substance sources but to create a superfund for the clean-up and response and to seek liability against those causing the hazard to pay for the response cost and any damage to natural resources. Those who could be liable were present or past owners of hazardous waste facilities, those who arranged the disposal or treatment of such waste, and those transporting the waste. Liability for these responsible parties was strict, joint and several, and could not be contracted away and assigned to third parties. Hooker was trying to do this, claiming it was the actions of others that destroyed the secure containment it had placed around the hazardous materials in 1953.

The court granted the partial summary judgment[67] against Hooker and its corporate parent Occidental, dismissing the assertion of a third-party defense, as it had a direct relationship with the school board when the land was deeded and an indirect relationship when the school board transferred some of the unused land to the city. The court said even if there were no relationships, this defense would still fail, as Hooker was at a minimum partly responsible, so its liability was strict, joint, and several. The court in a later ruling addressed the government's motion for a partial summary judgment for the common law nuisance claims against Hooker.[68] The court held it was a public nuisance, as, "We have no doubt that the release or threat of release of hazardous waste into the environment unreasonably infringes upon a public right and thus is a public nuisance as a matter of New York law."[69] In this litigation, the limitation of liability clause in the contract transferring the property to the school was presented as part of the defense's assertions,

---

[67] United States v. Hooker Chemicals & Plastics Corp., 680 F. Supp. 546 (W.D.N.Y. May 1988).
[68] United States v. Hooker Chemicals & Plastics Corp., 722 F. Supp. 960 (W.D.N.Y. Aug. 1989).
[69] *Id.* at 966.

Prior to the delivery of this instrument of conveyance, the grantee herein has been advised by the grantor that the premises above described have been filled, in whole or in part, to the present grade level thereof with waste products resulting from the manufacturing of chemicals by the grantor at its plant in the City of Niagara Falls, New York, and the grantee assumes all risk and liability incident to the use thereof. It is, therefore, understood and agreed that, as a part of the consideration for this conveyance and as a condition thereof, no claim, suit, action or demand of any nature whatsoever shall ever be made by the grantee, its successors or assigns, against the grantor, its successors or assigns, for injury to a person or persons, including death resulting therefrom, or loss of or damage to property caused by, in connection with or by reason of the presence of said industrial wastes. It is further agreed as a condition hereof that each subsequent conveyance of the aforesaid lands shall be made subject to the foregoing provisions and conditions.[70]

The defense denied liability because the new owner had notice from this clause and an opportunity to remediate. The plaintiffs viewed it as an admission Hooker was aware its dumped wastes were a potential harm to others, so a public nuisance. The court ruled against the defense,

[in] affirmative acts of negligence in the actual creation of a nuisance or dangerous condition... ownership or possession of the property upon which the condition is found, is not necessarily a prerequisite to responsibility for injury or damage which results therefrom... The claim here is based solely on allegations of affirmative acts of negligence in the creation of a dangerous condition on the... property. Under this theory, ownership is immaterial and the fact that defendant transferred his interest in the property prior to the dates in question does not render the complaint insufficient as a matter of law."[71]

The state and the federal government both settled, with Hooker agreeing to pay remediation and damages of more than $100 million each, and the city subsequently was found jointly liable for part of those costs.[72]

---

[70] *Id.* at 962.
[71] *Id.* at 962.
[72] United States v. Occidental Chemical Corp., 965 F. Supp. 408 (W.D.N.Y. July 1997).

## 4.2 AIRBORNE AND INDUSTRY

### A. Mid-Air Collison

| **LEGAL ISSUES** |
|---|
| ❖ Required compliance with visual flight rules<br>❖ Non-compliance with overtaking regulations causing liability |

On June 30, 1956, after both had departed the airport at Los Angeles, a United Airlines (UAL) DC-7 struck a TWA Lockheed Super Constellation over the Grand Canyon in Arizona, killing 128 people. This was the first airline accident where more than 100 people died. On December 16, 1960, with both airplanes destined for airports in New York City, a UAL DC-8 struck a TWA Lockheed Super Constellation, again killing 128 on the aircraft and six people on the ground. Given its remote location, the former crash had occurred in uncontrolled airspace, where it was up to the pilots to watch out for other airplanes. The latter crash, occurring over a large city, was within controlled airspace. Both accidents would result in federal investigations, litigation, and changes to air traffic safety regulations.

In 1956, TWA 2 was flying on an instrument flight rules (IFR) plan from Los Angeles to Kansas City. It took off at 09:01. En route, its climb to the planned 19,000 feet cruising altitude was changed by local controllers to visual flight rules (VFR) while ascending out of LA, requiring it to be aware of traffic around it. The pilots soon requested to air traffic control (ATC) a change in altitude from 19,000 feet to 21,000 feet. This was denied due to other air traffic, which was explained to TWA 2. It then requested "1,000 feet on top" (of the cloud cover), which the controller understood they were already at and approved it. This required the pilots fly under VFR. The pilots reported to their company as flying at 21,000 feet. UAL 718 took off at 09:04, flying to Chicago. Its flight plan's cruising altitude was 21,000 feet. The controller had the flight switch to VFR for its climb to its cruising altitude. A final radio message from UAL 718 ended with "we are going in," which was interspersed with another voice saying, "[pull] up, [pull] up."[73] When word got out that the planes were missing, a local pilot located the planes in difficult terrain, and it was ascertained by military personnel that no one had survived. There were no surviving witnesses to this collision.

---

[73] CAB, ACCIDENT INVESTIGATION REPORT, TWA N 6902C AND UA N 6324C, GRAND CANYON, ARIZONA, JUNE 30, 1956 (Apr. 17, 1957), p. 12.

The flight regulations at that time allowed for "off airways" uncontrolled flying using direct routes, based on a filed flight plan, to allow pilots to find the best weather, winds and shortest routes. UAL company rules did not allow flying off airways in instrument weather conditions, regardless of whether the flight plan called for VFR or IFR. TWA rules allowed flying off airways in instrument weather conditions, but only under an IVF flight plan at an assigned altitude. Flying 1,000 on top required adhering to VFR, with the onus on the pilot to see and be seen, avoiding other aircraft without ATC assistance. There was no clear definition of what "1,000 feet on top" meant, in lieu of an assigned cruising altitude. It apparently allowed the pilot to fly at any altitude above their filed cruising altitude at least 1,000 feet above the cloud cover, based on their direction (eastward used odd altitudes, westward even). It required approval from ATC but then the pilot had all the responsibility for visually providing separation between aircraft. Communications with ATC were relayed through intermediaries such as a company operator, leading to delays. The controller who had originally denied the 21,000-foot level clearance to the TWA flight then received, at about the same time, reports from both aircraft that put them on converging courses. They were headed for the same target line at the same altitude, but ATC gave no warning.

ATC at that time were not required to notify planes of this, because the targeted line was very long (175 miles) and the planes were in uncontrolled airspace, off airways. The controller had no idea what routes they would be taking to the line. They did not provide advisories to planes in uncontrolled airspace as a policy. ATC policy, in instrument weather conditions was to separate all traffic in controlled airspace. When visual weather conditions existed, only IFR traffic was separated, with VFR traffic having to fend for itself. Most air traffic was of the latter variety. The CAB report noted studies had shown pilots in VFR could typically not see other planes quickly enough to avoid accidents, both for a variety of physiological and weather reasons and because they had other duties in operating the aircraft. The lack of ATC control of all U.S. airspace would soon lead to the creation of the FAA, to be given total control of all airspace.[74]

---

[74] Pub. L. 85-726, An Act to create a Civil Aeronautics Board and a Federal Aviation Agency, to provide for the regulation and promotion of civil aviation in such manner as to best foster its development and safety, and to provide for the safe and efficient use of the airspace by both civil and military aircraft, and for other purposes.

In *Matland*,[75] the widow of a man killed in this collision first settled with the two airlines for $75,000. In exchange for this payment, she signed a release form that stated,

> I do hereby release and forever discharge [United Air Lines, Inc. and Trans World Air Lines, Inc. and their employees] from any and all actions, causes of actions, claims and demands for, upon or by reason of any damage, loss or injury, which heretofore have been or which hereafter may be sustained by me in consequence of an accident which occurred on or about June 30, 1956, Grand Canyon, Arizona.[76]

She then filed a claim under the Federal Tort Claims Act (FTCA) against the government, for the negligent part that ATC played in the collision. The court noted that the common law rule was a release against one of the tortfeasors in an incident releases all of them. The plaintiff's assertion was that the FTCA created a new right, but the court said there was disagreement whether this was a new right or simply a waiver of sovereign immunity. The court said it had to look to state law, some of which had changed the common law rule by statute. However, it was not clear which state's law to use. The court determined it should be where the flight passed over, California, Arizona, and Utah. At that time, all these still followed the common law rule, so the plaintiff's release with the airlines also released the United States and the federal tort claim was dismissed.

In *Ahmann*,[77] the estates of the TWA pilot and co-pilot sued UAL, accusing it of "negligently failed to keep a proper lookout, negligently failed to give way when overtaking the rear of the TWA Constellation occupied by plaintiffs' decedents, and negligently collided with the rear of the TWA plane when the defendant saw or should have seen said plane in time to avoid striking it."[78] The jury awarded the pilot's representative $64,000 and the co-pilot's $45,000. The defendant airline moved for a judgment notwithstanding the verdict, which the court granted. Left with

---

[75] Millicent K. Matland, of the Estate of Carl G. Matland, Deceased v. United States of America, and Third-Party v. United Airlines and Trans World Airlines, Inc., Third-Party, 285 F.2d 752 (3rd Cir. Jan. 1961).
[76] *Id.* at 753.
[77] Elmer W. Ahmann, Jr., Administrator of the Estate of James H. Ritner, Deceased v. United Air Lines, Inc., a Corporation, Jane F. Gandy, of the Estate of Jack S. Gandy, Deceased v. United Air Lines, Inc., a Corporation, 313 F.2d 274 (8th Cir. Feb. 1963).
[78] *Id.* at 275.

nothing and their complaints dismissed with prejudice, the plaintiffs appealed. The court of appeals reviewed all the evidence to see if the trial court had erred. The relevant flight rules were defined,

> Permission was granted, however, for TWA Flight 2 to 'maintain at least 1,000 feet on top'. This meant that if Visual Flight Rules conditions (VFR) existed and could be maintained, the TWA Constellation was free to occupy any odd-numbered altitude while traveling in a generally easterly direction. Had TWA been granted the requested 21,000 feet altitude, that would have allowed it to travel through clouds at that altitude and it would not have been necessary to maintain VFR conditions… The collision of the two planes, however, occurred in what is known as uncontrolled air space; that is, an area outside of any controlled zone or controlled airway. In such uncontrolled air space, the only means of avoiding collision is to maintain Visual Flight Rules conditions; that is, the 'see and be seen principle'. Section 60:30(b)(1), Civil Air Regulations, provided that planes outside of control zones 'shall not be flown less than 500 feet vertically under, 1,000 feet vertically over, and 2,000 feet horizontally from any cloud formation'; and Section 60.31(d) thereof provided that, 'When outside of control zones and control areas, no person shall operate an aircraft in flight when the flight visibility is less than one mile.' Flying in 'VFR' conditions means flying in air space where the foregoing minimums can be maintained. Being in uncontrolled air space, both planes were required to stay where they could fly VFR.[79]

The court undertook a detailed analysis of aircraft pieces recovered, the planes' relative capabilities, and the flights plans, and concluded that it was reasonable for the jury to conclude the UAL DC-7 was flying faster, approaching from the rear, and based on the relative angles of the planes to each other, that the UA pilots had sufficient time to see the TWA plane and react, if both followed VFR rules. An aircraft being overtaken had the right of way, so there was a duty of care for the other plane. The court said the jury was free to choose among alternative versions of what happened and assign negligence accordingly. Ruling that there was sufficient evidence for a jury to decide, the court of appeal reversed the judgment notwithstanding the verdict and remanded to reinstate the jury awards.

---

[79] *Id.* at 276.

In 1960, UAL 826, a DC-8 jet aircraft, was flying from Chicago to Queens Idlewild Airport (later JFK) and TWA 266, a propellor aircraft, was flying from Ohio to Queens but to LaGuardia Airport. As both approached the airport, they were in IFR. The UAL flight had told its company one of the VHF radio navigational receivers was not working, meaning it would be more difficult and time consuming to triangulate is position. ATC was not made aware of this. When the collision occurred, UAL 826 was 11 miles beyond the point where it was supposed to have gone into a holding pattern awaiting landing permission and flying much faster than had been instructed. UAL 826 was not taking radar vectors from ATC but doing its own navigation. The handoff from ATC to the airport approach controller was not a radar handoff, which was optional at the time. ATC had given a shorter clearance to UAL 826, saving 11 nautical miles but the crew apparently did not account for this in determining the vector where it was supposed to enter its holding pattern. This plus additional work in determining their location required by the defective equipment accounted for their being off-course. In the aftermath, the FAA revised several rules, including reporting of in-flight malfunctions, installation of distance measuring equipment in all aircraft, radar handoffs between controllers, and reductions in speed when approaching airports and holding patterns.

In *Buckheit*,[80] the administratrix of a passenger killed in this collision sued both airlines and the United States. The federal government moved to dismiss for failing to meet venue requirements, as she sued in the southern district of New York. She was allowed to sue where the accident occurred, so asserted that the radio waves from the ATC locations she said were negligent crossed over the southern district. As it was a failure in communications using those radio waves that was at the root of the negligence action, this district was appropriate. The court said that the ATC locations were in Queens County and New Jersey, so those would be appropriate venues, as would Staten Island, where the collision occurred and where the wreckage of the plane her son was on landed, while the other plane's wreckage landed in Brooklyn. Given that none of those locations were in the southern district of New York, it was not the appropriate district to litigate in. The motion to dismiss was granted.

---

[80] Buchheit v. United Air Lines, Inc., 202 F. Supp. 811 (S.D.N.Y. Mar. 1962).

In *Sawyer*,[81] the administratrix of the UAL 826 pilot sued the United States under the FTCA. The court noted that ATC requirements for aircraft separation in controlled airspace was "minimum of 1,000 feet vertical separation or 10 minutes of longitudinal separation if the aircraft did not have vertical separation, or by a minimum of 3 miles using radar. It was the responsibility of the controller to issue clearance which would provide this separation."[82] A pilot in controlled airspace could only enter with controller approval, who would give a vector and altitude to the next clearance limit. Without an additional approval, a plane reaching its clearance limit was required to fly an elliptical pattern at the cleared altitude no more than 4 miles northeast of the clearance limit. This meant UAL 826 was 7 miles outside its permitted holding pattern. The court noted it was the pilot who was responsible for safe operation of the aircraft; ATC's only responsibility was separating aircraft from each other. Pilots were able to disregard ATC instructions if their plane was in danger. The court charged the pilot with contributory negligence for excessive speed and being beyond the assigned clearance; rejecting the plaintiff's assertion that ATC had a last clear chance to save the plane but did not do so. The court held there was no negligence on the part of the United States. This decision was unsuccessfully appealed, where the court of appeals investigated the alleged negligence of each controller involved but found none.[83]

In *Cattaro*,[84] in a near mid-air collision in 1960, a commercial airliner was forced to take drastic evasive action to avoid a military bomber. One of the passengers sued the airline and the United States for his injuries, asserting the ATC did not adequately account for the bomber being in the same airspace. The court noted that two different controllers were dealing with the commercial and military aircraft but had not communicated with each other. The bomber pilot was told the commercial flight was at 25,000 feet, when it was at 23,000 feet. One controller also had both planes on his monitor but did not warn them. The court found both pilots and ATC directly contributed to the plaintiff's injuries, assigning 65% of the negligence to the federal government and 35% to the airline.

---

[81] Sawyer v. United States, 297 F. Supp. 324 (E.D.N.Y. Mar. 1969).
[82] *Id.* at 328.
[83] Patricia Sawyer, Administratrix of the Estate of Robert H. Sawyer, Deceased v. United States, 436 F.2d 640 (2nd Cir. Jan. 1971).
[84] Cattaro v. Northwest Airlines, Inc., 236 F. Supp. 889 (E.D. Va. Dec. 1964).

## B. Skydiving Errors

| LEGAL ISSUES |
|---|
| ❖ Releasing skydivers in clouds generating pilot legal liability<br>❖ ATC misidentification of planes giving rise to legal liability |

On August 27, 1967, a group of 20 sport skydivers boarded a World War 2 era B-25 Mitchell bomber plane to jump. The advice from ATC was that the plane was nearing the intended drop zone. In the first group, after receiving clearance from the pilot, 18 of the 20 sport parachutists jumped from 20,000 feet, believing that they were headed for a landing zone near a local airport. Instead, they had been dropped out over Lake Erie, miles from the shoreline. Fortunately, 2 of the 18 were rescued by boaters, but the other 16 were not, and drowned. The parachutists had jumped through a cloud cover, which was prohibited for sports jumpers. The same cloud cover had prevented the pilot from confirming what was beneath him before giving the signal that it was safe to jump. The intended landing site was more than 11 miles away. ATC had mistaken another plane for what it thought was the B-25 on its radar and issued directions accordingly. This other plane may have been a Cessna sent up to photograph the jumps. Fault was attributed to the pilot, ATC, and the jumpers themselves.[85]

The National Transportation Safety Board (NTSB) report stated the plane could only take 20 jumpers, so 3 of the 23 jumpers were offloaded. This was a military bomber, so the jumpers left from different locations on the plane. Two departed from a hatch in the forward section, 9 departed through the bomb bay, and the rest from a waist gunner's hatch or an aft section hatch. The first 18 jumpers left the plane at 20,000 feet. The other two were to jump at 30,000 feet. During the ascent, due to the cloud cover, the pilot had to switch from VFR to IFR then switched back after topping the clouds. The Cessna had taken off from the intended landing zone at Ortner Airport and circled around the airport at 12,000 feet, waiting for the jump. The B-25 meanwhile had to wait 15-20 minutes for the cloud cover to sufficiently clear for the jump. During this interval, the controller he had previously spoken to was relieved, and a new controller took over. There was confusion as to which plane was which on the radar.

---

[85] NTSB, SPECIAL INVESTIGATION REPORT OF A PARACHUTING ACCIDENT NEAR HURON, OHIO ON AUGUST 27, 1967 (Sept. 25, 1967).

The two surviving parachutists who landed in the water testified that they went into a cloud cover at 6,000 feet, came out at 4,000 feet, and opened their parachutes at 3,000 feet. It was only after coming out of the cloud cover that they realized the difficulty they would soon be in. One of these was among the first to leave the plane while the other was the last. One of the offloaded jumpers had remained at the airport. He stated that, as he was listening to the radio traffic, when the group of 18 were jumping, he could not hear the engines of the plane. However, when the final two jumpers, not part of the original 18, departed the plane, he could hear the plane's engines. A test flight using the recorded communications, plus what the pilot could remember of his route, ended up 11 miles away from the designated landing area at the drop time. FAA rules did not allow jumps that created a hazard to others. Jumps required the plane have two-way radio communications with ATC, provide a one-hour advanced notice to ATC, not be made into congested areas or control zones without FAA authorization, and not be made through clouds or in violation of VFR conditions. These rules applied to pilots as well as jumpers.

The NTSB concluded the ATC's radar misidentification was most likely that of the Cessna, not the B-25. FAA rules for radar identification included clear phraseology, identifying a primary target by the position and track corresponding with a direct report from the aircraft or having the aircraft make an identifying turn of at least 30 degrees. More than one method of identification was required for the identity when any doubt was raised. Reidentification was required when clutter on the radar scope or merging targets made the identity questionable. If it was not possible to reidentify, the radar service was to be terminated.

As the pilot could not use his radio to navigate while communicating with ATC, and with the cloudiness, the NTSB said the pilot should have terminated the jumps. The NTSB found: the pilot was not rated for the B-25; the plane was not equipped to carry passengers; the radio not being able to simultaneously communicate and navigate was not made known to ATC; the pilot had to remove his oxygen mask to communicate; ATC did not take adequate measures to positively identify the B-25 or Cessna; cloud cover precluded both a visual reference to the ground and that a jump could be successfully made under VFR separation; the pilot's decision to release the jumpers was faulty; and the jumpers were also in error.

In *Dreyer*,[86] all the jumpers that day, either through their representatives or themselves, sued the federal government under the FTCA. They asserted the proximate cause was the misidentification of the B-25 on radar by ATC. The government attributed it to pilot error, possibly from hypoxia due to taking off his oxygen mask to communicate. Further, all the jumpers were contributorily negligent. The court noted that the 18 skydivers who went first were intending to engage in something called "relative work," which was formation jumping requiring the jumpers to perform free-fall maneuvers near to each other. Both the B-25 and the Cessna had headed first over to the Cleveland VOR (or Vortac, the navigational aid that sends out radios signals in a 360-degree circle) to get their bearings after reaching their intended altitudes. The court also noted testimony that the free fall lasted about 90 seconds, and the surviving parachutists estimated they had three and a half minutes until landing on the water. To prepare, they discarded their boots and heavy clothing and loosened chute releases to escape from them on touchdown in the water. The two other jumpers who intended to jump at 30,000 feet were denied permission, so they jumped at a lower altitude over the airport.

As the alleged negligence concerned the ATC, the court discussed what they could see on their radar screens. Airplanes with transponders appeared differently than those without transponders, which were referred to as primary targets, whose aircraft type could not be identified on radar. The quality of the primary target information returned varied, due to many factors, and there also was ground clutter from terrestrial obstructions. The court noted that the controller tracking the plane, a 43-year-old former World War 2 fighter pilot, had said that there was significant ground clutter. However, the court's view was that the regulations for identifying a flight (discussed above) had not been followed by the controller. Due to misidentifying the plane and not following one of the techniques to ascertain its identity or terminate radar service, the controller provided incorrect information that led to the flight dropping the skydivers over the lake. The government asserted the intervening negligence of the pilot and at least that of the head skydiver, if not all the skydivers. The court held that the acts of others were not intervening acts sufficient for the government to avoid its own liability for negligence.

---

[86] Dreyer v. United States, 349 F. Supp. 296 (N.D. Ohio Oct. 1972).

In *Freeman*,[87] the government appealed, asserting that there was no duty of care owed to the parachutists, they were contributorily negligent when skydiving through clouds, and the intervening negligence of the pilot and jump master. On the first issue, the government claimed ATC's duty was only to planes to avoid crashes, not instructing skydivers when to jump. The court of appeals ruled a duty extends to the plane and its crew, passengers, and cargo. On the second issue, the plaintiffs had argued the regulation was only to protect others from parachutists jumping through clouds, not the safety of parachutists. The court agreed; it was not negligence per se or contributory negligence. On the third issue, the court, in affirming the lower court, said an intervening cause had to arise independent of the original negligence, ruling the negligence of the pilot and jump master did not alone cause the accident. The United States was sued the same year for ATC failings in a separate case, but that court held the proximate cause was the acts of the pilot and not the controllers.[88]

In *Northwest Airlines*,[89] the most famous skydiving incident ever was the subject. On November 24, 1971, Dan (later D.B.) Cooper hijacked a Boeing 727, demanding $200,000 cash and four parachutes through a flight attendant. These were eventually delivered to him after the plane landed at Seattle-Tacoma Airport, and the passengers were released. The plane then took off again with a skeleton crew, directed by Cooper on a route to the south, but with the added instructions that the plane was supposed to fly at a slow speed and with the rear stairs extended. This plane uniquely had inbuilt stairs as part of its design. When the latter was rejected by the pilot as impossible when taking off, Cooper relented. However, while alone in the rear of the plane about 30 minutes after departing, wearing a parachute and bundling up the money, he lowered the stairs. Into the rain, wind, and dark night, dressed only as he first boarded the plane, Cooper jumped off the stairs, into legend. The FBI has never been able to either find him or his body or even his identity. The insurance company here denied a claim for the ransom money, as it was not in the bank's premise when the hijacker exercised dominion over it. The state supreme court held that when the bank agreed to provide the ransom money, it was still on their premise, affirming the claim for the $200,000 D.B. Cooper ransom.

---

[87] Ramona Freeman, Etc. v. United States, 509 F.2d 626 (6th Cir. Jan. 1975).
[88] In Re Air Crash Disaster at New Orleans, Etc., 422 F. Supp. 1166 (W.D. Tenn. June 1975).
[89] Northwest Airlines, Inc. v. Globe Indemnity Co., 225 N.W.2d 831 (Minn. Jan. 1975).

## C. Helicopter Crashes

| LEGAL ISSUES |
|---|
| ❖ Need to exchange tickets to extend insurance coverage<br>❖ Helicopter landings bringing about operator legal liability |

After World War 2, the Civil Aeronautics Board (CAB) tried to promote the usage of civilian helicopters, which had been so successfully developed and deployed by the military. To encourage this usage, the government subsidized the development and awarded public contracts in three major cities for delivering the U.S. mail via helicopter, in New York, Chicago, and Los Angeles. Later, these companies would branch out into carrying passengers as well. Los Angeles Airways (LAA) was certified to deliver mail in 1947 and for passenger service in 1951. Helicopter Air Services (to become Chicago Helicopter Airways) was certified the following year. New York Airways was certified in 1951 for both mail and passengers. The subsidies ended in 1965,[90] with a final payment for mail services.[91]

However, these helicopters were to be involved in several crashes and incidents. The worst occurred to LAA. On May 22, 1968, a Sikorsky S-61L model, carrying 20 passengers and 3 crew, on a flight from the heliport at Disneyland to Los Angeles International Airport (LAX), suffered mechanical failure and crashed over Paramount and burned. The NTSB report[92] noted the failure began at 2,000 feet, in the five main rotor blades, about two miles from where it crashed. The pilots were able to bring the aircraft down to 600-800 feet before losing control. The yellow main rotor blade over-traveled and due to the stress, detached from the main rotor rotating swashplate. The black, blue, red, and white main rotor blades followed, crashing into the fuselage, detaching the tail rotor pylon, and the now completely uncontrollable craft plunged earthward nearly vertical. This was blamed on a loss of damper integrity in the other rotor blades, but the cause of that was to be undetermined. Tests at the manufacturer Sikorsky found no metal fatigue and all parts were within their service windows.

---

[90] National Capital Airlines, Inc. v. Civil Aeronautics Board, Washington Airways, Inc., Intervenor, 419 F.2d 668 (D.C. Cir. Mar. 1969), at 671.
[91] New York Airways, Inc. v. The United States. Los Angeles Airways, Inc. v. The United States. Chicago Helicopter Airways, Inc. v. The United States, 369 F.2d 743 (Ct. Cl. Dec. 1966).
[92] NTSB, AIRCRAFT ACCIDENT REPORT, LOS ANGELES AIRWAYS, INC., SIKORSKY S-61L, N303Y, PARAMOUNT, CAL., MAY 22, 1968 (Dec. 18, 1969).

In *Daburlos*,[93] the mother/mother-in-law of two victims of this crash was seeking payment under four insurance policies they purchased. The insurance companies rejected the claims based on the ticketing used. Her son and daughter-in-law had purchased the four policies from the two defendants at the airport in Philadelphia on the 19th, with a benefit payment of $75,000 each, for a premium of $2.50 per policy, and mailed them to her. Prior to this purchase, the couple had purchased round-trip tickets from Philadelphia to Los Angeles. On the 22nd, they purchased round-trip tickets from LAX to Disneyland on LAA. The outbound leg occurred without incident, but they were killed in the crash on the inbound leg. The policies were to insure for one airline roundtrip, Philadelphia to Los Angeles, requiring the insured be traveling on a ticket for that whole trip. If there was an itinerary change, the coverage would continue if the old ticket was exchanged for a new ticket on a scheduled carrier. Because LAA was an IATA member, it could have written a new ticket for this couple for the unused part of their trip, that is, LAX to Disneyland to LAX to Philadelphia. There was no additional insurance premium if they did so.

However, as this seemed to violate the requirement the original departure was not on the ticket, the court ruled it could not grant summary judgment for either party without additional evidence being presented. The following year, the case was tried before the court without a jury.[94] Contrary to the policy, the court said the couple did not die using tickets that covered their whole trip from Philadelphia to Los Angeles nor did they exchange their tickets. The court found that it would be impossible for the couple to comply with the express terms of the policy, as all IATA members would have only issued a new ticket for the unused portions of the trip. Because it was impossible, it was not necessary to comply with it. Because they were still on their original round trip at the time of the accident, the court held their beneficiary had a right to collect fully on all the policies from the two defendants.

In *Kronfeld*,[95] another insurance case related to this crash was in the New York, instead of federal, courts. The plaintiff's deceased spouse had purchased two insurance policies from the two defendants before flying

---

[93] Daburlos v. Commercial Insurance Co. of Newark, NJ, 367 F. Supp. 1017 (E.D. Pa. Dec. 1973).
[94] Daburlos v. Commercial Insurance Co. of Newark, NJ, 381 F. Supp. 393 (E.D. Pa. Sept. 1974).
[95] Kronfeld v. Fidelity & Casualty Co., 81 Misc. 2d 557 (N.Y. Sup. Ct. Feb. 1975).

from New York to Los Angeles on May 20th. He had a round-trip air ticket, but the dates of his return were not set. After a few days in Los Angeles, he purchased a ticket for the ill-fated LAA flight from Disneyland to LAX and was killed in the crash. The court noted that the process of buying flight insurance was intended to have the purchasers mail the policy home (they even sold the stamps there), and so he would not have a copy with him to refer to its terms to protect his coverage. No one could read through such a long and complex policy in the short time available at the airport. The policies had the same terms as described in *Daburlos*. The court said state law required giving clear notice of such clauses. The issue was whether the non-exchange of his ticket would exclude coverage. The court referred to other cases holding that the exchange requirement had no impact on the insurance risk, so this court refused to enforce it and entered judgment for the plaintiff on both policies. The appellate division affirmed,[96] with slightly different reasoning, because there was no valid reason for insurance companies to require the ticket exchange.

On August 27, 1969, on a LAA flight flying this time from LAX to Disneyland, a Sikorsky S-61L model, carrying 18 passengers and 3 crew, suffered a mechanical failure and crashed and burned, over Compton, killing everyone aboard. The NTSB report[97] noted that once again, the problem seemed to be with the yellow main rotor blade. This time metal fatigue was indicated as the problem, arising from insufficient metal hardness and inadequate shot peening (to increase resistance to stress). As the flight had left the radar-controlled area, its altitude was derived from the statements of many witnesses, estimated to be at 1,200-1,500 feet. The FAA required immediate inspections for fatigue cracks.

In *Roberts*,[98] an Oregon realtor on this flight had traveled from Portland to Los Angeles on business and was to take her two nephews to Disneyland. She booked roundtrip air tickets and before departing, spent 50 cents on a $15,000 insurance policy from a vending machine, neglecting to fill in the destination. The insurance company refused to pay. The court agreed, as the travel was not on a ticket that covered the entire airline trip,

---

[96] Kronfeld v. Fidelity & Casualty Co., 53 A.D.2d 190 (N.Y. App. Div. July 1976).
[97] NTSB, AIRCRAFT ACCIDENT REPORT, LOS ANGELES AIRWAYS, INC., SIKORSKY S-61L, N300Y, COMPTON, CAL., AUGUST 14, 1968 (Aug. 27, 1969).
[98] Verna Roberts v. The Fidelity and Casualty Company of New York, 452 F.2d 981 (9th Cir. Dec. 1971).

ticketed before her original departure, and her original ticket was not exchanged for a new one including the helicopter trip to Disneyland.

On July 27, 1960, a Sikorsky S-58C, flying from Chicago Midway Airport to Chicago O'Hare Airport, operated by Chicago Helicopter Airways (CHA), experienced a mechanical failure at 1,500 feet and crashed, killing all eleven passengers and two crew. The CAB report[99] attributed the crash to metal fatigue in a rotor blade, so the FAA issued an airworthiness directive requiring changing these rotor blades at 1,000 hours.

In *Franklin*,[100] CHA was sued for creating turbulence that caused a small plane to crash on March 31, 1959, along with the United States for controller errors. The controller had directed the S-58 CHA helicopter to land on the taxiway, crossing the runway about half a minute before the plaintiffs arrived. The court of appeals said the plaintiff could hear the conversations between the controller and the helicopter. The court held the helicopter was not negligent, as it was flying properly, following controller instructions, and checking in to receive a second clearance when hearing a plane was in the area. The court held the controller was not negligent, as he properly handled the required separations and communications. He could not be held liable for helicopter wake vortices, which were not generally known until several years later. As helicopter vortices travel with the wind, and the wind was blowing away from the path of the airline, the court ruled they could not have been the proximate cause of the plane's crash landing. The Supreme Court denied certiorari.[101]

In *New York Airways*,[102] the plaintiff sued for damages in landing his helicopter on a truck in Newark Airport on October 17, 1953. The court found the pilot did not engage in maneuvers to decrease his blind spots and see where he was landing. The court, affirming the decision, thought it incredible to assert that a controller dedicated to ensuring safe aircraft takeoffs and landings should devote time to keeping track of ground traffic.

---

[99] CAB, AIRCRAFT ACCIDENT REPORT, CHICAGO HELICOPTER AIRWAYS, SIKORSKY S-58C, N879, FOREST PARK, ILL., JULY 27, 1960 (Aug. 8, 1961).
[100] Siesel A. Franklin and Helen W. Franklin v. United States of America and Hugh Riddle, Jr., and Chicago Helicopter Airways, Inc., and Richard R. Creighton, 342 F.2d 581 (7th Cir. Apr. 1965).
[101] Franklin v. United States, 382 U.S. 844 (Oct. 1965).
[102] New York Airways, Inc. v. United States of America and the Port of New York Authority, United States of America v. Eastern Airlines, Inc., 283 F.2d 496 (2nd Cir. Nov. 1960).

## D. Asbestos

| LEGAL ISSUES |
|---|
| ❖ Not warning of the asbestos dangers creating legal liability<br>❖ Statute of limitations and discovery date of disease |

From the early 20th century, evidence of asbestos poisoning was first known, and it solidified over the next few decades. By the 1930s in the United States, there were public health warnings of the dangers and documented cases of asbestos industry workers being affected. It did not lead, though, to abandoning a mineral with useful features like non-flammability. It did result in significant litigation, as insulation and factory workers and others in contact with asbestos developed asbestosis, mesothelioma, and other related diseases and died. The problem has not diminished, as "Asbestos causes an estimated 255,000 deaths (243,223–260,029) annually according to latest knowledge."[103] The government would pursue criminal charges and a Superfund cleanup in one situation.[104]

In *Borel*,[105] the plaintiff had worked around asbestos for 33 years and sued insulation manufacturers for not warning workers about the dangers of asbestos. He had contracted both asbestosis and mesothelioma from the asbestos dust in his job and was seeking damages. The trial court held this to be a matter of strict liability and awarded him damages. Varied methods of protection, when offered, were not effective and difficult to wear in all conditions. The plaintiff had his right lung removed and eventually succumbed to these diseases. Medical testimony stated that even light exposure can cause these illnesses, but it was difficult to diagnose early, due to a long latency period, sometimes up to 25 years. The disease is both cumulative and irreversible, from the damage asbestos fibers do to the lungs, so it was not possible to pinpoint which exposure(s) caused the diseases. The court asked how long the defendants knew of these properties of asbestos, as the U.S. public health service had documented this issue by 1938. The court ruled the defendants were aware of the risks, but Borel and his fellow workers were never warned.

---

[103] Furuya S, Chimed-Ochir O, Takahashi K, David A, Takala J. *Global asbestos disaster*. INTL. J. ENVIRON. RES. PUBLIC HEALTH. 2018;15(5):1000.
[104] United States v. W.R. Grace, 06-30472 (9th Cir. Sept. 2007).
[105] Clarence Borel v. Fibreboard Paper Products Corporation, Nationalsurety Corporation, 493 F.2d 1076 (5th Cir. Sept. 1973).

The plaintiff initiated the lawsuit before his death against 11 asbestos-producing manufacturers, asserting negligence, gross negligence, and breach of warranty or strict liability. Negligence included failure to warn of the dangers, failure to inform of proper protective equipment, failure to test their products to ascertain the dangers, and failure to remove the products from the market. The defendants asserted the plaintiff's contributory negligence and assumption of risk. The jury found the defendants negligent but not grossly negligent and Borel contributorily negligent. The defendants were found strictly liable and damages were awarded. The court of appeals said the issue was putting a defective product on the market, meaning it was unreasonably dangerous to consumers. A seller had a duty to warn of a reasonably foreseeable danger of their product, after using reasonable care to discover such dangers. The failure to warn made the product unreasonably dangerous. While the utility of an insulation product containing asbestos could outweigh the risk to insulation workers and so enable its lawful marketing, it became unreasonably dangerous without a warning, giving insulation workers the knowledge and right to choose whether they wished to be exposed to it.

The defendants asserted that it was the duty of insulation contractors to warn their workers, not the manufacturers. The court of appeals rejected this, saying their duty was to the ultimate consumer. The court said the assumption of risk defense required knowing, understanding, and appreciating the danger and consenting to exposure. The contributory negligence defense was objective and requiring unreasonableness. The court rejected the assertion that Borel not wearing a mask was a defense, as it was not a strict liability defense. After this court affirmed, several of the defendants asserted they had had warnings on their products for several years (below), but the court dismissed these as not communicating the gravity of risk of serious disease and death to the reader:

> This product contains asbestos fiber. Inhalation of asbestos in excessive quantities over long periods of time may be harmful. If dust is created when this product is handled, avoid breathing the dust. If adequate ventilation control is not possible wear respirators approved by the U.S. Bureau of Mines for pneumoconiosis producing dusts.[106]

---

[106] *Id.* at 1104.

In *Velasquez*,[107] the plaintiff had worked as an insulator for more than 30 years and was suffering from asbestosis. The trial court had granted summary judgment to the defendants, asserting the claims for negligence and strict liability were filed after the one-year statute of limitations period. The court of appeals described the disease,

> Asbestosis, which is characterized by pleural thickening, reduced elasticity of lung tissue, reduced total lung volume and reduced ability to transfer oxygen, is commonly progressive. It may be detected before there has been significant respiratory impairment. Impairment itself does not immediately cause either a partial or total inability to work.[108]

He was examined by doctors in 1967, who could view his chest X-rays back to 1957, and saw a progression in the disease. In 1971, he was diagnosed with moderately severe asbestosis, which his doctors were told but he only heard he had indications of asbestosis. He was urged to continue working while minimizing dust inhalation. He was examined again in 1973 and was diagnosed with further progression of the disease and could only work until early 1974, when the illness forced his retirement. He filed his lawsuit later that year. The defendant asserted that he had to file suit in 1971, not 1974. The court said with this disease, there was no one specific date when the injury could be said to occur. The court rejected the plaintiff's assertion that the action accrued from either the dates of disability or substantial harm, instead believing the date of discovery was appropriate. The open question was when the plaintiff discovered his condition such that it was appropriate to seek legal remedy. As there were still facts to ascertain, the court of appeal reversed and remanded for trial.

In *Migues*,[109] the question was whether *Borel* was precedential for all asbestos products, as a matter of law. The decedent had worked cutting asbestos for over 30 years and subsequently died after a mesothelioma diagnosis. The trial court granted partial summary judgment on whether products containing asbestos were unreasonably dangerous and said the triable issues were whether: the defendants manufactured asbestos, the decedent was exposed to it, and such exposure caused his death.

---

[107] Velasquez v. Fibreboard Paper Products Corp., 97 Cal. App. 3d 881 (Cal. App. Oct. 1979).
[108] *Id*. at 883.
[109] Alberta Migues v. Fibreboard Corp., Nicolet Industries, 662 F.2d 1182 (5th Cir. Oct. 1981).

The court of appeals said the judge had precluded the fourteen defendants from litigating whether asbestos was unreasonably dangerous by splitting them into two groups. Eleven of them had been involved in prior litigation determining that it was unreasonably dangerous, so based on collateral estoppel, they could not relitigate this issue. For the other three, including the sole remaining defendant, the judge ruled the matter to be stare decisis based on *Borel* and the plaintiff only had to show these three defendants manufactured and sold asbestos products. The court of appeals disagreed with this ruling, saying,

> In *Borel*, this Court said: "the jury was entitled to find that the danger to Borel and other insulation workers from inhaling asbestos dust was foreseeable to the defendants at the time the products causing Borel's injuries were sold." We did not say that the jury was compelled, as a matter of law to reach this result, or that it could not have reached another result. On the issue of plaintiff Borel's possible voluntary assumption of risk, this Court stated, "we cannot say that, as a matter of law, the danger (of asbestos inhalation) was sufficiently obvious to asbestos installation workers to relieve the defendants of the duty to warn." This Court did not say that, as a matter of law, the danger of asbestos inhalation was so hidden from every asbestos worker in every situation as to create a duty to warn on the part of all asbestos manufacturers.[110]

In *Brisboy*,[111] the widow of an asbestos worker who died of lung cancer sued nine companies he worked for from 1951 to 1977, eight of which settled with the plaintiff. The defense asserted he died of lung cancer due to his heavy smoking habit. Medical testimony was conflicting on whether the asbestosis was the sole cause or whether smoking was the sole, contributing, or not a cause in his death. The jury found the decedent 55% contributorily negligent but the judge overruled this, as there was no way the decedent could know that asbestos would increase the risk of smoking related disease. The defense asserted that the 6-9 months he worked there was not the proximate cause of his death, but the court said even a brief exposure could lead to death. The court, in affirming, also agreed with the trial court's denial of the contributory negligence defense.

---

[110] *Id.* at 1188-89.
[111] Brisboy v. Fibreboard Paper Products Corp., 384 N.W.2d 39 (Mich. App. Oct. 1985).

In *re Asbestos*,[112] a multi-district panel was trying to determine if the varied lawsuits should be consolidated. Statistics included: 103 suits against 80 defendants in 19 judicial districts, 94 of the plaintiffs were tradesmen who worked with asbestos and 9 were asbestos factory workers. Johns-Manville was named in 91 of the lawsuits, 7 companies were named in more than 50 suits, and 7 other companies were named in 30 or more suits. The lawsuits asserted strict liability, negligence, and breach of warranty. The panel had issued a show cause order why the actions should not be consolidated. The responses included: discovery already advanced, different defendants in each action, a non-homogenous group of plaintiffs, different circumstances of asbestos exposure, causation was an individual issue, liability was also an individual question, and local issues would predominate in discovery. The panel then determined to vacate the order, as the only common issue was the state of scientific and medical knowledge concerning the risks of exposure to asbestos.

In *Cathey*,[113] the question for the court was whether punitive damages were appropriate in a mass tort case where the defendants were dealing with so many legal actions. The court of appeals rejected the so-called "overkill doctrine" as something that should be taken up with the legislature, not the courts. The exhaustion of finite corporate resources was also rejected as a public policy argument. The court noted evidence from a former director of the defendant who stated, "in the late 1940's Johns-Manville was aware that it was producing disease in employees who manufactured the [asbestos-containing] products" and that "disease [was] being produced in non-JM employees who may use certain of these products."[114] Based on this, the court of appeals held that it was reasonable for a jury to determine that it was a reckless disregard of social obligations or a conscious indifference to the consequences, sufficient for the jury to award punitive damages. The court also held it was also not a violation of due process, just because there were so many victims.

---

[112] In Re Asbestos & Asbestos Insulation Material, Etc., 431 F. Supp. 906 (J.P.M.L. Apr. 1977).
[113] Martha Jo Cathey, (82-5393), (82-5425), Mary Cavett, Administratrix, (82-5580) v. Johns-Manville Sales Corporation Raymark Industries the Celotex Corporation Pittsburgh-Corning Corporation Owens-Corning Fiberglass Corporation Fibreboard Corporation Gaf Corporation Nicolet, Inc. Southern Asbestos Company and Owens-Illinois, Incorporated, Defendants- (82-5393), Johns-Manville Sales Corporation, (82-5425, 82-5580), 776 F.2d 1565 (6th Cir. Nov. 1985).
[114] *Id.* at 1571.

In *W.R. Grace*,[115] after finding significant amounts of asbestos in the ground and air around the small town of Libby, Montana, the federal government sued to gain access to three sites which were long used to produce a significant amount of the world's vermiculite. The court said the EPA needed to prove its authorized right of access was denied by the defendants and the EPA believed there was a release or a threatened release of a hazardous substance. The court found that the authorized EPA access was denied to all sites, as it needed to enter to respond to what it believed was an asbestos problem in Libby. Access to the sites was ordered by the court. The government later sought reimbursement under CERCLA for its remediation costs from the defendant and the court awarded $55 million. Its liability included remediation of the mine, many schools, and dozens of residential and commercial properties. The EPA removed material that was disposed in and near Libby from the mining, processing, and sale of vermiculite. Despite defendant protests, the court ruled "All of the Superfund program's costs, including the indirect costs of those who have performed services for the Superfund program, are necessary to produce the cleanup of contaminated sites."[116]

W.R. Grace filed for bankruptcy, due to a tsunami of litigation claims against it. The federal government then filed a criminal case against certain executives of the company.[117] The defendants were continually attacking the indictment, trying to whittle down the charges and were ultimately able to minimize the counts and defendants, and avoid criminal consequences. There were originally ten counts to the indictment,

> The defendants are charged with conspiracy to violate the Clean Air Act and to defraud the United States in violation of 18 U.S.C. § 371 (Count I); violation of the Clean Air Act, 42 U.S.C. § 7413(c)(5)(A) (Counts II, III and IV); wire fraud in violation of 18 U.S.C. §§ 1343, 2 (Counts V and VI); and Obstruction of Justice in violation of 18 U.S.C. §§ 1505, 2 (Counts VII, VIII, IX and X). The charges relate to the Defendants' alleged role in the release and distribution throughout the Libby area of asbestos contaminated vermiculite.[118]

---

[115] United States v. W.R. Grace & Co., 134 F. Supp. 2d 1182 (D. Mont. Mar. 2001).
[116] *Id.* at 1169.
[117] United States v. Grace, 401 F. Supp. 2d 1103 (D. Mont. Nov. 2005).
[118] *Id.* at 1106.

## E. Exploding Cars

| LEGAL ISSUES |
|---|
| ❖ Known fuel tank defects defining civil liability<br>❖ Recklessly failing to warn leading to criminal liability |

In April 1974, the Center for Auto Safety wrote[119] to the National Highway Traffic Safety Administration (NHTSA), Office of Defect Investigation, asking that they open a defect investigation into the Ford Pinto. Beyond their own concerns, they cited recent letters they had received from attorneys. One attorney said the gas tank of a Pinto was forced into the passenger compartment in a recent rear-end collision, spewing fuel, leading to death and severe burns. Three deaths and four serious injuries were cited from five lawyers in New Jersey, Ohio, Alabama, Michigan, and Florida. The letter cited other studies that called out the Pinto's gas tank rupturing. The NHTSA declined to open a defect investigation at that time.

In August 1977, a detailed article[120] was published that asserted Ford Motor Company had rushed the Pinto into production, had found the problem with the gas tank ruptures before launching, decided to make no changes as the production lines were already configured, and lobbied ferociously for eight years to avoid being required to install a safer fuel tank. The article claimed there had been at least 500 burn deaths from the Pinto and the number could be higher. The reason no changes were made was due to an internal cost benefit analysis regarding this best-selling subcompact car. It found that the cost of litigation damages was less than installing an inexpensive part to prevent tank ruptures. Secret crash tests at greater than 25 mph resulted in ruptured Pinto fuel tanks. The only tests that did not rupture were when additions not on the mass-produced versions were added, such as a one-dollar plastic baffle. The article quoted an auto safety expert who studied the Pinto's fuel system "It's a catastrophic blunder," he says. "Ford made an extremely irresponsible decision when they placed such a weak tank in such a ridiculous location in such a soft rear end. It's almost designed to blow up—premeditated."[121]

---

[119] Letter from David Whitman, Center for Auto Safety to Andrew Detrick, Acting Director, Office of Defect Investigation, NHTSA (Apr. 9, 1974).
[120] Mark Dowie, *Pinto Madness*, MOTHER JONES, Sept./Oct. 1977.
[121] *Id.*

This article finally spurred the NHTSA to investigate, looking for any violations of the National Traffic and Motor Vehicle Safety Act of 1966. The result of its investigation was a report[122] that asked all interested parties for inputs. Ford claimed there had been 57 injuries and deaths to Pinto occupants in read-end collisions, of which 25 were fatalities. From this, there had been 29 legal claims arising from 35 rear-end accidents, 8 of which were settled out of court or which Ford lost, 2 which were pending investigation or Ford won, and 19 cases that were still pending trials. More than 2 million Pintos were produced in the 1971-76 model years, most of which were still on the road. Ford had done internal tests, which consistently showed the tank punctured in collisions under 22 mph, the fuel filler pipe was pulled out (spilling fuel), and the passenger doors jammed. This led to a recall of most Pintos to retrofit the relatively inexpensive parts that should have been installed initially.

In *Grimshaw*,[123] on May 28, 1972, a 1972 Pinto stalled on the freeway and was rear-ended by another vehicle that after braking was still traveling at 28 to 37 mph. The driver of the Pinto was killed, and a 13-year-old occupant was severely burned when the fuel tank ruptured and caught fire. The jury awarded him $2.5 million in compensatory damages and $125 million in punitive damages. The punitive award was reduced to $3.5 million as a condition to denying a motion for a new trial. All parties appealed. The court of appeals noted the faults described, but also that the Pinto's bumper was weak comparted to any other car. Ford's testing with additional components showed Pintos could survive the crash tests. The court noted a long list of inexpensive items that could have been added,

> Design changes that would have enhanced the integrity of the fuel tank system at relatively little cost per car included the following: Longitudinal side members and cross members at $2.40 and $1.80, respectively; a single shock absorbant "flak suit" to protect the tank at $4; a tank within a tank and placement of the tank over the axle at $5.08 to $5.79; a nylon bladder within the tank at $5.25 to $8; placement of the tank over the axle surrounded with a protective barrier at a cost of $9.95 per car; substitution of a rear axle with a

---

[122] INVESTIGATION REPORT, ALLEGED FUEL TANK AND FILLER NECK DAMAGE IN REAR-END COLLISION OF SUBCOMPACT PASSENGER CARS, 1971-1976 FORD PINTO, NHTSA OFFICE OF DEFECTS INVESTIGATION ENFORCEMENT (May 1978).
[123] Grimshaw v. Ford Motor Co., 119 Cal. App. 3d 757 (Cal. App. May 1981).

smooth differential housing at a cost of $2.10; imposition of a protective shield between the differential housing and the tank at $2.35; improvement and reenforcement of the bumper at $2.60; addition of eight inches of crush space a cost of $6.40. Equipping the car with a reinforced rear structure, smooth axle, improved bumper and additional crush space at a total cost of $15.30 would have made the fuel tank safe in a 34 to 38-mile-per-hour rear-end collision by a vehicle the size of the Ford Galaxie. If, in addition to the foregoing, a bladder or tank within a tank were used or if the tank were protected with a shield, it would have been safe in a 40 to 45-mile-per-hour rear impact. If the tank had been located over the rear axle, it would have been safe in a rear impact at 50 miles per hour or more.[124]

The court noted that the highest Ford executives were aware of the fuel tank issues but signed off on taking it to market, knowing inexpensive fixes were available. The testimony of the executive in charge of the crash testing program was particularly damning. Ford tried very hard to get his testimony excluded. Ford also attempted to get evidence excluded, the opposing counsel sanctioned, complained about jury instructions, and juror misconduct. The court rejected all claims of error, affirming the judgment. To Ford's protest about the size of punitive damages, the court said,

> The conduct of Ford's management was reprehensible in the extreme. It exhibited a conscious and callous disregard of public safety in order to maximize corporate profits. Ford's self-evaluation of its conduct is based on a review of the evidence most favorable to it instead of on the basis of the evidence most favorable to the judgment. Unlike malicious conduct directed toward a single specific individual, Ford's tortious conduct endangered the lives of thousands of Pinto purchasers. Weighed against the factor of reprehensibility, the punitive damage award as reduced by the trial judge was not excessive. Nor was the reduced award excessive taking into account defendant's wealth and the size of the compensatory award. Ford's net worth was $7.7 billion and its income after taxes for 1976 was over $983 million. The punitive award was... .005 percent of Ford's net worth and... .03 percent of its 1976 net income.[125]

---

[124] *Id.* at 775-76.
[125] *Id.* at 819-20.

In *Indiana v. Ford*,[126] the state indicted Ford Motor Company for a Pinto rear-end collision fire that killed three young women, sisters Judy and Lyn Ulrich, and their cousin Donna Ulrich, on August 10, 1978. The indictment from the grand jury[127] was three charges of reckless homicide for recklessly designing and building this 1973 Pinto so it would burst into flames upon rear impact, and then letting the car remain on the road not fixing or warning the owner, as legally mandated. Because of these actions and inactions, the three girls were burned to death. Recklessly was defined as "A person engages in conduct "recklessly" if he engages in the conduct in plain, conscious, and unjustifiable disregard of harm that might result and the disregard the involves a substantial deviation from acceptable standards of conduct."[128] There was also a misdemeanor charge of criminal recklessness,[129] later dropped for fear Ford would plead guilty to it in lieu of the other charges. The maximum penalty for the felonies was a fine of $10,000 each.[130] Ford, whose financial resources and legal talent would dwarf those of the small rural courts and part-time prosecutor, tried to have this unique criminal indictment of a major corporation dismissed.

Indiana had a vehicular reckless homicide law since 1939.[131] As Indiana codified its laws from July 1977, a reckless homicide felony was added when a person recklessly killed another human.[132] An omission to perform a statutory or contractual duty was also an offense.[133] Ford had such a duty under the Highway Safety Act to immediately fix and notify of defects.[134] Corporations could be criminally liable for the acts of its agents in the context of their employment.[135] The effective date for the revised versions of these provisions was July 1, 1978. Ford challenged the meaning of the word "person," trying for a narrow definition meaning only a human,

---

[126] State of Indiana v. Ford Motor Co, No. 11-431 (Ind. Super. Ct. Apr 1980).
[127] State v. Ford Motor Co., No. 5324 (Ind. Super. Ct., Sept. 1978).
[128] Ind. Code 35-41-2-2(c) Culpability.
[129] Ind. Code 35-42-2-2 Criminal recklessness.
[130] Ind. Code 35-50-2-6 Level 5 felony.
[131] Cichos v. Indiana, 385 U.S. 76 (Nov. 1966), at 78.
[132] Ind. Code 35-42-1-5 Reckless homicide.
[133] Ind. Code 35-41-2-1 Voluntary conduct.
[134] Pub. L. 89-563, An Act to provide for a coordinated national safety program and establishment of safety standards for motor vehicles in interstate commerce to reduce traffic accidents and the deaths, injuries, and property damage which occur in such accidents.
[135] Ind. Code 35-41-2-3 Liability of Corporation, Partnership, or Unincorporated Association.

which the court rejected.[136] The company's lawyers next asserted the design and build of the 1973 Pinto was done long before any liability arose under the 1977 law. To charge Ford for prior acts would be an unconstitutional ex post facto law. To keep the indictment from being dismissed, the court narrowed its focus to what was effective state law on July 1, 1978. That was, a corporation omitting to perform a legal duty to fix and warn of a defect in its cars was liable for reckless homicide. This was true only between July 1, 1978, and the crash date, a period of 41 days.

Ford next tried to get the case moved from the small rural Indiana county of Elkhart to an even smaller county by requesting a change of venue due to pretrial publicity. The was granted, moving the trial to Pulaski County, in a city of about 2,500 people. At trial, Ford challenged every prosecution witness, refused to authenticate its own internal documents, challenged the introduction of other prosecution evidence, and generally pressed home its superior advantage in legal manpower and money against a judge and prosecutor not experienced in product liability. The mother of Judy and Lyn testified she received a recall notice in February 1979, seven months after the crash. If she had received one before that, she would have gotten rid of the Pinto. Ford had its parts supervisor testify that, given the early June recall, it would take until the middle of September to get replacement parts to all dealers for 2 million Pintos. It would not have been possible to have fixed the Ulrich's Pinto before the accident. The prosecution tried unsuccessfully to introduce evidence showing Ford had known about this problem for years but had not acted.

A key issue was the speed differential between the Pinto and the van that hit it. Ford asserted the speed differential was at least 50 mph, as the Pinto was stationary. Ford was allowed to introduce films of vans traveling at 50 mph crashing into a stationary Pinto. Clearly a vehicle of this weight crashing into a stationary object like a Pinto would demolish it and crush the fuel tank, so the evidence was important to bolster the defense's case. The national standard at the time was for vehicles to be able to withstand a rear collision of 30 mph, so Ford was able to show no similar vehicle could take a 50-mph collision and not have it fuel tank explode. Ford showed videos of other car models and in all their staged crashes at Ford facilities, their test fuel escaped from the fuel tank.

---

[136] Ind. Code 35-41-1-2 Definitions.

The judge had allowed these films to be shown to demonstrate it was not industry practice at the time to have cars withstand a crash at 50 mph, in addition to showing why the fuel tank ruptured. The defense asserted even if the car had been recalled and retrofitted, it would not have survived this crash, as damage at that speed would always reach the fuel tank. Ford said the 1973 Pinto was within the federal standards. Also, it had issued a much-publicized press release about the recall in June, and the NHTSA did not dictate more warnings. Conversely, the prosecution had a difficult time getting the judge to admit evidence used in the *Grimshaw*.

The judge ruled that videos showing 1971 and 1972 Pintos in crash tests were not relevant to a crash involving a 1973 Pinto, especially as the earlier models had slightly worse safety features. The judge did not allow testimony that Ford had doctored prior Pinto tests to meet safety standards. The judge did not admit internal Ford documents showing they understood the fuel tank issue and their suggested improvements, as these related to the 1971 and 1972 models. The judge believed that design issues from the earlier models might be appropriate for a product liability civil case, but this was a criminal case was about a failure to warn. The state's case was that the Pinto was moving and the speed differential between the two vehicles was 30-35 mph. If it was 50 mph as the defense asserted, why were the girls missing those types of injuries? Ford's 350 convictions of the Clean Air Act in 1973 were cited to question the company's honesty.

As was typical of the whole 10-week trial, the prosecution had seven rebuttal witnesses, but the court only allowed two to testify, and the scope of their testimony was limited. In the end, the prosecution's hands tied for several reasons. These included its limited budget; the lack of relevant legal experience; a pared down indictment; regularly disallowed evidence and testimony; and a series of ambiguous rulings by a judge unfamiliar with these types of cases. This meant that the full case for the prosecution was not laid before the jury. Over several days of deliberation, the jury was unable to reach a unanimous decision, until instructed to focus on the triable issue, which was not Ford's design issues. It was Ford's efforts in the limited 41-day window to fix the affected Pintos. The jury could not, beyond a reasonable doubt, agree that Ford's failure to warn during that time had reached the required level of recklessness, and so had to acquit the company of criminal liability in the deaths of the three girls.

In *Stubblefield*,[137] the court of appeals was reviewing a verdict for wrongful death for a 15-year-old girl. On July 10, 1977, she was sitting in the backseat of 1975 Ford Mustang II which was rear-ended, and exploded into a ball of flames. The appellant car company was asserting that the expert witnesses had reached conclusions, which was a function for the jury. The court said without the help of the experts, there was no way the jurors would have comprehended all the technical details. The court also agreed with the denial of the motion for a directed verdict, as it was up to a jury to determine factual issues such as Ford's negligence in design and whether that was the proximate cause of the harm. Knowledge of this unsafe condition and lack of warning left these issues for the jury. Ford also objected to the playing of a tape of President Richard Nixon, Lee Iacocca, and Henry Ford where it was agreed that regulators were supposed to "cool it" as to safety requirements, but the court found it relevant. Ford also objected to crash tests of Pintos being introduced. The court said any evidence that supported a material fact was relevant and admissible and as the Mustang II that crashed evolved from the Pinto, this demonstrated Ford's continued negligence, failure to warn, and marketing of a dangerous product. The judgment for the negligence of Ford was affirmed.

In *Hasson*,[138] the state supreme court affirmed a judgment for a 19-year-old who suffered permanent brain damage when a Lincoln Continental's brakes failed when driving down a steep hill. The suit was based on strict liability and negligence, asserting that Ford could have either warned buyers to use a different brake fluid or installed a dual master cylinder at minimal cost to avoid this problem. The long trial with many conflicting experts led to the jury awarding compensatory and punitive damages of more than $9 million. Ford's appeal tried to re-litigate the facts, which the court rejected, as brake fluid vaporization on the new disc brake system in the car was a reasonable inference from the facts presented. The same former Ford engineer who had testified in the Pinto trials testified here to the lack of adequate testing by Ford on the brake system and a refusal to install a more expensive solution, the dual master cylinder. Ford's assertions of juror misconduct for reading books or doing crossword puzzles during the presentation of evidence were unsuccessful.

---

[137] Ford Motor Co. v. Stubblefield, 319 S.E.2d 470 (Ga. App. June 1984).
[138] Hasson v. Ford Motor Co., 650 P.2d 1171 (Cal. Sept. 1982).

## *Chapter 5*

# 1975 – 1999

Mankind's ascent to the heavens, and on to the final frontier of space, finally began in 1783. In pre-revolutionary France, a balloon built by paper-making brothers Joseph-Michel and Jacques-Etienne Montgolfier kicked off a national craze for ballooning. After flying upwards, the next challenge was to fly a distance. The journey across the English Channel was first accomplished in January 1785. Later that year, the first ballooning deaths occurred for two Frenchmen trying to cross the Channel. It would be more than a century before other lighter- and heavier-than-air craft like dirigibles, airplanes, and helicopters overtook ballooning as the principal means to reach the sky. Then another half century before rocket ships took mankind to outer space. Hauntingly, the risk of tragic death always lurked around the daring new adventures of humans ascending from terra firma.

On August 13, 1989, several hot air balloons ascended into the morning sky above Alice Springs in central Australia, carrying passengers. One, VH-WMS, ascended to about 2,000 feet, with clearance from ATC within controlled airspace, and a filed flight plan. A second one, VH-NMS, ascended slightly later, with 12 passengers on board. The two pilots, from the same company, were connected by a wireless radio system, but were not in communication. Both were pointing out the landscape below to their passengers. VH-NMS, still lower, could not see around its envelope to spot the upper balloon. Suddenly, it impacted the basket of the upper balloon, VH-WMS. This tore a hole in panels of the lower balloon, which the upper balloon's basket briefly entered inside of. When VH-WMS finally freed itself, the hole in VH-NMS's panels widened, and it began to lose the air inside its envelope. The balloon then collapsed and began to plunge rapidly, falling 2,000 feet to the ground. All 13 people aboard were killed.

The Australian Transportation Safety Bureau report said VH-WMS did not have a mandatory instrument package to indicate altitude and vertical movement. The company's manual dictated an upper balloon had to give way, and avoid basket to envelope contact when flying in formation. The report specified the accident factors as: "1. The pilot of the upper balloon failed to maintain an adequate lookout and control of his aircraft in that he did not give way to the lower balloon. 2. The pilot of the lower balloon did not adequately assess the position of the upper balloon before climbing in close proximity with it. 3. The pilots of the two balloons involved in the collision were not in radio contact with each other. 4. Collision damage to the lower balloon was such as to render it uncontrollable."[1]

The VH-WMS pilot, Michael Sanby, was criminally charged with 13 counts of manslaughter and committing a dangerous act for not keeping a proper lookout for, and giving way to, the other balloon, not staying in radio contact, and not having the necessary equipment. He was arrested as he boarded a flight to Africa. At trial, he was found not guilty of the manslaughter charges but was guilty of the dangerous act and sentenced to prison in 1992. This was appealed to the territorial court of criminal appeals, which noted he was convicted for violating the following statute,

> Any person who does or makes any act or omission that causes serious danger, actual or potential, to the lives, health or safety of the public or to any person... in circumstances where an ordinary person similarly circumstanced would have clearly foreseen such danger and not have done or made that act or omission is guilty of a crime.[2]

The court believed the initial impact did not cause a serious danger. It was the fouling of the lines when the upper balloon entered the other balloon's envelope that caused the fabric to tear, leading to the fatal plunge. The sudden rise of the lower balloon, as testified by many witnesses in other balloons, was also not foreseeable. As there was insufficient evidence for a jury to find beyond a reasonable doubt he had violated the statute, the conviction was quashed. The first section of this chapter covers disasters from nature and affecting the environment while the second section presents disasters related to structures and flight.

---

[1] ATSB, Aviation Safety Investigation Report 198900820, Kavanagh Hot Air Balloon E-260 13 August 1989.
[2] Michael Winston Sanby v. The Queen., No. CA8 of 1992 (NTCCA 84, Australia May 1993).

## 5.1 ENVIRONMENT AND NATURE

### A. Volcano

| LEGAL ISSUES |
|---|
| ❖ Restrictions for volcanic eruptions giving rise to legal liability<br>❖ Exemptions for discretionary emergency measures |

On May 18, 1980, a significant earthquake led to the eruption of Mount St. Helens, a composite volcano in the Cascade Mountains in Washington State, and part of the Ring of Fire around the Pacific Ocean. The blast, equivalent to at least 25 megatons of TNT, took more than 1,300 feet off the top of the mountain. The lateral blast obliterated everything for 8 miles, leveled everything for 19 miles including 4 billion board feet of timber, and seared trees beyond that. The subsequent ash cloud reached an altitude of 12 miles and circled the earth, depositing over 500 million tons of ash. More than 50 people died from asphyxiation from the hot ash, the historically large debris avalanche, the pyroclastic flow, mudslides, and flooding, and airborne trees and rocks. Among the dead was a geologist monitoring the volcano 6 miles away, hikers 13 miles away, an 83-year-old long-time mountain resident named Harry R. Truman, loggers still trying to harvest old-growth timber before the eruption, and various onlookers.

Part of a mountain chain of mostly dormant former volcanoes, Mount St. Helens became active again in late March with smaller earthquakes and eruptions of steam and ash. The northern side began to swell with magma. Most of this area was inside a national forest managed by the United States Forest Service (USFS), with the rest under state control. Following United States Geological Survey (USGS) and USFS advice, the governor declared the whole state under a state of emergency on April 3, 1980. On April 30, when subsequent volcanic activity indicated an increased risk of avalanches, mud flows, and flooding, the governor issued an executive order limiting access. The "red zone" around the volcano was only for select government personnel such as the USGS, USFS, law enforcement, and search and rescue. Within an outer "blue zone," only red zone personnel and homeowners could enter in daylight hours. An executive order extending the zones was ready for the governor to sign on May 17, but was not signed until May 25, a week after the eruption. This executive order extended the red zone to 20 miles from the center of the volcano.

In *Cougar Business Owners*,[3] the town of Cougar, Washington, 11 miles southwest of Mount St. Helens, was in the red hazard zone. Those running businesses there sued, complaining that the restrictions were imposed too early and lifted too late. The trial court granted summary judgment for the state and so the plaintiffs appealed. The state supreme court reviewed the timeline of what had occurred, including additional eruptions and modifications of the hazard zones by further executive orders. In early September, public hearings asked whether Cougar should be removed from the red zone. With a public consensus, it was removed within a few weeks of the hearings. The governor filed her affidavit with the court,

> As the summer progressed I was aware of the concern of some elements of the business people in Cougar that the restricted entry to their area was depressing their economy. I was also being advised of the continuing hazard to the Cougar area that the mountain posed. In making my judgments I weighed opinions both for and against opening access to Cougar... In each of these decisions affecting the Town of Cougar and its residents I weighed the advice of federal, state and local officials as well as the scientific community and made my decision exercising my best judgment based on the then current state of information and opinion. I acted at all times out of regard for what in my considered judgment was necessary to preserve and maintain life, health, property and the public peace. I acted at all times in good faith and without malice toward any person. Throughout this period of time it was my firm belief that the Mt. St. Helens disaster created the need for a continuing state of emergency necessitating in certain areas of this state at certain times restrictions on access such as those imposed by me on the Cougar Area.[4]

The court ruled that her actions were supported by statute, were entirely discretionary, and were proper exercises of the police power. The court said that while there may have been a case earlier, there was not one in waiting until no further eruptions of the magnitude of the May 18 eruption had occurred before suing. The court held that discretionary functions of government could not be tortious. The court defined those discretionary functions as meeting the following criteria,

---

[3] Cougar Business Owners Ass'n v. State, 97 Wash. 2d 466 (Wash. June 1982).
[4] *Id*. at 470.

(1) Does the challenged act ... necessarily involve a basic governmental policy, program, or objective? (2) Is the questioned act ... essential to the realization or accomplishment of that policy, program, or objective ...? (3) Does the act ... require the exercise of basic policy evaluation, judgment, and expertise ...? (4) Does the governmental agency involved possess the requisite constitutional, [or] statutory ... authority ... to do or make the challenged act ...?[5]

The court ruled that the governor had met all these criteria and had the statutory authority to act in an emergency. The plaintiffs then asserted that there was no disaster before May 18. The court responded that the disaster was not the eruption on May 18, but the reactivation of a dormant volcano. The plaintiffs' definition would mean the governor's only role would be in cleanup operations, as she could do nothing preventively. The plaintiffs also asserted the disaster was over by June, but the court said the authority to end the emergency measures was the same as to start them. The governor had the discretion to determine this, considering the subject was an active but not currently erupting volcano. The court also held this to be a valid exercise of police power and so dismissed the complaint.

In *Karr*,[6] representatives of decedents killed in the eruption sued the state but lost on summary judgment and appealed. The court noted the varied preparatory activities by federal, state, and local governments, including the USGS issuing a press release that those at least 20 miles from the volcano should be safe. However, no agency was sure when an explosion would take place. It could be years or even decades later. Recreational activities in the area were closed and roadblocks set up on roads in the area and criminal penalties set out for violators. After a bulge had begun to build on the north side of the volcano, there was concern that an earthquake could lead to an avalanche, which would in turn push debris into Spirit Lake, causing mudslides and flooding. Based on USGS advice, the USFS had designated red and blue hazard zones for federally controlled areas in the national forest and asked the governor to order the same for state-controlled lands, which she did by executive order. Further bulging on the northside of the volcano led to the May 17 proposed expansion of the hazard zones and the new executive order.

---

[5] *Id.* at 471.
[6] Karr v. State, 765 P.2d 316 (Wash. App. Dec. 1988).

The plaintiff's decedents were outside the existing hazard zones when they were killed and so the plaintiffs asserted the governor was negligent in setting the hazard zones. The trial court had held the state had sovereign immunity and was not subject to tort liability. The court of appeals noted that the blast happened without warning and the blast area was at least 10 times larger than any prior eruption, and at least 15 times worse than the worst estimates by experts. The governor was ruled to have made a policy decision, a discretionary function that had immunity. The court had applied the factors from *Cougar Business Owners* and reached the same conclusion. The appellant asserted she had not met the third prong in that she had not engaged in due consideration. The court, affirming the lower court, said there was no such evidence, and a decision had been made based on all the inputs from both the scientific community and citizens.

In *Johnson*,[7] a film crew tried to visit the volcano five days after the explosion. When spotted by a search and rescue helicopter on their way up, they refused an offer of evacuation. After completing their filming and on the way down, they were served citations by a deputy sheriff landing in a helicopter, who refused to give them a ride and directed that they take a different route down the mountain. This required spending a night on the mountain, during which the volcano erupted again, and ash and mud landed on them. The crew were forced to seek a helicopter rescue. They were never prosecuted and instead filed a civil suit. Among the claims were false arrest, but the court rejected this, as they were never detained, merely given citations. They also asserted negligent failure to rescue, but the court rejected this, as a negligent act of an official causing unintended injury did not invoke due process concerns.

In *Graham*,[8] plaintiffs were seeking insurance payments for their houses swept away by mudflows and flooding after the eruption. Pyroclastic flows along with the hot ash melted glacial ice, which combined with water from Spirit Lake, rainfall from the eruption cloud, and existing ground water to create the mudflows which eventually damaged their homes. Their insurance policies did not cover for earth movement (earthquake, volcanic eruption, landslide, mudflow) or flood but did cover for explosions. The supreme court remanded for a jury trial to decide,

---

[7] Johnson v. Barker, 799 F.2d 1396 (9th Cir. Sept. 1986).
[8] Graham v. Public Employees Mutual Insurance, 98 Wash. 2d 533 (Wash. Jan. 1983).

whether the movement of Mount St. Helens was an "explosion" within the terms of the insurance policies; whether that "explosion" was preceded by earth movement, and whether appellants' damages were proximately caused by the eruption of Mount St. Helens on May 18, 1980.[9]

In *Keetch*,[10] motel owners claimed business interruption after their premises were inundated with six inches of ash on May 18. By July 1, they had cleaned up the original ash fall, but had to continue to clean up throughout the year as ash blew in from other sites. The insurer refused to pay that part of the claim, but the court held that there should be partial interruption damages payable under the policy, as the motel's appearance was damaged by all the ash. The insurance company said as they were not forced to close, their business was not interrupted. The court of appeals agreed that there needed to be an inability to use a premise. None of the motel rooms had become unavailable due to the ash on the grounds. A diminished quality of service was not sufficient. The lower court's holding allowing the business interruption claim was reversed.

In *Furlow*,[11] a criminal defendant was asserting a violation of the right to a speedy trial. The defendant was apprehended on February 22 and his trial did not start until June 17, a period of 116 days. The applicable speedy trial statute required a trial take place within 90 days of apprehension. However, he was released from federal detention and re-arrested for other charges, so this rule did not apply to his apprehension in federal custody. The statute also required a trial within 70 days of arraignment on March 12, meaning he would need to be tried by May 21. Except that he filed a motion, which took 12 days to resolve, so that reset his last required trial date to June 2. Then there was the impact of the eruption on May 18, due to "interrupted transportation, communication, etc. (affecting the abilities of jurors, witnesses, counsel, officials to attend the trial)."[12] The trial date could now be extended to June 17, allowing for the eruption. The court of appeals affirmed the lower court's judgment, finding no presumptive prejudice or violation of a Sixth Amendment right for these relatively brief delays, including the delays caused by the eruption of Mount St. Helens.

---

[9] *Id.* at 539.
[10] Keetch v. Mutual of Enumclaw Insurance, 831 P.2d 784 (Wash. App. June 1992).
[11] Ross Furlow v. United States, 644 F.2d 764 (9th Cir. May 1981).
[12] *Id.* at 767-68.

In *Ladum*,[13] the plaintiff sought recovery from the federal government for rent related to a lease agreement for a USFS ranger station in Cougar. The tender required the building to be available by the beginning of 1980. The lease agreement gave the government the right to terminate the lease with 90 days' notice. The plaintiff was not able to obtain financing, so the government delayed their expected tenancy to October 1980. After the eruption, the government notified that it was terminating the lease. As the facility was never completed, the government denied that it owed any rent. The court of claims agreed, as the right of cancellation was properly exercised after the eruption had obviated the need for a station in Cougar.

In *Mining & Recovery Ltd.*,[14] Congress had passed the Mount Saint Helens National Volcanic Area Act of 1982,[15] which preserved the unique ecosystem around the mountain and made it part of the national forest. Any mining leases in this area had to be acquired by purchase, exchange, or donation. Dan Fer Investment Company agreed to donate its interests but never actually did so, because it insisted on a tax valuation so it could properly take a tax deduction. The government said that it never promised such a valuation. Due to the slow pace of acquisition, in 1998 Congress passed the Mount St. Helens National Volcanic Monument Completion Act[16] to complete these additions. The court concurred that the agreement was valid, and the government was under no obligation to provide a valuation for tax purposes. The court of appeals[17] noted the owner's $321 million valuation of the property did not consider the realities of extraction, the speculative nature of finding minerals in the claim, and the impact of the eruption. The USFS offered $242,000 worth of property outside the monument area. The court concurred that the USFS could exchange property inside the monument for property outside that did not contain minerals. In affirming the district court, it held the appraisal done for the USFS was not arbitrary and capricious or contrary to law.

---

[13] Ladum v. United States, 32 Cont. Cas. Fed. 72,456 (Ct. Cl. May 1984).
[14] Mt. St. Helens Mining & Recovery Ltd. Partnership v. United States, 177 F. Supp. 2d 1143 (W.D. Wash. Nov. 2001).
[15] Pub. L. 97-243, An Act to designate the Mount St. Helens National Volcanic Monument in the State of Washington, and for other purposes.
[16] Pub. L. 105-279, An Act to provide for the expeditious completion of the acquisition of private mineral interests within the Mount St. Helens National Volcanic Monument mandated by the 1982 Act that established the Monument, and for other purposes.
[17] Mt. St. Helens Mining and Recovery v. United States, 384 F. 3d 721 (9th Cir. Sept. 2004).

## B. Platform Collapse

| LEGAL ISSUES |
|---|
| ❖ Indemnities to negligent operator from legal liability<br>❖ Platform operations giving rise to full statutory legal liability |

On July 6, 1988, the Piper Alpha oil drilling platform in the North Sea caught fire after several explosions and eventually collapsed and capsized, leading to the deaths of 165 of the 226 people on the platform. A public inquiry was to establish the accident's circumstances and cause, led by W. Douglas (Lord) Cullen. His report[18] explained that gas and water were separated from drilled oil in production separators. A liquid condensate (mainly propane), extracted by cooling the gas, was injected back into the oil sent by pipeline 128 miles to the Orkney Islands. The remaining natural gas (primarily methane) went via pipeline to Aberdeen. Four modules sat on the production deck 84 feet above mean sea level. Module A contained the well heads, Module B the separators, Module C the gas compressors, and Module D the electrical plant and control room. The 107-foot level contained other modules, on top of which was the crew quarters.

A platform emergency shutdown system was intended to stop flows from the wellhead and to/from the pipelines. The platform had 6 lifeboats for 47 people each, 13 life rafts for 25 people each, plus life buoys, life jackets, and knotted ropes. Work by permit mandated advanced written approval for dangerous work, device isolation, safety precautions during the work, and approval of the work done, with three different managers responsible. The initial explosion in Module C was fed by condensate from a pump undergoing maintenance, leading to a fire in Module B, and then large explosions fed by gas already in the pipeline risers igniting. Some men lower on the rig descended to escape but fire prevented most of those higher up, including those in the crew quarters, from reaching the lifeboats. Rescue boats tried to attend but were driven back by fire. The living quarters eventually fell into the sea, where half of all victims perished while sheltering there, waiting for evacuation. Of the survivors, some jumped off the platform from as high as 175 feet; others died in doing so. The report concluded the senior leader, the offshore installation manager (OIM), had ineffectively led the platform's evacuation.

---

[18] THE PUBLIC INQUIRY INTO THE PIPER ALPHA DISASTER, THE HON LORD CULLEN (Nov. 1990).

In *Elf Enterprise Caledonia*,[19] the plaintiff (the successor to Occidental Petroleum Caledonia, OPCAL) pursued indemnity from many of the contractors who had employees on the platform the night of the explosion. After the disaster, the representatives of deceased victims and survivors had threatened to litigate their claims in Texas, the location of Occidental's headquarters, due to an increased likelihood of significant damage payouts. An agreement was reached, on what was termed a "mid-Atlantic formula," to settle the victims' claims, at a mid-point between what could be awarded in Texas courts and in Scottish courts. After paying out these claims to victims, the plaintiff then pursued their claims against various contractors to claw back their respective shares of the payouts to victims for their employees. Of the decedents on the platform, 31 were employed by Occidental and 134 by contractors and of the survivors, 6 were employed by Occidental and 55 by contractors.

The plaintiff asserted that they were bound to compensate the victims and that the amount they paid were reasonable. The plaintiff also claimed that the contractors were liable per contractual terms to indemnify the plaintiff for payouts related to their employees, plus their share of legal expenses. The defendants responded that they had no such liability and further, the awards given were too high, as the plaintiff over-estimated what a Texas court would award. There were 146 actions outstanding and the court proposed to try seven cases, each representing a distinct set of legal issues and contractors. The court, which did not use the Cullen report, ruled OPCAL was in control of the platform and was responsible for the safety, health, and welfare of persons on the platform, through the OIM. OPCAL had a comprehensive responsibility to see that the Offshore Installations (Operational Safety, Health and Welfare) Regulations 1976, enacted under the Mineral Workings (Offshore Installations) Act 1971, were followed. Each contractor was liable only for the acts of their own employees. It was the OPCAL operations staff who operated the platform, everyone else provided support. OPCAL safety staff also oversaw the work of contractors. The contractors worked under OPCAL's specifications, control and inspection, being required to conform to OPCAL's safety and operations procedures manuals. This included the work by permit system, which the defendants asserted was knowingly and regularly disregarded.

---

[19] Elf Caledonia Ltd v. London Bridge Engineering Ltd & Ors [1997] ScotCS 1 (Sept. 1997).

The plaintiff asserted the explosion was caused when a condensate injection pump, taken out of service in Module C but not correctly sealed by a contractor's employee, was restarted by OPCAL's lead production operator. Th plaintiff relied on proof of gas detection alarms going off in Module C and the testimony of witnesses on nearby ships. The defendants said the disaster could just as easily have started in Module B, which had a higher danger rating, or from the excessive amount of natural gas being flared during gas compressor maintenance. In the end, the defendants asserted that it was not possible, with the key participants all dead and the relevant equipment on the seabed, to definitively know what happened,

> Thus, it was contended, on the limited and inconclusive evidence which remains available any decision ascribing a specific cause to the accident is essentially speculative and thus unjustified. The defenders are correct to the extent that there is less evidence about the accident than the Court would like to have seen and that is an unfortunate but inevitable consequence of the catastrophic nature of what happened. However there is some evidence and the question is what can be taken from it when it is pieced together. If more evidence had been available then no doubt it would not have been necessary to spend almost four years on the proof.[20]

The defendants claimed OPCAL's lead production operator restarted the out-of-service pump knowing it violated safety protocols as there was no pressure safety valve in place. This would constitute willful misconduct and alleviate their obligation for indemnity. If he did not have this knowledge, then OPCAL had not ensured proper safety, handover, and work by permit practices were followed by its employees, so it was willful misconduct. The plaintiff was happy just to have their former employee be considered negligent in re-starting this pump, as that would not relieve the defendants of their obligation to indemnify. The defendants asserted that, even if the contractor's valve fitter had not properly tightened the blind flange used on the out-of-service pipe section, he could not be negligent if he could not foresee that it could lead to catastrophe for the platform. Further, it was the acts of the OPCAL lead production operator in restarting the out-of-service pump which broke the chain of causation.

---

[20] *Id.* ch. 5.1.2.

The court held it was the OPCAL's lead production operator's act in re-initiating the out-of-service pump that caused the initial explosion in Module C. The court then looked to the indemnity clauses. One example,

> The Contractor shall indemnify, hold harmless and defend the Company... from and against any claim, demand, cause of action, expense or liability (including but not limited to the costs of litigation) arising (whether before or after completion of the work hereunder) by reason of:-... Injury to or death of persons employed by or damage to or loss or destruction of property of the Contractor... irrespective of any contributory negligence, whether active or passive, of the party to be indemnified, unless such injury, death, damage, loss or destruction was caused by the sole negligence or wilful misconduct of the party which would otherwise be indemnified... For the purpose of this Article "wilful misconduct" shall mean an intentional and conscious disregard for:-... a. good and prudent practices normally associated with the type of operations envisaged herein, or b. of any of the terms of this contract, not justified by any special circumstances, but shall not include any error of judgement or mistake made either in acting or failing to act by any director, officer, employee, agent, contractor or subcontractor of the party to be indemnified provided such party acted in good faith... injury to or death of persons employed by or damage to or loss or destruction of property of the Company... irrespective of any contributory negligence, whether active or passive, of the party to be indemnified, unless caused by the sole negligence or wilful misconduct (in case of injury or death) or wilful misconduct (in the case of property damage, loss or destruction) of the party which would otherwise be indemnified"[21]

The court said the plaintiff's argument was that there would be indemnities due even if OPCAL was negligent, as OPCAL would be legally required to pay victims under the offshore platform laws and regulations. The defendants' argument was that they were only liable for indemnities for their own employees where they contributed to their death or injury. The defendants also urged the application of res ipsa loquitur, given the lack of evidence and the need for the plaintiff to prove the lack of negligence. The court agreed, and said the fact that all the people working

---

[21] *Id.* ch. 9.2

on the platform were not OPCAL employees was not an issue, as OPCAL had assumed responsibility for everyone working on the platform. However, the court held the contractor's pipe fitter was also contributorily negligent and the conduct of the plaintiff's operator was not willful, so the indemnities must be paid. The court discussed whether the potential use of U.S. courts should have influenced the victims' awards. He focused on whether Texas courts would accept jurisdiction when the events happened in Europe. In the end, the court accepted the settlement amounts were reasonable. The court ruled that the indemnity clauses applied only to a real loss, one not covered by insurance. In concluding, the judge said, "it rather concerns me that after a proof of inordinate length (over four years) six of the seven test actions have been decided by what very much appears to be a preliminary point." The plaintiff appealed the ruling that the contractors did not have to indemnify if insurers had already paid the claims. The court of sessions reversed and the House of Lords affirmed, requiring the contractors to indemnify despite the insurance payouts.[22]

In *McFarlane*,[23] the plaintiff was on one of the boats that attended after the Alpha Piper explosion. He did not suffer physical injuries but did suffer psychiatric injury. The ship was the *Tharos*, which was multi-functional, including fabrication facilities, machine shop, diving support, a crane, a helipad and helicopter, fire suppression devices and monitors, a platform gangway, living quarters, and a hospital. It was not intended as an initial responder due to its slow speed, and non-essential personnel like the plaintiff were to be evacuated before starting rescue operations. The trial court found the plaintiff, a painter, more susceptible to psychiatric injury than average. The court agreed that he was in fear for his life and safety that night, as he had not been evacuated before fire fighting started. The *Tharos* got to within 50 meters of the burning platform but could not advance, as three major explosions from the gas pipeline risers occurred. The scene in front of him included men jumping from high on the platform, some waving for help, and others on fire, and a rescue vessel engulfed in a fireball. The court of appeals reversed, holding the plaintiff was just a witness but not in actual danger nor did he feel so, as he never sheltered.

---

[22] Caledonia North Sea Limited v. British Telecommunications Plc (Scotland) and Others [2002] UKHL 4 (Feb. 2002).
[23] McFarlane v EE Caledonia Ltd. [1993] EWCA Civ 27 (July 1993).

## C. Chemical Poisoning

| LEGAL ISSUES |
|---|
| ❖ Chemical poisoning of nearby residents causing legal liability<br>❖ Multi-country litigation arising from a single disaster |

On December 2, 1984, a chemical plant in Bhopal, India, suffered a release of a highly toxic gas in a densely populated area, which lead to the deaths of thousands (the estimates vary widely) and sickened up to half a million people. The gas, methyl isocyanate (MIC), was an intermediate product of a process to create a pesticide, using practices that were no longer state of the art. The slow reaction to the disaster by both the company and local authorities meant that citizens living nearby were not quickly notified, and deaths and injuries rapidly mounted. The legal ramifications were significant, as the operator of the plant was a joint venture between Union Carbide (UC) and Indian entities, with UC having a slightly larger percentage, making it the majority owner. This entity was Union Carbide India Limited (UCIL). There were to be criminal charges and civil litigation filed, with plaintiffs trying to use U.S. courts but being sent back to India for adjudication, and then trying again, and again, and again, and again.

In *Gas Plant Disaster*,[24] the court was dealing with 145 individual lawsuits, which had been joined and consolidated. The Indian government had, in March 1985, passed the Bhopal Gas Leak Disaster (Processing Of Claims) Act,[25] which replaced an ordinance promulgated the prior month by the Indian president. The act gave the central government of India the exclusive right to stand in for all claimants and to initiate litigation, to reach a settlement, or take whatever action a private plaintiff might undertake. It also created a scheme to register and process claims related to this disaster. With that authority, the central government filed suit against UC in U.S. federal court, after registering nearly half a million claimants. It was also added to this litigation in the district court. UC then moved to dismiss the two complaints based on *forum non conveniens,* citing certain Supreme Court cases in support, to move the matter back to India for trial.

---

[24] In Re Union Carbide Corporation Gas Plant Disaster, 634 F. Supp. 842 (S.D.N.Y. June 1986).
[25] An Act to confer certain powers on the Central Government to secure that claims arising out of, or connected with, the Bhopal gas leak disaster are dealt with speedily, effectively, equitably and to the best advantage of the claimants and for matters incidental thereto, Bhopal Gas Leak Disaster (Processing Of Claims) Act, No. 21 of 1985.

The district court analyzed the guidance from these two cases.[26] One issue was the impact of a change in law when moving to a different jurisdiction. The court said this would negatively impact the plaintiffs, given the liberality of many American legal procedures such as strict liability, jury trials, extensive discovery, and contingency fees. However, courts were not to engage a conflict of law analysis but only determine that there were adequate remedies in the other jurisdiction. The court said UC had agreed it was amenable to service of process within India and Indian jurisdiction. Among the many substantive and procedural deficiencies that the plaintiffs, including ironically the Indian government, asserted regarding the Indian legal system were lack of legal innovativeness; endemic delays; lack of lawyer legal specialization; undeveloped substantive tort law; limitations on discovery; lack of class actions; lack of juries; and judgments could not be enforced in the United States. The court rejected all these because there were Indian alternatives for each. The court did require, as a condition of dismissing the complaint, that UC agree to broad discovery and that it would be bound by any judgment made in the Indian courts.

Other factors the court considered were that almost all the sources of evidence were in India; the witnesses were all in India so their availability could be easier to compel by Indian courts; and the ability to view the plant where the explosion occurred was easier in India. The court ruled the administrative burden would be easier in India; that Indian government involvement, at all levels, in setting up and licensing the plant and in investigating the accident, was far greater than it was in the United States; and *lex loci*, using the law where the tort took place, applied. In conclusion, as India was the most appropriate forum, the complaint was dismissed,

> The Court thus finds itself faced with a paradox. In the Court's view, to retain the litigation in this forum, as plaintiffs request, would be yet another example of imperialism, another situation in which an established sovereign inflicted its rules, its standards and values on a developing nation. This Court declines to play such a role. The Union of India is a world power in 1986, and its courts have the proven capacity to mete out fair and equal justice. To deprive the Indian judiciary of this opportunity to stand tall before the world and to pass judgment

---

[26] Piper Aircraft Co. v. Reyno, 454 U.S. 235 (Dec. 1981); Gulf Oil Corp. v. Gilbert, 330 U.S. 501 (Mar. 1947).

on behalf of its own people would be to revive a history of subservience and subjugation from which India has emerged. India and its people can and must vindicate their claims before the independent and legitimate judiciary created there since the Independence of 1947.[27]

In *Bano Bi*,[28] the court of appeals reviewed what had occurred since the dismissal of the complaints. The litigation had moved to India, where the Indian Supreme Court of India had approved a settlement of $470 million against UC and UCIL, saying,

> The basic consideration motivating the conclusion of the settlement was the compelling need for urgent relief. The suffering of the victims has been intense and unrelieved. Thousands of persons who pursued their own occupations for a[n] humble and honest living have been rendered destitute by this ghastly disaster. Even after four years of litigation, basic questions of the fundamentals of the law as to liability of the Union Carbide Corporation and the quantum of damages are yet being debated. These, of course, are important issues which need to be decided. But, when thousands of innocent citizens were in near destitute conditions, without adequate subsistential needs of food and medicine and with every coming morrow haunted by the spectre of death and continued agony, it would be heartless abstention, if the possibilities of immediate sources of relief were not explored. Considerations of excellence and niceties of legal principles were greatly over-shadowed by the pressing problems of very survival for a large number of victims.[29]

That court had also ended all civil and criminal litigation in the matter. However, two class action lawsuits were filed in Texas state courts, asserting that the Indian government had a conflict of interest due to its ownership interest in UCIL; the settlements were grossly inadequate; and their due process rights were violated due to inadequate notice, representation, and lack of opt out. The district court, pointing to its prior

---

[27] In Re Union Carbide Corporation Gas Plant Disaster, at 867.
[28] Bano Bi, Individually and on Behalf of the Children of Rashid Kahn, and as Representative of the Estate of Rashid Kahn v. Union Carbide Chemicals and Plastics Company Inc., Abdul Wahid v. Union Carbide Chemicals and Plastics Company Inc., 984 F.2d 582 (2nd Cir. Jan. 1993).
[29] Union Carbide Corporation vs Union Of India, A.I.R. 1990 S.C. 273 (Sup. Ct. of India, May 1989).

judgment, dismissed the complaints. The court of appeals said the Indian Supreme Court had upheld the Bhopal Act while rejecting many of these same arguments.[30] The court, deferring to the law of a democratic country in resolving disputes for a disaster occurring within its own borders, affirmed the dismissal, holding that the plaintiffs lacked standing.

In *Bano I*,[31] the court of appeals was reviewing a 1999 lawsuit from the disaster victims. They made claims under the Alien Tort Claims Act (ATCA) for the Bhopal disaster; asserted UC had not abided by the conditions under which the complaints were dismissed in 1986; and asked for damages for environmental damage from that plant unrelated to the 1984 disaster. Additionally, because the Supreme Court of India later allowed criminal prosecution against UC and its CEO at the time, and they did not appear in India to answer those charges, the plaintiff asserted that the fugitive disentitlement doctrine should be applied. The court of appeals affirmed the doctrine did not apply, as it was for fugitives from the court that was ruling, not those moving under its jurisdiction. The court also affirmed the dismissal of the ATCA claims, as they were fully litigated and settled in India. The court said that while the Supreme Court of India allowed the criminal proceedings to go forward in their revised decree, there was no agreement by UC to comply with the revised decree. Further, the dropping of criminal investigations was not part of the bargain with UC, so they had broken no contractual commitment. The court of appeals affirmed the lower court, except in not addressing the environmental claims, and so vacated and remanded for a determination on those issues.

In *Bano II*,[32] the case was back before the court of appeals after the district court had ruled against their revised complaint. The complaint

---

[30] Charan Lal Sahu v. Union of India, A.I.R. 1990 S.C. 1480 (Sup. Ct. of India Dec. 1989).

[31] Sajida Bano, Haseena Bi, Sunil Kumar, Dr. Stanley Norton, Asad Khan, Shiv Narayan Maithil, Devendra Kumar Yadav, Bhopal Gas Peedit Mahila Udyog Sangathan, (Bgpmus), Gas Peedit Nirashrit Pension Bhogi Sangharsh Morcha,(gpnpbsm), Bhopal Gas Peedit Stationery Karmachari Sangh,(bgpmsks), Bhopal Gas Peedit Sangharsh Sahayog Samiti,(bgpsss), Bhopal Group for Information and Action (Bgia), on Behalf of Themselves and All Others Similarly Situated v. Union Carbide Corporation and Warren Anderson, 273 F.3d 120 (2nd Cir. Dec. 2001).

[32] Sajida Bano, Haseena Bi, Sunil Kumar, Dr. Stanley Norton, Asad Khan, Shiv Narayan Maithil, Devendra Kumar Yadav, Bhopal Gas Peedit Mahila Udyog Sangathan (Bgpmus), Gas Peedit Nirashrit Pension Bhogi Sangharsh Morcha (Gpnpbsm), Bhopal Gas Peedit Mahila Stationery Karmachari Sangh (Bgpmsks), Bhopal Gas Peedit Sangharsh Sahayog Samiti (Bgpsss), and Bhopal Group for Information and Action (Bgia), on Behalf of Themselves and All Others

asked for injunctions to remediate the plant site and for health monitoring for those impacted by the disaster, for personal injury and property damages for the lead plaintiff, and damages asserted by local organizations for area residents. The district court held the personal injury claims were barred by the statute of limitations, that the property claims, because they also arose from the same groundwater contamination as the personal injury claims, should also be barred. As UCIL no longer operated at the Bhopal site, which was taken over by the state, it would be impractical to fashion an injunction in New York addressing a foreign government at such a distance. It was similarly infeasible to implement medical monitoring by locating thousands affected by the disaster over decades living so far away. And these local organizations did not have standing to represent individualized claims. The court of appeals concurred on the bodily injury claims but as there was no record of when the class representative became aware of her property damage, that issue was remanded. The ruling that the organizations could not represent others was upheld, as organizations could not seek damages for its members and the injunctive relief was individualized. Remediation of the plant site was affirmed as impracticable.

In *Sahu*,[33] a Bhopal property owner whose medical issues were not time barred sued for monetary damages and injunctive relief for the groundwater pollution. Among the theories the plaintiffs argued included that UC was directly liable for a nuisance, or that UC was indirectly liable, as either a joint tortfeasor with UCIL, acting in concert with UCIL, or had total domination over UCIL and so the plaintiffs should be able to pierce the corporate veil to place the actions of the subsidiary on the parent. The district court granted summary judgment against all but veil piercing, which it later also granted. The court of appeals reversed due to a lack of notice. After a long discovery, the district court again granted summary judgment, and the court of appeals affirmed.[34] The final summary judgment was in 2014,[35] some 30 years after this disaster had occurred.

---

Similarly Situated, Haseena Bi, Bhopal Gas Peedit Mahila Udyog Sangathan (Bgpmus), Bhopal Gas Peedit Mahila Stationery Karmachari Sangh (Bgpmsks), Bhopal Gas Peedit Sangharsh Sahayog Samiti (Bgpsss), and Bhopal Group for Information and Action (Bgia), on Behalf of Themselves and All Others Similarly Situated v. Union Carbide Corporation and Warren Anderson, 361 F.3d 696 (2nd Cir. Mar. 2004).

[33] Sahu v. Union Carbide Corp., 548 F.3d 59 (2nd Cir. Nov. 2008).
[34] Sahu v. Union Carbide Corp., No. 12-2983 (2nd Cir. June 2013).
[35] Sahu v. Union Carbide Corp., No. 07 Civ. 2156 (S.D.N.Y. July 2014).

## D. Tanker Spill

| LEGAL ISSUES |
|---|
| ❖ Oil tanker spill resulting in captain's criminal liability<br>❖ Level of punitive damages for maritime disaster |

On March 24, 1989, the Exxon Valdez oil tanker, more than 900 feet long, ran aground in the dark on Bligh Reef in Prince William Sound, Alaska. Capt. Joseph Hazelwood had veered out of the normal shipping lane to avoid ice. He, the only one aboard with the special license needed to navigate in these waters, had left the bridge before the required turn to avoid this well-known reef. This lack of judgment was attributed to his renewed drinking, as he was an alcoholic. Those on the bridge could not turn the slow-turning vessel in time to avoid hitting the reef. The result was a hole in the tanker that allowed 11 million gallons of oil to spill into the sound, contaminating 1,500 miles of coastline, and affecting wildlife, the environment, local natives, and commercial fishermen. Litigation would eventually split the groups seeking damages into those same cohorts.

The federal and state governments, after suing Exxon and its shipping subsidiary under the Clean Water Act, reached an agreement for payments of $900 million over ten years, to pay for the two governments' cleanup costs and for further remediation efforts. Exxon had spent more than $2 billion on the cleanup and could offset future payments to the government with further remediation efforts. The agreement also included a reopener clause that could specify another $100 million was due if other unforeseen damages were later discovered. In addition, to drop the criminal litigation against the company, Exxon agreed to pay an additional $125 million in fines and restitution. The civil agreement emphasized its timeliness,

> the recovery afforded by this settlement is worth far more to the public because it comes relatively soon after the Oil spill, instead of after many years of litigation, and because it will make substantial sums available for restoration work immediately, with the remaining payments scheduled to correspond to the Governments' expectation of when they will be needed.[36]

---

[36] Governments' Memorandum in Support of the Agreement and Consent Decree (Oct. 1991), p. 26-27.

In *Baker*,[37] the district court had segregated the classes into commercial fishermen, Alaska Native, land owners, and punitive damages. The land owners had settled before trial. Exxon admitted its negligence caused the oil spill. The jury determined Exxon and Hazelwood had acted recklessly. It awarded the commercial fishermen $287 million in compensatory damages, which after credit for payments already made, was about $20 million. The jury awarded $5 billion in punitive damages. The court was clear these punitive damages only concerned commercial fishing, not environmental damage, which had been addressed in the settlement between Exxon and the two governments. Exxon appealed the punitive damages award, assigning several errors. The court of appeals rejected Exxon's first contentions, that it had already been criminally fined and the cost of the cleanup was so significant that it would deter future offending or that punitive damages were not allowed in maritime law. Exxon asserted res judicata based on its agreement with the government. The court rejected that as it dealt with compensatory and remedial damages, not punitive, and only applied to the parties to that agreement.

Exxon's claim that the Clean Water Act precluded common law remedies was also rejected, as the punitive damages were related to private, not public, interests. Exxon's asserted punitive damages could not be accessed against an employer that had not directed or condoned the acts. The court said that Exxon had been adjudged reckless and its prior caselaw allowed for the situation when a manager in the scope of his employment and using his discretion was reckless. Exxon also was appealing the punitive damage amounts. The court of appeals, noting recent Supreme Court cases, said that the circuit courts were now required to de novo review punitive damage awards. So the court remanded this back to the district court, with the following guidance. The lower court was to focus on reprehensibility, the ration of punitive damages to compensatory damages, and comparable civil or criminal penalties. The case was remanded a second time by the court of appeals, for intervening Supreme Court decisions and so came back for a third review.[38] The court reduced the punitive damages to $2.5 billion, giving credit for Exxon's costs of cleanup, which had lessened the need for deterrence in the future.

---

[37] Baker ex rel. Mandatory Punitive Damages Class v. Hazelwood, 270 F.3d 1215 (9th Cir. Nov. 2001).
[38] In Re: The Exxon Valdez, 472 F.3d 600 (9th Cir. Dec. 2006).

The case came to the Supreme Court, after an en banc hearing was denied.[39] The Court reviewed the history of punitive damages, deciding they were awarded both as punishment for past acts and as a deterrent for future behavior.[40] While the median punitive damage award was less than the median compensatory award, the mean punitive damage award was higher, due to some outlier cases with very high punitive damage awards. Based on these experiences, the court said that for maritime cases like this, under federal common law, the upper limit for punitive damages should be not higher than the compensatory damages, in a ratio of 1:1. The court recounted all the compensatory damage payments: $287 million to commercial fisherman, $23 million to Native Alaskans, $13 million to other claimants, $133 million to Native and commercial fish processors, $21 million to Native corporations, $13 million to municipalities, $16 million to cannery workers and seafood brokers, and $1 million to others, for a total of about $507 million.[41] The court set that total as the upper limit, and reversed and remanded in line with that amount, based on the defendant's behavior it judged to be not as bad as intentional or malicious, but worse than negligent. Recklessness lay in between the other two levels of fault. The case then returned to the appellate court, where the district court's new punitive damage award of $507 million was affirmed but an interest cost was to be added, from the date of the original decision.[42]

In *Hazelwood*,[43] the state had criminally prosecuted the captain of the Exxon Valdez and he appealed his conviction for negligent discharge of oil, a misdemeanor. He asserted immunity, because he had immediately notified the government, under the federal Water Pollution Control Act. The state asserted both independent source and inevitable discovery to overcome this immunity, the former because a state law without immunity required reporting the grounding, so Hazelwood had two independent legal duties to report. The court of appeals rejected both and reversed the conviction. The state supreme court[44] affirmed the independent source holding but reversed on inevitable discovery, saying that there were inducements to report beyond just immunity in the statute, as it would be

---

[39] Baker v. Exxon Mobile Corp., 490 F.3d 1066 (9th Cir. May 2007).
[40] Exxon Shipping Co. v. Baker, 554 US 471 (June 2008).
[41] In Re Exxon Valdez, 236 F. Supp. 2d 1043 (D. Alaska Dec. 2002).
[42] Baker v. Exxon Mobile Corp, 04-35182 (9th Cir. June 2009).
[43] Hazelwood v. State, 1992 A.M.C. 2423 (Alaska App. July 1992).
[44] State v. Hazelwood, 866 P.2d 827 (Alaska Dec. 1993).

a criminal act not to report the spill. On remand, the court of appeals reversed and remanded for a new trial, as the negligence standard was for civil rather than criminal negligence,[45] The state supreme court reversed again, holding that the state's criminal statutes meant ordinary or civil negligence unless criminal negligence was specified expressly.[46] On remand, the court of appeals held the open issues of introducing Hazelwood's immunized statements and blood alcohol tests were harmless error beyond a reasonable doubt and finally affirmed the conviction.[47]

In *Alaska Native Class*,[48] this litigant class asserted damages unique to their culture. About 3,500 Alaskan Natives complained that the oil spill had damaged their subsistence way of life, which was defined as,

> dependent upon the preservation of uncontaminated natural resources, marine life and wildlife, and reflects a personal, economic psychological, social, cultural, communal and religious form of daily living... The complaint alleges injury to the "subsistence way of life, archaeological sites and artifacts... natural resources and property upon which [plaintiffs] depend and/or which are part of their natural habitat and lives."[49]

The district court, acknowledging that the cultural claims were not economic, allowed Exxon's motion for summary judgment. The court ruled that a private litigant could not recover for a public nuisance unless it could show special injury. The court had already given damages for the economic losses from subsistence fishing. The court of appeals affirmed, saying,

> While the oil spill may have affected Alaska Natives more severely than other members of the public, "the right to obtain and share wild food, enjoy uncontaminated nature, and cultivate traditional, cultural, spiritual, and psychological benefits in pristine natural surroundings" is shared by all Alaskans... The Class therefore has failed to prove any "special injury" to support a public nuisance action.[50]

---

[45] Hazelwood v. State, 912 P.2d 1266 (Alaska App. Mar. 1996).
[46] State v. Hazelwood, 138 Oil & Gas Rep. 245 (Alaska Mar. 1997).
[47] Hazelwood v. State, 962 P.2d 196 (Alaska App. July 1998).
[48] In Re the Exxon Valdez, Alaska Native Class v. Exxon Corp., 104 F.3d 1196 (9th Cir. Jan. 1997).
[49] *Id.* at 1197.
[50] *Id.* at 1198.

In *SeaRiver Maritime*,[51] Exxon was complaining about a new law passed after the initial spill. The Oil Pollution Act had the following provision, "tank vessels that have spilled more than 1,000,000 gallons of oil into the marine environment after March 22, 1989, are prohibited from operating on the navigable waters of Prince William Sound, Alaska."[52] The district court did not agree that this was a bill of attainder or a violation of due process or equal protection under the Constitution. The court of appeals said because it did not punish the owners and operators, it was not a bill of attainder. Because it had a rational legislative purpose, it did not violate due process. Because Congress had a rational basis to conclude that excluding such ships served the legitimate purpose of protecting Prince William Sound, it did not violate equal protection. A bill of attainder had to identify specific persons and inflict punishment without trial but the court said this act did not inflict punishment on the plaintiff.

In *Seattle Seven*,[53] the exclusion of certain plaintiffs from the allocation of punitive damage awards was reviewed. These seven seafood processors had reached a cede back agreement with Exxon to not take further compensatory or punitive damages resulting from the class litigation. The punitive damages pact was kept secret from the jury, but to keep from being cut out of punitive damages, Exxon revised the agreement to allow the seven to retain part. This exposed the cede back plan to the other plaintiffs. The district court ruled the agreement unenforceable because the jury was not told that almost 15% of the award would go back to Exxon. The court of appeals held that cede backs on punitive damages encouraged settlements and so the jury did not need to be told. Otherwise, juries would increase the punitive damages to compensate, frustrating the desirability of settling. The court of appeals vacated and remanded, to include the seven in the punitive damages' allocation, which would primarily go to Exxon. The court also approved, for four other processors, assignment of their punitive damage awards over to Exxon.[54]

---

[51] SeaRiver Maritime Financial Holdings Inc. v. Mineta, 309 F.3d 662 (9th Cir. Oct. 2002).

[52] Pub. L. 101-380, An Act to establish limitations on liability for damages resulting from oil pollution, to establish a fund for the payment of compensation for such damages, and for other purposes, § 5007 Limitation.

[53] In Re: The Exxon Valdez, Icicle Seafoods, Inc. v. Baker, as Representatives of the Mandatory Punitive Damages Class, 229 F.3d 790 (9th Cir. Oct. 2000).

[54] In Re: The Exxon Valdez, Baker, as Representatives of the Mandatory Punitive Damages Class v. Exxon Corp. Exxon Shipping Co., 239 F.3d 985 (9th Cir. Feb. 2001).

E. Radiation Leak

| LEGAL ISSUES |
|---|
| ❖ Nuclear radiation leak bringing about owner's legal liability<br>❖ Statutory limit on liability for licensed nuclear plant operators |

On March 28, 1979, in the early hours of the morning, the Three Mile Island Nuclear Generating Station near Harrisburg, Pennsylvania suffered a partial meltdown. Within two days, due to the potential impacts that emitted iodine could have on undeveloped thyroids, the governor of the state had advised pregnant women and small children be moved outside a 5-mile radius from the plant. As the commission appointed by President Jimmy Carter stated,

> Thus began the accident at Three Mile Island. In the minutes, hours, and days that followed, a series of events -- compounded by equipment failures, inappropriate procedures, and human errors and ignorance -- escalated into the worst crisis yet experienced by the nation's nuclear power industry. The accident focused national and international attention on the nuclear facility at Three Mile Island and raised it to a place of prominence in the minds of hundreds of millions. For the people living in such communities as Royalton, Goldsboro, Middletown, Hummelstown, Hershey, and Harrisburg, the rumors, conflicting official statements, a lack of knowledge about radiation releases, the continuing possibility of mass evacuation, and the fear that a hydrogen bubble trapped inside a nuclear reactor might explode were real and immediate. Later, Theodore Gross, provost of the Capitol Campus of Pennsylvania State University located in Middletown a few miles from TMI, would tell the Commission: "Never before have people been asked to live with such ambiguity. The TMI accident -- an accident we cannot see or taste or smell... is an accident that is invisible. I think the fact that it is invisible creates a sense of uncertainty and fright on the part of people that may well go beyond the reality of the accident itself.[55]

The site had two nuclear power plants, TMI-1 and TMI-2, which were operated by Metropolitan Edison and owned by General Public Utilities.

---

[55] REPORT OF THE PRESIDENT'S COMMISSION ON THE ACCIDENT AT THREE MILE ISLAND (Oct. 1979), p. 81.

The plants were driven by nuclear reactors that heated water which produced steam after interacting with cool water, to drive a turbine that turned a generator producing electricity. The reactor's heat was generated through nuclear fission of uranium atoms. The amount of heat and therefore electricity generated from fission reaction was restricted using control rods containing cadmium and other metals. These were inserted into the same cooling water as the nuclear fuel rods. Based on how many were inserted and their depth of insertion, the nuclear chain reaction was controlled. In an emergency, the control rods would fall into the water and stop all fission. To prevent the release of nuclear materials, three devices are employed: fuel rods which held the nuclear fuel pellets, the reactor vessel, and a containment building with 4-foot-thick concrete walls. The vessel has 8-inch steel walls, surrounded by 9 feet of concrete and steel shields. There were also several types of safety systems deployed.

In this accident, pumps feeding cool water into the steam generator tripped, and the stream turbine and electrical generator were properly shut down. Without the cooling effect of steam, pressure began to build in the water pressurizer tank, leading to a release valve opening as intended. Steam and coolant water came pouring out into a designated tank on the floor. The control rods then dropped into the water with the fuel rods, stopping the fission process, as intended. Emergency feedwater pumps providing water to the steam generator activated. All had worked as intended up to now. Then the errors began. The valves on the lines providing the emergency feedwater pumps were closed, so no water was being provided but the plant operators did not notice this. The pressure release value should have closed as pressure decreased but instead stayed open, leading to a significant loss of reactor coolant. This was again not noticed by the operators. Emergency injection of water onto the core itself was minimized by the operators, who mistook rising pressure to mean less water was needed. Loss of water coolant would lead to the fuel rods being uncovered. The operators remained ignorant of the true situation for several hours. The coolant in the reactor did not reach the fuel rods due to a steam bubble and the emergency water being switched off. Radiation levels in the containment building began to rise. The building automatically isolated except for runoff water going to an auxiliary building, where high radiation levels would also be found. A controlled release of the radiated water led to some externalized radiation, which then led to the evacuation.

In *Susquehanna Valley Alliance*,[56] area residents sued the plant's owners/operators and the Nuclear Regulatory Commission (NRC) but their complaint was dismissed for lack of subject matter jurisdiction.[57] This concerned nearly 1,000,000 gallons of radioactively contaminated water remaining in the containment and auxiliary buildings. and a plan to treat and release it into the Susquehanna River. The plaintiffs asserted this unproven technology violated federal statutes and the Constitution. The court of appeals agreed that the Atomic Energy Act provided no jurisdiction, as it prohibited private enforcement. The court reversed, holding that the National Environmental Policy Act (NEPA) and the Water Pollution Control Act did allow private enforcement, so the district court had subject matter jurisdiction. The Supreme Court denied certiorari.[58]

In *Three Mile Island Litigation*,[59] a class action lawsuit against the plant's owners/operators had to determine the appropriate classes. Classes I and II comprised individuals and businesses who suffered economic losses from the shutdown and evacuation of the area. A third class had been proposed but the master disagreed that a class for physical health-emotional distress concerns was possible, as each litigant's medical issues were unique. He instead proposed one for medical detection services, which were common. The plaintiffs' proposed class was,

> All those individuals within a twenty-five-mile radius of Three Mile Island who suffered personal injury, incurred medical expenses, are threatened with medical expenses and/or illness, suffered emotional distress and/or will require medical detection services, including independent inspections and surveys, for a reasonable number of years in the future to monitor the possibility of latent defects of said exposure, as a result of the nuclear incident.[60]

---

[56] Susquehanna Valley Alliance, Davis, Ronald L., Tompkins, Betty, Hess, Beverly M., Snell, Doreen E. v. Three Mile Island Nuclear Reactor, General Public Utilities, Metropolitan Edison Company, Jersey Central Power & Light Co., Pennsylvania Electric Co., Nuclear Regulatory Commission, Hendrie, Joseph A., Dieckamp, Herman, Creitz, Walter M., Verrochi, W. A., Bartnoff, Shepard, 619 F.2d 231 (3rd Cir. Mar. 1980).
[57] Susquehanna Valley Alliance v. Three Mile Island Nuclear Reactor, 485 F. Supp. 81 (M.D. Pa. Oct. 1979).
[58] General Public Utilities Corporation v. Susquehanna Valley Alliance, 449 U.S. 1096 (Jan. 1981).
[59] In re Three Mile Island Litigation, 87 F.R.D. 433 (M.D. Pa. July 1980).
[60] *Id.* at 435.

The district court initially focused on the Price-Anderson Act under which the nuclear plant licensee was indemnified by the NRC for amounts more than the insurance they were required to carry. This was for nuclear incidents, defined as "any occurrence within the United States causing bodily injury, sickness, disease, or death, or loss of or damage to property, or for loss of use of property, arising out of or resulting from the radioactive, toxic, explosive, or other hazardous properties of source, special nuclear, or byproduct material."[61] Losses for businesses, Class I, included lost revenues due to the high percentage of the population who evacuated. For individuals, Class II, it included loss of real estate values. The first two classes were certified, after finding common questions of law and fact predominated and was the most efficient way to litigate for these plaintiffs. For the proposed class III, the court said the claims for personal injury and emotional distress were diverse and personal, so class action was not the more efficient way to litigate those claims. However, a class was certified for the medical detection monitoring, as these issues were common and with tens of thousands of potential litigants, joinder of so many people was impractical. and class action was more efficient.

The question of punitive damages then came before the district court.[62] The court looked to the recent *Silkwood*[63] decision by the Supreme Court. There, Karen Silkwood was contaminated by plutonium while working in a nuclear plant. She then died in an unrelated car accident and her father sued and was awarded $10 million in punitive damages. The Supreme Court held that there was nothing in existing federal law that preempted the award of state-law punitive damages. Congress did not need to expressly allow punitive damages; it merely had to not to preempt them. The instant court could not find any intent though on the part of Congress to have punitive damages paid out by the U.S. Treasury. As the Price-Anderson Act set the limit of liability for plant owners/operators at $60 million and the government was liable for the next $500 million, the court disallowed punitive damages that would be paid by federal monies. This holding was eventually affirmed by the court of appeals.[64]

---

[61] Pub. L. 85-256, An Act to amend the Atomic Energy Act of 1954, as amended, and for other purposes, § 3.
[62] In Re Three Mile Island Litigation, 605 F. Supp. 778 (M.D. Pa. Feb. 1985).
[63] Silkwood v. Kerr-McGee Corp., 464 U.S. 238 (Jan. 1984).
[64] In Re Three Mile Island Litigation, 67 F.3d 1119 (3rd Cir. Oct. 1995).

In *General Public Utilities*,[65] owners/operators GPU sued the federal government under the FTCA for more than $4 billion, asserting the NRC did not follow its own regulations. The complaint alleged that the NRC had not informed the operators of a similar incident 18 months prior and had approved the plant when it knew or should have known the pressure release valve had failed. The incident was disseminated under other general information, not by the more urgent notice types: a bulletin requiring action or a circular that did not. Recent Supreme Court holdings said that Congress intended to shield the discretionary acts of government, if acting as a regulator, from tort liability, included reaffirming *Dalehite* (see Chapter 3). The court of appeals held that both counts were within the discretionary role of regulator NRC, and so reversed and remanded.

In *Babcock & Wilcox*,[66] GPU also sued the plant's manufacturer for $4 billion, alleging a failure to warn. The counts asserted strict liability, gross and ordinary negligence, and reckless misconduct. The defendants alleged GPU was negligent in maintaining the equipment, training their employees, and following their own procedures. The court held strict liability did not apply, because the parties could allocate risk between themselves contractually, were large corporations of similar strength, and had both participated in the design of the nuclear steam supply system, so would similarly know of design defects. As the parties were of equal power who had negotiated the design of specialized equipment, summary judgment was granted. Summary judgment was denied on the other claims, as there were arguable facts as to the contractual language disclaimers,

> B&W shall not be liable in any event for... loss by reason of Plant shutdown... or damage of any nature arising out of the construction or operation of the Plant... [GPU] indemnifies and holds harmless B&W... against all losses, claims, damages... due to the negligence of [GPU] or its employees... in the operation of the Plant... when resulting... from nuclear reaction, nuclear radiation, or radioactive contamination resulting from incidents at the site.[67]

---

[65] General Public Utilities Corporation, Jersey Central Power & Light Company, Metropolitan Edison Company, Pennsylvania Electric Company v. United States, 745 F.2d 239 (3rd Cir. Sept. 1984).
[66] General Public Utilities Corp. v. Babcock & Wilcox Co., 547 F. Supp. 842 (S.D.N.Y. Sept. 1982).
[67] *Id.* at 846.

In *Three Mile Island Alert*,[68] the group of residents had opposed a limited release of radioactive gas more than a year after the initial incident. The NRC has modified the operator's license to allow this but the plaintiff demanded a public hearing, which the NRC refused to call. The release occurred in the summer of 1980 and the hearing requirement was later changed by Congress. The plaintiffs then sued for damages. The district court dismissed due to the qualified immunity of the NRC officials. The court of appeals said this immunity applied to not violating clearly established statutory or Constitutional rights. In looking at the caselaw at the time, different courts had made differing decisions as to the need for a hearing. The court of appeals held that the law was not clearly established and so there was qualified immunity for the NRC officials.

This group later opposed the 1985 re-opening of the (other) reactor TMI-1 and again demanded a hearing. The court of appeals affirmed the district court's approval of the re-opening order, holding it was not contrary to law nor arbitrary or capricious.[69] The court noted the operator had been changed to a completely new subsidiary and legal entity. There had also been a complete change in personnel involved in operations, there were 155 conditions placed on the operator in the restart of TMI-1, and there had been extensive hearings lasting years and multiple levels of review that had examined this from every aspect. The falsification of leak rate data at TMI-2 that occurred before the disaster was the biggest issue, which had led to Metropolitan Edison pleading guilty to criminal charges. The court of appeals deferred to the NRC's showing that none of the same personnel were to be involved in TMI-1, the organizational structure had changed, and the operating procedures had changed, leading to a reasonable assurance that these types of violations would not re-occur.

---

[68] The People of Three Mile Island Acting Through Three Mile Island Alert, Inc., Bradford, Louise and Kline, Michael, Class Co-Representatives v. Nuclear Regulatory Commissioners Joseph M. Hendri, Richard T. Kennedy, John Ahearne, Victor Gilinsky, Peter A. Bradford, and Metropolitan Edison Company, General Public Utilities, Robert Arnold, Herman Dieckamp, and John Herbein, 747 F.2d 139 (3rd Cir. 1984).

[69] In Re Three Mile Island Alert, Inc., No. 85-3301. In Re Commonwealth of Pennsylvania, No. 85-3302. In Re Union of Concerned Scientists, No. 85-3310. Norman O. Aamodt and Marjorie M. Aamodt, No. 85-3315 v. United States Nuclear Regulatory Commission, Nunzio J. Palladino, Chairman, and United States of America, Metropolitan Edison Co., Jersey Central Power & Light Co., Penna. Electric Co., and Gpu Nuclear Corp., Intervenors, 771 F.2d 720 (3rd Cir. Sept. 1985).

In *People Against Nuclear Energy*,[70] the court of appeals had extended environmental law to include psychological health impacts. The Supreme Court believed that was not Congress' intent, holding the NEPA did not require the NRC to consider psychological health damage, and reversed,

> it is difficult for us to see the differences between someone who dislikes a government decision so much that he suffers anxiety and stress, someone who fears the effects of that decision so much that he suffers similar anxiety and stress, and someone who suffers anxiety and stress that "flow directly,"... from the risks associated with the same decision. It would be extraordinarily difficult for agencies to differentiate between "genuine" claims of psychological health damage and claims that are grounded solely in disagreement with a democratically adopted policy. Until Congress provides a more explicit statutory instruction than NEPA now contains, we do not think agencies are obliged to undertake the inquiry.[71]

In *TMI Litigation*,[72] the plaintiffs were 2,000 residents who complained of contracting neoplasm, ten of whom were selected for a test trial. The plaintiffs used expert testimony to assert there was a sufficient release of radiation to cause their illnesses but the district court struck most of this testimony and granted summary judgment to the defendants, saying "that despite finding the vast majority of Plaintiffs' experts to be well qualified, the court found many of their opinions to be based upon methodologies that were scientifically unreliable and upon data that a reasonable expert in the field would not rely upon.[73]" The court's judgment included both the test trial and non-test trial plaintiffs. The court of appeals examined in great detail both the science and the experts, finding them properly excluded except for one expert, which was harmless. The court of appeals affirmed, except reversing summary judgment on the non-trial plaintiffs.

---

[70] Metropolitan Edison Co. v. People Against Nuclear Energy, 460 U.S. 766 (Apr. 1983).
[71] *Id.* at 777-78.
[72] In Re: Tmi Litigation Lori Dolan Joseph Gaughan Ronald Ward Estate of Pearl Hickernell Kenneth Putt Estate of Ethelda Hilt Paula Obercash Jolene Peterson Estate of Gary Villella Estate of Leo Beam, No. 96-7623 in Re: Tmi Litigation All Except Lori Dolan, Joseph Gaughan, Ronald Ward, Estate of Pearl Hickernell, Kenneth Putt, Estate of Ethelda Hilt, Paula Obercash, Jolene Peterson, Estate of Gary Villella and Estate of Leo Beam, No. 96-7624 in Re: Tmi Litigation, 193 F.3d 613 (3rd Cir. Nov. 1999).
[73] In Re TMI Litigation Consolidated Proceedings, 927 F. Supp. 834 (M.D. Pa. June 1996), at 839.

## 5.2 STRUCTURES AND FLIGHT

### A. Walkway Collapse

| LEGAL ISSUES |
|---|
| ❖ Walkway collapse leading to loss of engineer's license<br>❖ Competing federal and state class actions |

On July 17, 1981, two suspended walkways in the atrium of the Hyatt Regency Hotel in Kansas City, Missouri, one hanging from the other, collapsed, killing 114 people and injuring nearly twice that. Many people were attending a tea dance being covered by local television crews,

> As the July 17 tea dance went on, the crowd grew in the lobby as well as on the skybridges, where onlookers gathered to get a bird's-eye view of the festivities below. Then, suddenly, the second- and fourth-floor skybridges began swaying before collapsing and crashing down into the lobby, killing some revelers and trapping others beneath the broken concrete. Dr. Joseph F. Waeckerle, who had recently resigned as Kansas City's medical director to take a position at a local hospital, was among the first responders on the scene. "You have to understand the chaos and the carnage that had gone on in that lobby. The water was flowing, the mains were cut when the skywalks collapsed. Electrical wires were hanging and arcing and sparking. There were no lights," Waeckerle said. He said he spent roughly 12 hours in the hotel lobby, overseeing rescue triage operations for those who had survived the collapse. Even for Waeckerle, who had responded to other disasters, the scene at the Hyatt Regency came as a shock. "Like everybody else, I shut my eyes for a moment and said, 'Gee whiz, what am I doing here?' and said a little prayer and prayed that I could do the best I can," he said. "And then got on with it." Rescue workers toiled throughout the night, using cranes and other heavy machinery to move the massive pieces of concrete that made up much of the pile. First responders went to great lengths to extract victims who were pinned under immovable debris, at times amputating their limbs to get them out.[74]

---

[74] *One Of The Deadliest U.S. Accidental Structural Collapses Happened 40 Years Ago Today*, NPR (July 17, 2021).

According to the investigatory report done by the National Bureau of Standards (NBS, later NIST), the problem was with the hanger rods supporting the walkways, and their connection to box beams in the walk ways. The fourth-floor walkway collapsed and the second-floor walkway, which it supported, then also collapsed, both falling to the atrium. It concluded that the collapse happened at loads less than those specified under city building codes; that the box beam-hanger rod connections in the walkways and those from the fourth-floor walkway to the ceiling did not comply with the city building code; the change in the original design that had the second floor walkway connected to the ceiling instead of the fourth-floor walkway doubled the load on the fourth-floor walkway; the original design would have been able to resist the loads at the time of the collapse, despite not complying with the city building code; and the quality of workmanship and materials was not a factor in the collapse.[75]

In *Federal Skywalk Cases*,[76] a mandatory class action lawsuit was initiated by certifying a class with representatives diverse from all defendants. The court certified classes for compensatory and punitive damages for business invitees at the hotel at the time of the collapse. The court of appeals vacated this order for interfering with state court lawsuits.[77] The district court was unwilling to certify a new class action, with the state court cases not participating. The court was concerned that funds available for punitive damages might all be used by the first claimants, and for the uncertainty whether multiple punitive damage awards were possible under state law. Instead, the claims were consolidated for trial.[78] Another plaintiff then came forward requesting class action certification, and a class was again certified.[79] In crafting a letter notifying claimants of the class action, the court made it clear this was to determine liability for compensatory and punitive damages and the amount of punitive damages (compensatory damages would be determined later). Participation in the class action was now voluntary.[80]

---

[75] NBS, Investigation of the Kansas City Hyatt Regency Walkways Collapse (May 1982).
[76] In re Federal Skywalk Cases, 93 F.R.D. 415 (W.D. Mo. Jan. 1982).
[77] In Re Federal Skywalk Cases. In Re Melanie Hanson Johnson and Gerard Stanley Johnson, in Re Federal Skywalk Cases. In Re Jacqueline N. Rau, 680 F.2d 1175 (8th Cir. June 1982).
[78] In re Federal Skywalk Cases, 95 F.R.D. 479 (W.D. Mo. Sept. 1982).
[79] In re Federal Skywalk Cases, 95 F.R.D. 483 (W.D. Mo. Oct. 1982).
[80] In re Federal Skywalk Cases, 97 F.R.D. 365 (W.D. Mo. Nov. 1982).

After the class certification, apparently defense counsel tried to entice absent class members to opt out of the federal class action. The plaintiffs then sought several sanctions against the defendants, asking the court to,

> (1) Declare all post-December 6,1982 opt-outs and releases from the federal class void; order defendants to send a corrective notice at their expense; and require any class member who still seeks to opt out to appear at a hearing so that the Court can determine whether the choice is informatively made; (2) Enter default judgments against the defendants on the issues of compensatory and punitive liability; (3) Disqualify counsel for defendants for violating Disciplinary Rule 7-104; (4) Withhold full faith and credit from any state court judgment that might issue in this matter; and (5) Award costs to the plaintiffs and assess attorneys' fees against the defendants and their counsel.[81]

The actions taken by counsel and class representatives for those filing claims in a proposed class action in state court included going on national television to claim those agreeing to the settlement of the state court class action would partake in the $20 million fund when, in reality, all they would get was $1,000. A notice was sent to those in the federal class action to induce them to drop out of the federal class action in favor of the state class action and the $1,000 settlement. The federal district court agreed this was worthy of an order of contempt for communicating with federal class members without consent of class counsel and the supervision of the federal court, and so voided any drop outs that occurred after the state court preliminarily approved a start class action.

On the first day of the federal trial, the defendants proposed a settlement, which the court then reviewed.[82] It said the terms offered to the federal class action were similar to the state class action. It had the additional features that members could choose arbitration, or the choice of being paid $1,000 without proof of injury, or to have a jury trial and be paid from a supplemental fund. Hallmark Cards, the ultimate owner, also agreed to make a significant contribution to charity. Finding the settlement agreement fair, reasonable, and adequate, the federal court approved it, while all claims for punitive damages were dismissed with prejudice.

---

[81] In re Federal Skywalk Cases, 97 F.R.D. 370 (W.D. Mo. Jan. 1983), at 372.
[82] In re Federal Skywalk Cases, 97 F.R.D. 380 (W.D. Mo. Jan. 1983).

In *Kenton*,[83] the plaintiff was a law student injured in this disaster who won an award of $4 million in damages at trial. The trial ordered a remitter of $250,000 in exchange for denial a motion for a new trial. She was one of those who chose a trial by jury. The case would come before the state supreme court on appeal. The first error raised was, as the defendants had admitted liability, that evidence not directly concerning the plaintiff's injuries should not be admitted and was inflammatory. This included testimony from a first responder and from her sister who was with her, video and still images of the scene, and the NBS report. Given that the witness suffered a severe cervical injury leading initially to paralysis and had suffered the highest grade of psychosocial stress, the court ruled that,

> the jury was entitled to consider the evidence of the scene of the collapse, the utter chaos that prevailed, and the effect upon respondent of being pinned beneath the debris, amidst blood, dead and injured bodies, and the sheer terror of the voices around her, in evaluating her physical and mental injuries for the purpose of fixing her compensation. The evidence was relevant, material, and appropriate. Its probative value far outweighed any prejudicial effect it might have had on the jury. There was no error in admitting the evidence.[84]

The defendants also objected to the testimony of law school professors on the demands of law school and practicing law and their opinions that she would unlikely be able to return to law school fulltime or practice law fulltime. The court disagreed that they were giving medical testimony and overruled the objection. The defendants further objected that the award was more than the approximately $2 million loss in her projected lifetime earnings. The court responded that including her future medical needs would increase it to $3 million. Further, the jury was allowed to consider the plaintiff's past and future pain and suffering and the many changes to her lifestyle that these injuries entailed. The court ruled in the companion case (see following) that the state no longer allowed trial courts to use remittiturs, so it reinstated the full amount of the jury's award of $4 million.

---

[83] Kenton v. Hyatt Hotels Corp., 693 S.W.2d 83 (Mo. June 1985).
[84] *Id.* at 89.

In *Firestone*,[85] the plaintiff won an award of $15 million for her injuries suffered in the disaster but the trial court ordered a remittitur of $2.5 million based on the weight of the evidence. The appeal reached the state supreme court. The court rejected the appellants' challenge to the rejected venue change motion, as the survey that was used was insufficient to truly gauge feeling among potential jurors. The trial took place more than two years after the disaster and local feelings had cooled in the interim. The appellants' claims that the plaintiff alluded to her poverty were rejected by the court, as each was appropriate in framing some current aspect of her life situation, including her total and permanent disability and need for ongoing medical attendance and expensive equipment. The court restored the jury award in full, which included her economic losses and future medical care. It abolished the use of remittitur in the state, calling it an invasion by trial judges of a jury's right to consider and award compensation. The usage had become too confusing and inconsistent. The granting of a new trial was still available to trial court judges if appropriate.

In *Phillips*,[86] a fireman who attended the rescue asserted permanent mental and physical injuries and emotional distress. The trial court dismissed due the fireman's rule precluding recovery during rescue operations. The supreme court agreed, as this was his job to take these risks, for which there was workmen's compensation for injuries. For injuries in a voluntary capacity, remedy could be sought in the courts. However, the court held that doing one's job during off duty hours was not volunteering. A professional rescuer could not assert he was a volunteer and so affirmed the trial court's dismissal. In *Occidental*,[87] one of the insurers refused to reimburse settlements paid to rescuers. The state supreme held subsequently that rescuers who were not police or firemen could litigate their injuries during a rescue.[88] A settlement was then reached with all rescuers who were not police or firemen. When presented with the rescuer claims, one insurer refused to pay and filed suit but the trial court issued a summary judgment against them. The court of appeals affirmed, rejecting the appellants' claims of error, including rulings that emotional distress claimants had to be within the zone of danger.

---

[85] Firestone v. Crown Center Redevelopment Corp., 54 U.S.L.W. 2056 (Mo. June 1985).
[86] Phillips v. Hallmark Cards, Inc., 722 S.W.2d 86 (Mo. Dec. 1986).
[87] Hyatt Corp. v. Occidental Fire & Casualty Co. of N.C., 801 S.W.2d 382 (Mo. App. Nov. 1990).
[88] Krause v. US Truck Co., Inc., 89 A.L.R. 4th 1067 (Mo. Mar. 1990).

In *Wintz*,[89] the plaintiff was awarded $1.5 million for her injuries. The plaintiff's physician had supplied her medical records to the defendants. Later, he found an x-ray taken before the disaster showing no compression fracture of her spine existed and so added it to her medical records. The plaintiff had this x-ray but the defendants did not. This prior x-ray was produced at trial before a doctor who in a deposition had previously said that her current fracture was not caused by the fall of the walkway. This new x-ray caused him to change his opinion, saying now that her fracture was caused by the fall of the walkway. The defense moved for a continuance, which was denied. The court of appeals said surprise coupled with prejudice was a valid reason for continuance, or an adjournment. The court reversed the judgment and remanded for a new trial.

In *Duncan*,[90] the Missouri Board for Architects, Professional Engineers and Land Surveyors, with voluminous findings of fact and law, revoked the certifications of the engineers involved with the walkways. Jack Gillum was a certified structural engineer and Daniel Duncan was a professional engineer and project manager under Gillum. The court of appeals affirmed, noting the facts were essentially uncontested. The board had found,

> Duncan... guilty of gross negligence in the preparation and completion of a structural drawing... and in failing to review shop drawings of the Hyatt project... guilty of misconduct in misrepresenting to the architects the safety of a connection (the double hanger rod-box beam connection) when he was ignorant of the safety due to a failure to perform engineering tests and calculations to determine such safety. Gillum was found vicariously liable and responsible for the acts and omissions of Duncan which liability and responsibility he assumed by affixing his professional engineering seal on the structural drawings... He was further found grossly negligent in failing to himself review or assure that someone had reviewed [the] drawing[s]... before affixing his seal thereto. Gillum was also found to have engaged in unprofessional conduct in failing and refusing to take responsibility for the entire engineering project as... required by [statute].[91]

---

[89] Wintz v. Hyatt Hotels Corp., 687 S.W.2d 587 (Mo. App. Jan. 1985).
[90] Duncan v. Missouri Board for Architects, Professional Engineers & Land Surveyors, 744 S.W.2d 524 (Mo. App. Jan. 1988).
[91] *Id.* at 528.

## B. Crowd Crush

| LEGAL ISSUES |
|---|
| ❖ Stadium crush generating legal liability for police<br>❖ Private prosecutions when public prosecutions not started**Error! Bookmark not defined.** |

On April 15, 1989, during the early stages of an FA Cup semi-final between Liverpool and Nottingham Forest, held at the neutral Sheffield Wednesday football ground, there was a crush in the standing-room-only pens for Liverpool supporters, leading to the immediate deaths of 95 people. More would die subsequently and hundreds were injured. The match was abandoned and inquiries, investigations, criminal proceedings, and civil lawsuits would soon follow. The government appointed a commission headed by a court of appeal justice, Peter (Lord) Taylor, to investigate. The interim report focused on the policing practices of the South Yorkshire Constabulary (SYC), responsible for certain crowd control that day. The SYC had insisted on the separation of the respective teams' fans, based on the direction they would arrive by train, and thereafter be channeled to their ticketed location on the grounds. The result was that Liverpool fans, despite a typically larger home crowd, had fewer total tickets and fewer of the cheaper standing places, but more of the more expensive assigned seats. As supporters arrived for their standing-room-only spots, there was a surge to get into already crowded terrace pens for the 15:00 kickoff.

> To escape the crush, fans began climbing the radial fences out of pens 3 and 4 into pens 2 and 5. Others tried to get over the front perimeter fence but were at first turned back by police who feared a pitch invasion. Near the front, fans, mostly youngsters, were weakened to the point of collapse and in some instances death but they were held upright by pressure all round. Further back, most were so preoccupied with the pain of being pressed against barriers and with breathing problems that they saw nothing of the game. But at the rear there were many who, although cramped, were watching the football unaware of the distress at the front… the final surge… caused a

horrendous blockage of bodies. The dead, the dying and the desperate became interwoven in the sump at the front of the pens.[92]

Autopsies found the causes of death as "crush asphyxia due to compression of the chest wall against other bodies or fixed structures so as to prevent inhalation."[93] The report broke the periods into two, the time up to the opening of an external gate at 14:52, and afterwards. Before that gate was opened, the issues identified were the lack of a fixed capacity in each pen where spectators stood and the lack of effective monitoring. After the gate was opened, due to many late arrivals, the issues became: diverting the massive influx of fans into empty pens, the internal barriers, the crushing not being recognized, the size of perimeter gates, and the police response. There was a similar incident in the same location, without deaths, eight years prior. The police then had opened the perimeter gates and closed off further ingress when crushing became clear. This standing area had undergone several revisions over the years, some at the request of the police. However, its safety certificate was never updated to reflect these changes nor the diminished crowd capacities they implied. There was no method other than visual monitoring to prevent overcrowding.

Apparently, the SYC had assumed control of the west-end terraces, which housed away supporters, while club stewards took the responsibility elsewhere in the stadium, with home supporters, seats, and gangways. The typical practice was to fill one of the standing-only pens before closing it and filling the next one. That practice was not followed on this day. The police did not have a good idea of what full meant, especially during an FA Cup semi-final. The sense was to let each pen fill to being overcrowded,

> Over the years, spectators on terraces have come to accept conditions which are often very uncomfortable and not infrequently downright dangerous. They are subjected to buffeting and squeezing to get in and out of the terraces. They are packed tightly and exposed to surging and swaying during the match. They put up with these conditions because they are devoted to the game and because there is little they can do about them. They believe the discomfort will pass and nothing very untoward will happen. Usually that is the case and

---

[92] THE HILLSBOROUGH STADIUM DISASTER, 15 APRIL 1989, INQUIRY BY THE RT HON LORD JUSTICE TAYLOR, INTERIM REPORT (Aug. 1, 1989), para. 74 and 81.
[93] *Id.* para. 109.

they are reassured by it... close proximity, shared discomfort, weathering sways and surges together and chanting the same songs and slogans en masse do evoke good humour.[94]

In *Alcock*,[95] the SYC chief constable was sued by survivors of those killed or injured that day, for nervous shock arising from SYC's negligence. The trial court queried whether the police owed a duty to the plaintiff, which it answered in the affirmative in 10 of the 16 cases. The court of appeal reversed all the successful plaintiffs, who then appealed to the House of Lords along with the unsuccessful plaintiffs. The plaintiffs included those who had lost brothers, sons, grandsons, and a fiancée. The court outlined four requirements for the claims: the plaintiff's relationship had to be close ties of love and affection; the plaintiff had to be proximate to the accident; had to directly perceive the accident or its aftermath; and theirs was a reasonably foreseeable injury. While some lords considered the claims of those who lost a son or a fiancée sufficient for the first prong, only a few of the plaintiffs were at the stadium while others saw it on television that did not identify individuals. This tended to disqualify their claims. As no plaintiffs met all the prongs, all the appeals were dismissed.

In *Hicks*,[96] the parents to two girls who died in this disaster sued for damages, claiming that before death the girls suffered injury and so accrued a cause of action before dying. The trial court dismissed the complaint, the court of appeal affirmed, as did the House of Lords, saying,

> The evidence here showed that both girls died from traumatic asphyxia. They were in the pens at one end of the Hillsborough Stadium to which access was through a tunnel some 23 metres in length. When the pens were already seriously overcrowded a great number of additional spectators, anxious to see the football match which was about to start, were admitted through the turnstiles and surged through the tunnel causing the dreadful crush in the pens in which 95 people died. Medical evidence which the judge accepted was to the effect that in cases of death from traumatic asphyxia caused by crushing the victim would lose consciousness within a matter of seconds from the

---

[94] *Id.* para. 175-76.
[95] Alcock v Chief Constable of South Yorkshire [1991] UKHL 5 (Nov. 1991).
[96] Hicks v Chief Constable of the South Yorkshire Police [1991] UKHL 9 (Mar. 1992).

crushing of the chest which cut off the ability to breathe and would die within 5 minutes. There was no indication in the post mortem reports on either girl of physical injuries attributable to anything other than the fatal crushing which caused the asphyxia.[97]

In *Duckenfield*,[98] a support group for Hillsborough families was trying to bring private prosecutions against the two SYC officers in charge the day of the disaster. The court recounted what had happened legally since the disaster, including that the DPP decided not to bring criminal charges and the coroner's jury returning verdicts of accidental death. Duckenfield retired and the so disciplinary proceedings before the Police Complaints Authority went nowhere as they could not prosecute a retired officer, and the other was his subordinate. A request for judicial review to quash the inquest verdict was denied. After a 1996 documentary raised additional evidence, a new inquiry under Lord Justice Stuart-Smith again found no basis to initiate a prosecution against Duckenfield and Murray, saying,

> "The causes of the disaster were many and complex. So far as these two officers… were concerned, the prosecution would have to prove to the high standard required for a criminal conviction that the failure to give the order to close off the tunnel when Gate C was opened amounted to the serious degree of recklessness necessary to constitute manslaughter… I have come to the clear conclusion that there is no basis upon which there should be a further judicial inquiry."[99]

Private prosecutions against them were then started, charging the two with manslaughter, willful neglect to perform a public duty, and for Duckenfield, attempting to pervert the course of justice. The court at length examined the two's request to have the DPP take over and then discontinue the private prosecutions against them but the court did not agree, as this was a decision for the DPP to make. While the DPP did not find sufficient evidence to bring the charges itself against the two, it also did not find that there was no evidence as to the first two charges. The

---

[97] *Id.*
[98] Duckenfield & Anor, R (on the application of) v Director Of Public Prosecutions [1999] EWHC Admin 286 (Mar. 1999).
[99] *Id.*

court did quash the third charge, on perverting the course of justice, which the DPP had been opposed to bringing in the first place.

In *White*,[100] police officers were asserting their own injuries from the disaster, seeking to recover for a breach of duty owed to them, and as rescuers. They claimed it was a breach of duty for the chief constable to expose these officers in the course of their employment to the risk of serious psychiatric harm, and he was vicariously liable for the decision to open the gate. The cases of officers who were directly involved in removing bodies from the pens were settled. Four test cases survived to appeal to the House of Lords. Most of the justices there held that the police should not be able to recover for psychiatric injury from the same incident if bystanders and others working there could not. As far as being rescuers, that was part of what they were trained to do. The court noted that the police could retire on a disability pension, so were much better off than the relatives of victims who could not get such a pension and could not collect damages for their psychiatric injuries. The appeals were allowed and the complaints dismissed for the police officers' claims for psychiatric injury.

In *Williams*,[101] after the unsuccessful efforts to get the cases tried in the UK, the mother of a 15-year-old boy who had died in the disaster appealed to the European Court of Human Rights (ECtHR). The court recited how the opening of the gate allowed 2,000 additional fans to move into the already full middle pens, causing the crush as the crowd surged at the start of the match. The original testimony of two police officers was that her son Kevin was alive after 15:30, and after 16:00. The coroner determined this must be in error, having concluded that all the deaths occurred by 15:15, when the first ambulances arrived. The two police officers changed their statements, but one admitted only doing so after being harassed by another police officer. Specialist pathologic evidence showed that Kevin could have been alive after 15:15. The plaintiff alleged that the authorities did not properly investigate her son's death and,

> there was no effective investigation, in particular (i) that there was no independent public investigation into the emergency response and planning; (ii) that there was no independent public investigation into

---

[100] White and Others v. Chief Constable of South Yorkshire and Others [1998] UKHL 45 (Dec. 1998).
[101] Anne Williams v the United Kingdom - 32567/06 [2009] ECHR 478 (Feb. 2009).

whether any failings by state agents had an impact on the death of her son; and (iii) that no criminal or disciplinary charges were pursued by the authorities against the two police officers involved. The applicant complains about the lack of independence of the West Midlands police, the narrow scope of the inquest, the inadequate opportunities for participation and cross-examination in the inquiries, the fact that the inquiries were not public and the fact that the impact of new evidence on the death of Kevin Williams has not been adequately considered.[102]

The court noted it was only allowed to try cases when all domestic remedies had been exhausted and it was within six months of that final decision. Because the new evidence was investigated under the Stuart-Smith inquiry, and the appeal to the ECtHR did not happen within six months of that, the case was held to be inadmissible.

In *Harrison*,[103] there was another appeal to the ECtHR regarding the lack of prosecution in the UK. In 2012, another government-initiated investigation, the Hillsborough Independent Panel, reported there was a significant police coverup, as many witness statements had been altered, searches were done to try and prove the intoxication of the victims, and that a good number of the victims might have survived if properly and timely cared for. Another outcome of this new report was an official attempt to quash the prior coroner's inquests. In 2012, the attorney general asked the original inquest to be quashed.[104] The court cited the 15:15 cutoff imposed by the prior coroner and new medical testimony produced by the panel that many of the victims survived past that time, calling it seriously flawed. This decision had precluded any investigation into the acts of the police and emergency services after that time. The court quashed all the inquests and ordered new ones. The Lord Chief Justice had asked that the parties not make the new inquest adversarial in the manner the prior one had been. Because those inquests were ongoing at the time this case came before the ECtHR, the court deemed the matter inadmissible as premature, as the new inquests had not yet been finalized.

---

[102] *Id.*
[103] Harrison and Others v. the United Kingdom - 44301/13 44379/13 44384/13 - Admissibility Decision [2014] ECHR 511 (Mar. 2014).
[104] Attorney General v Coroner of South Yorkshire (West) & Anor [2012] EWHC 3783 (Admin) (Dec. 2012).

In *Chief Constable*,[105] the head of the SYC was forced to resign and asked for a judicial review of the police and crime commissioner's actions. The court first reviewed the findings of the new coroner's jury,

i) By a majority of 7 to 2, the jury indicated that they were satisfied, so that they were sure, that those who died in the disaster were unlawfully killed.

ii) They determined that there was no behaviour on the part of football supporters which caused or contributed to the dangerous situation at the Leppings Lane turnstiles at Hillsborough.

iii) They determined that there had been a number of errors and omissions by South Yorkshire Police that had caused or contributed to the deaths.

iv) They found in particular, that there were errors or omissions by the police after the crush in the West Terrace at the ground which caused or contributed to the loss of lives.

v) They concluded that, after the crush in the West Terrace had begun to develop, there were errors or omissions by the ambulance service which caused or contributed to the loss of life.

vi) They concluded there were features of the design, construction and layout of the stadium which were dangerous or defective and which caused or contributed to the disaster.

vii) They concluded that there were errors or omissions in the safety certification and oversight of the stadium that caused or contributed to the disaster.

viii) They found that there were errors or omissions by Sheffield Wednesday Football Club in the management of the stadium and preparation for the match which caused or contributed to the dangerous situation which developed on the day of the match.

ix) They concluded that there were errors or omissions by Sheffield Wednesday Football Club on 15 April 1989 which may have caused or

---

[105] Crompton, R (on the application of) v Police and Crime Commissioner for South Yorkshire & Ors [2017] EWHC 1349 (Admin) (June 2017).

contributed to the dangerous situation that developed at the Leppings Lane turnstiles and in the West Terrace.[106]

Despite what the Lord Chief Justice had requested, the inquests turned adversarial. As agreed, the chief constable made an announcement of apology and accepting the findings of the inquest. Then however, he issued a second statement, which was generally viewed as being defensive and SYC failing to accept its responsibilities. It was widely criticized by MPs in Parliament. With the chief constable refusing to resign, the commissioner suspended him and he did then resign. The court found the commissioner's actions irrational, as the second statement was reasonably within the chief's powers and an appropriate response considering the SYC's conduct had been challenged by an MP. The court found the demand to resign disproportionate and quashed all the commissioner's decisions.

In *Metcalf*,[107] a solicitor for SYP's insurer and two senior police were charged with perverting the course of public justice in altering police witness statements collected after the disaster. Specifically, these were accounts provided to the Taylor inquiry. The solicitor's bad acts included putting words in the mouths of witnesses, having an unresolved conflict of interest, and demonstrating a lack of candor, thereby breaching his professional responsibilities as a solicitor. Reading all 467 accounts from various SYP officers, he advised revisions to 167 of them, removing criticism of the SYP, especially of senior officers. The court ruled that the Taylor inquiry was not a civil or criminal prosecution but a departmental inquiry. As such, he could not be perverting the course of public justice when the proceeding was not such. As to whether the intent was to pervert the follow-on proceedings where the accounts might be used at, the court ruled that the altered accounts could not affect the coroner's inquest or any civil or criminal proceedings. On the latter, because the originals had not been destroyed, they were available for use, as the inquest's assisting police officers knew. Therefore, it was insufficient for a jury to reasonably conclude there that was a tendency to pervert the course of public justice. The indictments for all three men were dismissed.

---

[106] *Id.*
[107] Metcalf & Ors, R. v (Hillsborough) [2021] EW Misc 8 (CC) (May 2021).

## C. Severe Weather

| LEGAL ISSUES |
|---|
| ❖ Flying into severe weather causing airline legal liability<br>❖ Not disseminating tornado data creating legal liability |

Outbreaks of tornadoes are common in the U.S. Midwest, due to geography and climatic conditions. Between 1950 and 1974, there were seven outbreaks in which more than 100 people were killed. On March 21-22, 1952, outbreaks in the southern United States killed more than 200 people. On May 11, 1953, in Waco, Texas, more than 110 people died from tornadoes. On June 8-9, 1953, more than 200 were killed in states ranging from Michigan to Massachusetts. On May 25-26, 1955, more than 100 people fell victim to tornadoes across the Great Plains. More than 260 people died during outbreaks on April 11-12, 1965, across the Midwest. On February 21-22, 1971, more than 120 people were killed by tornadoes in the Mississippi Delta. On April 3-4, 1974, more than 330 people died from these storms. Tornadoes did not typically produce significant legal issues, mostly just claims for property damage or workmen's compensation.[108]

In *Lirchhult*,[109] parents sued after a tornado struck and knocked down a school cafeteria wall in Coldenham, New York, on November 16, 1989, killing nine children and injuring many more. The defendant county asserted that they had no duty to disseminate the weather despite its emergency management plan, its discretionary acts were immune, and it owed no special duty of care. The state court ruled that there needed to be sufficient evidence of that exercise of discretion at trial, so refused to dismiss the complaint. On appeal,[110] the court reversed, saying a tornado watch, not a tornado warning, was issued, and the county had to use its discretion in determining what actions to then take. In federal court,[111] the district court ruled that because of compulsory education laws, there was a duty of care to protect the children from foreseeable risks of death. The court held that while a state agency voluntarily providing protection against a danger had a duty under state tort law, the agency failing to act in providing that protection did not automatically violate Due Process.

---

[108] Transport Insurance Co. v. Liggins, 625 S.W.2d 780 (Tex. App. Dec. 1981).
[109] Litchhult v. Reiss, 149 Misc. 2d 584 (N.Y. Sup. Ct. Jan. 1991).
[110] Litchhult v. Reiss, 183 A.D.2d 1067 (N.Y. App. Div. May 1992).
[111] Lichtler v. County of Orange, 813 F. Supp. 1054 (S.D.N.Y. Feb. 1993).

Between 1975 and 1999, there were no tornado events causing more than 100 deaths. However, tornadoes or other severe weather events like thunderstorms, snowstorms, or wind shear did cause significant loss life when they interacted with commercial aviation. In this period, there were several airplane crashes in the United States with more than 100 fatalities that were directly linked to other severe weather events, including: Eastern Airlines (EAL) 66 where 113 were killed in New York on June 24, 1975; Pan Am 759 with 153 fatalities near New Orleans on July 9, 1982; and Delta 191, with 137 people dying at Dallas-Fort Worth on August 2, 1985.

In *Air Crash Disaster*,[112] the NTSB attributed[113] the EAL 66 crash to a thunderstorm astride the ILS localizer for runway 22L. Another plane had decided to go around, after encountering severe wind shear and a third did land but reported the same wind shear. Both had experienced significant air speed loss and increased rate of descent and had to apply near maximum thrust to counter these. Experienced pilots took 54 flights in similar conditions in simulators and only 5 were successfully landed. The controller testified he did not change runways because the surface winds were most nearly aligned with 22L. Doing so would cause delays of up to 30 minutes. Despite this knowledge, the pilot continued the approach and the ATC continued to use 22L. The plaintiffs alleged negligence of both the EAL management in allowing pilots to land during thunderstorms; ground crews in not providing updated weather information; and the pilots for trying to land in such weather; not reading out the altitude, the rate of descent, and air speed; setting too low a landing speed; and proceeding below the decision height without having the runway clearly in view. With the government stipulating to their liability, this court then affirmed EAL's.

In *Domangue*,[114] EAL paid the widow of an overseas-bound passenger $75,000, the maximum under the Warsaw Convention (see Chapter 3). The federal government had already admitted liability, so the court was determining its damages. Based on Louisiana state law, she was claiming loss of love, affection, companionship and grief and mental anguish, and loss of past and future support. The court, citing the closeness of the

---

[112] In Re Air Crash Disaster at John F. Kennedy International Airport on June 24, 1975, 635 F.2d 67 (2nd Cir. Oct. 1980).
[113] NTSB, AIRCRAFT ACCIDENT REPORT, EASTERN AIRLINES, INC. BOENG 727-225, JOHN F. KENNEDY INTERNATIONAL AIRPORT, JUNE 24, 1975 (Mar. 1976).
[114] Domangue v. Eastern Airlines, Inc., 542 F. Supp. 643 (E.D. La. June 1982).

husband, wife, and children, awarded $200,000 for lost love and grief. For the loss of past support, based on this 29-years-old barge-anchor operator's income before trial, the court awarded $126,000. For future support, $311,000 was awarded, which would take the children up to the age of 18. The plaintiff also asked for pre- and post-judgment interest from EAL but the court rejected this, as the Warsaw Convention's financial limits were fixed. The court of appeals reversed this part of the judgment, in that having interest penalties ensured funds were paid more quickly to the survivors, when they needed such monies the most, which was a key intent of the Warsaw Convention and its Montreal Agreement revisions.[115]

In *Caldarera*,[116] the plaintiff had lost his mother, wife, and son in the crash. The district court determined the damages owed by the United States under the FTCA, while a jury determined what EAL owed. After describing how close-knit the family was, the district court calculated an appropriate award to him would be, for the loss of love and affection, $400,000 for his wife, $100,000 for his mother, and $150,000 for his son, and $400,000 to his son for loss of his mother. The father was also awarded for the loss of his wife's services but not his mother's support, nor for pain and suffering of the victims, as there was no evidence that they survived the crash briefly. Because the jury had awarded an amount to the husband within an allowed deviation, the court left that jury award alone. Because the jury awarded the same amount to the son, the court reduced that award to be more in line with its calculation above. The district judge arrived at about $1.2 million in liability for the United States and the reduced jury award was about $1.54 million against EAL. The court held that both the United States and EAL were jointly liable for the amounts it calculated of $1.2 million but only EAL was liable for the excess, $0.34 million. On appeal, the award for the loss of the love and support of his wife were reduced to $250,000, as being the maximum amount the court would allow, at least in this case. Similarly, the court of appeals reduced the award to the son for loss of his mother to $300,000.[117]

---

[115] Mrs. Evelyn H. Domangue, Individually and on Behalf of the Minors, Barry Joseph Domangue, Jr. And Michelle Marie Domangue v. Eastern Air Lines, Inc., 722 F.2d 256 (5th Cir. Jan. 1984).
[116] Caldarera v. Eastern Airlines, Inc., 529 F. Supp. 634 (W.D. La. Jan. 1982).
[117] Peter Joseph Caldarera, Jr., Etc. v. Eastern Airlines, Inc., and United States of America, 705 F.2d 778 (5th Cir. May 1983).

In *Haley*,[118] the parents of a 25-year-old man who died on Pan Am 759 were awarded $15,000 for his mental anguish prior to the first impact and $350,000 each for the loss of their son's love and companionship. The court of appeals could not find cases regarding the fear a victim felt before impact and death but there were cases for negligently-induced fright. Because it took 4-6 seconds from the plane first hitting the trees until the final impact, the court held that was sufficient time for this fear to have manifested. The defense complained about the damage awards for a man of his age who had lived away from home the last eight years. The court agreed, looking to other awards in prior state cases and found $150,000 to be the largest such award. After adding one-third to it as was what a reasonable jury would have found, the court of appeals ordered a new trial, unless the parents accepted the revised amounts of $200,000 each.

In *Turgeau*,[119] the NTSB attributed[120] the Pan Am crash to windshear. The plane only rose to an altitude of about 100 feet, then hit trees about 50 feet high, and crashed into houses, killing people on the ground. The report said the plane experienced a strong headwind, then a downdraft, then a decreased headwind, which required an increased pitch attitude and added thrust. Current low-level windshear technology did not provide sufficient advice for pilots and ATC to avoid wind shear encounters. The plaintiffs were homeowners at the crash site whose home was covered in aviation fuel and was bulldozed. In addition to the cost of their home and temporary living expenses, they were awarded damages for mental pain and anguish. The court of appeals reversed the mental anguish award for the father, as he was not present during the crash and there was no strong causation in watching his house later be bulldozed. The mother was present, with her child, afraid the plane would strike them, so the court let her larger mental anguish award stand. The award for temporary living expenses was also reversed, as Pan Am paid for the first seven months, sufficient time for the plaintiffs to find a new dwelling. The court rejected the city's bulldozing as a superseding event cutting off Pan Am's liability.

---

[118] Thomas W. Haley, Ann S. Haley v. Pan American World Airways, Inc., 746 F.2d 311 (5th Cir. Nov. 1984).

[119] In Re Air Crash Disaster Near New Orleans, La. On July 9, 1982. Darryl Turgeau and Dolores v. Turgeau v. Pan American World Airways, Inc., United States Aviation Underwriters, Incorporated and the Boeing Company, 764 F.2d 1084 (5th Cir. June 1985).

[120] NTSB, AIRCRAFT ACCIDENT REPORT, PAN AMERICAN WORLD AIRWAYS, INC. BOENG 727-235, NEW ORLEANS INTERNATIONAL AIRPORT, JULY 9, 1982 (Mar. 1983).

In another homeowner case,[121] the Pan Am plane destroyed the plaintiff's home and killed his wife and three children. The jury awarded him $1 million for the loss of love and affection, $100,000 for her pain and suffering, $400,000 for the loss of each child, and $50,000 for his own mental anguish for the loss of his house and contents. In lieu of granting a new trial, the plaintiff was given the choice to accept remittiturs on all the awards. He accepted then appealed. The court of appeals ruled the award for loss of love and affection to be excessive, and after reviewing other cases, held that $500,000 was the maximum amount awardable for the loss of his wife and $250,000 per child. The award for her pain and suffering was also reversed, as there was no evidence she survived the initial impact. The award for anguish at the loss of his house was reversed, as he was not present during the crash and there was no strong causation.

In *Pregeant*,[122] the district court awarded the parents of a former flight attendant who died on this Pan Am flight damages for both pre-crash mental anguish and post-crash suffering. The court of appeals affirmed both awards, saying the jury could reasonably infer the post-crash suffering from the events that occurred on the plane's path after striking the ground. On the pre-crash mental anguish,

> when the left wing of the plane struck a tree at an altitude of 53 feet and rolled to the left, the passengers "certainly would have been thrown about and fighting for their lives and experienc[ing] a whole different situation." It is only reasonable to assume that at this point they despaired of their lives, realizing that death was imminent. In addition, the jury was aware that Susan Savoie was a former flight attendant. Such an experienced flier would be expected to detect danger sooner than the average passenger. To an experienced flier, a quick, unexplained descent on take-off can be nothing less than a panic-inducing event.[123]

---

[121] In Re Air Crash Disaster Near New Orleans, Louisiana on July 9, 1982. Robert Giancontieri, Cross-Appellant v. Pan American World Airways, Inc., Cross-Appellees, 767 F.2d 1151 (5th Cir. Aug. 1985).
[122] Judy Pregeant, Individually and as the Administratrix of the Estate of Susan Savoie, Ruth Toups, Janice Martinez, Bernice P. Savoie and Antoine R. Savoie v. Pan American World Airways, Inc., 762 F.2d 1245 (5th Cir. June 1985).
[123] *Id*. at 1249.

In *Larsen*,[124] the NTSB attributed[125] the Delta 191 crash to the pilot traveling through a rapidly developing thunderstorm with lightning in the landing flight path. The plane encountered windshear, then wind vortices, then hit a car, a light pole, and a water tank before exploding into fire. The rear fuselage separated and half the people in it survived. The report noted that the lower-level windshear detection system at the airport had certain deficiencies, such as not being able to report winds above the 20-foot-high sensors, and updrafts and downdrafts not being detectable. The plaintiff was the widow of a passenger killed on this flight. Delta had stipulated to its liability, with compensatory damages to be determined by the court, and punitive damages waived. The court awarded damages to the widow for loss of companionship, loss of care and maintenance, and mental anguish. His estate could have been awarded for the conscious pain and mental anguish of the decedent but due to the conflicting testimony of survivors and with no testimony of his situation, the court found it was precluded from awarding for pre-impact suffering.

In *Christy*,[126] the issue was whether the children and the father of a Delta passenger could recover care and support and mental anguish damages under Texas law. She had not died, but suffered permanent and severe brain injury. The court of appeals could find no state cases awarding damages to non-bystanders when there was no death involved, and so affirmed the summary judgment grant to Delta. In *Miller*,[127] a victim's daughter won an award representing his estate. His parents then filed suit but the district court granted summary judgment to Delta for the res judicata effect of the daughter's suit. The plaintiffs asserted they were different parties and it was a different cause of action. In affirming, the court of appeals disagreed, as this lawsuit arose from the same set of facts, and the estate had represented all parties pursuing wrongful death claims.

---

[124] Larsen v. Delta Air Lines, Inc., 692 F. Supp. 714 (S.D. Tex. July 1988).
[125] NTSB, Aircraft Accident Report, Delta Air Lines, Inc. Lockheed L-111-385-1, Dallas-Fort Worth International Airport, August 2, 1985 (Aug. 1986).
[126] In Re Air Crash at Dallas/Fort Worth Airport on August 2, 1985. Robert Bruce Christy v. Delta Air Lines, Inc., Michael Thomas McGee as Conservator and Next Friend of Jodi Michelle McGee and Jayme Bruce McGee v. Delta Air Lines, Inc., 856 F.2d 28 (5th Cir. Oct. 1988).
[127] In Re Air Crash at Dallas/Fort Worth Airport on August 2, 1985. David C. Miller, Jr., and M. Dorothy Miller v. Delta Air Lines, Inc., 861 F.2d 814 (5th Cir. Jan. 1989).

In *Connors*,[128] the widows of the Delta pilot and second officer filed suit against the United States for the alleged negligence of the FAA controllers and the National Weather Service. Delta joined as a plaintiff. The court explained the three level structure for ATC: the route controllers, split into one of 20 contiguous regions within the United States, bringing flights to within 35 miles of the airport; the approach controllers taking flights from there to within 7 to 10 miles of the airport to sequence them for landing; and the tower directing final approaches and landings from that point to the airport, along with handling takeoffs. The weather service assisted ATC at various points. It also explained that radar could only see precipitation but not wind. The court noted repeatedly that the pilots could see the developing thunderstorm on their onboard radar and could see the storms out the window. Other planes had reported seeing it painted all red on their radars. The court said the crew had sufficient weather information to decide on whether to continue the approach or not.

The court held that crew was negligent in attempting to land and this was the proximate cause of the crash. Even after their initial encounter with wind shear, the pilots did not abandon their approach. This was contrary to Delta's operating manual and FAA's advisories if at less than at 500 feet. The court ruled that doing so in such weather conditions was negligence and the failure to execute a missed approach was the proximate cause of the crash. The court did find the weather service and tower controllers had breached their duties in supplying comprehensive and updated weather information but it was not consequential, as the pilots already knew all this. ATC was not held negligent for not using a different runway. Any negligence by ATC was bracketed by the pilots' decision to enter the thunderstorm and then to continue landing in the face of significant wind shear. Accordingly, the court held the United States was not liable, as its negligence was not the proximate cause of the crash. The court of appeals affirmed.[129]

---

[128] In Re Air Crash at Dallas/Fort Worth Airport, 720 F. Supp. 1258 (N.D. Tex. Sept. 1989).
[129] In Re Air Crash at Dallas/fort Worth Airport on August 2, 1985. Kathleen E. Connors, on Behalf of the Beneficiaries Of, and as of the Estate of Edward M. Connors, Deceased, and Delta Air Lines, Inc. v. United States of America, Jean R. Nassick, on Behalf of the Beneficiaries Of, and as of the Estate of Nick N. Nassick, Deceased v. United States, 919 F.2d 1079 (5th Cir. Jan. 1991).

## D. Pilot Error

| LEGAL ISSUES |
|---|
| ❖ Pilot errors in flight giving rise to airline legal liability<br>❖ Willful misconduct negating the limitation of liability |

It is not only weather that is a primary factor leading to disasters in commercial aviation. Pilot error, that is, aviator negligence, has also been the proximate cause in several airplane crashes. There are many types of pilot error that have led to the deaths of 150 or more people, including: pilots taking off without ensuring there is a clear runway ahead of them; navigational errors leading to crossing a belligerent's borders; neglecting to undertake items on the pre-flight checklist leading to stalling the plane on takeoff; piloting a plane under control into terrain; and possible intentional criminal acts by a pilot. Examples of each of these types of pilot error that occurred during this period include, respectively: KLM 4805 and Pan Am 1736 on the island of Tenerife in 1977, with 583 killed; Korea Airlines (KAL) 007 over Kamchatka in 1983, with 269 deaths; Northwest Airlines (NWA) 255 in Detroit in 1987, with 156 fatalities; American Airlines (AA) 965 near Cali, Columbia in 1995, with 159 dead; and EgyptAir 990 off the Massachusetts coast in 1999, where 217 people died. Each of these aviation disasters will be presented in that order.

For KLM 4805 and Pan Am 1736, the Spanish aviation authority, *Subsecretaria de Aviacion Civil*, determined the fundamental causes of the March 27, 1977, collision between the two 747s on the runway of the Spanish island of Tenerife. These were: the Dutch captain took off without clearance; he did not obey the tower's instructions to stand by for takeoff; he did not stop the takeoff when the Pan Am plane reported still being on the runway; and, without knowing, answered "Yes" to his flight engineer's query if the Pan Am plane had left the runway. Other factors included the low-lying clouds that covered the runway, minimizing visibility; two important transmissions occurring simultaneously; and the strict KLM flight hour rules, which the crew would have exceeded with further delays. Also contributing was the crowded taxiway at this small airport, requiring use of the runway to taxi planes for takeoff; use of non-standard ATC language; Pan Am missing their turnoff exit; and terrorist bombings at the planes' intended destination, Gran Canaria, requiring re-routing planes to Tenerife.

With so many possible claimants, insurance underwriters decided to try to settle as claims quickly. Still, many lawsuits were filed and the multidistrict litigation panel had to decide the most appropriate forum to consolidate the lawsuits. Despite most lawsuits being filed in California, as many survivors and claimants resided there, the panel chose the southern district of New York, because the surviving Pan Am pilots, the NTSB and FAA investigators, the Pan Am's headquarters, and so many relevant documents were all there.[130] After the stipulations of liability for compensatory damages, the panel could transfer cases back to the original district for discovery for damages and trials for each specific plaintiff.[131] Otherwise, the district court would apply the law of each plaintiff's state to determine damages.[132] The court meantime denied plaintiff requests for a corporation to recover for the death of a key officer[133] and for a victim's twin sister's emotional injuries due to their "extrasensory empathy."[134]

In *Sibley*,[135] the plaintiff sued in Massachusetts for punitive damages, and was transferred to New York. While the plaintiff and KLM both agreed to use Massachusetts' choice of law rules, they came to different conclusions. The plaintiff asserted these rules indicated use of Massachusetts' wrongful death statute, which allowed punitive damages. KLM asserted that Dutch law should apply, which did not allow for punitive damages in wrongful death cases. The court noted that the state had until recently used *lex loci*, meaning Spanish law would control, which did not allow punitive damages. However, recent state decisions allowed for an interests' analysis. The court said that, as the purpose of punitive damages was to punish, the jurisdiction where the accident occurred had the predominant interest in punishment. The court held that Massachusetts interest in controlling a foreign company's actions in the Canary Islands was clearly overridden by the Dutch interest in protecting its own companies, so punitive damages would not be allowed. Suits by surviving flight attendants for punitive damages were denied under California law.[136]

---

[130] In Re Air Crash Disaster at Tenerife, Etc., 435 F. Supp. 927 (J.P.M.L. Aug. 1977).
[131] Ridout v. Pan American World Airways, Inc., 461 F. Supp. 671 (J.P.M.L. Nov. 1978).
[132] Vogel v. Pan American World Airways, Inc., 450 F. Supp. 224 (S.D.N.Y. May 1978).
[133] Bowen v. Pan American World Airways, Inc., 474 F. Supp. 563 (S.D.N.Y. Mar. 1979).
[134] Burke v. Pan American World Airways, Inc., 484 F. Supp. 850 (S.D.N.Y. Mar. 1980).
[135] Sibley v. KLM-Royal Dutch Airlines, Etc., 454 F. Supp. 425 (S.D.N.Y. Aug. 1978).
[136] Jackson v. Koninklijke Luchtvaart Maatschappij N. V., 459 F. Supp. 953 (S.D.N.Y. Nov. 1978).

The KAL 007 flight had gotten off course on its flight from Alaka to Seoul, South Korea, when the pilots had neglected to select the proper settings on the autopilot. It subsequently flew over prohibited military airspace in the Soviet Union and was shot down by a military aircraft on September 1, 1983. In *KAL Disaster*,[137] the issue was summary judgment on KAL's liability under the Warsaw Convention. The plaintiffs asserted that because the font on the ticket was 8-point instead of the required 10-point, the tickets were defective and so invalid for the limitation of liability. In analyzing the Convention's history, the court denied the motion, ruling that nothing in it specified a loss of the liability limitation if 10-point font was not used. This was affirmed on appeal.[138] The Supreme Court affirmed, ruling that not providing adequate notice was not equivalent to non-delivery of a ticket, for which there was unlimited liability.[139] A four-judge concurring opinion disagreed with this interpretation, but saying it would not obviate the limitation based on the small difference in font sizes.

The United States was accused of both not effectively utilizing its military capabilities and not warning the plane it was off course.[140] The court ruled military matters were non-justiciable, belonging to a separate government branch. On the government's motion for summary judgment on the latter issue, the court ruled there was not enough evidentiary record to decide. Two years later, after significant discovery, the government again motioned for summary judgment and the court granted it.[141] The plaintiffs had found no duty of the government to warn the plane it was off course. The court said that even if there was such a duty, the actions of the Soviet fighter pilot in shooting down the plane was a superseding event that was not reasonably foreseeable by the United States. This was same finding the court had previously held for defendants Boeing and Litton, and for mapmaker Jeppesen, who was accused of not having an explicit warning of the consequences of straying over Soviet-controlled areas printed on the charts and maps it provided to KAL.[142]

---

[137] In Re Korean Air Lines Disaster of September 1, 1983, 664 F. Supp. 1463 (D.D.C. July 1985).
[138] In Re Korean Air Lines Disaster of September 1, 1983. Appeal of Plaintiffs Steering Committee, 829 F.2d 1171 (D.C. Cir. Sept. 1987).
[139] Chan v. Korean Air Lines, Ltd., 490 U.S. 122 (Apr. 1989).
[140] In Re Korean Air Lines Disaster of September 1, 1983, 597 F. Supp. 613 (D.D.C. April 1984).
[141] In Re Korean Air Lines Disaster of September 1, 1983, 646 F. Supp. 30 (D.D.C. May 1986).
[142] In Re Korean Air Lines Disaster of September 1, 1983, 597 F. Supp. 619 (D.D.C. June 1984).

KAL later moved to bar damages greater than $75,000.[143] The court did not grant the motions, as there were reasonable inferences from the evidence that a jury could conclude there was willful misconduct. The court said while it might be merely negligence to fail to notice the plane being off course at point A or point B or point C, failing to notice this at all three could lead to the reasonable inference that the crew knew they were off course and did nothing to fix it. Knowing that their inertial navigation system was not working properly and then not turning back was willful misconduct. As was failing to perform mandatory cross-checks or not reacting to them if done. That the crew could not communicate with certain ground-based systems should also have alerted the crew that they were off course. The results of using their weather radar again would have told the crew they were off course. The actions of the Soviet pilot were not superseding causes here due to KAL's higher degree of misconduct, experience with Soviet fighter interceptions, and nexus to being off course.

In *Boyar*,[144] KAL was seeking to have three plaintiffs excluded for buying tickets outside the United States. The court ruled that the ticket was merely a representation of a contract, not the contract itself. However, the contract was modifiable and the actions for the two passengers who had entered these contracts outside the United States were dismissed for falling outside the Waraw Convention but the one passenger whose sister had purchased the ticket for him in the United States, despite the ticket being issued in South Korea, was not dismissed.

Upon the main case finally going to trial, a district court jury found KAL guilty of willful misconduct (removing the limit of liability) and granted $50 million in punitive damages. The court of appeals affirmed the willful misconduct finding but remanded the punitive damages award, as such awards were not part of the Warsaw Convention.[145] Each case then had to return to its originating district court for the plaintiffs' damage awards. In responding to varied motions by KAL in the trial of one victim,[146] Muriela Kole, the New York district court overruled the motions, saying,

---

[143] In Re Korean Air Lines Disaster of September 1, 1983, 704 F. Supp. 1135 (D.D.C. Nov. 1988).
[144] Boyar v. Korean Air Lines, 664 F. Supp. 1481 (D.D.C. Feb. 1987).
[145] In Re Korean Air Lines Disaster of September 1, 1983, Korean Air Lines Company, Ltd., 932 F.2d 1475 (D.C. Cir. July 1991).
[146] In Re Korean Air Lines Disaster of September 1, 1983, 807 F. Supp. 1073 (S.D.N.Y. Nov. 1992).

"that survival actions are permitted under the Warsaw Convention; that the estate may recover for decedent's conscious pain and suffering prior to her death; that the estate cannot recover for decedent's loss of the quality or enjoyment of life; that estate may recover for loss of support, lost services and loss of inheritance for any dependent survivors or beneficiary of the estate; that the individual non-dependent plaintiffs suing in their individual capacities may recover for mental injury connected to physical injury, loss of love and affection, lost inheritance, and lost services. [Mother] Muriel Mahalek may, therefore, proceed as a party plaintiff."[147]

The court of appeals[148] said the district court jury had awarded her mother damages for mental injury and loss of society, her sister for mental injury and loss of society, inheritance and support, and the estate for the victim's pain and suffering. The court affirmed only the pain and suffering award, reversing the awards for mental injury awards, and for loss of society to the mother, as there was no dependency on her daughter proven. The awards to her sister for loss of society, support, and inheritance were remanded for evidence of dependency. The Supreme Court reversed, holding that loss of society was not a pecuniary award and so not available under the applicable U.S. law, the Death on the High Seas Act (DOHSA).[149] The same court of appeals had similarly reversed an award for grief for another plaintiff.[150] The Supreme Court had not ruled on the pain and suffering award but KAL then tried, unsuccessfully, to challenge these awards as not being pecuniary.[151] The D.C. court of appeals, the following year, held that because DOHSA was a wrongful death statute and not a survival statute, pre-death pain and suffering could not be awarded.[152]

---

[147] *Id.* at 1078.
[148] Marjorie Zicherman, Individually and as Under the Estate of Muriel A.M.S. Kole Muriel Mahalek, Mother and Next of Kin of Muriel A.M.S. Kole, Plaintiffs- Appellees/cross- Michael Kole v. Korean Air Lines Co., Ltd., Defendant-Appellant/cross-Appellee, 43 F.3d 18 (2nd Cir. Dec. 1994).
[149] Zicherman Ex Rel. Estate of Kole v. Korean Air Lines Co., 516 U.S. 217 (Jan. 1996).
[150] Barbara Swift Hollie v. Korean Air Lines Co., Ltd., 60 F.3d 90 (2nd Cir. July 1995).
[151] Daisy E. Bickel v. Korean Air Lines Company, Ltd., 96 F.3d 151 (6th Cir. Oct. 1996); Eric W. Forman v. Korean Air Lines Co., Ltd., 84 F.3d 446 (D.C. Cir. July 1996).
[152] In Re Korean Air Lines Disaster of September 1, 1983. Philomena Dooley v. Korean Air Lines Co., Ltd, 117 F.3d 1477 (D.C. Cir. Aug. 1997).

The NTSB attributed[153] the NWA 255 crash on August 16, 1987, which occurred shortly after takeoff, to a failure to use the Taxi checklist to ensure the flaps and slats were properly extended for takeoff. The checklist's first item required the first officer to call out "flaps" and then check the flaps and slat settings and call it out (e.g., "Flaps 11"). The captain would then check that setting and if correct, respond with "Flaps 11". The cockpit voice recorder had no mention of the flap callouts by either pilot. The After Start and Before Takeoff checklists were also not called for, the steps were not called out, nor their completion called out. The flaps and slats were always in the retracted position, when they typically would be set for 10-15 degrees on takeoff.

In *Polec*,[154] after an 18-month trial, the district court jury found Northwest to be entirely negligent and that airplane maker McDonnell Douglas had no liability, so it could collect from Northwest on claims it had settled in strict liability suits it faced. McDonnell Douglas' assertions at trial were that this crew had a history of negligence in not following checklists. This issue could have been notified by an aural warning system, but the crew had a habit of pulling the circuit breaker to the system because its noises irritated them. Further, after they were notified by the stick shaker when the plane stalled upon takeoff, their consequent actions in those few seconds were the wrong ones to save the plane. Among the many issues raised by Northwest and rejected by the court of appeals included that violations of FAA regulations could not be used to prove negligence while not allowing proof that McDonnell Douglas' plane itself violated FAA regulations. The court ruled the testimony about Northwest's vice-president of operations negative reaction after seeing the flap setting post-accident should not have been admitted. However, it did not affect the result due to significant other evidence. Northwest also asserted that allowing a series of incidents to be categorized as willful misconduct should instead have been evaluated individually. This finding meant the Warsaw Convention's limited liability was not available. The court of appeals did not agree with Northwest assertions, and so affirmed both judgments.

---

[153] NTSB, AIRCRAFT ACCIDENT REPORT, NORTHWEST AIRLINES, INC. MCDONNELL DOUGLAS DC-9-82, DETROIT METROPOLITAN WAYNE COUNTY AIRPORT, AUGUST 16, 1987 (May 1988).

[154] In Re Air Crash Disaster. Chester H. Polec Kris Grigg, Mary Kahle, James Wennen, Earl Pearson, Carolyn Johnson, Suzanne Redd Ross, Victor Elfering, Marilyn Blakley, Bonnie Royden, David Charles Morris, Patricia Roundy, and Janet D. Cook v. Northwest Airlines, Inc., McDonnell Douglas Corporation, 86 F.3d 498 (6th Cir. June 1996).

The NTSB summarized the Columbian investigation of the AA 965 crash on December 20, 1995. The crash was attributed to errors by the pilots in planning and executing their approach and failure to discontinue it, lack of situational awareness of the nearby mountainous terrain, and failure to revert to more basic navigation when their flight management system (FMS) navigation became confusing and time demanding. In *Crash Near Cali*,[155] the district court granted summary judgment on American's liability, saying "No reasonable jury could find that acts of the pilots of Flight 965 and in particular the pilots' decision to continue their descent at night from a grievously off course position in mountainous terrain amounted to anything less than willful misconduct, whether that term is construed to require an objective or a subjective inquiry. Moreover, no reasonable juror could find that the pilots' conduct was not among the proximate causes of the crash."[156] The court of appeals[157] noted American told its pilots not to rely on ATC landing clearances in South America. After an ATC offer of a short cut, these pilots entered the wrong waypoint into the FMS, and started a turn away from their course and into the surrounding mountains. To make it worse, they had deployed the speed brakes while dealing with the FMS, which hindered their ability to quickly climb when confronted with the aural "Pull Up, Terrain" warnings.

The legal issue was whether the test for willful misconduct that barred the Warsaw Convention's limitation of liability was a subjective or objective test. A new revision to the Convention since the case began required the court to determine whether it clarified or revised the law. Finding it clarified the law, the court then ruled that the issue was whether the pilots knew they were significantly off course such that they were recklessly endangering their passengers. Holding that this was a subjective query to be decided by a jury, not an objective legal decision a judge could make, the court of appeals remanded for the jury finding. In *Carlson*,[158] after the judgment on American's willful misconduct, the court rejected summary judgment for the FMS manufacturer and the database maker. They had tried to avoid contributing to the plaintiffs' damages payouts.

---

[155] In Re Air Crash Near Cali, Colombia on December 20, 1995, 985 F. Supp. 1106 (S.D. Fla. Oct. 1997).
[156] *Id*. at 1109.
[157] Cortes v. American Airlines, Inc., 177 F.3d 1272 (11th Cir. June 1999).
[158] Carlson v. American Airlines, Inc., 24 F. Supp. 2d 1340 (S.D. Fla. Feb. 1998).

The NTSB determined that[159] the loss of EgyptAir 990 on October 31, 1999, was due to the deliberate actions of the relief first officer. According to the transcripts of the cockpit voice recorder, the 59-year-old relief first officer had relieved the younger command first officer much earlier than planned (20 minutes instead of 3-4 hours) without prior notification to and over the protests of the latter. Shortly thereafter, the command pilot left to use the restroom. While he was gone, the autopilot was disconnected and an abrupt nose-down elevator movement was input, resulting in a 40-degree downward trajectory. The plane began to descend rapidly, eventually reaching a descent rate of 20,000 feet per minute. All the while, the relief first officer was repeating the phrase "I rely on God." The captain returned as the G force became negative and the plane exceeded its maximum operating airspeed, causing the master alarm to sound. The engines were switched off and the captain asked why they were shut off. The two elevator surfaces then began to receive opposing up and down inputs as the two pilots fought each other for control of the plane.

In response to the EgyptAir assertions of mechanical failure, Boeing said there was none and each asserted failure type could be recovered with normal flying techniques. The report noted the relief first officer had not responded appropriately to the initial nose-down situation, did not show anxiety or call for help, and did not answer the command captain's queries. This was viewed as being inconsistent with a sudden unexpected mechanical problem. The cockpit voice recorder showed the relief first officer's seat moving forward to manually fly the plane and being alone at the time the descent input were entered. The report noted there was no logical reason to disconnect the autopilot or move the throttle levers to idle. The report concluded that the airplane could have been recovered if the relief first officer had been working with, instead of opposing, the command captain's efforts. The NTSB determined that the probable cause,

> is the airplane's departure from normal cruise flight and subsequent impact with the Atlantic Ocean as a result of the relief first officer's flight control inputs. The reason for the relief first officer's actions was not determined.[160]

---

[159] NTSB, AIRCRAFT ACCIDENT BRIEF, EGYPTAIR FLIGHT 990 BOEING 767-366ER, 60 MILES SOUTH OF NANTUCKET, MASSACHUSETTS, OCTOBER 31, 1999 (Mar. 2002).
[160] *Id.* p. 67.

In *Crash Near Nantucket Island*,[161] the personal representative of two of the victims of this crash sought non-pecuniary damages under DOHSA. The court noted that DOHSA was amended in 2000 to permit non-pecuniary damages for wrongful death, for loss of care, comfort, and companionship, for aviation accidents occurring more than 12 nautical miles from the U.S. shoreline. This was to be retroactive to any deaths occurring after July 16, 1996. The parties agreed that the loss of care, comfort, and companionship equated to what courts in maritime cases had long termed the "loss of society." The parties varied widely in their estimates of the value of the loss of both parents for two families. The plaintiffs asked for, on average, more than $700,000 per parent per child while the defendants offered $75,000 per parent per child. The court looked at the remaining life expectancies for these four parents ranging from about 10 to 20 years and the added significance of losing both at the same time. It awarded about $200,000 per parent per child.

Two Egyptian passengers[162] who tried to litigate in the United States were dismissed, as their travel did not end in the United States or their contract with EgyptAir start there. Boeing and Parker Hannifin, responding to suit by Egyptian, Syrian, and Canadian plaintiffs, cross-claimed for contribution and indemnity against EgyptAir. The response was that if those plaintiffs had sued EgyptAir, there would be no subject matter jurisdiction under the Warsaw Convention, as above, so there should be no jurisdiction over contribution and indemnity claims by the manufacturers. This would indirectly impose passenger claims on EgyptAir. Boeing asserted the indemnity was contractual and further the manufacturers were not part of the Convention. The court ruled that the Convention was not applicable to the relationships between the airline and manufacturers and denied the motion for summary judgment against the manufacturers. A son whose two parents died on this flight received compensation directly from EgyptAir.[163] He then, on legal advice, tried to join the litigation but he had never legally become a personal representative of his parents' estates. The court held he lacked standing to sue. He then tried to sue the lawyer for malpractice but this claim would be barred by the statute of limitations.

---

[161] In Re Air Crash Near Nantucket Island, Mass., on 10/31/1999, 307 F. Supp. 2d 465 (E.D.N.Y. Mar. 2004).
[162] In Re Air Crash Near Nantucket Island, Mass., 340 F. Supp. 2d 240 (E.D.N.Y. Aug. 2004).
[163] Mohamed v. Donald J. Nolan, Ltd., 967 F. Supp. 2d 647 (E.D.N.Y. Aug. 2013).

E.  Spaceship Explosion

| LEGAL ISSUES |
|---|
| ❖ Spaceship explosion giving rise to government legal liability<br>❖ Differing legal protections based on an astronaut's employer |

On January 28, 1986, in the 25th space shuttle launch, Challenger exploded a little more than one minute into the flight, killing all seven astronauts. This was mission 51-L, each letter signifying: the year, that it launched from Kennedy Space Center, and was the 12th launch that year. Challenger was on its 10th flight, the most heavily used of the four space shuttles. By executive order, a presidential commission concluded that the fault lay with the seal from an O-ring in a solid rocket booster which had failed and allowed hot gases to escape, causing the explosion.[164] The report explained that the shuttle rode piggyback on an external liquid-fueled, expendable storage tank and two solid-fueled, recoverable booster rockets. The crew was comprised of a commander, a pilot, mission specialists, and payload specialists, the latter not career astronauts. The three main shuttle engines were fed by the external fuel tank, while the solid rocket boosters provided 80% of the takeoff thrust for about two minutes before being separated.

It was a very cold day, 36° F, 15° F colder than any prior launch. Evidence showed that upon liftoff, smoke came from the aft field joint of the right solid rocket booster, facing the external fuel tank, indicating the joint sealing was not complete. These puffs occurred in synch with the liftoff load dynamics and resultant flexing of the joint. This suggested the rubber O-rings in the joint seal were being burned by hot propellant gases. This led to a flame from the right solid rocket booster escaping and mixing soon with hydrogen in the external fuel tank. The commission concluded,

> the cause of the Challenger accident was the failure of the pressure seal in the aft field joint of the right Solid Rocket Motor. The failure was due to a faulty design unacceptably sensitive to a number of factors [including]... the effects of temperature... the character of materials... and the reaction of the joint to dynamic loading.[165]

---

[164] REPORT OF THE PRESIDENTIAL COMMISSION ON THE SPACE SHUTTLE CHALLENGER ACCIDENT (June 1986).
[165] *Id.* p. 73.

The government tried to settle with the families of the astronauts. The status of these seven differed. Two were current members of the military (Navy Cmdr. Michael J. Smith and Air Force Lt. Col. Ellison S. Onizuka), three were employed by NASA (Francis R. (Dick) Scobee, Ronald E. McNair and Judith A. Resnik), and two were civilians (Gregory B. Jarvis and Christa McAuliffe.). The latter was the first school teacher sent into space and unlike the others, a relative novice to the space program. The military personnel's survivors would be compensated under standard military programs, while the NASA employees would be subject to the Federal Employees' Compensation Act of 1916.[166] The National and Aeronautics Space Act of 1958[167] also provided for the payment of limited death benefits (§203.a) and potentially more for meritorious claims (§203.b). The representatives of the two civilians were under no such restrictions.

The government negotiated settlements with representatives of Onizuka, Scobee, Jarvis, and McAuliffe. These were reached in both its name and that of rocket booster manufacturer Morton Thiokol, with the payouts allocated between them 40%/60%. The offers were based on the number and ages of their dependents. Offers made to the other three representatives were rejected. Resnick, for example, had no spouse or children and would have likely received less. The representatives of Resnick and Adair then decided to settle solely with Morton Thiokol, as the government would not agree to a settlement that did not employ the same formula used by the other families. Smith's widow decided to litigate, perhaps using the example of widow from a prior NASA program. When three astronauts were killed in a fire on the launchpad of Apollo 1 on January 27, 1967, the widow of Virgil I. "Gus" Grissom sued NASA contractor North American Rockwell for wrongful death.[168] They had manufactured the space capsule with the pure oxygen atmosphere feeding the fire, from which the astronauts were unable to escape due to the door latching mechanism. The Grissom lawsuit was not successful, as it was held to be barred by the statute of limitations but the widow and the manufacturer later reached a settlement.

---

[166] 5 U.S.C. § 8102 Compensation for disability or death of employee.
[167] Pub. L. 85-568, An Act to provide for research into problems of flight within and outside the earth's atmosphere, and for other purposes.
[168] Grissom v. North American Aviation, Inc., 326 F. Supp. 465 (M.D. Fla. May 1971).

In *Smith*,[169] the shuttle pilot's widow sued Morton Thiokol, the federal government, and the manager of NASA's solid booster program, Lawrence Mulloy. The latter had been on the call the night before the launch, known to have urged Morton Thiokol managers to change their decision not to launch, due to concerns of the Morton Thiokol engineers about the impact of the cold temperatures on the O-ring. He was asked by the commission,

> Kutyna: Larry [Mulloy], let me follow through on that, and I am kind of aware of the launch decision process, and you said you made the decision at your level on this thing. If this were an airplane, an airliner, and I just had a two-hour argument with Boeing on whether the wing was going to fall off or not, I think I would tell the pilot, at least mention it. Why didn't we escalate a decision of this importance?[170]

The government responded that the *Feres*[171] Supreme Court case, recently reaffirmed,[172] did not allow claims by servicemen. The plaintiff asserted her husband was not performing activities incident to his military service when he died. The court noted that he was detailed from the Navy to NASA under an agreement dating to the Eisenhower administration. Further, he was a member on active service in that branch, subject to its rules, retained his military rank and privileges, and his dependents received military death benefits. The court ruled that while his NASA duty was in lieu of his normal military duty, he was still under military control. The court also ruled he was piloting the shuttle because he was part of a military program detailing pilots to NASA and therefore it was incident to his military service. The court held that under the *Feres* doctrine, it had no subject matter jurisdiction to hear claims under the FTCA. The claims against the government and Mulloy were then dismissed. She subsequently settled with Thiokol but appealed against this judgment. The court of appeals affirmed, holding that this claim against the government or its employee were barred by *Feres*.[173] Additionally, a new statute, retroactively applicable, would serve to bar any claims against Mulloy.[174]

---

[169] Smith v. Morton Thiokol, Inc., 712 F. Supp. 893 (M.D. Fla. Feb. 1988).
[170] PRESIDENTIAL COMMISSION REPORT, p. 101.
[171] Feres v. United States, 340 U.S. 135 (Dec. 1950).
[172] United States v. Johnson, 481 U.S. 681 (May 1987).
[173] Jane J. Smith, of the Estate of Michael J. Smith v. United States of America, Lawrence B. Mulloy, 877 F.2d 40 (11th Cir. July 1989).
[174] Pub. L. No. 100-694, Federal Employees Liability Reform and Tort Compensation Act.

In *Boisjoly*,[175] Morton Thiokol was sued by a former employee who had testified to the problems with the O-rings before the commission,

> Mr. Boisjoly: I expressed deep concern about launching at low temperature. I presented... the chart that summarized the primary concerns, and that was the chart that I pulled right out of the Washington presentation without changing one word of it because it was still applicable, and it addresses the highest concern of the field joint in both the ignition transient condition and the steady state condition, and it really sets down the rationale for why we were continuing to fly. Basically, if erosion penetrates the primary O-ring seal, there is a higher probability of no secondary seal capability in the steady state condition. And I had two sub-bullets under that which stated bench testing showed O-ring not capable of maintaining contact with metal parts, [and a] gap opening rate to maximum operating pressure. I had another bullet which stated bench testing showed capability to maintain O-ring contact during initial phase (0 to 170 milliseconds of transient). That was my comfort basis of continuing to fly under normal circumstances, normal being within the data base we had. I emphasized, when I presented that chart about the changing of the timing function of the O-ring as it attempted to seal. I was concerned that we may go from that first beginning region into that intermediate region, from 0 to 170 being the first region, and 170 to 330 being the intermediate region where we didn't have a high probability of sealing or seating.[176]

He sued, under what the court termed the "private" action and the "qui tam" action. The former included defamation, intentional infliction of emotional distress, civil conspiracy, antitrust, and witness tampering. The court dismissed the first cause of action due to a lack of specificity and not meeting the slander per se requirements. The second was dismissed, because Morton Thiokol's decision to launch, contrary to his strenuous objection, was not directed at him with the intent to cause emotional distress and the alleged acts were not outrageous. The third was dismissed because the alleged conspiracy between Morton Thiokol and NASA was not directed at him. The fourth was dismissed as either he had no standing

---

[175] Boisjoly v. Morton Thiokol, Inc., 706 F. Supp. 795 (D. Utah Sept. 1988).
[176] PRESIDENTIAL COMMISSION REPORT, p. 80.

or was not directly injured by the alleged anticompetitive behavior. The fifth was dismissed as there was no private right of action. For the qui tam action, under the False Claims Act, specifically the false claims were in supplying defective second-stage boosters and Morton Thiokol agreeing to the launch under cold temperatures it knew were dangerous. However, this claim could not go forward because NASA knew of such issues, being informed by Morton Thiokol. The court dismissed all claims in both actions.

In *New York Times*,[177] the newspaper fought a several-year battle to get copies of the voice communications tape of this mission. The reason they proffered was to understand the inflections in the astronaut's voices and any background noises such as those related to the rocket boosters that would not be on a transcript. The newspaper requested this information under the Freedom of Information Act, for both a transcript and the actual tapes. NASA provided the transcript but the rejected the demand for the tapes, under an exception that it would violate the privacy of the astronauts' families. The court granted summary judgment to the Times because the recording had to contain personal information about a person to be protected but because the tapes did not contain such personal information,

> It is an undisputed matter of record that the tape at issue here contains no information about the personal lives of the astronauts or any of their family members, but only the comments, observations, and communications of certain of the Challenger astronauts concerning the launching and flight of the Shuttle on the date of the accident.[178]

NASA appealed,[179] saying that although the information itself was not personal, when uttered by one of the identifiable astronauts, it was. A split court of appeals affirmed 2-1, saying that the tape contained information that was unrelated to any particular person. The dissenting opinion would have not read the exemption so narrowly. The full court of appeals vacated that decision then convened en banc and reversed the district court by a 6-

---

[177] New York Times Co. v. National Aeronautics & Space Administration, 679 F. Supp. 33 (D.D.C. June 1987).
[178] *Id.* at 35.
[179] New York Times Company v. National Aeronautics and Space Administration, 852 F.2d 602 (D.C. Cir. July 1988).

5 vote, remanding to the district court to undertake for the second step in the analysis, a balancing of the public and private interests involved.[180] It held that the astronauts' voices, "and whatever those voices may reveal of their thoughts and feelings at the very moment of their deaths,"[181] were personal information. To underline its point that inflections are personal, the court described what the New York Times had published on the information it had obtained from NASA after the Apollo 1 fire,

> Lest there be any doubt that voice inflections can contain personal information, recall the 1967 fire in the cockpit of the Apollo 1 spacecraft, which killed Edward H. White, 2d, Roger B. Chaffee, and Virgil I. (Gus) Grissom. In that tragedy, too, NASA had a tape of the last moments of the astronauts' lives. The New York Times was then content, however, to publish an article based solely upon the verbal description given by NASA, without gaining access to the sounds on the tape. Here is how the Times recounted the last few seconds in the cockpit: "Fire ... I smell fire," an unidentified astronaut reported over the intercom. Two seconds passed. "Fire in the cockpit!" cried Colonel White. This time the voice was sharp and insistent. It was identified as Colonel White's by Donald K. Slayton, a former astronaut and now chief of crew operations. There was silence for three seconds--then a hysterical shout from an unidentified astronaut: "There's a bad fire in the spacecraft!" A longer gap followed, about seven seconds. There were sounds of frantic movement, unintelligible shouting. Finally, after four more seconds, Commander Chaffee cried out the last words of distress: "We're on fire--get us out of here!" N.Y. Times, Jan. 31, 1967, p. 1. The description alone is chilling. One can hardly doubt that the horror in the voices on the tape would convey additional information that applies to the astronauts in the throes of their deaths.[182]

On remand, the district court[183] recounted that these digital tapes were recovered from the ocean floor about six weeks after the disaster. The district court found substantial privacy interests of the families,

---

[180] New York Times Company v. National Aeronautics and Space Administration, 920 F.2d 1002 (D.C. Cir. Dec. 1990).
[181] *Id.* at 1010.
[182] *Id.* at 1005-06.
[183] New York Times Co. v. National Aeronautics & Space Administration, 782 F. Supp. 628 (D.D.C. Dec. 1991).

The Challenger families potentially face a far more disruptive assault on their privacy than the employees in *NARFE,* should the tape be disclosed. They may be subjected not just to a barrage of mailings and personal solicitations, but also to a panoply of telephone calls from media groups as well as a disruption of their peace of mind every time a portion of the tape is played within their hearing.[184]

The court did not find that there was a significant public interest in discovering how NASA operated during this brief mission. NASA had several people listen to the tapes whose affidavits asserted there was nothing about the booster rockets that could be heard on the tapes. The court ruled that the public interest was minimal. The court held the substantial privacy interests of the families outweighed the minimal public interest. With a transcript of the flight already publicly released, the court granted summary judgment to NASA, ending this long legal battle.

In *Hughes Communications*,[185] NASA was hit with a series of lawsuits from companies who had entered contracts with NASA to launch satellites from the space shuttles. The court of claims began by discussing how NASA had transformed from a space research and development organization into a space shuttle service for commercial interests, especially in satellite launches for private companies. This would help fund the space shuttle program, help develop new technologies, and keep the United States in the forefront in space exploration and technology. After this disaster, a presidential directive stated that NASA was to no longer use the space shuttles in the commercial satellite launch business. This would be turned over to the private sector. At that time, there were 44 commercial payloads already scheduled and plans had to be made about what to do with them. They were broken into four categories: shuttle unique (8), national defense or impacting foreign policy (12), costly to retrofit to a private sector expendable launch vehicle (ELV) (11), and remainder (13). The plan adopted was to have the first two groups assigned to fly on the shuttles, while the latter two groups would be assigned to ELVs. All ten of the plaintiff's planned satellites belonged in the latter two groups. This led plaintiff Hughes to file a lawsuit against the government for its losses.

---

[184] *Id.* at 632.
[185] Hughes Communications Galaxy, Inc. v. United States, 37 Cont. Cas. Fed. 76,307 (Ct. Cl. Apr. 1992).

The allegations were for breach of their agreement and a taking under the Fifth Amendment. The court noted several features of their agreement, including making only best efforts to launch; a fixed termination date even if the satellites were not launched; rights to delay or postpone a launch; NASA's ability to terminate the agreement for reasons beyond its control; a limited ability for Hughes to sue the government; termination if NASA could not obtain government appropriations; and the launch services were subject to government policy and the law. The court found that the change of policy was a sovereign act and the plaintiff's interest in its launch slots was not a property interest under the Fifth Amendment, so not a taking. As the contract subjected the launch services to government policy that had changed, the court granted summary judgment to the government. The court of appeals reversed and remanded,[186] as it held the contract's key provision specified its 1982 policy, not that provision that allowed changes. On remand the government was found liable.[187] Damages were assessed, as the difference between what it would have cost to launch five satellites, the likely number NASA could have launched on the shuttle, and what it did cost to launch these on ELVs, plus reconfiguration costs.[188] The judgment was affirmed.[189] Other satellite companies also sued NASA.[190]

In *Lovingood*,[191] a former NASA manager did not like how he was portrayed in a BBC docudrama on the Challenger disaster and sued for defamation and false light. The show had him representing to the commission that the probabilities of a total mission failure including deaths of the astronauts was 1 in 100,000 while NASA engineers had said it was 1 in 200. The real-life query had concerned main engine failure, which was much lower due to several redundancies. The film noted some scenes were created for dramatic purposes. As he was deemed a public official and actual malice was not proved, and there was no evidence of reckless disregard demonstrated in broadcasting it, the court denied both claims.

---

[186] Hughes Communications Galaxy, Inc. v. The United States, 998 F.2d 953 (Fed. Cir. Oct. 1993).
[187] Hughes Communications Galaxy, Inc. v. United States, 40 Cont. Cas. Fed. 76,906 (Fed. Cl. Nov. 1995).
[188] Hughes Communications Galaxy, Inc. v. United States, 47 Fed. Cl. 236 (Fed. Cl. June 2000).
[189] Hughes Communications Galaxy, Inc. v. United States, Defendant-Cross, 271 F.3d 1060 (Fed. Cir. Nov. 2001).
[190] American Satellite Co. v. United States, 37 Cont. Cas. Fed. 76,308 (Ct. Cl. Apr. 1992); New Valley Corp. v. United States, 34 Fed. Cl. 703 (Fed. Cl. Jan. 1996).
[191] Lovingood v. Discovery Communications, Inc., 275 F. Supp. 3d 1301 (N.D. Ala. Aug. 2017).

# *Afterword*

Not every disaster or disaster type was able to be presented in this book. Some topics that were not addressed included building elevator failures, cable car detachments, mountaineering accidents, levee breaks, avalanches, wildfires, droughts, blizzards, tanker truck explosions, blackouts, school building fires, nursing home fires, power line or tower collapses, famines, amusement park accidents, and PFOA and other environmental poisonings. The significant number of airplane crashes meant that only representative examples of the varied categories of aviation disasters could be presented. HIV/AIDS was an intended topic, but the consequences of this disease played out over decades and was so widespread, that it would be difficult to document in a few pages. This was also true of varied outbreaks of other diseases that ravaged the world at different times. Disasters from armed engagement between combatants, mass suicides, and terrorist incidents were topics intentionally excluded.

There were other specific disasters that were not presented because: (1) the legal documents were not still extant or not readily available; (2) there were no legal issues to discuss, as liability was clear, and settlements were quickly made; or (3) no legal remedy was pursued. An example of the first type was the 1971 Ibrox stadium disaster where criminal liability was found in a trial in Scotland for the deaths of 66 people at a match but those records were hard to obtain. An example of the second type was the 1972 Big Dipper amusement park disaster in Battersea, England, where five children died on a roller coaster. Examples of the third type included the 1943 Bethnal Green tube station crush where 173 died, the 1955 Le Mans racing disaster where 84 people were killed, and the 1996 Mt Everest climbing disaster, where 8 climbers died over 24 hours. There were other disasters that deserved a presentation, like the 1995 collapse of Sampoong Department Store in Seoul, South Korea that killed 502 people. However, the largest category of omissions were the many types of disasters which already had an example presented. Besides aviation disasters, there were many mine explosions, railroad crashes, and building fires not covered.

The 21st century has already seen a list of disasters that is too long. The Covid 19 pandemic, the HIV/AIDS pandemic, the acts of terrorism on 09/11/2001 and 07/07/2005, the Space Shuttle Columbia explosion when reentering the Earth's atmosphere, the Deepwater Horizon oil spill, the devastating consequences of Hurricane Katrina and the levee breaks, the Fukushima nuclear accident, the West African Ebola outbreak, Hurricane Sandy, the earthquakes in Kashmir, Haiti, and Nepal, the Indian Ocean earthquake and tsunami, the Kaprun funicular disaster, and many aviation disasters, including American Airlines 587, Air France 447, and Malaysian Air 370. The human impacts of these disasters are well known but the legal stories likely less so. There could easily be another volume covering these.

As disasters do not seem to be in any manner diminishing, just changing their manifestations or locations, it is perhaps appropriate to conclude by discussing one final disaster type unique from the incidents already presented. This was a personal tragedy instead of a large-scale disaster, but also a bit of a legal oddity, and a story that seemingly needed to be told. In *Reich*,[1] the decedent Steven had been struck by lightning and killed August 8, 1968. His widow Sandra filed for workmen's compensation. The only issue before the court was whether his death arose out of his employment. He was a vice-president of a family food growing business. He had gone to a hay field to direct his workers to cease working, as a storm was brewing. He was standing in the field next to his car. The one worker not yet in a vehicle was standing five feet from him when lightning struck Steven. The defendant company acknowledged that he died of being struck by lightning while working, yet he was no more at risk that anyone else in the general population from lightning. As an act of God, lightning was not compensable unless the character of the employment was such that it subjected the employee to risks greater than those in the same vicinity. The referee ruled being in an open, flat and unprotected field met that criterion. A lighting expert testified that being a grounded person surrounded by several nearby taller farm vehicles meant lightning would seek out the person instead of vehicles with rubber tires (a poor ground). Because Steven was 6 feet tall and the other man outside a vehicle was 5 feet 4 inches tall, lighting would seek the tallest grounded object around, which was Steven. The appeals court affirmed the judgment for his widow.

---

[1] Reich v. A. Reich & Sons Gardens, Inc., 485 S.W. 2d 133 (Mo. App Sept. 1972).

# Index

(Abridged: includes only the initial / primary references to legal issues, disaster types, and certain high appellate courts or regulatory/investigatory institutions.)

Acts of God not always a defense, 53
**After Death**, 45
**Air Pollution**, 184
**Airplane Crashes**, 140
**Airship Explosion**, 119
Airship explosion investigations not determining causation, 119
Altering approved construction plans causing criminal liability, 124
Applying the Warsaw Convention for international travel, 140
Arbitration agreement to handle tort claims, 130
**Asbestos**, 218
ATC misidentification of planes giving rise to legal liability, 210
Board of Trade inquiry, 38
**Bridge Collapse**, 17
Bridge designer being culpable after collapse, 17
Bureau of Mines, 69
Challenging the public health officers' authority, 107
**Chemical Dumping**, 199
**Chemical Poisoning**, 244
Chemical poisoning of nearby residents causing legal liability, 244
**Circus Fire**, 130
Civil Aeronautics Board, 142
Common carriers' passenger liability, 21
Competing federal and state class actions, 261
Consequences of violating airship conditions of passage, 119
Construction of a faulty LNG tank giving rise to legal liability, 157
**Coupling Loss**, 8
Creating common operating rules and regulations, 12
**Crowd Crush**, 267

**Dam Failure**, 171
Damage from oil well blowouts resulting in legal liability, 194
**Derailment**, 21
Differences between two nations' maritime judgments, 31
Differing judicial interpretations of operator's liability, 69
Differing legal protections based on an astronaut's employer, 291
Diseases arising from tunnelling work resulting in legal lability, 152
Disregard of patron's safety giving rise to criminal liability, 124
Duties owed to a theater audience, 58
Duty to deploy improvements in safety technology, 12
**Earthquake & Fire**, 63
Enforcing current fire codes on older buildings, 135
Environmental Protection Agency, 187
Equal protection violations arising from hotel fire, 135
Exemptions for discretionary emergency measures, 233
**Exploding Cars**, 224
Explosions in mines generating legal liability, 69
**Factory Fire**, 74
Federal maritime and admiralty law overriding state law, 41
**Fertilizer Explosion**, 166
Final actions taken before collision defining legal liability, 37
**Flood**, 53
Flying into severe weather causing airline legal liability, 275
**Fog Collision**, 31
Food and Drug Administration, 146
**Helicopter Crashes**, 214

Helicopter landings bringing about operator legal liability, 214
**Hotel Fire**, 135
House of Lords, 243
**Hurricane**, 179
**Iceberg**, 79
Impact of pandemics on contractual obligations, 107
Impact of venue change on jury verdicts, 102
Impact on consumer protection statutes for drugs, 146
Indemnities to negligent operator from legal liability, 239
Issuing bonds to fund the cost of claims, 171
John Doe hearing, 103
Judicial Committee of the Privy Council, 33
Known fuel tank defects defining civil liability, 224
**Lake Collision**, 26
**Landslide**, 189
Leaseholders of railroads having legal liability, 21
Level of punitive damages for maritime disaster, 249
Liability standards for carriers of goods vs people, 3
Limitation of liability for foreign ships striking an iceberg, 79
Limitations on fire insurance liability for earthquakes, 63
Limiting liability for chemical waste transferred, 199
**LNG Explosion**, 157
Mass corporate poisoning bringing about criminal liability, 146
**Mass Poisoning**, 146
**Mid-Air Collison**, 204
**Mine Explosions**, 69
Misrepresentation exception to federal tort claims, 179
Multi-country litigation arising from a single disaster, 244
Mutual liability for damages in collisions, 26

National Highway Traffic Safety Administration, 224
National Transportation Safety Board, 210
National, state and local laws to prevent air pollution, 184
Need to exchange tickets to extend insurance coverage, 214
Neglect of train signaling rules causing legal liability, 90
Negligence in braking train leading to criminal liability, 8
Negligence in government program resulting in legal liability, 166
**Nightclub Fire**, 124
No responsibility for unauthorized post-disaster acts, 53
Non-compliance with overtaking regulations causing liability, 204
Not disseminating tornado data creating legal liability, 275
Not warning of the asbestos dangers creating legal liability, 218
Nuclear radiation leak bringing about owner's legal liability, 254
Nuclear Regulatory Commission, 256
Oil tanker spill resulting in captain's criminal liability, 249
Owner's liability for locking in factory workers, 74
**Pandemic**, 107
Passenger ticket provisions excluding negligence, 79
Paying off damage awards in installments, 130
**Pilot Error**, 282
Pilot errors in flight giving rise to airline legal liability, 282
**Platform Collapse**, 239
Platform operations giving rise to full statutory legal liability, 239
Private claims process used to quickly provide relief, 171
Private prosecutions when public prosecutions not started, 267
Proof of negligence not required for damages, 189

Protection from legal liability by statute, 41
Proving airline negligence in plane crashes, 140
Proving guilt as a public nuisance, 74
Proving survivorship of shipwreck victims, 45
Putting a monetary value on lives lost at sea, 95
**Radiation Leak**, 254
Railway Inspectorate, 9
**Rapid Transit**, 102
Recklessly failing to warn leading to criminal liability, 224
Recreating an accident to verify witness testimony, 8
Releasing skydivers in clouds generating pilot legal liability, 210
Replacing legal records loss in a conflagration, 63
Required compliance with visual flight rules, 204
Requirement for public hearings before oil lease approval, 194
Requirements to indict for manslaughter due to fire, 58
Requiring implementation of pollution control devices, 184
Restrictions for volcanic eruptions giving rise to legal liability, 233
Right to administer a victim's estate, 45
Rights of way on rivers, 37
**River Collision**, 37
Rules for avoiding collision between ships in fog, 31
Rules for avoiding collisions between ships, 26
**Running Aground**, 41
Sailing a ship into a warzone generating legal liability, 95
**Severe Weather**, 275
Signalman criminal liability not extended to railway, 90

**Silicosis**, 152
Siting and managing coal tips defining operator legal liability, 189
**Skydiving Errors**, 210
**Spaceship Explosion**, 291
Spaceship explosion giving rise to government legal liability, 291
Stadium crush generating legal liability for police, 267
Statute of limitations and discovery date of disease, 218
Statutory limit on liability for licensed nuclear plant operators, 254
Strict liability or negligence for latent defects, 3
**Tanker Spill**, 249
**Theater Fire**, 58
**Torpedo**, 95
Tort Claims Act limited by acts of discretion, 166
**Train Collision**, 12
**Triple Collision**, 90
U.S. Supreme Court, 35
Use of new technology not part of custom leading to liability, 157
Use of statutory courts of inquiry, 17
Use of Superfund law to remediate and recover funds, 199
Use of uncertified drivers creating operator criminal liability, 102
Use of workmen's compensation laws to avoid liability, 152
**Volcano**, 233
**Walkway Collapse**, 261
Walkway collapse leading to loss of engineer's license, 261
Weather forecasts and warnings giving rise to legal liability, 179
**Well Blowout**, 194
Willful misconduct negating the limitation of liability, 282

www.ingramcontent.com/pod-product-compliance
Lightning Source LLC
Chambersburg PA
CBHW052141220526
45471CB00004B/1472